O'Connor
FLANNERY

FLANNERY O'CONNOR

A Life

Jean W. Cash

THE UNIVERSITY OF TENNESSEE PRESS

Knoxville

CONTENTS

ILLUSTRATIONS

ACKNOWLEDGMENTS

H aving completed this project after more than ten years of writing and research, I gratefully acknowledge the help of numerous people, particularly those whom I have interviewed. I have listed all of them in the "Sources Cited" section of this book, but I would like to give special recognition to some: from Savannah, the late Hugh R. Brown Jr.; the board of the Childhood Home Foundation for permission to quote from interviews conducted by Hugh R. Brown Jr.; O'Connor's Savannah cousins, the three Persse sisters; and Sister Consolata, Mary Flannery O'Connor's third grade teacher; from Milledgeville, Mary Barbara Tate, Elizabeth Horne, Kitty Smith Kellam, Helen I. Greene, and the late Rosa Lee Walston; from O'Connor's years at Iowa, James B. Hall, Walter Sullivan, Herbert Nipson, the late Robie Macauley, and the late Andrew Lytle; Stephen Wilbers wrote a history of the Iowa Writers' Workshop and deposited papers in the University of Iowa Library that led me to many of O'Connor's contemporaries at Iowa. Later O'Connor friends and acquaintances whose help was invaluable include Thomas and Louise Gossett, Ted R. Spivey, Robert Drake, Ashley Brown, Louise Abbot, William Kirkland, and the late George Beiswanger.

Others whose permissions have been vital to my work include Robert E. Lee, who both granted me an interview and graciously allowed me to use the complete file of letters between O'Connor and his sister Maryat Lee as well as Maryat Lee's personal journals. Hualing Engle (Mrs. Paul Engle) generously permitted me to quote from her husband's papers at the University of Iowa library. Robert Cowley allowed me to quote from his father's papers at Newberry Library, Chicago; Nancy Tate Wood granted permission for me to quote from her mother's letters to Brainard Cheney at Vanderbilt; Roy M. Neel permitted me to quote from the letters of Brainard and Frances Neel Cheney at Vanderbilt; and Fr. Robert McCown, S.J., allowed me to quote from the unpublished letters of his brother, the late Fr. James McCown.

No unpublished primary quotations from O'Connor letters, juvenilia, or other material appear in this manuscript because the Mary Flannery O'Connor Charitable Trust, advised by O'Connor's current literary agent, Ben Camardi, refused to grant this permission; however, the following are reprinted by permission of Farrar, Straus and Giroux, LLC: Excerpts from *The Complete Stories* by Flannery O'Connor. Copyright 1971 by the Estate of Mary Flannery O'Connor. *Everything that Rises Must Converge* by Flannery O'Connor. Copyright 1965 by the Estate of Mary Flannery O'Connor. Copyright renewed 1993 by Regina O'Connor. *The Habit of Being: Letters of Flannery O'Connor,* edited by Sally Fitzgerald. Copyright 1979 by Regina O'Connor. Excerpt from "Introduction" from *A Memoir of Mary Ann* by the Dominican Nuns of Our Lady Perpetual Help Home. Introduction by Flannery O'Connor. Copyright 1961 by Flannery O'Connor. Copyright renewed 1989 by Regina O'Connor. *Mystery and Manners* by Flannery O'Connor. Copyright 1969 by the Estate of Mary Flannery O'Connor.

A number of libraries allowed me to read primary material found in their archives: the William E. Perkins Library at Duke, the Jean and Alexander Heard Library at Vanderbilt, the University of Iowa Libraries, Iowa City; Washington and Lee University, the Newberry Library, the Robert W. Woodruff Library, Emory University, the McFarlin Library, the University of Tulsa, the John M. Olin Library, Washington University, the McKeldin Library, the University of Maryland, and, most significant, the Ina Dillard Russell Library at Georgia College and State University, Milledgeville. Nancy Davis Bray, curator of the O'Connor Collection there, has been a constant aid and inspiration both during my many trips to Milledgeville and via telephone and e-mail. John M. Meador, dean of the libraries at the University of Mississippi, led me to late letters between O'Connor and Louis Dollarhide. Courtesy of the Atlanta History Center, I read O'Connor letters included in their collection. The Ford Foundation also granted me permission to use material from O'Connor's application for her 1958 Ford Foundation grant and the archives, Marillac Provincial House, St. Louis, sent me a copy of the letter O'Connor wrote to Sr. Bertrande Myers in 1961.

The O'Connor Collection at Georgia College and State University owns most of the photographs (identified in text) that I have used in the book; I gratefully acknowledge permission to use photographs from this collection. Dr. William C. Harris graciously permitted me the use of his photograph of the Cathedral of St. John the Baptist in Savannah. Joe McTyre of Atlanta, Georgia, also permitted me to use three photographs of O'Connor that he took in 1962. Thomas and Louise Gossett allowed me to reproduce the photograph of O'Connor and Katherine Anne Porter that appears in the book, and Cynthia Gilliatt permitted me to use her photograph of the O'Connor home in Savannah. I also wish to acknowledge the assistance of David Breneman, digital artist, of King Photo in Harrisonburg, Virginia, whose computer expertise helped me reproduce many of the photographs that appear in the book.

James Madison University awarded me a study grant in the summer of 1990 that enabled me to begin serious work on this project; a faculty educational leave in the fall of 1992 resulted in the first chapters of the book. Three different department heads of English at JMU have facilitated my efforts: Peter Hager, Karyn Z. Sproles, and David Jeffrey. In the summer of 1993, NEMLA, the northeastern branch of the Modern Language Association, awarded me a travel grant that financed my trip to the University of Iowa. I would also like to acknowledge the support of the University of Tennessee Press, whose representatives patiently waited for the completed manuscript. Most recently, Joyce Harrison and Stan Ivester functioned as expert guides.

Other scholars of O'Connor's work, colleagues, students, family, and friends have also given me unqualified support. Sarah Gordon at Georgia College and State University published a number of my early efforts in *The Flannery O'Connor Bulletin* and granted permission for me to use material from these articles in my study; J. Wallace Donald, editor of *English Language Notes,* also granted me permission to use quotations from three articles published in that journal; Virginia Wray of Lyon College, Sura Rath of

Louisiana State University, Shreveport, and Marshall Bruce Gentry of the University of Indianapolis have long supported my efforts. At James Madison University, I have received particular encouragement and editorial help from colleagues including Jeanne R. Nostrandt, Jacqueline Brice-Finch, Cynthia Gilliatt, Ron Nelson, Joan Frederick, Robert Hoskins, Cameron Nickels, Mark Facknitz, and the late David Hallman. Scores of students have studied O'Connor's work with me and added to my knowledge; members of my June 2000 seminar were particularly astute—and patient. Several past students of O'Connor's work have become encouraging friends as well as teachers, scholars, and writers themselves: Keith R. Perry, Shawn Miller, and Dale Smith are three of them. Finally, my husband, Lloyd, has recognized my dedication to O'Connor, and my son, Gordon, has cheered me on at every stage of the process.

THE WOMAN

Throughout her lifetime and in the thirty-six years since her death, Flannery O'Connor has remained a partial enigma to readers despite the incredible lucidity of her work. Even to the biographer, she remains an elusive subject because, first of all, she was a product of the New Critical approach to literary study. O'Connor felt that knowledge of the personal lives of writers is of little value in understanding their works. Louise Westling is correct in her assessment that O'Connor "seemed to think of her art as a force above or outside conditions of gender. When she spoke of 'the writer,' she always referred to an anonymous, rather objective intellect, whose personal life was irrelevant to 'his' work" (Westling, "Mothers and Daughters" 510). During her lifetime, O'Connor, then, was quite wary of disclosing personal facts to the public. Reacting angrily when *Time* magazine overemphasized her suffering from lupus in a review-article of *The Violent Bear It Away,* she wrote to Elizabeth Fenwick Way that "the full medical report [. . .] was [. . .] in very bad taste" (*HB* 378). When an acquaintance from Atlanta sent O'Connor a "folksy" portrait of the writer that she wanted to publish in the *Atlanta Journal-Constitution,* O'Connor thanked her for writing the "piece" but would not permit her friend to publish it, asserting that she didn't mind people writing about her work but that anything personal increased her blood pressure, caused her hair to turn gray, and brought out her "latent hives."[1] O'Connor was also dubious about the prospect of later biographies, declaring that future readers would have little interest in "'a life spent between the house and the chicken yard'" (Alexander 1B).

Close study, however, of O'Connor's self-proclaimed uneventful life reveals that she lived a vital existence and that her distinctive personality, the result of both genetics and heritage, dominated every period of life; neither the vicissitudes of illness nor the loneliness of insularity squelched her intellectual curiosity. Even as she approached the age of forty, she remained open to new ideas and concepts of human, philosophical, and theological meaning. To the benefit of her readers, O'Connor was able to assimilate whatever she learned into the ultimate richness of her writing—both fiction and nonfiction.

What then were the essential features of O'Connor's unique personality, qualities which allowed her to create literary works of enduring value? Even Cleanth Brooks, with his firm emphasis on formalist criticism, asserted, "In her instance, I find it hard to separate the person from the artist. Certainly the character of both was an invincible integrity" (Brooks, "Flannery O'Connor— A Tribute" 17). Spiritual certainty established the basis for this "invincible integrity." O'Connor possessed a deep and abiding faith that even transcended the boundaries of the Roman Catholicism into which she was indoctrinated at an early age. Her heritage, on both sides of her family, was Roman Catholic; for seven years she attended parochial schools in her native Savannah, even though she may have been something of a renegade there. As she herself asserts, the strict nuns in her earliest schools in Savannah must have considered her strange when Mary Flannery in the third grade substituted "St. Cecilia" for "Rover" in a grammar sentence.[2] Though O'Connor could look a bit critically at the restrictive dogmas of her faith, she never faltered in her fundamental Christian belief. In her most famous statement on the subject, O'Connor proclaimed: "I see from the standpoint of Christian orthodoxy. This means that for me the meaning of life is centered in our Redemption by Christ and that what I see in the world I see in relation to that. I don't think that this is a position that can be taken halfway or one that is particularly easy in these times to make transparent in fiction" (*MM* 32). O'Connor's deep spiritual commitment was both personal and intellectual; at the personal level, she practiced her faith with an almost obsessive dedication. Wherever she was—at Iowa, in Connecticut with the Robert Fitzgeralds, or in Milledgeville—she attended mass nearly every day; though she asserted that she did not pray in a conventional, dogmatic sense, she kept *A Short Breviary* by her bed: "I say Prime in the morning and sometimes I say Compline at night" (*HB* 159). Little evidence exists to suggest that O'Connor ever suffered from any sort of religious doubt. Only once in a letter to Alfred Corn, a young student at Emory who was having serious religious doubts himself, did she reveal that she herself experienced some problems with faith when she studied other religions in college. She told him that the "clash of different religions was a difficulty for me. [. . .] [but . . .] What kept me a skeptic in college was precisely my Christian faith. It always said: wait, don't bite on this, get a wider picture, continue to read" (*HB* 477). The only other evidence—and it's clearly tangential—that might indicate doubt occurs in O'Connor's letters to Fr. James McCown in the O'Connor Collection at Duke University. Before he placed the letters in the collection, he literally cut two or three sentences in individual letters that he felt might have been too personal for the public exposure.

Beyond her personal practice of Roman Catholicism, however, O'Connor was also deeply committed to understanding twentieth-century Catholic theology. As her comments in her letters and her reviews for the diocesan paper *The Bulletin* clearly demonstrate, she was particularly interested in the ideas of Karl Adam, Jacques Maritain, Romano Guardini, and Teilhard de Chardin. She read these theologians to enhance her own understanding of contemporary trends in Roman Catholicism. Later, after she began to review their works, she hoped she could also help other Catholics discover them and their importance. Through the years, she consistently recommended works by these writers to friends troubled by spiritual doubt; it is certain that the theologians she read helped O'Connor herself to remain both intellectually and spiritually alive to the major currents in twentieth-century Catholic thought. O'Connor was not, however, exclusively interested in Roman Catholic theologians: after reading the Jewish theologian Martin Buber's *The Eclipse of God* in 1958, she wrote to Fr. McCown, "These boys have a lot to offer us" (*HB* 303).

A second trait of great importance to O'Connor the artist was her consummate individualism; O'Connor recognized early that she was different from others but accepted that uniqueness as a positive quality rather than as a source of embarrassment. Throughout her life, she took an almost perverse pride in having been discovered by Pathé News as the little Georgia girl who taught a bantam rooster to walk backward. Interest in exotic fowl became her lifelong avocation. The bantam who walked backward becomes an interesting analog to many of her characters who, too, often walk in reverse until grace touches their lives. Her individualistic interest in exotic fowl also provided her most adept fictional symbol for transcendent glory, the peacock.

O'Connor demonstrated her unique individualism in another significant way: she refused to accept the 1940s notion of Southern womanhood with its roots in the pre–Civil War South. She also showed little interest in the typical concerns of teenagers in the 1940s. Even before the onset of her illness, she considered fashion or dating unimportant and found the idea of marriage shocking. From an early age, her chief interests were in reading and telling stories and writing and illustrating them herself. She knew that the focus of her life would be Art.

Intellectual versatility and extraordinary intelligence were other significant characteristics of O'Connor's sensibility. As a high school and undergraduate student, she was as interested in cartooning as she was in writing. She was the regular cartoonist for the college newspaper at GSCW and even sent some of her efforts to *New Yorker* magazine. As Robert Fitzgerald wrote in his introduction to *Everything That Rises Must Converge* in 1965, "She was a girl who started with a gift for cartooning and satire, and found in herself a greater gift, unique in her time and place, a marvel" (R. Fitzgerald, "Introduction" vii). O'Connor possessed a breadth of intellect that enabled her to appreciate works of fiction as disparate as those of Sophocles, Georges Bernanos, François Mauriac, William Styron, and Walker Percy. For her the only relevant criterion was that the writer possess a vision that reached beyond the topical and ordinary. Those writers who troubled her most were people like Carson McCullers, Truman Capote, and Tennessee Williams, whose works were so mired (she felt) in the secular world that they displayed no transcendent vision. Additional proof of her intellectual versatility lies in the public lectures and readings that she gave, the numerous reviews she wrote for the diocesan papers *The Bulletin* and *Southern Cross,* and the magazine articles she produced. She remained also, throughout her life, an amateur painter who covered the walls of Andalusia with her striking works.

An extraordinary sense of humor permeates O'Connor's fiction. Wryly stated turns of phrase certainly evoke appreciative response from her readers. It was not, however, until the collection of O'Connor's letters *The Habit of Being* appeared in 1979 that the full range of O'Connor's personal sense of humor became apparent. Readers of her fiction alone might label O'Connor a dour religious fanatic whose only pleasure evolved from her treatment of spiritual themes. On the contrary, her letters reveal that she was also a warm-hearted woman with a balanced outlook on both the lupus that mandated her return to Milledgeville and on the narrowness of life in that small Georgia town. She obviously enjoyed sharing her sense of fun in the letters to her numerous correspondents.

Besides revealing that O'Connor possessed a strong and enduring sense of humor, the letters of *The Habit of Being* also reveal another major quality of her sensibility. Though in person O'Connor was reticent—Rosa Lee Walston once described her as being as "laconic as Coolidge"—the numerous, and revealing, letters she wrote to so many different correspondents prove that O'Connor possessed an extraordinary capacity for friendship (Walston, "Flannery O'Connor" 17). As a young girl growing up in Savannah and Milledgeville, O'Connor experienced difficulty relating to people her own age. Whatever friendships she formed were superficial, promoted mainly by her mother; however, once she had published her stories and began to travel throughout the country to promote her fiction, O'Connor established the genuine friendships she had long secretly desired. These friendships led to rich correspondences with a wide range of people: Andrew Lytle, Caroline Gordon, and Robert Lowell were only three of the well-known writers who became her lifelong friends; she also established strong relationships with academic scholars like Tom and Louise Gossett, Ted Spivey, Ben Griffith, and William Sessions. Her rich and revealing exchanges with young, beginning writers like herself (among them, John Hawkes) provided the intellectual stimulation she so much desired; she also established personal friendships with several women, particularly Louise Abbot, Elizabeth "Betty" Hester, Maryat Lee, and Cecil Dawkins. Finally, she developed her own system of mentorship with young college students who asked her for either literary or theological advice; contemporary poet Alfred Corn was one of these students. Overall, then, O'Connor was neither mysterious nor strange: She was an intelligent, good-humored artist, vitally concerned with both the mission of her art and with the people who occupied her world—relatives, close friends, and the secular humanists so clearly in need of spiritual reawakening.

The chapters that follow first proceed chronologically from O'Connor's birth and early years in Savannah through her adolescence and young adulthood in Milledgeville and the five years she spent at the University of Iowa and in New York and Connecticut. Illness then forced O'Connor to return to Milledgeville. At this point my narrative changes to focus on how she managed to maintain her creativity under this circumstance. I have included chapters on her return and on her accommodation to living permanently with her mother, Regina Cline O'Connor. I have also dealt extensively with the previously mentioned friendships that sustained O'Connor during her years in Milledgeville. Two chapters also detail O'Connor's many trips away from Milledgeville to read from her works or to lecture about them and on Southern fiction in general. The next chapter describes and briefly analyzes the many book reviews she wrote for the Roman Catholic diocesan paper *The Bulletin*. Her reviews, too, added to the variety and intellectual substance to her existence. The final chapter of my study focuses on the role of illness in her life, particularly her ability to control and transcend it for thirteen years before her untimely death in August 1964; the study ends with an assessment of her expanded reputation achieved in the thirty-eight years since her death.

CHAPTER ONE

SAVANNAH, 1925~1938

I n her essay "The Nature and Aim of Fiction," first presented as a lecture at Emory University in February 1957 and later included in *Mystery and Manners,* Flannery O'Connor asserted that any writer "who has survived his childhood has enough information about life to last him the rest of his days" (*MM 84*). She elaborated on this idea in an early letter to Maryat Lee in February 1957: "I think you probably collect most of your experience as a child—when you really had nothing else to do—and then transfer it to other situations when you write" (*HB* 204). O'Connor spent the first twelve and a half years of *her* childhood in Savannah, Georgia, where she was born 25 March 1925 and lived until 1938. Because she spent her productive years as a writer in Milledgeville, Georgia, readers associate her with that town rather than Savannah, erroneously assuming that she collected the vital information about life that permeates her fiction during the years she spent there.

With the exception of her five years in Iowa, New York, and Connecticut, Flannery O'Connor lived in Milledgeville, from the age of thirteen until her death from lupus in the Baldwin County Hospital in August 1964. More significantly, she completed her first novel, *Wise Blood,* in Milledgeville and went on to write *The Violent Bear It Away* and the stories collected in *A Good Man Is Hard to Find* and *Everything That Rises Must Converge* there. As Hugh R. Brown pointed out, however, in an unpublished essay on O'Connor's years in Savannah, Mary Flannery O'Connor (as she is still known there) spent the first third of her life in Savannah, the city of her birth. Having been born in St. Joseph's Hospital, O'Connor then lived on historic Lafayette Square at 207 East Charlton Street under the loving and protective eyes of her parents, Edward F. and Regina Cline O'Connor. O'Connor's early years in Savannah were vitally important to her development. As Brown so succinctly wrote: "She was born there; her first impressions of the world were gathered there; she learned to read and write in Savannah; she learned about God and grace and salvation and judgment there" (H. Brown, "Flannery O'Connor" 2).

Certainly, Mary Flannery O'Connor was at least partly shaped by the city of Savannah itself, which in the 1920s and 1930s was a quite different place from the bustling seaport of its early years or the rather sprawling city popular with today's tourists—readers of *Midnight in the Garden of Good and Evil.* Economically, during the 1920s and 1930s the city was not prospering. Its great years as a port in the late nineteenth century had ended—the few shipping agents and cotton dealers had left partly because of problems with the boll weevil and partly because patterns of economic development had changed. In the 1920s, Savannah had few factories, no major industries, and little tourism (H. Brown 4). The economic decline of the city obviously contributed to Edward F. O'Connor Jr.'s lack of business success there in the 1930s and to the concern with financial security that permeated the life of his wife, Regina, and, to a lesser extent, that of his daughter, Flannery.

Racially the city was totally segregated; even the Roman Catholic Church had four churches for whites and three for blacks (H. Brown 4). O'Connor's third cousins on the O'Connor side of the family, Patricia and Winifred Persse and Margaret P. Trexler, provide insight into race relations within their family during the 1920s and 1930s. They talk about how little housework any white person had to do then, asserting that even white families with modest incomes could afford servants: "It was amazing. You could always have someone there to cook, and somebody to come in once a week and wash clothes, and do the ironing."[1] Though they are not absolutely certain, they assume that the O'Connor family employed at least one black servant. One of O'Connor's earliest playmates in Savannah, Elizabeth Maguire Johnson, lived on the same block as the O'Connor family. She says that though *her* family was not wealthy they employed "two Negro servants."[2] O'Connor's lifelong tendency to categorize most Southerners of African descent as servants, then, likely had its beginning in Savannah.

Natives of the city during the years O'Connor lived there provide additional insights into what the town was like then. Elizabeth Maguire Johnson says: "The sidewalks and streets were made of bricks. Negroes with baskets on their heads roamed the streets selling vegetables, crabs and oysters. They sang their wares. There were still some horse drawn vehicles. We played in the squares under the magnolia trees." The Persse sisters recall that during the 1920s and 1930s all the "nice" stores and movie theaters (the Odeon, the Bijoux, the Arcadian, the Lucas, and the Savannah) were in downtown Savannah. They recall going to the movies every Saturday, dressed in hats and gloves. The Savannah Theater catered to children, providing a serial, double features, Pathé News, and giveaway contests. Though Mary Flannery may have gone to the movies with others, she never went with the Persse sisters, who always "went as a family."

Daniel O'Leary, who attended the Marist School for boys on Lafayette Square, recalls that it was "pretty grim around here" during the depression days of the 1930s, though he asserts that the block where the O'Connor's lived was not so rough as the 300 block of Charlton Street, then an area of cold-water flats. Declaring Lafayette Square "a real paradise for boys," he remembers coming to school early and staying late to play football and softball in the middle of the square, then a sandy plot, just "crawling with boys." He speaks enviously of the rowdiness of the area, recalling his boyhood desire to live in the Lafayette Square area rather than farther out of town. Almost as an afterthought, he says that he seldom saw the girls who lived there.[3] O'Leary's description of the rough, masculine quality of Lafayette Square helps explain the protective home environment in which Mary Flannery O'Connor grew up. His comments may also help explain why the adult O'Connor referred so seldom to her years in Savannah. Beyond scant references to her education in Catholic schools and to her episode with the chicken that walked backward, O'Connor left little documented comment on her childhood in Savannah.

One significant exception, a description of an orphanage in Savannah, however, occurs in a letter she wrote to her friend Betty Hester in October 1957:

> St. Mary's Home is the Catholic orphanage for girls in Savannah. When I was a child it was in a creaking house on a dreary street and I was occasionally taken there to visit the Sisters or some orphan distant-cousins; also probably as a salutary lesson. "See what you have to be thankful for. Suppose you were, etc."—a lesson my imagination played on exhaustively. I don't suppose that orphanage was so bad, there was doubtless plenty of love there but it was official, and you wouldn't have got yours from your own God-given source. Anyway to me it was the ultimate horror
>
> [. . .] I still remember. From time to time, they were allowed to spend the day with me—miserable occasions for me, as they were not other children, they were Orphans. I don't know if they enjoyed coming or not; probably not. [. . .] Anyway I have been at least an Imaginary Orphan and that was probably my first view of hell. Children know by instinct that hell is an absence of love, and they can pick out theirs without missing. (*HB* 244)

The poignancy of this description shows how strongly Mary Flannery valued the stability of her own family life, and the horror she imagined would result if she were suddenly orphaned. Hugh R. Brown uncovered additional evidence of Mary Flannery's special interest in the orphanage: "in 1936, when the Catholic paper carried the Roll of the Female Orphanage Society (the Contributors), neither Regina or Edward O'Connor is listed. But Mary Flannery is" (H. Brown, "Savannah Years" 13).

Another vital influence on Mary Flannery O'Connor's early development in Savannah was the Roman Catholic community into which she was born. Because her parents and other relatives in Savannah were devout, practicing Roman Catholics, Mary Flannery O'Connor herself early developed strong faith. Years later she wrote to William Sessions about the ease with which she took her first communion. It was "as natural" to her, she said, "as brushing my teeth" (*HB* 164). The insularity of the Catholic community in Savannah also had a lasting impact on O'Connor's life. Of being a born Catholic, she wrote: "what one has as a born Catholic is something given and accepted before it is experienced" (97).

Even though the Catholics in Savannah were a definite minority, they were devoted to the Church and to each other. The O'Connor home, located as it was on Lafayette Square just a block from St. John's Cathedral, placed Mary Flannery in the center of this community. St. Vincent's Grammar School for Girls, which she attended through the fifth grade, was adjacent to the cathedral. Diagonal to St. Vincent's was the Marist Brothers School for Boys. Sister Consolata, a Mercy nun who was Mary Flannery's third grade teacher at St. Vincent's, comments on the overall religious atmosphere in which Mary Flannery grew up: "there was a very close relationship between the people and the church in those days. [. . .] It [the Catholic community] was not large and the people knew each other. Today they don't."[4] Mary Flannery's childhood playmates recall that "she and her family seemed to be devout Roman Catholics, as was the whole neighborhood," and that she was "raised very religious."[5] Sister Consolata says: "She had a very deep religious background even within her own home and with her associates. All of her relationships, like with the Dowlings—they are very religious—[and] the Feugers were very religious, the Persse's were very religious. I think that her association with those people had a lot to do with Mary Flannery's religious training."

Certain of O'Connor's comments in letters clearly illustrate the importance of her early Catholic training. Most of these remarks are positive, but in a letter to Betty Hester in January 1956, O'Connor related a less positive, though amusing, result of her early indoctrination into Catholicism; she asserted that through the influence of the nuns, she "developed something the Freudians have not named—anti-angel aggression, call it." From the ages eight to twelve, she said, she would occasionally seclude herself in "a locked room [. . .] with a fierce and evil face [and] whirl around in a circle with my fists knotted, socking" her guardian angel, for whom she possessed a "poisonous dislike" (*HB* 131–32). Such an admission reveals the individuality of the young O'Connor's creative approach to religion. Its defiance also demonstrates that the young Mary Flannery did not accept every tenet of Catholic dogma without some show of rebellion.

The strong family structure O'Connor's Irish Catholic ancestors built in Georgia also surely influenced her early years in Savannah. Exclusively

Irish on both sides, her ancestors settled in Georgia, mostly in Savannah, during the nineteenth century. The Hartys, Treanors, Clines, Flannerys, and O'Connors—all Roman Catholics—came to Georgia during the heavy immigration of the Irish during that period. Sally Fitzgerald wrote that these Irish Catholics, "although always a distinct minority, have been assimilated into Georgia life and become and integral part of it."[6] Despite her Irish ancestry, O'Connor, in a late letter to her friend Janet McKane in New York, disclaimed that Irish connection, asserting that she had no emotional or sentimental ties to her Irish background: "I was brought up in Savannah where there was a colony of the Over-Irish. They have the biggest St. Patrick's Day parade anywhere around and generally go nutty on the subject" (*HB* 531).

Sally Fitzgerald traced the first of O'Connor's ancestors to the several Roman Catholic "families of English descent" who emigrated from Maryland to Locust Grove, near the present town of Sharon in Taliaferro County in the late eighteenth century. They built the first church there in 1792. Fitzgerald determined that among these settlers was the first of Flannery O'Connor's ancestors to arrive in Georgia: Patrick Harty, of County Tipperary, Ireland, who in 1824 joined the settlement at Locust Grove. Patrick Harty's daughter Johannah, born in Ireland, would become Flannery O'Connor's great-grandmother on the maternal side of the family.

Hugh Donnelly Treanor, who was to marry Johannah, also came to the United States from Tipperary in 1824, at the age of twelve; he, too, probably came to the Locust Grove settlement in Georgia. Treanor eventually moved to Milledgeville in 1845, where he bought and operated "a prosperous water-powered grist mill on the Oconee" River. He and Johannah Harty married in 1848. Of their involvement with Roman Catholicism in Milledgeville, O'Connor, in a letter to Janet McKane, wrote: "Mass was first said here [in Milledgeville] in my great-grandfather's hotel room, later in his home on the piano" (*HB* 520).

O'Connor's great-grandfather, Peter Cline, came directly from County Tipperary, Ireland, to Georgia in 1845 to teach Latin at the Richmond Academy in Augusta. Though he died at the early age of thirty-nine in 1848, his son Peter James Cline survived to become Flannery O'Connor's grandfather. Peter J. Cline studied at the Sharon Academy in Georgia and at St. Vincent's College in Pennsylvania; stranded there when the Civil War started, he left a biographical note, published in *Memoirs of Georgia* (1895), in which he tells of difficulties he encountered returning to Georgia; after the war he clerked in a dry-goods store and later established a similar store in Milledgeville in 1871, with a branch in Eatonton. Cline had great success as a merchant, farmer, and politician. Elected in 1888, he, as mayor of Milledgeville, was instrumental in putting in the city water system in 1891. Cline successively married two of Hugh and Johannah Harty Treanor's daughters, Kate and Margaret Ida. He fathered a total of sixteen children, of whom one of the younger was Regina Cline O'Connor.

Still another significant, though tangential, O'Connor ancestor was John Flannery, who came to the United States from Ireland in 1851 at the age of sixteen; in 1854, Flannery moved to Savannah, where he worked as a clerk and bookkeeper until the Civil War started. In 1861, he enlisted in the Confederate army and later fought with Generals Johnston and Hood before leaving the army in 1865 because of serious illness. He returned to Savannah, where he founded and was president of the Southern Bank of the State of Georgia; he was also active as a cotton broker, railroad director, and member of the Roman Catholic Church. He helped build the Cathedral of St. John the Baptist in the 1870s and was on the building committee for the present cathedral, built after the original burned in 1898. In 1867, John Flannery married Mary Ellen Norton, a granddaughter of Patrick Harty of Locust Grove; their daughter Kate, the Cousin Kate of Flannery O'Connor's letters, married Raphael Semmes of Savannah, a nephew of the Confederate admiral.

On the O'Connor side of the family, Flannery O'Connor was the descendent of one of two brothers, Daniel and Patrick, who came to Savannah from Ireland in the post–Civil War era. Patrick, a wheelwright who eventually manufactured carriages and wagons and operated a livery service, was Mary Flannery's great-grandfather. Patrick's son Edward Francis, born in 1872, became a prominent businessman and banker in Savannah. His daughter Nan married Herbert Cline, son of Peter J. and Margaret Ida Cline, and, in 1922, his son Edward Francis Jr. married Herbert's sister Regina, whom he met at Nan's wedding. Edward Francis O'Connor Jr. attended Catholic schools in Savannah and St. Mary's College in Maryland. In 1916 he "joined the American Expeditionary Force as a Lieutenant in the 325th Infantry

Regiment of the 82nd Division and served in France with distinction in the First World War." After the war, he first worked for his father, "who owned a wholesale distributorship for candies and tobacco"; then, "financed by a gift from Mrs. [Kate] Semmes in honor of O'Connor's birth," he started a real estate business in Savannah (H. Brown, "Savannah Years" 14). He seems, however, to have been more interested in American Legion activities than selling real estate. In 1935 Chatham Post No. 36 in Savannah elected him commander, and the next year he became commander of the American Legion for the state of Georgia. Traveling widely, he made a number of speeches on legion matters (*CW* 1237). In a letter to Betty Hester in July 1956, O'Connor herself commented on her father's activities with the American Legion and admitted that she was impressed by the patriotism that he displayed in some of the speeches he made to the organization (*HB* 166). The O'Connor Collection at Georgia College and State University holds two letters written by Edward O'Connor in December 1937. Both letters reveal his desire to attain a political position under the expanding bureaucracy created by the New Deal. In one letter, O'Connor solicits Erwin Sibley of Milledgeville to ask Georgia's U.S. senators (Walter F. George and Richard B. Russell Jr.) and Congressman Carl Vinson to write letters in his behalf. In the other letter, to Senator George himself, O'Connor described his qualifications for the hypothetical position.[7] His appointment as a real estate appraiser for the Federal Housing Authority in Atlanta in 1938 proves that his perseverance paid off; however, that O'Connor did not intend to move his family from Savannah permanently seems indicated by his having listed himself in the city directory for 1939 as living at 207 E. Charlton Street. Instead of giving the usual information about employment, his listing says "'on temporary duty in Atlanta'" (H. Brown, "Savannah Years" 14).

With a father who was struggling for business success during the depression, Mary Flannery, then, grew up in a community that was strongly Catholic (hence patriarchal), yet in a family that was markedly matriarchal, a quality at least partly related to the mores of the time, which eliminated many fathers from the most intimate family affairs. Savannah cousins and other acquaintances remember the central position Regina Cline O'Connor occupied in the family; Edward F. O'Connor was peripheral. O'Connor's distant cousin Katherine Doyle Groves has distinct memories of Edward O'Connor. About seven years older than Mary Flannery, Groves asserts that she was "surprised to read that they [father and daughter] were close." To her, Edward O'Connor always seemed "aloof."[8] Admitting that she herself "wasn't crazy" about him, she describes him as a man with his head "sort of in the clouds." She remembers that he failed in one financial scheme after another and that his strongest interest was in veterans' affairs. To Mrs. Groves, he seemed a bit pompous, with his nose always "a little elevated."[9]

Mary Flannery's early playmates, who often visited in the O'Connor home, provide other information about Edward F. O'Connor Jr. Loretta Feuger Hoynes remembers him as a hard-working man; she also recalls that, unlike her own father, Ed O'Connor always napped after the midday meal. She, a nurse, interprets this habit as early evidence of his illness; she believes that he was suffering from lupus long before his condition was diagnosed and that his health was never openly discussed because, in the thirties, a veil of secrecy still covered topics like illness and death. Elizabeth Maguire Johnson says: "I don't remember much about her father. He was quiet and rather good looking," and Pat Persse asserts that she did not "really remember her [Mary Flannery's] father at all." Another early friend, Newell Turner Parr, has no memory of ever having seen Mary Flannery in public with him.[10]

It is clear, nevertheless, that Edward O'Connor doted on his daughter. Hugh Brown found that "from 1927 through 1931, The City Directory for Savannah carried a separate listing for Miss Mary Flannery O'Connor of 207 E. Charlton Street" (H. Brown, "Savannah Years" 13). In a few letters in *The Habit of Being,* the adult Flannery O'Connor also revealed the marked influence that Edward O'Connor had on her life. O'Connor's correspondent Betty Hester "elicited," as Louise Westling asserts, "a series of remarkable letters containing the most revealing personal comments O'Connor ever wrote" ("Revelations" 15). Among these comments are several that reveal the affinity she felt with Ed O'Connor, a closeness based on their mutual illness—lupus—and on their shared interest in writing. Though O'Connor asserted, "He died when I was fifteen and I really only knew him by a kind of instinct" (*HB* 166). She remembered that he "toted around some of my early productions. I drew—mostly chickens, beginning at the tail, the same chicken over and over, beginning at the tail. Also occasional verse" (167–68). In the same letter, O'Connor revealed her father's interest in writing and her own desire to fulfill what she perceived to be his unfulfilled longings; in addition, she discussed their shared disease, lupus. In still another letter to

9

Hester, written a month later, O'Connor elaborated on her father's (and her own) interest in writing, asserting that "he would have written *well* if he could have." She talked about the political writing he did and ended with one of her most poignant statements: "Needing people badly and not getting them may turn you in a creative direction, provided you have the other requirements. He needed people I guess and got them. I wanted them and didn't. We are all rather blessed in our deprivations if we let ourselves be I suppose" (169). O'Connor reveals here an intellectual and emotional understanding of her father that she developed during her early years with him in Savannah, for, after the family moved from Savannah to Atlanta in 1938, Edward O'Connor soon fell ill with lupus, dying in Milledgeville in 1941 at the age of forty-five.

Though O'Connor was close to her father, Regina Cline O'Connor and her cousin Kate Flannery Semmes created the matriarchal aura that permeated Mary Flannery's childhood. O'Connor's third cousin Tony Harty recalled that "women in the family were all very strong personalities."[11] Mrs. Semmes, one of these strong women, lived in the house adjacent to that of the O'Connors, separated only by the empty lot that the Persse cousins say became empty when Mrs. Semmes needed a place to park her electric car. Kate Flannery Semmes exercised considerable financial control over the O'Connor family. Hugh R. Brown wrote that as soon as Ed O'Connor bought the family's home on Charlton Street in 1923, he "conveyed it to Cousin Katie by a debt deed for $4,500." Not having paid this debt by the time the family left Savannah in 1938, Ed O'Connor relinquished the house to Katie Semmes, who later left it to Flannery O'Connor in her will (H. Brown, "Savannah Years" 14). Even earlier evidence of Mrs. Semmes's influence on the family derives from Regina Cline O'Connor's having named her daughter for Cousin Kate's mother, the previously mentioned Mary Norton Flannery. The Persse cousins think this naming was unusual, since Katie was a cousin only on Regina's side of the family. Katherine Groves, too, emphasizes that Mary Flannery had no Flannery blood; she believes that the name was given simply to honor Mrs. Semmes. Groves's first memory of Mary Flannery also involves Katie Semmes. She remembers visiting Mrs. Semmes in her former home on Bull and Taylor Streets just after Mary Flannery's birth. Ed and Regina came to call on Mrs. Semmes, bringing her with them "as an infant in a basket."

Regina Cline O'Connor, then, no doubt had dual motives in naming her daughter "Mary Flannery": she gave her the name both to honor Mrs. Semmes's mother and to influence Katie Semmes herself to assist the family financially. Sister Consolata tells a relevant anecdote: "I used to call her Mary O'Connor. And the mother came and she said, 'Sister, please, whatever you do, you can drop the Mary, but be sure to call her Flannery because of the income.'" Tony Harty asserted that the O'Connor family treated Mrs. Semmes with "all kinds of deference and respect. [. . .] She was a wealthy lady and [. . .] Regina and Cousin Kate had this understanding."[12] Loretta Hoynes agrees that Cousin Katie helped the family, but she also asserts, "You worked for what you got from her." Hoynes also believes that Regina cared a great deal for Mrs. Semmes, reciprocating the attention and financial support her cousin gave her by helping the older woman manage her affairs.

The enduring relationship that existed between Kate Semmes and the O'Connors (particularly Regina and Mary Flannery) proves that love as much as money undergirded the connection. Writing to Betty Hester in late 1957, after Mrs. Semmes insisted that she and her mother join a "diocesan pilgrimage" to Lourdes and Rome that a local priest had organized, O'Connor also revealed that a portrait of Mrs. Semmes hung in their home: "She is the child in the high chair in the picture in the parlor" (HB 250). O'Connor's cousin, Katherine Groves, recalls that though the O'Connor's left Savannah while she (Mrs. Groves) was in college, she remembers the letters Mary Flannery wrote to Mrs. Semmes, who "would read them to me, and they were so well written and had such a sense of humor in them and she'd do little pen and ink sketches and she would poke fun at herself" (Groves, Brown interview).

Regina and Mary Flannery continued to visit Mrs. Semmes through the years, including an extended visit in February 1952, while Flannery was reading the page proofs of Wise Blood. Mrs. Semmes financed their trip to Italy in 1958, obviously motivated by her desire to help Flannery benefit from the waters at Lourdes. When O'Connor inherited her childhood home in Savannah in 1958, she renovated it and rented out apartments during the last five years of her life.[13] Mrs. Semmes's influence, added to O'Connor's early education in the Catholic girls' schools administered and taught by nuns, helps clarify the matriarchal family structure in many of her stories; in fact, an early friend in Savannah, Lillian Dowling Odom, suggests that the "heavy, heavy" mothers of Savannah lay behind the mothers in her fiction.[14]

O'Connor's mother, Regina Cline O'Connor, however, exerted the prime matriarchal influence in O'Connor's early life, certainly dominating the life of her young daughter, who from childhood called her mother "Regina." O'Connor's Savannah acquaintances remember that Mary Flannery called both parents by their first names. When one friend asked her why she called her mother "Regina," Mary Flannery replied, "'Well, what would you have me call her, "Miss Regina" like you do?'"[15] This seeming idiosyncrasy in manners probably resulted from Mary Flannery's being an only child who grew up hearing her parents address each other by their given names, but it may also be early evidence of her independent nature.

Regina Cline O'Connor deeply cherished her only child. Loretta Hoynes even suggests that Mary Flannery remained an only child because Regina decided to have no more children when she learned of Edward's lupus: "She knew the lupus could be hereditary." Several of O'Connor's Savannah acquaintances remember how much protective control Regina O'Connor exerted over her daughter. Elizabeth Maguire Johnson says that Regina "was very particular with her," forcing Mary Flannery to lead "a very structured life." Katherine Groves suggests that, because Regina was afraid Mary Flannery would pick up germs, she forbade her to have cats and dogs as pets. She and other of O'Connor's early acquaintances also remember how strictly Regina monitored Mary Flannery's friendships. Apparently Regina had a list (either mental or written) of children she would allow to play with her daughter. The Persse cousins assert that her allowing only certain people to associate with Mary Flannery "proves how protective she [Regina] was." Elizabeth Johnson remembers how closely Regina watched Mary Flannery's diet by "making her eat all her vegetables first before she could eat anything [else] on her plate." Loretta Hoynes recalls the extra care Mrs. O'Connor exercised over Mary Flannery's brief walk to St. Vincent's: "School was really just a block away, and Regina took her to school every day. She walked her right over to the gate of the yard every morning. There were no automobiles, so it couldn't be that she couldn't go alone because a car might hit her. Cars were very few and far between in those days and the streetcars weren't going to get her because they went straight down Abercorn."[16]

Hoynes also remembers how tightly Mary Flannery held her pocket-book when they went out together and how she refused to take the shortcut across the cemetery from Broughton Street to Abercorn; she also recalls that Mary Flannery was not allowed to play on the local playground. Summarizing the protected quality of Mary Flannery's life, Hoynes calls her a "really secluded child," who never wandered freely through the community (Hoynes, Brown interview).

Despite noticing how protective of Mary Flannery Mrs. O'Connor was, Mary Flannery's teacher Sister Consolata also remembers that "Mary Flannery was not spoiled for an only child, [even though] [t]here was a great deal of love expressed between mother and child. She would come over at lunch time to see how she was doing. She watched out for her. [. . .] The mother idolized her. But the mother was most cooperative. No matter what you told her, she would follow up on it and check back the next day." Overall, the Persse sisters analyze the relationship between mother and daughter as mutually dependant. Pat Persse asserts, "She [Flannery] could not have lived without her mother."

Along with the parental and matriarchal influences, O'Connor's parochial school training in Savannah certainly contributed to her development. She began school in Savannah in 1931, entering first grade at St. Vincent's Grammar School just across Lafayette Square from her family's home. The school was run by the Mercy Order of Nuns, most of whom were young Irish girls brought to the United States and trained briefly in Baltimore before being sent to teach in grammar schools like St. Vincent's. Sister Consolata was one of these neophytes. Since O'Connor's cousins, the Persse sisters, spent all of their elementary school years at the Sacred Heart Academy, to which Mary Flannery transferred in 1936, they have clear recollections of what Catholic elementary schools in Savannah were like in the 1930s. They describe the parochial atmosphere as highly disciplined. In every classroom, the school day began with a formal prayer. Through the seventh grade, the same nun taught her class every subject. Behavior, they assert, was regimented in a positive sense. "There was just an aura about the nuns," created at least partly by the habits they wore, which inspired their students with awe. The Persse sisters emphasize the distance they felt between themselves and the nuns and the fact that the nuns lived such restricted lives: "They could never do anything. They could never go out alone. They always had to be with a companion."

Very few students ever dared "talk back to a nun," and those who did "didn't go home and get sympathy." In absolute silence, students lined up for various activities. Winifred Persse remembers being yanked out of line for saying "excuse me" after she had stepped on another student's foot. Her punishment was to stay after school. The nuns mandated total silence in the school. One of the Persse sisters recalls, "If a nun ever left a room and came back and you were talking, you were in real trouble." They also remember being struck across the hands with a ruler: "This was always done in the classroom where the other children could see it."

St. Vincent's in 1931 was in an old house built in the 1800s near the cathedral. Nuns at St. Vincent's provided their students with religious instruction, preparing them for their first Communion. They used the Baltimore Catechism, then the official explanation of church doctrine in parochial schools. Another part of the religious training was, according to the Persse cousins, that they early participated in church ritual. They sang the complicated Latin masses, participated in a "children's choir," and learned to sing anthems. Though they learned to recite masses, the Persse sisters do not recall reading any treatises by Catholic scholars. One of the Persse cousins recalls that the nuns put great emphasis on teaching the then-popular Palmer method of handwriting: "You could tell who went to Catholic schools because we all wrote alike." The Persses also remember with great enthusiasm spelling bees and the annual major money-raising shows that featured dancing, singing, and dramatics. Overall, the Persse sisters believe they received a good basic education, one superior to the training young people receive in Catholic schools today.

Several Savannah women remember Mary Flannery's early years at St. Vincent's: Loretta Feuger Hoynes, Elizabeth Maguire Johnson, Lillian Dowling Odom, and Lynette Jones, among them. Lynette Jones remembers that they started school together: "I was five and she was six and I lived out by the golf course, and Mary Flannery, of course, lived right here."[17] Odom remembers that Mary Flannery was never in on the customary play at school, asserting that "maybe she didn't fit any of the roles." She recalls that Mary Flannery often isolated herself from the other girls, presumably to read. Loretta Hoynes, on the other hand, remembers that Mary Flannery played normally during school recesses but went home for lunch, until the school changed the rules "because it was causing friction with other parents and children" (Hoynes, Brown interview). Both Odom and Hoynes remember how students at school often shared lunches, a tradition in which Mary Flannery refused to participate. Hoynes says: "She brought caster oil sandwiches so nobody would eat her lunch" (Hoynes, Brown interview). Odom also remembers that Mary Flannery, possibly copying household maids, chewed snuff in class and shot the rubber bands off her braces behind the nuns' backs.

Elizabeth Maguire Johnson was one of Mary Flannery's closest friends during her first three years at St. Vincent's. She says she and Mary Flannery were in the same class, but though she herself adjusted well to the school, "Mary Flannery didn't." She has a quite definite opinion regarding Mary Flannery's difficulties, asserting that the trouble was "her mother [who] antagonized the nuns" by not allowing Mary Flannery "to conform to their rules and regulations"; Johnson remembers that the church required children to attend a special mass at the Cathedral of St. John the Baptist in the lower church at 9:00 A.M., but "Mary Flannery always went to mass with her parents at 11:00 o'clock in the upper church." When they were in the third grade, Sister Consolata "would give Mary Flannery a bad time about this." Mrs. Johnson also recalls the difficulty Mary Flannery had with the compositions required of third graders: "Mary Flannery would always write about her ducks and chickens. The nun would fuss at her about this." Johnson also asserts, "I don't think Mary Flannery was good at spelling either," a speculation that relates to a favorite story Pat Persse tells about Mary Flannery's poor spelling: "She came home with her report card one day and she wanted to explain to the mother these marks, you know; in geography she got an 85 and 'Sister said that would have been a 95 except for my spelling and in history I got a 64 and Sister said it would have been better than that except for my spelling and in spelling she got a 40 and Sister said that would have been better if I could spell!'"

Sister Consolata has somewhat different memories of both the school and her young pupil. Of the school, she says: "It was a very good school. [. . .] We had good trained teachers, all Sisters. We were up-to-date in everything." Of the Mary Flannery in the third grade, she recalls: "She was just an ordinary child [but . . .] a good student." According to her teacher, Mary Flannery behaved well and caused no problems: "She took her place like everyone else, she got in line, she did what the others did. She was Mary Flannery O'Connor and that was it." Hugh Brown wrote that Sister Consolata also recalled that "young Mary Flannery O'Connor had a habit of speaking to adults as though she was on the same level with them. 'She was a little forward with adults'" (H. Brown, "Savannah Years" 9). Sister Consolata also recalls Mary Flannery's special interest in her chickens and her excitement in talking about them, though "she was a little awkward in expressing herself. She would go like this [hand gesture] when she was talking to you. Very demonstrative. Her speech was a little awkward, too." The nun remembers, too, that Mary Flannery was "interested in reading and writing" and adept at both. Since Sister Consolata's comments contradict some of those of Mary Flannery's classmates, it may be instructive to give, at this point, O'Connor's opinion of the veracity of nuns. In August 1959, she wrote to Ted Spivey: "I have been in the Church for 34 years and I have known many nuns, have gone to school to them, correspond with a few, and I have never found one who deliberately lied" (*HB* 347).

Mary Flannery transferred to the Sacred Heart Grammar School for Girls after she finished the fifth grade at St. Vincent's. Her Savannah acquaintances speculate about the transfer. Pat Persse suggests that she may have transferred to Sacred Heart because of her friendship with the Dowling sisters, Lillian and Anne, who had decided to change schools. Sister Consolata concurs. Persse also suggests that Sacred Heart was more socially pretentious, more "lace curtain" than St. Vincent's. Lillian Dowling Odom believes Mary Flannery may have left St. Vincent's because of the "strictness of a certain nun"—possibly Sister Consolata. Loretta Hoynes, too, asserts that the strict nuns were the main reason she left St. Vincent's; she expected them to do what she wanted. Dan O'Leary, who attended the Marist school for boys, suggests that Regina O'Connor might have transferred Mary Flannery to Sacred Heart because of its more genteel atmosphere: "this was a pretty rough and ready neighborhood down here" (O'Leary, Brown interview). Hugh Brown believed that the teachers at Sacred Heart were probably better. They belonged to the Order of St. Joseph and had received better training (including college degrees) than the Mercy sisters at St. Vincent's.[18]

Transferring to Sacred Heart mandated that Mary Flannery could no longer walk to school. Her mode of transportation was extraordinary—Katie

Semmes's anachronistic electric car that O'Connor's classmates at Sacred Heart remember with enthusiasm. The Persse cousins, who were already attending Sacred Heart, recall that the car was one of a kind in Savannah. Even Daniel O'Leary, who did not know Mary Flannery O'Connor personally, remembers the car and its owner: "Back in those days it was an oddity because everybody had gone gasoline. It must have been left over from about 1920; she was probably very set in her ways and didn't want to learn to drive with a clutch and a gear shift. She would walk out, [. . .] a very stately lady with a big hat and long white gloves and get in that car and drive off" (O'Leary, Brown interview). Schoolmates remember that Mrs. Semmes allowed Regina to use it to drive Mary Flannery to school. Mary Flannery's playmates during that period, including the Persse sisters, recall being driven around in the car.

Outside school, Mary Flannery formed friendships with the few girls from the neighborhood and school whom Regina Cline O'Connor found acceptable. Pat Persse asserts, "I think she was very sheltered, and she was around adults much more than she was around children except in school and with the 'Merriweather' girls." Sister Consolata believes that Mary Flannery "had very nice friends, well chosen." All her childhood friends remember that Regina was quite selective about which girls Mary Flannery could associate with. Though the Persse cousins, who occasionally came to the O'Connor house to play with her, were not aware of a written list of approved friends until later. They assert that "the mother checked out anybody who came in." They also suggest that, as relatives, they may have "made it on the approved list automatically." Loretta Hoynes says more emphatically of Regina's protective exclusiveness: "She had a list of girls allowed in the house. If you weren't on the list, you didn't get in" (Hoynes, Brown interview). One childhood friend who witnessed Regina's rigidity firsthand was Marguerite Pinckney Nolen, one of Mary Flannery's approved friends, who brought an uninvited friend of hers to the O'Connor home. Regina O'Connor sent the child home, making clear to Marguerite "that she did not want her to bring any other children with her when she came to play" (Walsh, Brown interview).

One group of Mary Flannery's friends called themselves the "Merri-weather girls," a name which Lillian Dowling Odom asserts Mary Flannery herself probably coined. The group included the two Dowling sisters, Loretta Feuger and two or three other girls. Mrs. Odom explains that the group met after school in a small clubhouse behind the O'Connor home, where they read Mary Flannery's early stories from the third grade on. Loretta Feuger Hoynes says that she knew Mary Flannery as far back as she could remember. She recalls that when she suffered a ruptured appendix at the age of three, Regina brought Mary Flannery to visit her. She says, "the last time I saw her was about a year before she died" (Hoynes, Brown interview). Hoynes claims that the young Mary Flannery was a "very lonely person," looking for friendship but not knowing how to get it. Her attitude, according to Hoynes, was, "You do what I say, or we don't play." Hoynes also says that she was Mary Flannery's only close friend in Savannah but implies that the friendship was promoted by her mother rather than chosen by herself. Hoynes's mother said, "You've got to go!" Hoynes says that the forced friendship between them continued even after the O'Connors left Savannah: she visited Mary Flannery every summer in Milledgeville until they were sixteen and her mother could no longer force her to go. Hoynes also tells how their relationship finally ended during her last visit to Milledgeville: a friend of Mary Flannery had a brother their age, who invited Loretta to go to the movies with him. When they returned and sat on the porch to swing and smoke, Mary Flannery became so angry that she put Loretta out of the house with her suitcase, declaring her a "wayward woman." Hoynes returned to Savannah by bus the next day. This experience later found its way into "A Temple of the Holy Ghost."

Another of Mary Flannery's early friendships in Savannah was with Newell Turner Parr, one of the few non-Catholic friends of whom Regina approved. Parr recalls a relationship much less forced and far friendlier than the one described by Loretta Hoynes. Parr first became acquainted with Mary Flannery when her family moved into a house just across the street from the O'Connors'. She remembers Regina O'Connor's graciousness to the family as Protestant newcomers to the neighborhood: "This whole area was really Catholic so I was a little bit like a fish out of water." She relates some of the details of their friendship, including her memory of spending time in Mary Flannery's upstairs bedroom. She recalls that Mary Flannery "wanted to read me her stories and unfortunately I was not that interested in stories. [. . .] I remember that she had pages and pages of handwritten-in-pencil stories, and she would try to get me interested. I wasn't quite smart enough to listen very attentively." Despite her inability to appreciate Mary Flannery's early literary efforts, Parr, who knew her only over a period of about two years, says: "I am very glad that I had the opportunity of knowing her because she was really a very special person." Incidentally, Parr also recalls that Loretta Feuger did, indeed, visit Mary Flannery every day (Parr, Brown interview).

Elizabeth Maguire Johnson was still another of Mary Flannery's early friends. A Roman Catholic like the O'Connors, Johnson went to school with her at St. Vincent's in grades one through four; the Maguire family lived near the O'Connors on Lafayette Square and their mothers were also friends. After they moved when Johnson finished the fourth grade, she never saw Mary Flannery again; however, during their early school years, Johnson visited the O'Connor family often to play after school. She recalls one particular incident regarding Mary Flannery's cruelty to another child: "I remember going to her house once with a little girl who was visiting me and Mary Flannery tied her up to a chair in her bedroom. I remember my mother saying if she acted like that not to play with her." Other friends recall less dramatic activities. Pat Persse remembers that when she visited Mary Flannery on Saturday mornings they listened to a radio program called "Let's Pretend," which featured a reader of fairy tales; the girls "had sort of 'let's pretend' parties. And we'd go up and sit around and listen and then we'd go down and the mother was making gingerbread men. I say that every time I go in that house I smell gingerbread." The Persse cousins also believe that the "let's pretend" kind of game was the sort Mary Flannery enjoyed most as a child. Another early friend, Marguerite Pinckney Nolen, recalls that she and Mary Flannery played on the unused third floor of the house, particularly in a bathroom with a huge tub; she remembers reading stories to Mary Flannery and getting annoyed "because in the middle of a paragraph, Flannery would stop her and say 'Read that over again,' almost as if she were pondering the sentence structure or the imagery or whatever" (Walsh, Brown interview).

As a result, then, of the combination of her native genius and the myriad influences of her early years in Savannah, Mary Flannery O'Connor developed a unique personality and unique interests, recalled by both her relatives who remain in Savannah and her early schoolmates. Her contemporaries retained distinct physical memories of the young O'Connor. A distant cousin remembers that as a child Mary Flannery was not pretty: "Her eyes were pretty, I guess, but other than that you wouldn't have singled

her out to say 'That is a pretty child'" (Brown interview). Lillian Dowling
Odom remembers her "large ears, large glasses, loping walk," and ortho-
dontic braces. She also suggests that Mary Flannery was aware of her
"afflicted" appearance. Pat Persse describes the shoes Mary Flannery wore as
"some sort of corrective shoes; they weren't braces or anything, but like Girl
Scout oxfords and they were real unattractive." Loretta Hoynes suggests that
the shoes were meant to correct her "pigeon-toed" feet (Hoynes, Brown interview). O'Connor herself substantiated some of these descriptions. In a brief
self-portrait she wrote for a magazine writing class at Iowa, she described
herself as being "pigeon-toed," having a "receding chin," and showing the antisocial tendencies of an only child.[19] Though some of O'Connor's Savannah
acquaintances speculate that the physical awkwardness they remember in
Mary Flannery might have been symptomatic of special health problems she
already had, Loretta Hoynes recalls her as a *healthy* (Mrs. Hoynes's emphasis)
child with a good appetite. She remembers that Mary Flannery was very active,
a lover of horses and pigs but "deathly afraid" of cats and dogs. O'Connor
herself, writing to Betty Hester in March 1960, supported Hoynes's memory
of her childhood healthiness: "I am wondering where you got the idea that
my childhood was full of 'endless illnesses.' Besides the usual measles, chicken-
pox and mumps, I was never sick" (*HB* 379).

Besides recalling her physical characteristics, Mary Flannery's relatives
and acquaintances in Savannah remember her unique personality. Sister
Consolata suggests that the basis of that essential difference may have lain in
her superior intelligence: "I imagine it was because she was brighter. She
caught on very quickly. You didn't have to go over things with her. She
knew them right away. You could tell that." One cousin recalls that Mary
Flannery was not popular with other children. Sheltered by her mother, she
grew to be an "odd child," who showed no particular talents, "only her pecu-
liarities." Loretta Hoynes concurs, asserting that the young Mary Flannery
was "very deep, [. . .] a really strange person [who was often] strong-willed
and intimidating." Elizabeth Maguire Johnson, too, says, "Mary Flannery
was a rather strange young child and she did seem to have a vivid imagination. I can remember her mother talking about the stories that she wrote—
although I never read them." Newell Turner Parr, however, views Mary
Flannery's uniqueness more positively, calling her "a very unpretentious
person, [. . .] committed to being genuine," an outlook which some adults

considered a fault: "She was a lot of fun because she saw things as they were, behind the pretention" (Parr, Brown interview). Parr also recalls how the two of them sometimes enjoyed making fun of adults: "She was very good at that because she could see the humor in things. She was not interested in all the little things that most girls were interested in at that time, being cute and pretty and attracting all the boys. She really had an awareness of the important things in life, which was a little unusual for a girl at that age" (Parr, Brown interview). Attesting to Mary Flannery's lack of interest in boys, a distant cousin remembers that her own brothers, O'Connor's contemporaries, *"did not like her at all"* (cousin's emphasis).

During her years in Savannah, Mary Flannery, like other preadolescents from socially conscious backgrounds, took obligatory dancing lessons. In a letter to Betty Hester in March 1956, the mature O'Connor, taking pride in having a "tin leg" in regard to dancing, recalled her disgust with the mandatory lessons: "Nothing I hated worse than the company of other children and I vowed I'd see them in hell before I would make the first graceful move. The lessons went on for a number of years but I won. In a certain sense" (*HB* 145–46). One cousin recalls that once, when Mary Flannery and a girlfriend were to attend a dance in Savannah, Regina brought them to Cousin Katie Semmes to show off their dresses. According to the cousin, Mary Flannery had somehow acquired a mouthful of snuff, which undercut any pretense of being ladylike. Lillian Dowling Odom also remembers the episode: "instead of turning out to be the pretty little girl, she had this mess in her mouth. She did things like this all the time. She didn't like being the pretty little girl" (Odom, Brown interview).

In a letter to Betty Hester in 1956, the adult O'Connor revealed her deliberate refusal to become a teenager: "When I was twelve I made up mind absolutely that I would not get any older. I don't remember how I meant to stop it. There was something about 'teen' attached to anything that was repulsive to me. I certainly didn't approve of what I saw of people that age. I was a very ancient twelve; my views at that age would have done credit to a Civil War veteran. I am much younger now than I was at twelve, or anyway, less burdened. The weight of centuries lies on children, I'm sure of it" (*HB* 136–37).

Mary Flannery's childhood interests also show her uniqueness. Her contemporaries remember her early interest in chickens and birds. Pat Persse says, while trying to remember the appearance of the O'Connor house, "The only thing that I could remember is that she had birds on the back porch" (Persse, Brown interview). When Mary Flannery was six years old, she gained a certain notoriety from owning a chicken that could walk backward. Loretta Hoynes, who was already Mary Flannery's friend, thinks that Katie Semmes was responsible for bringing a Pathé News photographer to Savannah to film the chicken walking backward. Hoynes claims to have been with Mary Flannery when the photographer arrived; she also asserts that he did not actually get it: "Mary Flannery did not like the photographer that came down here and she would not let the chicken walk backward. She had that chicken trained well. It did not do it" (Hoynes, Brown interview). O'Connor's own comment in a 1959 interview with Betsy Lochridge suggested (at least facetiously) that the filming was successful: "When I was six I had a chicken that walked backward and was in the Pathé News. I was in it too with the chicken. I was just there to assist the chicken but it was the high point in my life. Everything since has been anticlimax" (*Con* 38). Elizabeth Maguire Johnson remembers Mary Flannery's ducks and chickens: "She used to mimic the chicken that walked backwards. She would walk backwards, and I remember her mother saying that Mary Flannery was a mimic" (Johnson, Brown interview). Sister Consolata remembers her student's enthusiasm for chickens: "She always brought in chicken stories. When she talked about her chickens, she'd get very demonstrative and try to express herself." In an unpublished letter written to a relative in the summer of 1937, Regina O'Connor described Mary Flannery's enthusiasm for poultry—this time ducks; she told her correspondent that Mary Flannery had become so engrossed in her ducks that she could hardly separate her daughter from them. She also described Mary Flannery's pleasure in watching them take baths in the dirt that she had sifted into one of their cages. She admitted that she herself enjoyed the ducks' antics almost as much as her young daughter did.[20] O'Connor's early love for exotic fowl became a lifelong avocation, one that enriched both her later circumscribed life in Milledgeville and her fiction.

Except for those comments already included, O'Connor's early connections in Savannah have few memories of any special interests Mary Flannery displayed in either reading or writing, though her cousin Katherine Groves recalls that she wrote plays and had others take roles in them. In her autobiographical sketch from Iowa, O'Connor herself talked about how she used her early precocity to show her parents that God was just in giving them such a child. She wrote of how she used her early talent as a writer to prove her literary ability to them and subsequently received the sort of positive response at which she had aimed (O'CC, GCSU). Even her early efforts show her clever satirical ability.

In an unpublished letter to Maryat Lee in 1960, O'Connor talked about another of her early productions, a biographical study of her relatives that she wrote at the age of ten. She wrote that she printed and distributed seven copies that were too "naturalistic" to be well received by her subjects.[21] A diary-like notebook twelve-year-old Mary Flannery wrote and bound displays her independent turn of mind; she vents anger against education, both formal and social, reveals that she is a poor speller, and demonstrates a rather typical preadolescent resentment of her mother's control.[22]

O'Connor's relatives and acquaintances in Savannah have few recollections of her reading there, but in the summer of 1937, when she was twelve, Mary Flannery and her mother traveled to Atlanta to enroll Mary Flannery in a summer reading course offered at the Atlanta Public Library. The two apparently stayed with relatives in Atlanta while Mary Flannery completed the class; a certificate proving that she finished it is in the O'Connor Collection at Georgia College;[23] in addition, the Woodruff Library at Emory has thank-you notes from both Mary Flannery and her mother to the relative with whom they stayed in Atlanta. Mary Flannery's note is brief and to the point, showing that Regina probably forced her to write it; she bluntly thanked her relative for giving her the chance to read the books, said she appreciated the certificate, and ended by saying that "Regina" will write when she "has time."[24] In a letter to Betty Hester in 1955, however, O'Connor wrote disparagingly of her childhood reading, asserting that "[t]he only good things I read when I was a child were the Greek and Roman myths which I got out of a set of a child's encyclopedia called *The Book of Knowledge*" (*HB* 98). She wrote that she later developed an interest in Edgar Allan Poe

> which lasted for years and consisted chiefly in a volume called
> *The Humerous Tales of E. A. Poe.* These were mighty humerous—
> one about a young man who was too vain to wear his glasses
> and consequently married his grandmother by accident; another

about a fine figure of a man who in his room removed wooden arms, wooden legs, hair piece, artificial teeth, voice box, et. etc.; another about the inmates of a lunatic asylum who take over the establishment and run it to suit themselves. This is an influence I would rather not think about. (*HB* 98)

Disparaging or not, the young Flannery chose a fitting literary hero in Poe, one of the first U.S. writers to use elements of the grotesque for motives other than sensationalism.

One other area of interest involving Flannery O'Connor and Savannah evolves from the reactions of her relatives and acquaintances to the fame she achieved during her years in Milledgeville, which continues to increase both nationally and internationally. Her relatives and friends are unanimous in being surprised or shocked by her genius. Pat Persse declares: "There was certainly no one else in the family that had this kind of talent"; however, she also recalled that Mary Flannery possessed unique talent from childhood: "Even as a child she was doing something, illustrating children's books or even writing children's stories that may have been published. So I think her talent was evident." Elizabeth Maguire Johnson says simply, "I had no idea Mary Flannery would become a writer. This was especially so with the nun criticizing her compositions so much." The nun herself (Sister Consolata) concurs: "We never knew she was going to be a celebrity. [. . . But when it came] I was delighted, was very happy for the child and her mother. I was very close to the mother. I knew she was very supportive of me and of the school. No matter what we wanted, she was there. And that helped the child."

Natives of Savannah remember the community's reaction to *Wise Blood* in 1952. Hugh Brown asserted that when the novel came out, "Savannah was scandalized. It took a long time for people to begin to understand that book" (H. Brown, personal interview). The Persse sisters, though not invited, remember the book signing party held at GSCW: "When she wrote *Wise Blood,* everybody, all the family members were so proud of this relative, you know who had become famous and published a book. So the college, Georgia College for Women, had a literary tea and they invited all the family. [. . .] Miss Katie Semmes went and my aunt; they drove to Milledgeville for this occasion; and, of course, they all [. . .] got an autographed copy of the book. Mrs. Semmes read the book and [. . .] went to bed for a week" (Persse,

Brown interview). Katie Semmes had also, apparently, bought a number of copies of the novel and sent them to Monsignor James T. McNamara and other members of the clergy in Savannah before she had read the book herself. When she did read it, she was so shocked that she wrote letters of apology to the Savannah clergy (H. Brown, personal interview).

Gerry Sullivan Horne, who knew O'Connor slightly in Savannah but much better in Milledgeville, remembers her own thoughts about *Wise Blood:* "What is this thing that Mary Flannery has written here!" (Horne, Brown interview). An unidentified member of the audience at one of the sessions Hugh Brown held at the O'Connor home wittily exclaimed: "It [the content of *Wise Blood*] wasn't on the reading list at St. Vincent's" (H. Brown, personal interview). A distant cousin recalls that family members were aghast at the book, wondering where she "had ever learned anything like that—that they had never known people like that." She claimed in 1990 that she still did not care for Mary Flannery's writing. Though the Persse cousins grew to appreciate and understand O'Connor's fiction, Pat Persse's comment depicts the family's early astonishment with O'Connor's fiction: "Nobody could understand how this sheltered Southern girl had come up with this story and this language" (Persse, Brown interview). Obviously, this "sheltered Southern girl" had opened her senses to a world beyond the protected shell of her early upbringing, and yet incorporated the genuine spirituality of her Catholic faith to give her grotesque regionalism a universal dimension.

CHAPTER TWO

MILLEDGEVILLE, 1938~1942

When Edward O'Connor took a job with the Federal Housing Administration early in 1938 as a real estate appraiser in Atlanta, Regina and Mary Flannery O'Connor followed him there briefly; Mary Flannery completed seventh grade at the parochial school of St. Joseph's Church in Atlanta. When the school term ended, however, she and her mother moved to Milledgeville to live in the Cline family home on Greene Street; Edward O'Connor remained in Atlanta during the week, rooming at the Bell House, a boardinghouse where Regina's bachelor brothers, Dr. Bernard and Louis Cline, had lived for many years (*CW* 1238-39). Years later, in 1957, when the Bell House was bulldozed to make room for a parking lot, O'Connor wrote that her Uncle Louis "brought all of the furniture out of it—largely monstrosities—and it is arriving here this afternoon in a van" (*HB* 238). She mentioned further acquisitions from the Bell House in a letter to William Sessions on 1 September 1957: "We have come into the front-porch rockers from there so our front porch now looks like the entrance to an old ladies' rest home" (240).

Despite the inconvenience of having her husband live part time away from the family, Regina Cline O'Connor must certainly have welcomed the move to Milledgeville since her family's Roman Catholic roots were so deep in the former Georgia capital. Of the development of Roman Catholicism in the town and Peter Cline's early prominence in the town, Milledgeville historian James C. Bonner writes that in 1874 Roman Catholic members of the community dedicated "a Roman Catholic sanctuary" on the site of the old Lafayette Hotel. About sixty members formed the parish "known as the Sacred Heart of Jesus. Among these were the families of Treanor, Cline, O'Brien, Magill, Supple and Quinn." He relates that the "Catholic community grew steadily, and it made exceptional contributions to the civil and cultural life of the town," a town in which they experienced no "religious intolerance." Bonner asserts that the "leading Catholic, Peter J. Cline, was the unanimous choice for mayor in 1889; two of his wife's sisters taught in the local school" (Bonner 251–52).

When the O'Connor family arrived in Milledgeville, they joined two of Regina's unmarried sisters, who continued to live in the impressive house where Peter Cline's large family had grown up. Gen. John B. Gordon built the Gordon-Ward-Beal-Cline-O'Connor house, one of Milledgeville's oldest homes, in 1837. Of the illustrious early history of the house Bonner writes: "By 1820 the state had acquired a two-acre double lot on Clarke Street between Hancock and Greene on which there was a two-story frame house facing the latter street. Known as Government House, this building served as the residence of the chief executive until 1838 when the Executive Mansion was completed" (22).

The house where Mary Flannery O'Connor spent her teenage years was and remains a beautiful tribute to Milledgeville's past. The large, frame structure with many windows faces Greene Street with great dignity. Regina Sullivan and her sister Gerry Sullivan Horne recall the rather exalted social position of the Cline family in Milledgeville. Asserting that even though the Cline sisters were not wealthy—recall that Peter J. Cline had sixteen children from his two marriages—Gerry Sullivan Horne says, "You always thought of the family [. . .] as a very genteel, old Southern family" (Sullivan and Horne, Brown interview). O'Connor's Savannah cousin Tony Harty, who also visited his relatives in this house during his boyhood in the late 1930s and early 1940s, remembered the two unmarried sisters, Mary and Katie Cline. He said, "Mary—Sister they called her—the Matriarch, she was in control but she never wielded her authority in an offensive way. She was always pleasant, exerting gentle control." O'Connor's closest friend at GSCW, Betty Boyd Love, gave more information about Miss Mary: "[She was] quiet and retiring. She was like a tall, thin, austere nun, and in appropriate fashion Flannery called her 'Sister.' I think it isn't likely that Miss Mary wore only white, but my recollection of her is of a quiet, kindly woman always in white" (Love 65). In a note on the manuscript of an early version of Love's article, Regina Cline O'Connor revealed that Miss Mary gained her family nickname because she was the first daughter born into the family after five boys.[1] Elizabeth Horne, a longtime Milledgeville friend of the Clines and O'Connors—she too, is Roman Catholic—asserts that she loved both of the Cline sisters but that they were decidedly different in personality: "Miss Mary was a business man from the world 'go.' They tell me she took over [the family business] when her father died. From that point on, she was the head of the family. [. . .] She had a lot of strength. They used to say about Miss Mary that she said she wasn't going [to die] unless she could take her money with her, so she wasn't going."[2]

Miss Katie Cline, though "a little disabled," according to Tony Harty, worked in the post office in Milledgeville for many years. Elizabeth Horne recalls: "We used to call Miss Katie the Duchess of Bopshire. She had a coat that had a fur collar and I can see her right now—a long and regal image of a duchess." Horne found it rather strange that Miss Katie worked in the post office: she seemed too regal for such "lowly" employment. Betty Boyd Love also held a strong memory of Miss Katie: "Miss Katie was something of a 'character.' She bore a strong resemblance to illustrator Tenniel's Duchess in *Alice in Wonderland*. As a matter of fact, Flannery addressed her as 'Duchess.' She was a woman of vigorous appearance, vigorous language, and vigorous opinion" (Love 65).

One quality of O'Connor's family life, then, that remained stable when she moved from Savannah to Milledgeville was its matriarchy. She and her mother moved into a house inhabited only by women; since Edward O'Connor remained in Atlanta during the week and Regina's bachelor brothers also came to Milledgeville only on weekends, hers remained a family controlled by its female members. O'Connor's Milledgeville contemporaries clearly remember how Miss Mary Cline dominated the household.

Kitty Smith Kellam, though six years younger than Mary Flannery, grew up in a house near the Cline mansion. Of Miss Mary Cline, she says: "Miss Mary was very austere; her backbone was so straight. They never heard of osteoporosis when she came along. [. . .] She was one [. . .] commanding woman in her carriage and personality."[3] Kellam also speculates on the humorless life Mary Flannery must have lived in the Cline household: "I don't know whether there was too much excuse [for Mary Flannery] to laugh in that house or not, with her brilliance and being in a conservative home with these older aunts." The matriarchal Cline household, then, probably had both positive and negative influence on its youngest inhabitant. Certainly, her independent aunts and ambitious mother provided models of strong, self-sustaining women; however, at the same time, she was—because of their maturity—partly deprived of a normal girlhood. Still, O'Connor's Savannah friend Loretta Feuger Hoynes feels that Mary Flannery experienced "much happiness" in Milledgeville, where the Cline family was well known and connected: "They took care of each other."

Mary Flannery's father, Edward O'Connor, remained as distant a figure in Milledgeville as he had been in Savannah, particularly after he became seriously ill with lupus. None of O'Connor's Milledgeville acquaintances have strong memories of him. Kitty Smith Kellam says: "I don't remember anything about the man except seeing him walk out of Church. He was a [. . .] tall, good-looking man." Elizabeth Horne, four years older than O'Connor, also recalls Ed O'Connor only at Church with Regina. She believes that he and Mary Flannery shared a loving relationship, that "[t]hey were close [but] Regina, I'm sure ruled the roost." Elizabeth Shreve Ryan, a classmate of Mary Flannery's at Peabody, remembers that when Edward O'Connor died in 1941, she, as a class officer, attended his funeral, and Helen Greene, who took her meals in Milledgeville at the home of Mrs. Mag Stembridge (a Roman Catholic), remembers the Stembridges attending a Rosary for Ed O'Connor. She also believes that Mary Flannery "was devoted to her father" and speculates that "she was a lot like him."[4]

Her father's illness and death, then, brought the O'Connors to Milledgeville permanently, but Mary Flannery O'Connor apparently failed to develop a particularly warm emotional attachment to the town itself. Though she had visited Milledgeville during summer vacations while her family lived in Savannah, the move into the Cline household must have been somewhat traumatic, for at thirteen she was accustomed to living only with her parents; in addition, she was on the verge of adolescence, had been schooled to this point only in the Roman Catholic system, and had already established a number of acquaintances in her native Savannah.

As a thirteen-year-old, Mary Flannery O'Connor carried with her the qualities of personality she had already developed in Savannah. She was obviously precocious in her interest in reading and writing; she was also a loner who did not easily form friendships; her hobbies—particularly her interest in birds, ducks, and chickens—remained strong; as an only child, she was closely attached to her family: her rather domineering and overly protective mother and her loving but reserved father. Mary Flannery O'Connor was already a unique girl whose particular qualities and interests would sustain her through her high school and college years.

Having arrived in Milledgeville already molded by her childhood in Savannah, she could, then, view the town with an objectivity that later enabled her to live in and write about the South from a Georgia point of view but without personal reference to Milledgeville. In 1960 she wrote to her agent Elizabeth McKee about her reluctance to write directly about the town: "Milledgeville is the only Southern town I could write about and if I did that I'd not only have to please the editors of HOLIDAY but the 10,000 citizens here. I'm afraid it would activate my lupus" (*HB* 408). Though some of O'Connor's Milledgeville friends enjoy looking for Milledgeville connections in her stories, they have found few correspondences. Jay Lewis, for example, believes that "A Temple of the Holy Ghost" evolved from Mary Flannery's summer experiences with her Florencourt cousins from Boston, and that there is a good deal of O'Connor herself in Joy-Hulga Hopewell of "Good Country People."[5] Generally, however, her contemporaries feel that O'Connor's work is universal rather than limited to a depiction of life in Milledgeville. In a 1960 interview, O'Connor herself commented specifically on her universal use of her community in her work: "I don't feel that I am writing about the community at all. I feel that I am taking things in the community that I can show the whole western world, the whole edition of the present generation of people, of what I can use of the Southern situation" (*Con* 70).

When the O'Connors moved there in 1938, inland Milledgeville was quite different from the coastal city where Mary Flannery had spent her first years. Savannah, the first permanent settlement in Georgia, was far more cosmopolitan than this rather remote town of under ten thousand inhabitants. Savannah carried an aura of the Old World, with its seaport, its half dozen theaters, its almost European architecture and its Roman Catholic enclave. Though Milledgeville had its own illustrious history, having served as the capital city of Georgia from 1807 to 1877, it was much more provincial than Savannah, despite its beautiful antebellum homes like the former governor's mansion (1838) on Clarke Street and the Cline house on Greene Street.

According to James Bonner, Milledgeville became the capital as a result of the urge for western expansion in the state. Savannah, because of its early connections—political and commercial—with England, was not seriously considered. After the town of Milledgeville (named to honor John Milledge, then governor of the state) was established in 1803, the legislature, within two years (1805), designated it the state capital. Because Milledgeville virtually arose from the wilderness in the western part of the state, it maintained its frontier qualities, including little expansion, for many years.

Despite its relative remoteness, Milledgeville, as the state capital, saw considerable activity during the Civil War. The Secession Convention met there on 16 January 1861, attended by notables from other states, including Robert Barnwell Rhett from South Carolina, Edmund Ruffin from Virginia, and Judge W. L. Harris, representing Mississippi. After a three-day meeting the convention voted to secede, with considerable rejoicing among the populace. Shortly thereafter, local men activated several volunteer military units in support of the Confederate effort. The oldest, the Baldwin Blues, had been organized as early as 1848 and was formally incorporated in 1858. They were joined by the Black Springs Rifles, the Troup Artillery, and the University Guards, quickly formed at nearby Oglethorpe University (Bonner 156). Though not everybody in Milledgeville supported secession, once the war started, most inhabitants—male and female—contributed to the Confederate effort. In 1864, Milledgeville itself was invaded by "a roving band of cavalryman under George Stoneman" (164). Finally, Sherman, too, attacked Milledgeville, burning several residences, the Central Depot, the bridge spanning the Oconee River, and the town arsenal (177). Thus the town shares a heritage of devastation with many southern towns, a heritage celebrated often in works of both popular and literary southern fiction.

With the exception of one story, "A Late Encounter with the Enemy," in which she treats veneration for what she facetiously termed the "Wah Between the States" (*HB* 428), Flannery O'Connor showed little interest in Milledgeville's Confederate past. She, in fact, revealed her lack of knowledge of the history of the town as late as October 1958 in a letter to Betty Hester, when she wrote that she was reading Bonner's history of Georgia: "I am highly pleased with the Georgia past. I am trying to persuade my mother to read it. [. . .] It is full of eye-gougers and duelists" (300). Her revelation that she was trying to influence her mother to read the history also documents the lack of historical emphasis Regina Cline O'Connor must have placed on her daughter's education. In other of her letters, O'Connor clearly showed her indifference to the Civil War; when Hester offered to buy her copy of one of Bruce Catton's novels, O'Connor responded: "What do you want to read *A Stillness at Appomattox* for? Buy it for me but don't send it to me. I never was one to go over the Civil War in a big way" (309). A fragment titled "Reminiscence," preserved in the O'Connor Collection at Georgia College, further reveals her dichotomized view—she expresses some veneration for the historical South but a lack of appreciation for new southern customs. Her subject here is the pilgrimages to antebellum houses that became so popular in southern towns beginning, in the 1920s, with the women's club movement for the preservation of antebellum houses. O'Connor recalled that older homes, including her own, were opened to the public during these pilgrimages and that the public "trouped" through the houses with an attitude of "respectful solemnity." She remembered her own attitude as proud, bored, and mocking. She signed her pet chickens' names into the guest book and added their addresses as "Hungry." She wrote that the pilgrimages had continued through the years and, as she believed, become even more replete with "fakery" than during her girlhood. She asserted that the motivation for these events was "romantic imagination"; they were best looked at with a "brutal" eye.[6]

O'Connor showed her clearest repugnance for glamorizing the war, however, when, in 1961, Milledgeville celebrated the Centennial of Georgia's secession from the Union. One of her Milledgeville friends, Lance Phillips, who was British, wrote the pageant. In various of her letters from the period, O'Connor ridiculed the whole affair: the "big parade in 20 [degree] weather with young ladies on floats freezing in their drafty dresses" (*HB* 428); the money spent—"$1,000 for fireworks and $600 for floats" (432); and, Phillips's pageant, which "was such a smashing success that the Chamber of Commerce hopes to put in on during the season and make this another Wm'burg" (432). In an unpublished letter to Maryat Lee, O'Connor admitted that she did not see the pageant,[7] though she did agree to welcome guests at the Cline home, which, of course, was open as part of the pilgrimage. She wrote to her friend Ashley Brown: "We have been vigorously celebrating Secession here. [. . .] I sat over the hole in the upholstery in the living-room sofa and shook the hands of all and sundry. About 500 people showed up" (431).

J. O. Tate, who was a young man growing up in Milledgeville himself during this period, elaborates on O'Connor's lack of enthusiasm for the Centennial events: "O'Connor's participation in the Tour of Homes (antebellum ones) was, I believe, a grudging one—a family obligation and no more; for she was not comfortable with the Old South Associations. She was not at home with the tone or style of the United Daughters of the Confederacy, which sponsored that Tour on Jan. 20 and 21, 1961. So she sat on the hole in the sofa, but she didn't go to the Square Dance at the National Guard Armory or the 'Old Fashion Ball' at the Auditorium of the Milledgeville State Hospital" (J. O. Tate 32). As Tate has asserted elsewhere, O'Connor "'virtually cut herself off from local history,'" instead becoming "'a citizen in good standing of the republic of letters'" (Day 1).

Milledgeville in the twentieth century has gained fame mostly for its institutions, not the least of them its most renowned writer. Its institutional prominence, however, began with the town's status as state capital and the early construction of government buildings. By 1830 three Protestant churches—the Methodist, the Baptist, and the Presbyterian—shared Statehouse Square with these buildings. The Episcopalians built their church in 1840 (Bonner 24–25). Another early institution in the town was the state penitentiary. One of the four original squares in Milledgeville was Penitentiary Square—called that as early as 1807—when there were already plans to build a state prison on it. The prison opened in 1817 with "fewer than a hundred inmates" (24); the square also held the Baldwin County courthouse and jail. When the O'Connors came to Milledgeville, the penitentiary, moved out of town, had evolved into the state penitentiary for men, women, and youthful offenders. In letters, O'Connor refers several times to the reformatory for juveniles, satirically citing it as one of the few outstanding features of the town or commenting about juvenile escapees; in July 1959, for example, she wrote to Maryat Lee that nine inmates of the reformatory had escaped during the week just past: "They track them down through the woods with other reformatory boys. We would much prefer they use dogs" (*HB* 339).

A third institution associated with Milledgeville was the Georgia Lunatic Asylum, a bill for which the legislature passed as early as 1837; it did not, however, admit its first patient until 1842 (Bonner 82). When the O'Connor family moved to Milledgeville, the hospital had become the Central Hospital for the Mentally Ill. Again, in her letters, O'Connor occasionally referred to this institution as one of the few intriguing features of her community; her Savannah friend Loretta Hoynes remembers Mary Flannery's adolescent enthusiasm for the asylum: "When you went to Milledgeville, her greatest thrill was taking somebody by the mental institution because the windows were all open and there was no air-conditioning [. . .] and those folks were just literally screaming, and she would love to take you by there. That was a lot of fun to take a new visitor, who hadn't been there" (Hoynes, Brown interview). Kitty Smith Kellam speculates that because of her superior powers of observation, O'Connor might have used eccentrics from the mental hospital as models for characters in her fiction. She wonders whether they "would have been different had not the state mental institution been in Baldwin County."

Finally, in relation to its institutions, Milledgeville was noted for its schools in a time when there were no public schools in Georgia. Bonner writes that as early 1810, "Mason Locke Weems appeared during the session of the superior court to take orders for his books, among which was his famous *Life of Washington*. Weems remained in Milledgeville through part of the legislative session. His lecture at the Statehouse on the importance of education was well attended" (67). During the 1820s, according to Bonner, there was a "paucity" of reading material in the town: "To fill this deficit several local citizens subscribed to a circulating library organized and run from Lucas' tavern" (*Georgia Journal* 10 May 1815: n. pag.). By 1820 Arthur Ginn had established a bookstore on Wayne Street that offered, among other books, *Wealth of Nations,* Plutarch's *Lives,* Locke's *Essays,* and works by Shakespeare, Cervantes, Goldsmith, Byron, Scott, Swift, and Coleridge (Bonner 67).

In 1816, William Montgomery Green and his wife opened two private academies—one for young men, the other for young women—in Milledgeville (Bonner 98). This early interest in education culminated, after the

Civil War, in Milledgeville's becoming the site of two colleges, the Georgia Military College (which continues to educate both secondary and junior college students—today young men *and* young women) and today's coeducational Georgia College and State University, which was Georgia State College for Women when O'Connor and her family moved to the town in 1938. Bonner calls the building of "two flourishing colleges [. . .] an exceptional achievement for a community of fewer than 1,700 inhabitants" (247). Though Flannery O'Connor uses neither Georgia State College for women nor its adjunct Peabody High School as direct settings in her fiction, they contributed to her development through the education she experienced and the accomplishments she recorded in both of these institutions between 1938 and 1945.

At that time the Catholic community was too small in Milledgeville to support parochial schools; therefore, Regina O'Connor had no choice but to send her daughter to the public Peabody High School. In 1938, O'Connor, along with her Roman Catholic kin, continued to attend mass in Milledgeville and to receive religious instruction from nuns who came to Milledgeville every Sunday from Mount DeSalles in Macon. Kitty Smith Kellam recalls how alien she felt as a Roman Catholic child in a predominantly protestant town: "You didn't know what was wrong with you. [. . . I felt there] were a lot of misconceptions. Things that seemed perfectly normal to me seemed like voodoo to other people and I didn't understand why because I had never been to a Protestant church so I couldn't understand all the mysticism that they felt and the secrecy involved, when to me it made perfect sense." Elizabeth Horne, however, believes that the small number of Catholics in Milledgeville helped to draw them closer together in their practice and in their faith. She recalls that because the Church has always regarded Georgia as a "mission territory," it was conscientious in serving the special needs of the congregation: nuns came to teach Sunday school, to play the organ for the choir on special occasions like midnight mass on Christmas Eve.

Horne, absolutely certain that O'Connor's faith never wavered throughout her life, remembers O'Connor's explanation for her lifetime of steadfast belief: "I heard her say once, in a conversation, she had investigated as thoroughly as she could the background of the Church, the credentials of the Church and had accepted them and as far as she was concerned from that point on in the Church, that was it, and I've always felt the same way." During her adolescent years in Milledgeville, then, Mary Flannery, though privately a devoutly practicing Catholic, seems to have lived publicly a mainly secular life. Peabody High School, which she entered as an eighth grade (freshman) student in 1938, was a laboratory school of Georgia State College for Women. When she attended Peabody it was primarily a girls' school. Elizabeth Shreve Ryan remembers only "one brave male" in their class; most young men from the town attended the Georgia Military Academy (Ryan 49). Elizabeth Horne, who graduated four years ahead of Mary Flannery, remembers two boys in her class who "absolutely refused to go to a military school." Of the strength of Peabody's program and its special value to O'Connor, Ryan asserts: "Peabody High provided Mary Flannery with a supportive and nourishing atmosphere [. . .]. The faculty of Peabody were teachers of teachers with a level of education and experience far above that of the average Georgia school teacher at the time" (49). Other contemporaries of O'Connor who also attended Peabody share Ryan's enthusiasm for the school. Yvonne Giles Armour says: "I just remember having a lot of real good teachers that were students, but most of our [supervising] teachers had advanced degrees—many of them had doctorates but at least a master's degree."[8] Elizabeth Horne also retains quite positive memories of the Peabody faculty. Because Peabody was connected with GSCW, a master teacher in each subject area supervised rotating student teachers. Horne remembers having "a different teacher every six weeks in each subject." Critics of the system have asked her how she received a good education in an environment in which unskilled teachers "practiced on" students. She says, "I reminded them that these people who taught us under the tutelage of the master teacher were out teaching *them* without anybody directing them."

One of the exceptional master teachers at Peabody was Lila Blitch, Mary Flannery's eighth grade Latin teacher.[9] Blitch, later a Ph.D. candidate at the University of Maryland, wrote a paper there, "The Southern Landlord and His Tenants," in which she says she tried to dispel the negative view of the South propagated by certain Southern writers including O'Connor. She says she was "terribly disappointed" in the type of person O'Connor chose as the main character of *Wise Blood*.

According to Blitch, Peabody in the 1930s and 1940s (when she taught there) had a strong academic focus, partly because it operated under strict government control as one of ten high schools in the state chosen to offer an experimental curriculum. For two or three summers selected teachers from Peabody met with teachers from the other nine schools to coordinate the experiment. Peabody teachers had to write reports to the government detailing their participation and progress. Blitch's pamphlet, for example, was later published in a North Carolina journal for high school teachers. She recalls that the principal of the school, Mildred English, urged teachers to "stick with the basics" as well as to use innovative ideas. Overall, Blitch feels that the cooperative effort paid off—she recalls her years in the program as an "interesting time."[10]

Peabody alumnae remember the experimental nature of Peabody. "They let you do so many different things," one recalls. "We never did anything by rote. The primary thrust of the school was to teach you to think which is the best education you can possibly get."[11] She also recalls never diagramming a sentence "until I had to teach it." Yvonne Giles Armour remembers that in Margaret Abercrombie's home economics class, students chose what they wanted to do: her group planned and executed a formal dinner at the home of one of the students. Elizabeth Horne, who later became a high school chemistry teacher herself, recalls her chemistry class at Peabody: "They asked us what we wanted to learn, so we told them we wanted to learn about photography and we wanted to learn about cosmetics. [. . .] I enjoyed it. We had a real nice year and the teacher did run in a little bit about the elements and the periodic table. [. . .] I learned my chemistry in college." Jay Lewis also remembers that Peabody had "a Verse Choir, [. . .] an a cappella choir" whose members recited poetry in harmony: "we would have our altos and sopranos."

In contrast with the enthusiasm of her classmates at Peabody, the adult O'Connor often mentioned the "sorry" quality of her Peabody education, particularly decrying her lack of instruction in the classics. The brief list of her entrance credits when she entered GSCW does show that the curriculum—despite innovative techniques—was uninspiring. She had earned four credits in English and History, two in French, one each in Latin, Art, Algebra, Plane Geometry, Biology, and Home Economics and a half credit each in Arithmetic and Commerce. In an unpublished fragment in the O'Connor Collection at GCSU, she lamented her lack of classical education, asserting that such an education is essential for the writer. The Dewey form of education, she asserted, left no trace of the classics; the system forced the writer to make up for the lack the "best way we can" (O'CC, GCSU). O'Connor also felt that the progressive system allowed immature students too much freedom to plan their own courses of study. In her lecture "The Total Effect and the Eighth Grade," she wrote:

> Ours is the first age in history which has asked the child what he would tolerate learning [. . .]. The devil of Educationism that possesses us is the kind that can be "cast out only by prayer and fasting." No one has yet come along strong enough to do it. In other ages the attention of children was held by Homer and Virgil, among others, but, by the reverse evolutionary process, that is no longer possible; our children are too stupid now to enter the past imaginatively. No one asks the student if algebra pleases him or if he finds its satisfactory that some French verbs are irregular, but if he prefers Hersey to Hawthorne, his taste must prevail. (*MM* 137)

Of the effect of this system on herself as one of its "victims," O'Connor asserted, in the unpublished autobiographical sketch from Iowa, that she became "a self-expressive adolescent" who could neither spell nor count, had a confused sense of history, and no knowledge of foreign languages.[12] O'Connor was also dubious about progressive attempts to integrate subject matter into what educators today term *interdisciplinary studies:*

> I once went to a high school [Peabody] where all the subjects were called "activities" and were so well integrated that there were no definite ones to teach. I have found that if you are astute and energetic, you can integrate English literature with geography, biology, home economics, basketball or fire prevention— with anything at all that will put off a little longer the evil day when the story or novel must be examined simply as a story or novel. (*MM* 127)

Of the organization of the Peabody system itself, O'Connor wrote to Cecil Dawkins that the whole idea of "'learning for life'" turned her stomach. She told how the teachers at Peabody studied under William Heard Kilpatrick during the summers and returned in the fall to ask their students "as mature children, what we ought to study." O'Connor asserts that the result for her of this "progressive" environment was that she learned neither Greek nor history (*HB* 249).

In a 1963 interview with Gerard E. Sherry, O'Connor talked about how being allowed to make choices about what to read negatively influenced her reading habits; she asserted that because she could read whatever she chose, she read nothing worthwhile. She remembered, for example, "reading a book of Ludwig Bemelman's about the hotel business. [. . .] About all I remember of those four years is the way the halls smelled and bringing my accordion sometimes to play for the 'devotionals'" (*Con* 99). In response to O'Connor's criticism of the Peabody system, Kitty Smith Kellam asserts that "if anybody would have rebelled at a list of books mandated it would have been Flannery." Elizabeth Horne, however, recalls that in one of their last conversations, O'Connor "was so disturbed about the trend of asking the children what they wanted to do. [. . .] She said there should be a list of books that everybody should read. [. . .] She felt there must be a basic knowledge in each discipline. She was very much upset about not having to read some things that everybody ought to."

Though O'Connor facetiously asserted that she was not hurt by this educational system because she was "blessed with 'Total Non-Retention,'" the progressive atmosphere did benefit her more than she was willing to admit— it allowed her to display her originality in ways that a more formal atmosphere might have stifled. Adding new details, Elizabeth Shreve Ryan retells the story of how Mary Flannery made clothes for her pet duck rather than an apron for herself in the experimental Home Economics class: "A prime example of this attitude [acceptance of] unique personalities and talents such as hers abounds in the now familiar story told by Mary Flannery's home economics teachers Margaret Abercrombie. When Miss Abercrombie instructed her students to make an apron, Mary Flannery asked if she might makes clothes for her pet duck. In following Peabody's philosophy of progressive education and granting permission, Miss Abercrombie reasoned that sewing clothes for a duck required more skills than creating a shapeless apron" (Ryan 50).

Lila Blitch also remembered Mary Flannery's early creativity, recalling her in the eighth grade as a good student, though a "quiet sort of child" who seemed to "stay to herself." Blitch's more specific recollections, however, were of how Mary Flannery's particular interest in a pet duck had a literary result. She remembers that it was then customary for parents to invite teachers to their homes for dinner. Just after Easter in 1939, Regina O'Connor invited Blitch to dine at the Cline house with her, Mary Flannery, and the two unmarried Cline sisters. The former teacher recalls a pleasant evening that included Mary Flannery's inviting her upstairs to her room. When they got to the room, Mary Flannery proudly showed Blitch a baby yellow duck. Blitch says that she didn't think much about this duck at the time; however, on the last day of school, Mary Flannery told her that she had something to show her: it was a book about the duck which she had written, illustrated and titled "Mistaken Identity." Today that piece of juvenilia (dated 1941) is part of the O'Connor Collection at GCSU. In the story, Mary Flannery writes of a duck named Herman who becomes Henrietta after presenting its owner with an egg. Besides demonstrating her incipient talent at as a writer, the book also shows Mary Flannery's artistic skill: it is replete with drawings of Herman in a variety of masculine poses. The final drawing, however, shows Henrietta nesting (O'CC, GCSU). "Mistaken Identity" also stimulates fascinating speculations about Mary Flannery's questioning of her own sexual identity. Alienated by her superior intelligence and talent from other young Georgia women of her era, she experienced great difficulty conforming to the conventional roles offered them. When she has her goose tell three eligible females, "You gals can go to Hades," she is no doubt expressing her own disdain for boys and dating. Decidedly not a Southern belle, she probably would have preferred to be a male like Herman: in the early 1940s men were the thinkers, questioners, and writers—what she herself wanted to become.

After her first year at Peabody, Mary Flannery apparently began to become fully involved in school activities and, as a result, accepted for both her talents and her unique personality. The 20 November 1940 issue of the *Peabody Palladium,* which lists Mary Flannery O'Connor as its art editor, features two of her linoleum cuts, one a tribute to Thanksgiving with the *s* reversed. The other, with the caption, "Just One More Day to Dream," shows a sleeping student dreaming of a huge roast turkey. "The First Book," a poem by Mary Flannery O'Connor appears in the same issue of the *Palladium*. The poem, though showing that Mary Flannery, like Faulkner, was no precocious poet, does reveal the high value she already placed on reading: she advised her readers to follow the example of her inventive caveman. More revealing, however, are her tone and use of language, both of which somewhat prefigure her later expertise. She rather ironically comments on human transience when she admonishes her readers to read while they still have time. She also displays a Roman Catholic doubt about human progress in the final lines of the poem (O'CC, GCSU).

Several of O'Connor's classmates at Peabody recall her publicly presented artistic and literary efforts. Gerry Sullivan Horne remembers her more for her art than her writing, but her sister Regina Sullivan remembers a review Mary Flannery wrote for the *Peabody Palladium* of *My Mother Is a Violent Woman,* the first writing she had ever seen by her (Sullivan and Horne, Brown interview). One member of the class of 1943 remembers, "We had a little weekly thing that we did on a piece of poster board, *The Chatterbox*. It was rotated among a lot of people. You worked it up and sometimes wrote all the articles yourself and you sometimes had other people do some of the thing, and a lot of it was gossip, who was dating whom and that sort of thing and who wore what to the prom. I knew her through that." Elizabeth Shreve Ryan, who still owns copies of the *Palladium* from 1940–42, says they show how Mary Flannery excelled in art as well as in "both creative and expository writing and won honors and recognition for her accomplishments." An art award that Ryan also remembers O'Connor received was "a five-week scholarship to the advertising Art School of Nashville, Tennessee" (Ryan 50–51).

In her senior year at Peabody, Mary Flannery won a prize in a statewide essay contest sponsored by Rich's Department Store in Atlanta. Students were to submit an essay on "The Citizen of My County Who Has Contributed Most to the State of Georgia." Top prize in the contest was a four-year scholarship, covering room, board, and tuition at any college in Georgia. J. Reynolds Allen, a contemporary of Mary Flannery, then attending Georgia Military Academy, also entered the contest. His essay on Carl Vinson won first prize in the state; O'Connor's essay on Dr. Marvin M. Parks, a former president of GSCW, won second place (to that of Allen) in Baldwin County and a prize of ten dollars (*Milledgeville Union-Recorder* 14 May 1942: n. pag.). Today Reynolds Allen takes considerable pride in having outwritten the future world-famous author when they were both seniors in high school.[13]

The most convincing evidence, however, of Mary Flannery O'Connor's creativity at Peabody occurs in a feature article about her published in the

Palladium on 16 December 1941. A photocopy of the article also appears in the 1990 issue of *The Flannery O'Connor Bulletin.*[14] Under the headline "Peabodite Reveals Strange Hobby," the story reveals that Mary Flannery's hobby is "collecting rejection slips." She told the reporter that she had begun writing at the age of six and had already produced three books, "Mistaken Identity," "Elmo," and "Gertrude," each of them about a goose. Mary Flannery, describing these books as "of a novelty type—too old for young children and two young for older people," asserted that her ambition was "to keep on writing, particularly satires."

The reporter details Mary Flannery's other creative interests including her collection of fowl—Herman the goose, which "Mary Flannery brought [. . .] to school last summer and painted its portrait"; Hallie Selassie, a pet rooster; Winston, a black crow; and the deceased Adolph, another rooster, whose "name was changed when neighbors began wondering about 'Here Adolph.'" At that time, Mary Flannery also owned 150 miniatures of fowl "in glass and china." The reporter praises Mary Flannery as a musician who plays "clarinet, accordion, and bull fiddle, 'because,' she said, referring to the latter, 'I am the only one who can hold it up.'" Although O'Connor took piano lessons both in Savannah and Milledgeville later, she claimed to have little interest in music, several times alluding to her "tin ear." One Milledgeville acquaintance remembers Regina O'Connor telling how she had to spank Mary Flannery to force her to wear hose to her first piano recital.

The *Palladium* article also mentions her cartoons for the paper, which show the "keen sense of humor characteristic of the cartoonist." The reporter envies Mary Flannery's unique notebook, "which she has painted with oils and covered with cellophane," and mentions that the young artist has recently designed "a collection of original lapel pins," now "on sale at a local store." The author's most revealing and prophetic statement about Mary Flannery, however, is her assertion that "nothing can be put beyond Mary Flannery—Nothing is impossible." A photograph, illustrating the article in the *Palladium* reveals a young girl who seems indifferent to her appearance. Looking even younger than her fifteen years, she faces the camera squarely with a set, determined expression. She wears what appear to be steel-rimmed glasses, and her hair is flat on top with bushy, rather unkempt-looking sides. She obviously had little interest in presenting herself as a Southern beauty.

The O'Connor Collection at GCSU contains manuscripts of two unpublished stories and a poem that Mary Flannery no doubt wrote while she was a student at Peabody.[15] Both stories, with clear autobiographical elements, show their young author's affinity for her feathered pets and her distinctly individual personality. Neither of the manuscript stories has a title. One of them features a protagonist named Mary Flemming, who has three pet chickens named for relatives who live next door—Cousin Annie, Aunt Edythe, and Helen. This story clearly shows Mary Flannery's adolescent angst, particularly her attitude toward being so closely supervised by a prim-and-proper mother, determined that her daughter be clean, have straight teeth, a flat stomach, and a graceful gait. Mary Flemming's antics in the story as she kisses her pets surely echo Mary Flannery's early deliberate attempts to maintain her individuality in spite of her mother's desire to raise a proper daughter. Having her heroine kiss chickens instead of boys may also show Mary Flannery's deliberate rejection of sexuality. A comic poem (full of misspellings) that O'Connor no doubt wrote about the same time as she wrote this story shows a similar individualism and evident self-satire; she declared that she was no "angle," that she lacked grace, had dirty hands and feet, talked little, was bad tempered, raspy voiced, and not musical; yet she managed to survive by eating good meals and breathing "plenty of fresh air."

Mary Flannery's second story also chronicles a young girl's love for a bird—this time a dead rooster. This story, however, seems less consciously autobiographical than the first presented here, though again Mary Flannery presents an obvious conflict between a mother and daughter; in fact, in this story the relationship becomes one of outright hostility. Caulda resents her mother's failure to understand her "sibling" love for her pet. When the rooster dies—possibly killed by either the family dog or the mother—the young girl tries to hold onto its corpse. Sillow has apparently been her only source of emotional warmth. When the mother tries to take the rooster's body from her, Caulda viciously attacks her. Caulda's reaction to the death of her pet may also be related to O'Connor's early loss of her father: it is tempting to interpret Caulda's sorrow and her subsequent fear of death as expressions of Mary Flannery's grief. In this story, the young author has created a rural setting with primitive, superstitious characters: death arrives as the "grim reaper" in white clothes, carrying "something at his side."

Despite writing stories like these, Mary Flannery did not show her private writing to classmates. Since none of them was a particularly close friend, they recall only the work—mainly cartooning—that she did for the school newspaper. Regina Sullivan remembers Mary Flannery for her intellect more than her appearance, asserting that her classmate possessed "a fantastic sense of humor, a great deal of dry wit and just always had a little twinkle to her eyes" (Sullivan and Horne, Brown interview). Probably because of her physical awkwardness, Mary Flannery showed little interest in athletics. Elizabeth Shreve Ryan tells of Mary Flannery's indifference to her gym classes at Peabody: "[S]he was far from enthusiastic about physical education. Nevertheless when the time came to head out to the volleyball or basketball court, she donned her blue gym suit and complied with grace, at the same time loathing every moment on the court. [. . .] Despite her good-natured acceptance of physical education, active participation in games was another matter. The closest she ever came to taking part was a nudge with her shoulder if the ball happened to come in her direction" (Ryan 50).

Mary Flannery's early Milledgeville acquaintances also remember her distinctive drawl. Reynolds Allen believes that she tried to sound as Southern as possible, using an accent "conspicuous to me." Kitty Smith Kellam describes Mary Flannery as "awkward in many ways. She was always immaculately groomed but she always looked like she wished she had on something else. It was like she [. . .] just didn't want to be bothered, and I remember how she used to despise to have to wear something on her head to go to Church. I think we kind of raced to see who could get it off first when we walked out the door." Elizabeth Horne believes such criticism of O'Connor's appearance, speech, and unusual behavior was clearly unjust. She says that she and her contemporaries—those who cared deeply about the somewhat unusual young girl—looked on these qualities "as [just] being Mary Flannery."

Because she was different then—physically, socially, and creatively—Mary Flannery apparently had few close friendships as a young girl in Milledgeville. Her acquaintances cannot recall her visiting other girls' homes. Jay Lewis remembers that Elizabeth Shreve walked up the hill to the Cline house to visit Mary Flannery, but "I never saw Flannery visit anybody." Another acquaintance asserts: "She never had any playmates. She never had what would be considered a close friend. We all knew her. We worked with her on various things, but [she never had] somebody that would go home to your house in the afternoons and then you would study together, go to the movies together." Though Regina Sullivan also says that she cannot remember that Mary Flannery had many close friends, she also asserts that "this didn't bother her" (Sullivan and Horne, Brown interview).

When Tony Harty visited Milledgeville during the summers he recalled that Mary Flannery was "always interested in doing something, [. . .] but she tended to just go her own way, and if you wanted to come along that was fine, but she was gonna get them done." Rather than forming close friendships, dating, and chatting with friends, Mary Flannery went her own way, participating in whatever activities interested *her*. The Sullivan sisters remember that, as a member of a Girl Scout troop in Milledgeville, she entertained the other girls by bringing one of her chickens, Aloisius, with her to the scout meeting: "He was dressed in his little gray shorts, a little white shirt, a jacket and a red bow tie. [. . .] He was not in a cage or a box; he just wandered around as we had our troop meeting and this always amused all of us" (Sullivan and Horne, Brown interview). Yvonne Giles Armour tells another anecdote that reveals O'Connor's continuing interest in her winged pets: "I remember long years ago going on a little field trip through Nesbit Woods, which no longer exists. It was really a nice area, and we were walking along and she had split off as some of us had from the group and she came running back to the teacher and said, 'Oh, I've found Amelia Earhart! I've found Amelia Earhart!' The teacher nearly fainted. She [Mary Flannery] had found a bird that had been missing. It was one of her birds, and she had named the bird Amelia Earhart, which would be very appropriate, of course."

Mary Flannery's closest acquaintance during her days at Peabody High may have been Mary Virginia Harrison, whose family lived near the Cline house. The same issue of the *Palladium* that carries the story about O'Connor's talents has, as its lead story, an account of that year's Christmas pageant at Peabody in which Mary Virginia Harrison was to represent "the Spirit of the Present." The accompanying photograph shows her to have been a young woman of grace and beauty. Mary Barbara Tate suggests that the friendship between Mary Flannery and Mary Virginia was likely one more promoted by their mothers than one the girls themselves might have chosen. Elizabeth Horne concurs. Other of their acquaintances feel that Mary Flannery and

Mary Virginia had too little in common to be genuinely close. O'Connor was intellectual and artistic while Mary Virginia's "aim was not to be intellectual but to be the Southern belle" (M. B. Tate, interview 1992). Alice Alexander, however, in an article published in the *Atlanta Journal* in 1979, asserts that a close friendship existed between the two girls:

> underneath the window [of the Cline house] met a secret society of two, Mary Flannery and her best friend Mary Virginia Russell [*sic*]. The society had an official flower, the dandelion.
>
> Mary Virginia was a pretty girl who loved to dance and flirted with the boys. A man who dated her [Reynolds Allen] said she and Flannery were as different as two friends could be. Flannery made a pin for her the color of a parrot, and the two would memorize the signs for Burma-Shave along the highway to Macon, where they went to visit the dentist. (Alexander 3B)

Recently discovered letters between O'Connor and Harrison found at Mary Virginia's childhood home in Milledgeville offer stronger proof of a friendship between them. Among the correspondence are three Christmas cards Mary Flannery made and sent to her friend in the early 1940s. Two other later letters are of particular interest. One reveals that while O'Connor was spending her last year in Iowa, Mary Virginia visited her there in October 1947. In the other, written in October 1949, O'Connor reacted to Mary Virginia's invitation to be one of her bridesmaids; she thanked Mary Virginia for having invited her to be in the bridal party, but she refused on theological grounds: she asserted that Church law forbade her from participating in religious services other than Catholic. She explained that a "conscious Catholic" must repress emotional wishes to whatever the Church demanded. Her final comment was that without this sort of devotion, the Catholic believer has nothing. To moderate her refusal, O'Connor joked that her lack of physical grace would have interfered with the ceremony, that she might have fallen through her skirt, and that her facial expression—looking as if she had "smelled something bad"—would not have been appropriate.[16] That communication between the two continued even after college proves its warmth; a friendship beyond that promoted by their mothers did, in fact, exist between the two young women.

Reynolds Allen, however, remembers that Mary Flannery was quite introverted as a young person and already seemed more "preoccupied with writing" than pursuing a social life. He does recall one occasion when he and Mary Virginia double-dated with Mary Flannery and his cousin Dick Allen. They went to a local juke joint, where Mary Flannery did very little talking. He does recall that once during the evening she stamped her foot and said, "'My dad-gum foot's gone to sleep!'" On hearing that anecdote, Kitty Smith Kellam says, "I'm glad I wasn't a fly on that wall."

O'Connor's cousin, Tony Harty, could not remember Mary Flannery's having shown any interest in boys as a teenager, and her Savannah friend Loretta Hoynes claims that Mary Flannery did not like men at all, probably because her only childhood association with a man was with her sick father. Hoynes says, "Men were not good in her opinion." One Milledgeville acquaintance suggests that Mary Flannery's awkwardness in forming relationships with the opposite sex may have resulted from her living in a household of adults. She has said, "To my knowledge, as long as I knew Flannery, she never had what I considered a date. Of course, the rest of us wasted an awful lot of time on that."

Adding variety, however, to Mary Flannery's summers in Milledgeville were the frequent visitors—young cousins, particularly—whom Mrs. O'Connor surely invited in order to provide her only child with companions. O'Connor's favorite visiting cousins were the Florencourt sisters from Boston, the daughters of Regina's sister Agnes. Tony Harty asserted that these "Yankee" cousins, Margaret, Louise, Catherine, and Frances, "were all roughly the same age." Kitty Smith Kellam, who recalls the Florencourt sisters as "outgoing and friendly," remembers playing with the two younger sisters, Frances and Louise, while the older girls and Mary Flannery sat on the porch of the Cline mansion:

> I think the times that I saw her talk the most was when the cousins were visiting. I can remember [that these] were the only times I ever heard her laugh. She seemed to be more relaxed. [. . .] You didn't hear her laugh very often except when they were there. They would sit on that porch and rock *all* day long and I used to think how horrible that would be—just watching

the world go by and rocking. We [the younger girls] were down at the other end [of the yard] playing all kinds of games. We would [also] go a lot of afternoons into the dining room for a tea party and they would join us.

Regina O'Connor also invited Regina Sullivan and Jay Lewis to these tea parties; Lewis recalls that "Flannery just hated them. She just didn't like anything like that, those kind of parties. [She sat over in a corner] and glowered and pouted." Another Milledgeville acquaintance remembers that when the Florencourts visited, it was "obligatory" for her mother to invite them and Mary Flannery to their home on the edge of town for horseback riding. She recalls that Mary Flannery accompanied her cousins only reluctantly. Her mother remembers one visit that coincided with a recent harvest of black cherries. Mary Flannery, she says, sat on the porch with her, while the Florencourts were riding horses, alternately ejecting cherry seeds with a terse mutter, "I didn't want to come." Commenting on Mary Flannery's behavior, this acquaintance suggests that childhood play meant nothing to her: "She was an adult, I think probably from the time she was about three years old because she lived only in the company of adults." Loretta Hoynes also asserts that Mary Flannery's behavior was not always ladylike during these summer visits: "If you wanted her to be a good girl, she was nothing. She enjoyed pushing people in the pig pen" or giving inexperienced riders "wild" horses. "She would laugh if you fell off" (Hoynes, Brown interview). Still another Milledgeville acquaintance, Lucia Bonn Corse, recalled Mary Flannery's social isolation: "I am not proud to say that I and my friends were unkind to Mary Flannery. She was always excluded from parties. Her Connecticut cousins visited during the summer and there were parties for them and she had to be included. She spent the evening in a corner by herself. She was physically unattractive and we (I) didn't explore her mind."[17]

On the other hand, Tony Harty remembered that as an adolescent Mary Flannery continued to love animals, especially the geese she kept in the yard of the Greene Street house. Kitty Smith Kellam also remembers noisy guinea hens: "When we played back there, we tried to stay away from them because of the noise and the odor." She also recalls how protective Mary Flannery was of her pets. As an out-of-town visitor only, Harty remembered the fun all the youngsters had together: trips to the farm, cardplaying, and going to movies together. "Mary Flannery was always pleasant to me," he said.

Overall, given time and place and circumstance, Mary Flannery O'Connor lived, it would seem, a secure but individualistic life as a young adolescent in Milledgeville. Though her particular interests and talents sustained her through her high school years, she was ready to move on to college almost as soon as she graduated from Peabody High School in June 1942. Mary Flannery may have considered schools other than GSCW as she finished her senior year but entered the freshman class at the college—just around the corner from her home—for the first summer session that began on 9 June. Milledgeville acquaintances say that her staying on in Milledgeville to attend GSCW was not at all unusual; in fact, they assert that most town girls who went to college during World War II attended the local women's college. Expense, transportation difficulties associated with the war, and small-town insularity all contributed to their decisions to stay on in Milledgeville. O'Connor's classmate Yvonne Giles Armour says, "We just sort of automatically went here. It was a sort of extension of high school. As a matter of fact, only one person in our graduating class went off to college. One girl went to a school in Alabama." Elizabeth Horne also recalls that attending GSCW was almost automatic for Milledgeville girls; she suggests that being a student at the local college eliminated any necessity for adjustment since Peabody graduates had learned to know many of the professors. Another acquaintance feels that O'Connor would not have considered any other college because of the expense of going elsewhere: "She and her mother still were not well off, and any money had to come from largesse from other sources." Jay Lewis recalls how little tuition was in those years: $67.50 for the full year. These general influences and more specific ones like her being an only child—rather overprotected—and only sixteen years old surely led Mary Flannery O'Connor to choose to remain in Milledgeville to begin her advanced study at GSCW.

CHAPTER THREE

MILLEDGEVILLE, 1942~1945

I n 1942, when Mary Flannery O'Connor entered its freshman class, Georgia State College for Women, as its name then clearly indicated, was a women's college founded mainly to train teachers. During the years that O'Connor attended, its president was Dr. Guy Wells. According to members of the GSCW class of 1945, most students were from "small towns and rural areas throughout Georgia."[1] They came from "middle income families" and had attended eleven-year secondary schools. Several of O'Connor's classmates, who, like her, attended these schools, felt somewhat disadvantaged in college but most survived to graduate. Recollections of the difficulty of the curriculum vary according to who is responding, but most students felt that the course offerings were sufficiently rigorous to promote learning. Elsie Parker Danielly says, "The basic curriculum did not deviate from the norm for women's colleges of that era. Even though I came from an economically poor country high school, I never felt particularly challenged, except in the field of science." Retired army major Grace Womble remembers that all students studied in the same basic courses during their first two years—Social Science, English, Humanities, General Math, Biology, Health, and Physical Education—and then moved on to specialize during their junior and senior years. Sarah Rudolph Miller, who majored in Food and Nutrition, recalls that her upper-level classes included "nutrition, microbiology, quantitative/qualitative organic chemistry, physiology and advanced math. [. . .] I had to spend considerable time studying, writing, and in labs." Fran Richardson, who attended the University of Georgia one summer to take two courses she needed to graduate from GSCW in three years, feels that "[t]heir academic requirements were much easier than those at G.S.C.W. The curriculum at G.S.C.W. was broad and interesting. Good Teachers."

GSCW alumnae from the Class of 1945 remember several outstanding professors at the college. One asserts that it did not matter that there were relatively few doctorates among the faculty: "Most of my professors were women who had Masters' degrees and loved teaching. I did not have a 'bad' non-caring professor in undergraduate school." Of particular interest among the outstanding professors are those from social science, English, and education, Mary Flannery O'Connor's two majors and minor. Supporting Lena Jo Tabb Chambers, who asserts that "most of the education classes were pretty dull, but the English and library science classes were great," only one alumna remembers an outstanding professor of education—her supervising teacher at Peabody, Elsie Calhoun.

Administrators exerted strict control over the academic and social lives of the young women at GSCW. Students arrived at GSCW and stayed there: they were not allowed to use cars on campus "until the last 2 weeks of Senior year. [. . .] We could go home for two weekends each quarter and *everybody* rode Trailways and Greyhound." Men visited the campus only on weekends. Hazel Smith Ogletree writes, "I liked the total concentration on academics during the week with only the 'distraction' of *men* on the week-ends!" To help enforce learning, evening study halls in the dormitories were mandatory. Mary Boyd Gallop recalls that "the honor system was in effect & worked well." GSCW also enforced rules concerning dress and social behavior. Marion Nelson Poats remembers "having to wear hose on Sunday and we could never go to breakfast with hair in curlers under a scarf." "Jessies" (the students' unofficial nickname for themselves) also had to "sign in & out to leave campus."

During the years "town girl" Mary Flannery O'Connor attended GSCW, the most unusual feature of campus life was the encampment of WAVES who arrived after the U.S. Navy declared the college a clerical training center for storekeepers. Elizabeth Horne suggests that Baldwin County's influential congressman, Carl Vinson—"a very powerful man"—probably helped bring the WAVE encampment to Milledgeville. Bess Saye McFarland writes that the arrival of the WAVES put "G.S.C.W. on war-footing." Alumnae remember the WAVES marching in formation to and from their classes and several recall the crowding (three girls to a room) that resulted from the encampment. Edna S. Weiss, one of the WAVES trained at GSCW, says, "Many of the nearby stately homes were converted to offices and barracks, and I remember that the house I was billeted in was called 'Mansion House.'"[2]

Numerous references to and photographs of the WAVES in the school newspaper *The Colonnade* show the impact they had on the college.[3] When they arrived in early February 1943, a photograph of the first contingent appears on the front page with the caption "GSCW Welcomes the WAVES." Inside are more photographs of them on campus, including a group marching in front of the old governor's mansion—then the college president's home. The 1943 yearbook the *Spectrum* devoted two pages to the WAVE encampment, with photographs showing them marching on campus, relaxing, and making up their bunks, military style.

Most GSCW alumnae remember that having the WAVES on campus made them more aware of the reality of World War II. Elsie Parker Danielly writes: "The war greatly influenced our academic and social life. We spent many hours after classes in volunteer service. The arrival of the WAVES for training on our campus further kept the war effort foremost in our lives. The college seemed to have been in a 'holding pattern' from 1942–45." Alumnae also remember that, because the WAVES were on campus, the Bob Hope USO Show came to GSCW. The 15 May 1943 *Colonnade* carried a story about his appearance under the headline "Bob Hope Entertains the Navy Tonight." Attendance at his performance was limited to "the United States Naval Training School personnel and GSCW students."

Mary Flannery O'Connor viewed the WAVES on campus primarily as targets for her satirical cartoons in *The Colonnade*. More than a few show the military women marching in groups across campus, totally oblivious to the existence of the younger, civilian students. O'Connor's first cartoon with WAVES as its subject appeared in the 23 January 1943, *Colonnade.* As two students observe a group marching, one suggests that she is going to ask the WAVE to let her try on her military hat. Several other examples demonstrate O'Connor's satirical facility. In a cartoon of 20 February 1943, O'Connor drew two students observing a WAVE as she searches through her satchel; one wonders whether the WAVE is carrying gunpowder in the bag. In a 27 March 1943 cartoon, O'Connor depicts WAVES marching across campus. In the foreground a student archer aims her bow and arrow at them. In the 24 April 1943 *Colonnade,* O'Connor shows two students looking at a long row of WAVE hats and coats, hanging by assigned numbers. One gleefully asks the other whether they can still make the dean's list if they deliberately mix up the hats. In contrast with O'Connor's satirical depiction of the WAVES, photographs in both the *Colonnade* and the *Spectrum* show them to have been attractive young women, scarcely older than GSCW students. Elizabeth Horne recalls that since so many of the WAVES were Roman Catholics, "We [the Sacred Heart Catholic Church in Milledgeville] used to have open house for them every Sunday night. We served coffee, some played bridge, some played music, but they mostly visited. They were very prominent in our parish and in this college."

GSCW, then, as part military camp and part refuge for students, was the milieu the sixteen-year-old Mary Flannery O'Connor entered in the summer of 1942. In the three years she spent as a Jessie, she became an integral part of the school, one whose name and talents were known to nearly every student on the campus, though socially, at least partly because she lived off campus, she remained somewhat isolated and certainly individualistic. Alice Alexander in a feature on O'Connor in the *Atlanta Journal* tells a partially mythical story: as a freshman on "Rat Day," Mary Flannery "refused to wear an onion around her neck. When the sophomores commanded her to kneel and beg their pardon she replied, 'I will not'" (Alexander 3B). Margaret Uhler, who was a freshman at GSCW when O'Connor was a senior, identifies the original source of the anecdote as Miss Katherine Scott of the English department: "She told this story to illustrate Flannery's intelligent refusal to make herself look like a nut. Miss Katherine admired her for daring to stand up to the upperclassmen."[4] Other of O'Connor's classmates at GSCW cannot recall the episode, though Yvonne Giles Armour believes it quite possible that Mary

Flannery refused to wear the onion. Clearly, O'Connor's reluctance to conform shows her desire to distinguish herself from the typical freshman.

Still another classmate, Fran Richardson, recalls that town girls who lived off campus with their families and those who lived on campus comprised "two distinct groups. Flannery was liked by both groups but reserved with both. She enjoyed her privacy. Flannery was fun to be around because of her great sense of humor. She lived in town with her mother, though, so [I] never knew her like the other girls in our dormitories. She was never in on our late night "'bull sessions.'" Another anonymous classmate, now a guidance counselor, asserts that, though she was not in O'Connor's "group of friends," she realized early that O'Connor was "[i]ntellectually [. . .] far superior to most of us, and the spark of genius was there. [. . .] Her friends were mostly those people who were active in student government, the literary magazine and on the annual staff." Hilda Gray Mayo, an English major who studied in several classes with Mary Flannery, remembers her as "a brain. She seemed to be a loner, as I never saw her with a close friend. She wasn't a very attractive looking person but was very quick." Mildred Sauls Bradley recalls Mary Flannery as "intelligent, serious, reserved, yet witty. Not very interested in clothes, jewelry & the things college girls often spent too much time on." Kathryn Donan Kuck also recalls her classmate's uniqueness: "I admired her freedom of expression [because] I don't admire beauty queens." Bess Saye McFarland remembers that when Mary Flannery visited students in their dormitories "[s]he conveyed an unusual sense of humor in all her conversations and was considered by many to be 'far out' in her approach to things." Still another classmate recalls how O'Connor used her "dry, dry wit" in club meetings. She would listen to others talk at length and then "in one sentence Flannery could drawl, 'Well now, I really think'—and she'd hit the nail on the head." Overall, O'Connor's classmates seem to agree that she was an entertaining and talented individualist, who stood out as a student, a writer, and incipient artist but cared very little for the social conventions of the ordinary coed.

O'Connor's closest friend at GSCW was Betty Boyd Love, whom she met almost as soon as she started school. Love recalls their meeting during the summer 1942 session: "I first met Flannery O'Connor in the summer of 1942. We were both freshmen entering a new accelerated program at Georgia State College for Women. There weren't many of us in the program. Most of the summer students at GSCW were public school teachers returning to college to renew or upgrade a credential, so the small group of us who were 'regular' students got to know each other quite soon" (Love, "Recollections" MS 1). Love tells that she spent long hours with O'Connor both in class and working on the college literary magazine, the *Corinthian*. She also remembers that they both published "some rather dreadful poems" in an anthology of college poets. Describing herself as "devastatingly serious in those days," she recalls O'Connor's contrasting sense of humor: "I never knew Flannery to be without the same dry, whimsical humor that she later developed to such a fine degree and into such a fine art" (Love, "Recollections" 65). O'Connor recalled the "dreadful" poetry they wrote in a letter to Love in November 1949. She told her that Helen Greene had read a poem by her (O'Connor) in the fall issue of *Seydell's Quarterly;* O'Connor seemed embarrassed that it had been published: "I have only a vague recollection of what the poems were about but they were bad enough" (*HB* 19).

Besides their shared literary work, Love also became what she described as a "regular visitor" to the Cline house, where she often had Sunday dinner (at noon) with O'Connor; her mother, Regina; and her aunts. She remembered particularly "the long walnut table with its silver napkin rings and the little pot of demitasse coffee served to pour over ice cream at desert." Love recalled, too, the variety of guests who shared the meal: "There were often several students there, and other friends and perhaps a stray serviceman or two. Miss Katie would sit on the porch on Sunday morning and talk to the passersby, perhaps also inviting someone, either strange or old acquaintance, to dinner" (Love, "Recollections" 64). Mary Flannery also invited Betty Boyd's roommate, Mary Boyd Gallop, to Sunday dinner at the Cline house. Gallop recalls the warm affection apparent in the family: "She was very fond of her mother in Flannery's way of liking people. Being the only child, the mother seemed just as fond of her girl as were two maiden aunts living there."

Betty Boyd Love also described O'Connor's upstairs bedroom furnished with "a big high-legged clerk's desk at which she worked sitting on a stool. The rooms were all large, with high ceilings, and cool. It was a pleasant place to be in the Milledgeville summers." Overall, Love recalls feeling, only in retrospect, that the matriarchal household was "somewhat unusual." At the time the family arrangement "appeared perfectly unexceptional, and I'm sure they all looked on it as such. Flannery was the daughter of the house, loved and accepted. It was a quiet life, and a good one" ("Recollections" 65).

Love also remembered O'Connor's continued enthusiasm for fowl while she was at GSCW: she still kept ducks in the yard behind the Cline mansion and signed her drawings with "a chicken formed of her four initials" ("Recollections" 66). Aside from what she called O'Connor's "formidable talent," Love also recalled

> Flannery O'Connor [as a] quite unusual individual, and I was fond of her. She knew who she was, and what she was, and was neither over-pleased nor disturbed by either. There are critics who would have you believe that she was something of a freak herself. Not so! She was physically a bit awkward. She may have considered some social conventions absurd. But she never exhibited any open rebellion. She was probably merely amused. She "talked Southern," to use her own words. Well, yes, in a way— but mostly she talked Flannery. She drawled, she had a wry twist of humor, and she was delightful company. [. . .]
>
> Was Flannery an eccentric? Maybe. But she found acceptance of herself among her Southern neighbors even though they may not have understood her work in the least. (Love, "Recollections" MS 7)

That O'Connor clearly reciprocated Betty Boyd's friendship is proved by the letters she wrote to her while she was in New York after earning her MFA at Iowa. These letters reveal the warmth of their friendship, their shared ambivalence about GSCW—its classes, professors, and students— and O'Connor's increasing sophistication. Love asserts that their "divergent interests never detracted from the basic quality of our relationship, and I enjoyed her just as much in our brief later visits as I had done when we saw a great deal of each other in college years" (Love, "Recollections" MS 7).

Another close acquaintance—at least during their first year at GSCW— was the previously mentioned Mary Boyd Gallop, who writes, "I can't say I was as close as some of her friends, [but] Flannery invited Betty & me to eat Sunday dinners with her and we did many times." She remembers that O'Connor "seemed to take charge of anything she did" with a strong "sense of humor through it all." Gallop also recalls that O'Connor "never seemed interested in the opposite sex. She was happy just being herself." Gallop remembers that Mary Flannery once told Betty Boyd that she (O'Connor) thought Mary was "'just a bit too pedantic.' I never forgot that, but even then you could see how excessive her vocabulary was. To me she was some- one we loved because she was so honest." Other classmates remember Mary Flannery more for her artistic and literary talents than for being sociable. Kitty Smith Kellam says simply, "Flannery did not participate in any social activities." Another recalls with considerable pride her one conversation with Mary Flannery on a walk across campus; she says she "felt good that she walked with me." Hazel Smith Ogletree remembers how O'Connor signed her yearbook: "The usual bunk—M. F. O'Connor."

Besides developing a bit socially, Mary Flannery O'Connor certainly expanded her knowledge as a student at GSCW—this in spite of her later reluctance to give the college much credit for her education. During her first year there (GSCW then operated on the quarter system), she took Biology 100 (Human Biology), Chemistry 321 (Introduction to Geology), Mathematics 100 (Functional Mathematics), Humanities 101 and 102 (survey courses), Social Science 101 and 102 (introductory courses), Health 100 (orientation course in health), two courses in physical education for freshman, French 211–212 (Intermediate French), and three English courses: English 101–102 (General College Composition) and English 324 (Advanced Composition) (Transcript, O'CC, GCSU); in addition, she was a contributing staff member of the college literary magazine, the *Corinthian,* and cartoonist for the college newspaper, the *Colonnade.*

Fran Richardson recalls being a student in Miss Katherine Scott's English 101 with O'Connor; she remembers O'Connor's "creative mind" and that "she and Miss Scott had a great rapport in English 101. They would start talking and forget the rest of us were there. I told her once that I wished I could bor- row some of her creativity, and she replied, 'I'd exchange it for your ability to attract the men.'" A letter to Katherine Scott in the O'Connor collection at Georgia College proves that O'Connor maintained an acquaintance with Miss Scott, who died at ninety-two in 1988, for many years. In the note she thanks Miss Scott for lending her a book and comments on the professor's 1958 retire- ment from the faculty at GSCW.[5] Miss Scott revealed her own dichotomized feeling about her famous student in late interviews with journalist Bill Schemmel: "Even then, it was obvious she was a genius, warped, but a genius all the same. When I read her first novel I thought to myself that character who dies in the last chapter could have done the world a great favor by dying in the first chapter instead" (Schemmel 72). Mary Barbara Tate, who knew both O'Connor and Katherine Scott well, suggests that Miss Scott's acerbity may have been motivated partly by envy. Miss Scott also wrote, rather unsuccessfully; according to Tate, she may not have approved of Flannery's work because she did not conform to nineteenth-century style, "did not write the way Miss Katherine thought she should" (Tate, interview 1989). Elizabeth Horne, who was also well acquainted with Miss Scott, says that she believes it unlikely that Miss Scott would have recognized O'Connor's talent: "I would not have picked her as one who would have seen anybody's talent, especially. She made the line and others followed." Another contemporary says that she knew Miss Scott from childhood but tried to avoid taking classes from her because "she was one of those who could tell the same story fifteen times [until] our eyes glazed over."

O'Connor's second English teacher at GSCW was Dr. William Wynn in English 102. Kathryn Donan Kuck recalls studying in this beginner's writing course in the English department with her: "We looked forward to her papers. She read them to the class. Mr. Wynn was a gentleman of the old school who was soon to retire. [. . .] He did not enjoy her style of writing and he tried hard to change it. He wanted her to be lady-like and graceful." Another classmate recalls that Professor Wynn "had published a little grammar book and he used that as his text. He was another one of those [teachers] that I did my best to avoid because I thought he was dull." O'Connor never officially declared a major in English because she refused to take the required courses in grammar and Shakespeare that only Dr. Wynn taught. Mary Barbara Tate elaborates, "This is what I've been told by former members of the faculty. She told them if she declared the major, she would have to take Shakespeare with Dr. Wynn and maybe a grammar course and he was considered by some ineffective. Flannery was one" (M. B. Tate, interview 1992).

Hallie Smith, however, who may have been O'Connor's professor in English 324, was apparently more sympathetic to O'Connor's unique sense of humor. Elsie Parker Danielly remembers: "In creative writing classes, Miss Hallie Smith often stressed her aversion to the vague use of the words 'thing,' 'something,' 'everything,' or 'anything.' When Mary Flannery and I were assigned to work together in class on a short satire, she suggested that we use the word 'it' and 'its' throughout the paper. Miss Smith, having an appreciation of wit, loved it!"

The manuscript collection at GCSU holds several assignments, mainly descriptive and narrative, that O'Connor wrote for Smith's class. One exercise required her to write parallel versions—one objective, one subjective—of the same street scene. Calling it Raphael Street, O'Connor apparently chose to write a description of Charlton Street in Savannah. Both descriptions are far more vivid that those usually produced by first-year college students: O'Connor received a grade of A+ for her effort. Another assignment, this one a description of a country grocery store and its owner, includes a particularly good simile (O'CC, GCSU). Besides awarding O'Connor a top grade for this effort, Smith also urged her to submit her work to the *Corinthian*. A third passage, which O'Connor titled "The Cynosure," shows its author's early concern with hubris, the kind of excessive pride that almost damned Ruby Turpin (O'CC, GCSU). Again, O'Connor's efforts merited her a grade of A and the comment "Excellent!" Hallie Smith's enthusiasm and encouragement soon led Mary Flannery to become a contributing writer to the *Corinthian*.

During her first year at GSCW, O'Connor published three essays, a brief story, and a free-verse poem in this student literary magazine. In "Going to the Dogs," published in the fall 1942 issue, O'Connor ridicules the dog-like behavior of some students who rested on the grounds of the campus, reposed under radiators, or chased cats up trees. She coyly sidesteps her satire, however, by asserting that she isn't talking about students at all but only the "four-legged" intruders on campus. O'Connor contributed "Why Worry the Horse?" to the *Corinthian* for its winter 1943 issue. In this topical essay, occasioned by gasoline and parts shortages brought on by World War II, O'Connor facetiously addresses the problems of the reactivated horse as mode of transportation. O'Connor also contributed a book review of *The Story of Ferdinand* by Munro Leaf to the winter issue; she facetiously recommended the book to her classmates.

O'Connor's Poe-like "Elegance Is Its Own Reward" in the spring 1943 issue tells of a husband who claims to have killed his two wives for having been dull and unassuming; he actually kills the women when they fail to produce the money they promised as dowry. He decapitates the first, later regretting that action as "vulgar"; because he regrets his indelicacy, he adds finesse to the second killing by plying this wife with romantic language before wringing her neck. In the same issue of the *Corinthian,* O'Connor published a free-verse poem, "Effervescence," that begins as a parody of Lowell's line from "The Vision of Sir Launfal": "Oh, what is so lovely as a day in June?" The bit of doggerel, however, really targets the laziness of GSCW students.

Student reaction to O'Connor's writing in the *Corinthian* varied. One classmate recalls that she first heard of Mary Flannery when she read "Going to the Dogs" in the *Corinthian.* She declares that she was "amazed at the quality of the writing." Fran Richardson's comment about O'Connor's student writing gives an opposite perspective: "Her writings in Corinthian and Colonnade were always different and bizarre." Generally, however, those who recall O'Connor—and most of her classmates do—remember her for both her writing in the *Corinthian* and her cartoons in the *Colonnade* and the *Spectrum.*

During her first year at GSCW, O'Connor began her tenure as cartoonist for the *Colonnade,* the GSCW biweekly newspaper. Her first cartoon (in the 9 October issue), of a large, stiff student walking with a cane, illustrates campus reaction to "Physical Fitness Day." After drawing two more cartoons in October, Mary Flannery became art editor of the paper in November 1942, a position she held until her graduation in June 1945. During the 1942–43 school term she produced more than twenty additional cartoons for the paper, obviously helping to build her reputation as a talented satirical artist. One cartoon of personal interest during O'Connor's freshman year appears in the 9 January 1943 issue. Two students lament their omission from the dean's list for the fall 1942 semester. Mary Flannery O'Connor—during her three years at GSCW—failed to make the dean's list only for the fall 1942 quarter. Still another self-satirizing cartoon appears in the 3 April 1943 edition of the paper. The scene is a dance where everybody is dancing except a tiny, bespectacled wallflower who grins behind her hand and asserts that she can always pursue a Ph.D.

During her three years at GSCW O'Connor produced a linoleum block cartoon for each issue of the *Colonnade.* Her cartoons (as would be expected in a woman's college) almost always feature female students reacting to various campus events. There are, however, exceptions, such as the one in the 7 March 1944 issue, which features two plump adolescent boys walking past the college. One comments to the other that he hopes college rules become freer before they are old enough to date girls. O'Connor also directed many of these cartoons at the WAVES on campus. Of her use of the WAVES, Nelle Womack Hines has commented: "The appearance of several hundred WAVES on the campus of GSCW during the early spring gave new impetus to this freshman's talent and some of her cleverest cartoons have dealt with the WAVE situation." Hines applauds O'Connor for "fast making a name for herself as an up-and-coming cartoonist. A female Ogden Nash, Mary not only draws her pictures and writes her captions, but goes Ogden one better by carving her own cuts on linoleum block." Hines also asked Mary Flannery to describe how she "went about her work." O'Connor explained that "first—she caught her 'rabbit.' In this case, she explained the 'rabbit' was a good idea, which must tie up with some current event or a recent happening on campus" (Hines n. pag.).

In pictorial content, O'Connor's cartoons generally feature two students: one—tall, thin, and rather ungainly—often seems surprised or befuddled; the other—short and a bit pudgy—usually wears glasses and the harried expression of the incipient intellectual. Using these typical campus types, as Hines suggests, O'Connor employed her "keen sense of humor [. . .] to see the funny side of the situation which she portrays—minus a sting." O'Connor's classmate Hazel Smith Ogletree feels that Mary Flannery "patterned her cartoons after an exaggerated physical picture of herself. She could make us all look like her—yet keep our own special identity." Margaret Uhler attests to the popularity of O'Connor's cartoons, "My most vivid memory of her then was that we all scanned the Colonnade for her delightful cartoons before we read anything else." Sarah Rudolph Miller says, "I feel that Mary Flannery's art [at GSCW] reflected her true personality and genius far better than her writing." Margaret Meaders, then a faculty member at GSCW and faculty advisor to the *Colonnade,* describes O'Connor's cartoons as "wonderful" and "merry." She elaborates, "Penetratingly conceived and skillfully executed, those cartoons were the most professional student works I have ever seen" (Meaders 377–78). Helen Greene says that she "hoped Mary Flannery wouldn't drop it [her cartooning], but it was too light, I think. She was deeply serious." In her article, Hines related that in 1943 O'Connor indeed hoped to combine writing and cartooning in the future: "Miss O'Connor frankly states that her literary ambition is to be able to write prose satire. She plans to work hard and hopes some day to find a place where her satiric essays and cartoons will fit to good advantage" (Hines n. pag.).

The 1943 *Spectrum* gives further information about O'Connor during her first year at the college. Her freshman photograph shows her as bright-faced, wearing glasses and the typical pin-curled hairstyle of the 1940s and 1950s. Her eyes through the glasses reveal the clear, forceful intelligence that accounted for both Mary Flannery's academic success and her extracurricular involvement. She served as an editorial assistant for the 1943 *Spectrum;* she also appears in the club photograph of the Roman Catholic Newman Club, though Kitty Smith Kellam cannot remember her having been a member. As a freshman, Mary Flannery also joined the Allegro Club, meant for students with particular interest in the arts. Her interest in this group apparently waned, however, for she is not listed as a member in either 1944 or 1945, and Margaret Meaders recalls that O'Connor "produced none of the one-act plays performed annually in heated class competitions" (Meaders 377). Mary Flannery's enthusiastic participation in campus activities obviously enhanced both her sense of positive accomplishment and gave her a place in the GSCW community. Elizabeth Shreve Ryan writes that at GSCW: "Mary Flannery continued her artistic and literary contributions to student publications and her academic excellence, becoming more poised, more interested in her appearance, and more self-confident as she moved into the wider circle of college life (Ryan 51).

O'Connor's schedule during her second year at GSCW (1943–44) included French 322 (Survey of French Literature), French 421 (Drama of the Classical Period), Physics 100 (Survey in Physics and Astronomy), Education 104 (Introduction to Education), two courses in physical education for sophomores, Sociology 301 (Introduction to Sociology), Sociology 200 (Contemporary Georgia Problems), and four English classes: English 312 (Survey of English Literature), English 331 (The Short Story), English 360 (American Literature), and English 311 (Survey of British Literature) (Transcript, O'CC, GCSU). By her second year at GSCW, O'Connor seems to have conformed to the requirements of the college curriculum, realizing that she had to study in some troublesome classes in order to earn her degree. At Iowa, she wrote, in the previously mentioned autobiographical sketch, that as an undergraduate she read what was required for transforming herself into the typical, low-paid Georgia teacher of high school English (Transcript, O'CC, GCSU).

During her 1943–44 year at GSCW, O'Connor continued to participate in campus activities and to excel academically: articles in the *Colonnade* list her as a dean's list student for every quarter from spring 1943 through spring 1944. As literary assistant to the journal, Mary Flannery published three stories in the literary magazine during her second year at GSCW. In the longest of the three, "Home of the Brave," appearing in the fall 1943 issue, O'Connor satirizes home-front hypocrisy displayed by a group of small-town women who have gathered to wrap bandages for the war effort. Two of the women are jealous of the military positions of their respective sons: one woman's, too dull for officer's training, is headed for Guadalcanal; the other— brighter and of a superior social rank—has become an officer who trains recruits in Florida, sheltered from the killing. Ironically, O'Connor has the first soldier die of the mumps en route to Australia and the superior soldier's mother, who has been most critical of the lowly infantryman, learn that he has secretly married her daughter. The gossipy women also discuss their sly-ness in subverting rationing rules by hoarding food. The reader can feel O'Connor's disgust with home-front behavior, particularly the social snob-bery, which she no doubt witnessed in Milledgeville.

In a second contribution to the same issue of the *Corinthian,* "Doctors of Delinquency," the seventeen-year-old writer comments satirically on the lax moral and educational training of contemporary children. She begins with an anecdote about a child named Elbert who killed his brothers and uncle with a time bomb. Through this example, she states her strong disapproval of the self-expressive emphasis in modern education that has allowed chil-dren to control the adult world. She also takes swipes at modern nutrition and the media (billboards, radio, and movies) that alienate children from both nature and serious reading. "Biologic Endeavor" in the spring 1944 issue of the magazine was O'Connor's third contribution to the *Corinthian* during her second year at GSCW. This one is similar to the last in that she uses an anecdote to launch an attack at what she rightly perceives to be a foible of modern life. She talks of Great-Uncle Benedict, who dies in 1882 at the age of eighty-six after eating tainted meat. She argues that today's dietary habits are far more dangerous than those he practiced, as people eat too much processed food and then expect to alleviate the damage to their systems with a wide range of patent medicines, like Tums and Ex-Lax. Clearly, her criticism here was prophetic.

O'Connor also continued her work as art editor for the *Colonnade* during her second year at GSCW, producing her regular humorous vignettes of
campus life. In the 5 October 1943 issue she shows two students strolling
across campus, one heavily loaded with books; both look grouchy. One asks
the other whether she thinks teachers are even necessary. Another cartoon
has a Jessie trying to sell a WAVE a "Contemporary Georgia Syllabus." Just
ahead of student government elections in late February 1944, O'Connor
drew a cartoon of a political candidate delivering a typical windy harangue;
her final cartoon for the year, published in the 30 May 1944 issue shows a girl
bounding in the air, surrounded by others who display similar glee at leaving school for the entire summer.

O'Connor's expertise as a cartoonist enhances the quality of the 1944
Spectrum. She drew illustrations for the three major student groups at
GSCW: the SGA, the YWCA, and the Recreation Association; her student
government officer carries a huge gavel and wears a serious, grim expression
while her YWCA official bends over a symbolic candle; her beefy tennis
player, representative of the third group, stands, muscle bound, seemingly
facing her caricaturist. O'Connor also drew cartoons of the editors of the
three campus publications, all looking pretentiously harried. Another that
introduces the club section features a meeting at which all members appear
to be either asleep or monumentally bored. Her last illustration, for a feature
titled "The *Spectrum* Presents: The News and Views of Jessie Jones as
Recorded in her Diary," shows the diarist on her bed thinking and writing.
One event "Jessie Jones" refers to specifically is O'Connor's political cartoon
in the *Colonnade* that followed "election speeches before the student body."

Listed as a member of the yearbook staff, O'Connor also merited the
following special comment in the book itself: "Mary Flannery O'Connor, of
cartoon fame, was the bright spot of our existence. There was always a smile
in the *Spectrum* office on the days when her linoleum cuts came in." In addition to working with school publications, O'Connor was also active as a
member of the International Relations Club in 1944. Helen Greene, who
sponsored the club, remembers its beginning and Mary Flannery's involvement: "The first honor society in the College was the International Relations
Club, which R. Hoy Taylor, our dean, sponsored for several years. He asked
me to take it over [. . .] and the students, among them Mary Flannery, were
a joy to work with. I lived in Beeson Hall (a dormitory with a few faculty

apartments) after 1940 and often had meetings in my apartment there—meetings that Mary Flannery, an active IRC member, attended" (Greene, "Mary Flannery O'Connor" 45). Greene also recalls that after these meetings another student always walked home with Mary Flannery because even then it was not entirely safe to walk unescorted on the streets of Milledgeville after dark. Besides, Greene adds, O'Connor "was very carefully brought up." A fellow member of the IRC also recalls that when the group sponsored an appearance by journalist Robert St. John at GSCW, the next year the O'Connors held a reception for him at the Cline mansion: "Regina was supportive and good," she asserts, in entertaining such GSCW guests.

During her third year at GSCW, O'Connor's transcript shows that she set out to complete requirements for her degree in social studies, studying in eight courses in that department during 1944–45: Social Studies 454 (Current Social Problems), Economics 301–302 (Principles of Economics and Current Economic Problems), Political Science 324 (American National Government), History 307–308 (United States History), Social Science 412 (Philosophy), and Political Science 421 (Comparative Government). She also took Art 429 (Art Appreciation), Education 306 (School and Society), and three English Courses: English 308 (Spoken English), English 344 (Contemporary Literature), and English 328 (Tennyson and Browning) (Transcript, O'CC, GCSU).

Continuing to achieve academic excellence, Mary Flannery maintained her dean's list status every quarter (except her second) through her graduation with an A.B. in social science on 11 June 1945. O'Connor's classmates and teachers at GSCW remember her overall excellence as a student. Hazel Smith Ogletree recalls: "M.F. was brilliant—yet did not shine in class particularly—preferred to stay quietly in the background. Then she would 'ace' the tests—and her papers were always excellent—. When she did offer oral participation it was brilliant with her insight—and many times offered with a touch of humor. She *never* 'took over' any discussion, so teachers would often ask for her opinion on an interpretation." Hilda Gray Mayo, who studied in several English classes with O'Connor, also remembers her as a superior student: "Actually she was quite witty. When she had something to say, it was intelligent and quite often, that dry wit shocked us and left us laughing. Mary Flannery could write stories 'at the drop of a hat.' When our teachers gave a writing assignment, she would be writing away while I was still *thinking* about what I was going to write. She was an outstanding student, very quiet but very well prepared for class. She did not flaunt her intelligence but usually waited to be called upon." Mary Boyd Gallop adds another comment about Mary Flannery's modesty: "If she was the best in class you never heard it from her." Though O'Connor clearly dominated her classmates intellectually, she still had not improved in athletic skill. Her transcripts show that she participated in physical education classes during two of her three years at GSCW. A classmate recalls: "I only remember one class with her. It was P. E. (golf) and I remember she was considered dangerous with a golf club in her hand. She was apt not to look around or yell 'Fore.' [. . .] we were careful not to get too close—she was careless when swinging the club. She wasn't particularly athletic, [but] she was a good sport and laughed at herself." Another class which Mary Flannery took during her senior year was English 308 (Spoken English) with Mary Thomas Maxwell. Mary Barbara Tate, recalling a story told by Rosa Lee Walston, who joined the English faculty just after O'Connor graduated, describes O'Connor's experience in the course: "Though she cringed at public speaking, she signed up for a course in speech. When Miss Maxwell queried her, she said, 'Well, I know it won't do any good, but I have to show Regina and Sister.' At the end of the course she had an *A,* for though her voice had not noticeably improved, the content of her talks was splendid" (M. B. Tate, "Mary Flannery O'Connor" 34). Years later in a letter to Betty Hester, O'Connor herself commented on her senior English class in the poetry of Tennyson and Browning; she remembered that she took the course but little else about it: "All I remember from the whole course is 'Come into the garden, Maud, for the black bat, night has flown.' I thought that was hilarious" (*HB* 533).

Classmates, however, remember that O'Connor shared a special rapport with her teachers, though they cannot recall that faculty members singled her out for special attention. Still, to Mildred Sauls Bradley, "At times she seemed to be more on their level than on ours (students')." Besides her interaction with her teachers in freshman English, O'Connor established strong relationships with three other of her GSCW professors: George W. Beiswanger, her teacher in Social Science 412 (Philosophy); and history/ social studies professors Helen I. Greene and James C. Bonner. Greene asserts that "all the teachers liked her. She was a very serious student."

Beiswanger, who joined the faculty of GSCW in the fall of O'Connor's senior year, taught her only in Social Science 412 (Philosophy); he recalled O'Connor's participation in his class:

> Flannery's fall semester as a graduating senior coincided with my first semester on the GSCW faculty. She enrolled in a new Humanities course (which I had never taught before, having just returned to college teaching after five years at Theatre Arts Monthly as assistant editor and dance critic, following seven years on the philosophy faculty of Ohio Wesleyan University). The course was entitled Introduction to Modern Philosophy and used as its textbook John Herman Randall's "The Making of the Modern Mind," an academic best-seller whose viewpoint (and mine) was secular humanist (grounded in Pragmatism) and took for granted that the Renaissance and the Age of Enlightenment set the western mind free from the benightedness of Medieval thought (from Thomas Aquinas, etc.).
>
> Flannery sat in class, listened intently, took notes, and without her saying a word, it became clear that she didn't believe a word of what I was saying. It was philosophic *modernism* that had blinded the western mind. She knew Aquinas in detail, was amazingly well read in earlier philosophy, and developed into a first rate *"intellectual"* along with her other accomplishments. [. . .] It soon became clear to me that she was a "born" writer and that she was going that way.[6]

On the basis of his enthusiasm for O'Connor's intellect and talent, Beiswanger, who earned both an M.A. and Ph.D. in philosophy from the University of Iowa, told Flannery about the fellowships offered by the university. He also wrote a letter of support for her application, thus setting her on track to develop as a writer.

O'Connor showed her gratitude to Beiswanger later by trying to help him publish two scholarly essays. In the summer of 1952, she asked Robert and Sally Fitzgerald to read an article he had submitted to the *Kenyon Review*. She revealed her own mixed feelings about it in a letter to the Fitzgeralds: "I am not clear on how he uses such terms as contemplation &

meditation interchangeably, or whether he is making prayer & poetry the same thing or what. [. . .] But anyhow this guy is one of these learned gents & I don't aim to stick my neck out too far arguing with him" (*HB* 40). A few weeks later, she sent the Fitzgeralds another article, which she declared "shows him in a better light," though she was "hoping I don't have to talk any of this claptrap with him" (41).

James C. Bonner, the Milledgeville historian and a popular GSCW faculty member, taught O'Connor in four classes at GSCW; Charles E. Claffey interviewed Dr. Bonner, who died in 1984, for an article he published in the *Boston Globe* in 1981. Bonner asserted that O'Connor was "'an interesting girl with a great sense of humor. [. . .] Unfortunately, I never recognized her writing talents while she was in my class.'" Bonner, however, saved her evaluation of one of his classes, apparently that from Social Science 324 (American National Government): "'She gave a very sensitive explanation for her criticism of the course and hers was the only one of the evaluations that I saved'" (Claffey n. pag.). Today that evaluation is part of the O'Connor Collection at GCSU. That O'Connor read his history of Milledgeville in the mid-1950s indicates her continued respect for Professor Bonner.

O'Connor undoubtedly held more respect for Helen I. Greene than any other member of the GSCW faculty, writing to her friend Betty Boyd in November 1949: "I still think she's the brightest thing they have around" (*HB* 19). Greene shows that their admiration was reciprocal in her published reminiscence of O'Connor and in an October 1992 interview. Greene said, "She was a lovely person; she really was and, of course, always she was very flattering when she came to see me. Mary Flannery was herself, decidedly, from the time she was a little girl." Greene also remembers Mary Flannery as a student who never used her special abilities—her "wit" and "charm"—"to hurt feelings" or to take advantage of her classmates: "Always Mary Flannery was keen on the study of religions but it was not to impose her own ideas on others or to impress them with her convictions" (Greene, "Mary Flannery O'Connor" 44). Greene also recalls Mary Flannery's special enthusiasm for her survey of European history "because the author of our textbook [. . .] was a noted professor at Columbia University, who while working on his studies of Martin Luther in Germany, had changed his membership to the Roman Catholic Church" (44). When she returned to Milledgeville from Iowa and later Yaddo, O'Connor sought out Greene. Her former teacher remembers her enthusiasm for Iowa and her disgust with the secularism she encountered at Yaddo. Still, later when illness forced O'Connor to live in Milledgeville permanently, O'Connor continued to maintain her friendship with the history professor.

Outside the classroom, O'Connor continued her involvement in college activities during her senior year at GSCW. As editor of the *Corinthian,* she wrote an introductory note for the fall 1944 issue that shows the individualistic tone she hoped to give the magazine during her tenure. Other students who worked on the *Corinthian* with her that year recall that she occupied her position as editor with modesty and consideration. Hazel Smith Ogletree says, "When I worked [with her] on it my senior year, she was a 'pro'—yet helpful & encouraging." Besides producing a cartoon for the cover and writing the editorial note, O'Connor contributed an illustrated fashion essay, "Fashion's Perfect Medium," a poem "PFTT," and cartoon illustrations for Joyce Moncrief's satirical essay, "You Can Have My Share."

In "Fashion's Perfect Medium," O'Connor scores a direct hit on the universal concern of college students about their physical appearance. Trends popular in 1944 remain visible on today's campuses. She describes sweaters so outsized that they cover the students' entire bodies. O'Connor illustrates the popularity of these oversized sweaters with clever cartoons. One shows a sweater so long that, as she says in her essay, a skirt is no longer required, and another shows a sweater decorated with the long, knotted string of beads also popular in the 1940s. O'Connor noted students' preference for shoes they can easily walk out of, reversible raincoats with linings that hang far below the outer layer of the coat, and hairstyles resembling those of sheepdogs.

For the final issue of the magazine under her editorship, O'Connor drew the cover: a caricature of an overweight cowboy lounging, drink in hand, under a beach umbrella. In a note on the contents page, O'Connor—with considerable irony—explains the drawing as revealing the lassitude of most GSCW students. O'Connor also contributed a poem, "Higher Education," and an essay, "Education's Only Hope" to the spring 1945 edition of the *Corinthian.* O'Connor, in her two-quatrain "Higher Education," humorously gauges the distance between "internally cushioned" professors and their totally conventional students who are deaf to their instruction. In "Education's Only Hope," O'Connor, as a graduating senior about to leave

GSCW, launches a strong attack on the educational establishment. She criticizes chapel speakers who express unrealistic enthusiasm for the roles GSCW students will take after the end of World War II; she argues that current educational practice has not developed in these students the positive qualities like strong interest and "dauntless courage" that would have enabled them to become active participants in the real world. She asserts that if the false enthusiasts were to observe a classroom discussion at GSCW, they would realize how weak minded most students are. As an influence on student apathy, O'Connor also notes the lack of interest most students have in student government, the activity which *should* prepare them to participate in their political futures. She also chastises students who don't read daily newspapers, slyly suggesting that only a comic-book version of the news would attract their interest. Finally, O'Connor attacks the general apathy of both students and faculty. She particularly criticizes students who fail to voice their disgust with current pedagogy. No students, she asserts, have the courage to confront their professors about wasting class time by relating personal anecdotes. She ends by calling for dynamic reform, not "Progressive Education."

Besides editing the *Corinthian,* O'Connor continued as art editor of the *Colonnade* during her senior year. Her cartoon for the 28 September 1944 issue of the paper addresses a perennial campus problem: two students observe a third who is obviously desperately homesick. When a genuine health crisis, involving Para-B Typhoid, threatened GSCW students in October, O'Connor responded with a cartoon of her two favorite subjects eating in the dining hall; the bright one speculates about the number of paratyphoid bacilli they are ingesting and predicts that they'll be ill by the next morning. A third cartoon (14 January 1945) of particular relevance to O'Connor as a student at GSCW has a student standing before a quite impressive library checkout desk asking for books the faculty have not recommended.

The *Colonnade* from the 1944–45 school year also provides other evidence of O'Connor's success at GSCW. The 24 October 1944, issue reveals that she was one of twelve seniors selected for the 1944–45 *Who's Who in American Colleges and Universities.* The 1945 *Spectrum* explains her induction: "Mary Flannery O'Connor's cartoons have given laughs to all. Editor of the *Corinthian,* she is also a member of Phoenix and I.R.C." The 6 December issue of the *Colonnade* reveals that she was one of five students tapped for fall induction into the Phoenix Society, a prestigious GSCW honorary group composed of the upper 7 percent of students from the senior class. About 3½ percent of the membership was inducted during the fall of the senior year, the other half during the spring quarter. The 1945 *Spectrum* describes the group as "the only organization on the campus which is sponsored by the entire faculty. The Phi Beta Kappa members of the faculty serve as a permanent committee to select the members of the Phoenix Society." Another article in the 5 April 1945 *Colonnade* names O'Connor as one of three GSCW "art students [to] have had their work selected to be in a group of sixty art objects which will appear in an exhibit throughout Georgia." O'Connor's painting *Winter* was part of the exhibition which started its tour at the University of Georgia in Athens. Finally, an article in the 6 June issue of the paper about future plans of graduating seniors announces that Mary Flannery O'Connor will attend graduate school at the University of Iowa.

Some of O'Connor's most impressive work during her third year appears in the 1945 *Spectrum*, of which she was feature editor. The endpapers of the yearbook, which in earlier years were plain white paper, consist of an enlargement of a cartoon she drew to illustrate life at GSCW that spring. O'Connor's friend Betty Boyd Love describes the cartoon as one of her favorites: "There was a very large one, inside the covers of our senior yearbook, showing a hectic front campus, which for some reason was all torn up that spring—a scene of rain, mud, boards bridging holes in the lawn, WAVES marching, [. . .] dogs, girls in raincoats and boots—the whole thing brings to mind, with a minimum of linear detail, the entire confusion of that last spring" (Love, "Recollections" 65). In addition to the endpapers, on pages 4 and 5, Mary Flannery created a complete set of cartoons to illustrate all facets of life at GSCW under the title "A Pilgrimage through Jessieville." The first drawing caricatures Parks Hall, the chief administrative building on campus. Lying in front of it are two sleeping hounds. Its caption: "This is Jessieville." A second drawing features two women in caps and gowns; Betty Boyd Love writes, "[N]o student needed a caption to identify the Dean of Women [Adams] and the Academic Dean [Taylor]." (65). In her caption, O'Connor termed these women "guides." A group of four girls, one carrying a huge load of books, represent the student body; O'Connor called them "Wayfarers." Six other drawings refer to the WAVES on campus ("Our Naval Escort"), campus leaders ("We Learn to

Lead"), and various Jessieville activities: "We Record Our Travels," "Points of Interest," "Having a Wonderful Time," and "Where Our Pennies Go." Each of these drawings—enlarged—appears later in the *Spectrum* to introduce a section of the yearbook. O'Connor's 1945 classmates recall the yearbook drawings with approval even after more than fifty years. One of them, Maj. Grace Womble, has a copy of the endpapers on which several classmates made comments like that of Mary Louise Bobo Haley: "Her illustrations in our college annual are very humorous and depict college days on the GSCW campus well." O'Connor's artistry gives the 1945 *Spectrum* a continuity and sophistication lacking in most college yearbooks of that era.

In addition to her cartoons for the *Colonnade* and the *Spectrum,* O'Connor also created a mural for new campus student center in the basement of Parks Hall. Helen Greene writes: "When we acquired a student center in the basement of Parks Hall (then an administrative and classroom building), Mary Flannery decorated the walls with some of these Thurberesque types, and I wish they could have been preserved" (Greene, "Mary Flannery O'Connor" 45–46). Greene explains that they remained on the walls "a good many years," until a flood from pipes that exploded when the heat was turned off too early in the spring "ruined the walls." O'Connor's mural was then painted over.

O'Connor appears in a number of photographs in the 1945 *Spectrum*. She wears no glasses in her senior portrait. Her hair is fashionably arranged, and she appears to be wearing a bit of makeup; though not beautiful, she is more than passably attractive. As editor of the *Corinthian,* Mary Flannery appears in two staff photographs. In one, with her business manager, Peggy George, she hams it up for the camera. In a staged staff meeting photograph, she is dressed in typical college style—a dress with well-worn saddle shoes and socks. She looks attractive, confident, in charge. Though listed as feature editor of the *Spectrum* and a member of the Town Girls' Club, O'Connor does not appear in their photographs; however, looking particularly attractive, she was in both the Newman Club photo and that of the International Relations Club.

Of particular interest to O'Connor and other prospective writers was the visit of poet Robert P. Tristram Coffin to GSCW in early March 1945. The 7 March *Colonnade* announces that he would speak at two chapel programs and also be "available to small groups for lectures and discussions. The English and literature classes will have an opportunity to hear Mr. Coffin during class periods. Personal conferences may be scheduled during the week." In a letter to Janet McKane in December 1963, O'Connor remembered his visit: "Your quoting a poem of R. P. T. Coffin took me back. He visited our college when I was about 18, read some poems of mine and came to our house for some kind of program. That was the only time in my life when I attempted to write poetry. All my poems sounded like 'Minniver Cheevy.' Mr. Coffin was a striking-looking old man" (*HB* 554). Betty Boyd Love and Margaret Meaders also remember Mr. Coffin's visit and the party for him Mary Flannery held at the Cline mansion. Meaders writes:

> One spring Flannery had an evening get-together for him, with a few upperclassmen and faculty members present. Several students were members of the class that had been boning up on the Coffin poetry; and one of them—with that eager, bright-eyed undergraduate enthusiasm that all visiting celebrities are confronted with over and over—had a question for Mr. R. P. T. Coffin.
>
> "We have been studying the symbolism of your poetry," she said, a bit breathlessly but, oh, so charmingly in the manner of one poetic soul to another. "We think we know what most things represent." She named names and coupled them with meanings. Then, frowning prettily, she added, "But in the poem about the fox we couldn't ferret out what the fox himself is supposed to represent."
>
> There was an expectant silence, while most of the assembled company waited for Ultimate Truth from the horse's mouth. For one unguarded moment Mr. Coffin's blue sea-captain eyes blazed almost wrathfully, as he spat out ten short words. "My god!" the poet exclaimed, "just a fox, just an ordinary everyday fox!" I happened to look at our hostess then and found her busy disciplining the mirth that twinkled in her eyes. (Meaders 380–81).

Love remembers the episode a bit differently, suggesting that the question was a deliberate set up and that O'Connor asked it. She says, "That was probably the only unkind thing I ever knew her to do" (Love, "Recollections" MS 2).

Another classmate who attended the party for Coffin does not remember the episode but feels that it would have been like O'Connor to be involved: "She would have loved it."

Since by the time Flannery O'Connor began to write seriously and it was obvious that she had read rather widely, it is interesting to speculate about her extracurricular reading while she was at GSCW. One of her class-mates suggests that O'Connor read far more than other students since she had time for reading because of her limited social life. She recalls that Mary Flannery's responses in class indicated wide reading; she also remembers that Mary Flannery, like her caricature of her cartoons, always carried a large stack of books with her to class. In the 1960s Mary Barbara Tate, then teaching in the English department of Georgia College, tried to document O'Connor's college reading by collecting checkout cards from library books in the Ina Dillard Russell Library. Some years later, when a new librarian came to Georgia College, Tate's collection of cards disappeared; she says, "It was a great loss because I found her name in [books of] history, philosophy, criticism. It was a rich resource and I just grieve that it was lost" (M. B. Tate, interview 1989). The O'Connor Collection does contain a small stack of checkout cards from books O'Connor read at GSCW; the list, however, is not particularly impressive, as most books seem like those she would have checked out while doing research for either English or social science classes. Representative titles from the sixteen cards saved include Louis Untermyer's *Play in Poetry,* Kipling's *Selected Stories,* Henry Beston's *The Book of Gallant Vagabonds,* Evarts Boutell Greene's *The Foundations of American Nationality,* William McGovern's *From Luther to Hitler,* and Allan Nevins's *A Century of Political Cartoons.*[7]

A number of O'Connor's classmates at GSCW expected Mary Flannery O'Connor to achieve success and fame as either an artist or writer. One says of her cartooning, "We all thought maybe that's where she would gain her fame, at first. In the beginning, she came on stronger with her cartoons than she did with her writing." Others—English majors and women who worked with her on the *Corinthian, Colonnade,* and *Spectrum*—were not surprised by her success. Hazel Smith Ogletree recalls "her grasp of the written word"; Bess Saye McFarland feels that O'Connor's "contributions to our literary magazine should have been a clue"; and Carmen Singletary Schatz writes:

"I'm not surprised that she became a famous writer. She was considered very intelligent at G.S.C.W. I can believe that thoughts and ideas of writing were developing at the times that she seemed to be in a class of her own." Hilda Gray Mayo says that she "just *knew* she would be a writer. The words seemed to flow from her pen. Most of us struggled with writing assignments, but hers were so good and interesting." Though Maj. Grace Womble did not necessarily expect Mary Flannery to achieve success as a writer, she did expect "she would be very successful in something." Faculty member Margaret Meaders, however, little expected Mary Flannery to achieve fame so quickly: "I did not dream that in so short a while, the quiet, somewhat withdrawn, unhurried girl would go so far and—in one sense of the word—travel so fast" (Meaders 386).

Despite her considerable success as a student, writer, and artist there, O'Connor's later comments about her education at GSCW were primarily negative. She repeatedly emphasized her inability to retain what she read in college. To Betty Hester in 1955, she wrote that she had read both Aristotle and Plato in college but remembered little about them, declaring that "total non-retention has kept my education from being a burden to me" (*HB* 93). O'Connor, as an adult, was often critical of the depth and breadth of her reading in literature. Though her transcript reveals that she ostensibly studied contemporary literature at GSCW, she wrote to Cecil Dawkins in May 1957 that she had never heard of Porter, Faulkner, or Welty until she read their fiction at Iowa. She criticized English departments for their failure to teach "contemporary literature" (*HB* 221). Helen Greene recalled that when O'Connor was studying Southern literature at Iowa, she asked her why she hadn't read some of Katherine Anne Porter's work at GSCW. "'Honey,' she answered, 'she writes in *Harper's Bazaar.* You don't read that kind of literature.' She laughed and laughed so she knew what was funny." Greene's comment, however, also revealed how traditional the curriculum was at GSCW in the 1940s. Though O'Connor's course of study seems to have been typical of that of most potential teachers during the 1940s and 1950s, the fact that she completed requirements for the degree in three calendar years probably somewhat influenced her negative outlook on her education at GSCW; yet, despite her criticism of her undergraduate education, O'Connor's development in her second hometown was of pivotal importance to her life as a creative writer. Because Peabody and GSCW pre-sented a progressive approach to education and O'Connor was aware of it, she broadened her perspective. She knew that the two types of education—restrictive/parochial and progressive/secular—she had experienced were insufficient for the career that she proposed to follow. As she told Ralph Morrissey in a 1955 interview, "'After I graduated [from GSCW], I realized I needed expert advice if I were ever to be a real writer. So I entered Paul Engle's course in creative writing at Iowa State University.'"[8]

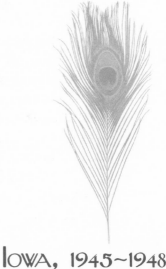

CHAPTER FOUR

IOWA, 1945~1948

When Flannery O'Connor enrolled in the State University of Iowa in Iowa City in September of 1945, she entered a university with one of the first established programs in creative writing in the United States. The English department there had begun to emphasize creative writing near the end of the nineteenth century with the rise of Midwest regionalist writing. Poet and collector of folk songs of the West, Edwin Ford Piper, who joined the faculty at Iowa in 1905, soon began to conduct informal workshop sessions with aspiring poets. John Towner Frederick, an early graduate of Iowa, returned to teach there in 1913; two years later he established *Midland: A Magazine of the Middle West,* which for more than thirty years published regional writing, including poetry and stories by Ruth Suckow, Raymond Weeks, James T. Farrell, Maxwell Anderson, Mackinlay Kantor, and Paul Engle (Wilbers 3, 4, 10, 13, 14, 15).

As early as the 1920s, the University of Iowa had begun to allow students to submit creative work as a master's thesis. When Norman Foerster joined the University of Iowa faculty in 1930, as director of the newly formed School of Letters, he convinced the administration to accept creative dissertations from Ph.D. candidates (Wilbers 43). This innovation ultimately led to the creation of the Iowa Writers' Workshop. Foerster was also influential in instituting literary criticism as a central focus in the English department. When, in 1939, he added both Austin Warren and Rene Welleck to the faculty, the department began to earn a nationwide reputation for its emphasis on literary theory (51). Because of its emphasis on creative writing, literary theory, and the success graduates had in getting their work published, Iowa quickly began to draw talented young writers from all over the country to its program. The name Writers' Workshop first came into university use in 1939, when Wilbur Schramm, its first official director (he served from 1939 to 1941), advertised his summer workshop in creative writing under that name. That summer eleven creative writers added their expertise, among them Donald Davidson, Wallace Stegner (who had presented a novel as his master's thesis in 1932), and Paul Engle (51).

Engle had also been one of the first Iowa students to earn an M.A. degree in English on the basis of creative writing: he submitted a collection of poems, *One Slim Feather* as his M.A. thesis in 1932. Under the title *Worn Leaves*, the collection was the first creative M.A. thesis from Iowa to be published. Engle, who would become the dominant figure in the history of the Iowa Workshop for Writers, was a native of nearby Cedar Rapids, Iowa. After his *American Song: A Book of Poems* had received early enthusiastic praise in 1934, he returned to the University of Iowa in 1937 to take a job as a writing teacher and lecturer in poetry in the English department. When Wilbur Schram left Iowa in January 1942 to become actively involved in the war effort in Washington, D.C., Engle was named acting director of the workshop (86–88). By 1965 Engle had transformed a program that had only 12 students when he took it over to one with 250 graduates students.

Members of the workshop during the years O'Connor was at Iowa have recalled both Engle's dedication to the program and his eccentricity. W. D. Snodgrass, who came to Iowa in 1948, just after O'Connor left, described Engle's rather peculiar mental habits: "[I]f there were two ways to do a thing—one, simple and straightforward; the other, complicated, difficult, underhanded but nearly as effective—Paul always took the latter. [. . .] That same penchant, however, made him a superb administrator. It may well be that such a large and costly program needs an impresario similarly gifted" (Snodgrass 447). Walter Sullivan, who entered the workshop in the fall of 1947, during O'Connor's final year there, also recalls Engle's absolute dedication to the welfare of his students, a dedication that became self-sacrificing in his desire to bring first-rate writers to Iowa City as guest lecturers in the workshop. According to Sullivan, Engle was well aware that some of these guests "had better reputations than he did but this did not deter him. He never tried to upstage any of the talent he brought in."[1]

Engle revealed his desire to publicize the workshop in December 1947, while O'Connor was still at Iowa, when he wrote two articles for a Des Moines, Iowa, newspaper.[2] These accounts provide considerable information about the operation of the program during O'Connor's years there. Of the value of Iowa's allowing graduate students to submit creative work for advanced degrees, he wrote, "In this way the student is enabled to go on with his writing while at the same time acquiring a more extensive background of literature." Engle's comments about the admissions policy in the program reveal how popular the program had become by 1947: "[A]t the graduate level, each year hundreds of students from most of the states" were seeking admission to the workshop. To be considered, applicants submitted "an extended piece of their writing," which the admissions committee "read carefully" before making a decision. "Normally," Engle asserted, "about two out of three are rejected in this manner." Engle also described the specific workshop method: participants read their manuscripts and then received detailed criticism from both the staff of the writing program and other workshop members. Engle wrote, "The students are quite merciless in criticizing each other's work [. . . but] often unexpectedly subtle and fresh viewpoints come up in this way" (21 December 1947).

In the second article, Engle gave information about his recent arrangement with Rinehart Publishers in New York, who were so impressed with the "soundness" of his program that they were offering two one-year fellowships of $750 each to students whose manuscripts showed promise of publishing success. Engle boasted that only the Writers' Workshop at Iowa had such an arrangement with a "commercial publishing house." At the end of the second article, he announced that "Miss Flannery O'Connor of Georgia won the Fellowship given in May, 1947, and is now completing her novel in the Workshop" (28 December 1947).

When O'Connor received this prestigious fellowship, she had already earned the M.F.A. (in June 1947) under the tutelage of Engle, who had discovered O'Connor after she had entered the school of journalism at the university in the fall of 1945. She started with a fellowship in journalism that waived her tuition and paid her a stipend of sixty-five dollars for the term (*CW* 1240). She must have arrived in Iowa City in mid-September 1945 since classes that fall began on the twenty-fourth. Regina O'Connor accompanied her daughter to Iowa City to help her settle into Currier House, the graduate dormitory. They must have traveled by bus from Milledgeville to Atlanta and taken a train from there to Iowa City.

Regarding his first meeting with O'Connor, Paul Engle often told the story of how she came to him shortly after the fall 1945 semester began and declared herself a writer with a desire to join his Writers' Workshop:

> She walked into my office one day and spoke to me. I understood nothing, not one syllable. As far as I knew, she was saying "Aaaraaaraaarah." My God, I thought to myself, this is a retarded young girl.
>
> [. . .] Finally, I said, excuse me, my name is Paul Engle. I gave her a pad—believe me, this is true—and said would you please write down what you're telling me. And she wrote, "My name is Flannery O'Connor. I'm from Milledgeville, Georgia. I'm a writer." She didn't say "I want to be a writer." She said, "I am a writer." (Qtd. in C. McCarthy 6)

When asked whether he could verify the authenticity of Engle's anecdote, Walter Sullivan responded that he believed the story was true: "That was one of the curious things about Flannery—that accent. She never lost one little inch of that. This was a Southern accent beyond Southern accents."[3] Engle also remembered that he read only a few words from O'Connor's writing sample before realizing that O'Connor possessed what he later called "pure talent." In a letter to Robert Giroux in July 1971, Engle described his perceptions of her work: "The stories were quietly filled with insight, shrewd about human weakness, hard and compassionate" (Giroux vii). In the same letter, Engle gave details of O'Connor's behavior in the workshop. She sat "silent" at the back of the room, untouched by the "exuberant talkers": "The only communicating gesture she would make was an occasional amused and shy smile at something absurd. The dreary chair she sat in glowed" (vii).

Another story that Engle often told about his interaction with O'Connor concerned his working with her to improve the seduction scene between Leora Watts and Hazel Motes in *Wise Blood*. Engle described a conference with O'Connor regarding the scene during which he told her that her depiction lacked authenticity. When he added that he had suggestions to make that might improve it, she was too embarrassed to discuss the passage in his university office. They went to his car, he said, to continue their discussion, but she would neither allow him to offer direct advice nor to talk about her own lack of sexual experience (Noguichi 60–61). The frank and gregarious Engle obviously intimidated the twenty-year-old.

O'Connor's relationship with Engle during her years in the workshop apparently was strong in the beginning; it weakened partly because Engle was so often away from Iowa City during her second and third years there. During the entire 1946–47 term, Engle was on leave from his position, spending time in Florida and elsewhere as he worked to publicize the program. Robie Macauley, O'Connor's close friend during her last year at Iowa, believed that, though she respected Engle as a teacher, she did not take him "very seriously as a critic. She thought that his suggestions for revision in *Wise Blood* were far off the mark, I remember"; however, Macauley also recalled that though workshop members—including O'Connor—joked about Engle's "mannerisms and pretensions," they realized that he was "the moving force behind the workshop."[4] O'Connor clearly acknowledged Engle's influence on her work by dedicating her MFA thesis to him: "To Paul Engle whose interest and criticism have made these stories better than they would otherwise have been."[5]

After she left Iowa, O'Connor maintained only occasional contact with Engle; however, in a letter to Sally Fitzgerald in December 1954, O'Connor described Engle as her "ex-mentor" (*HB* 74). In a handwritten postcard to Engle from Milledgeville in August 1948, she revealed the "dullness" of her current life—she described sleeping in a "coffin"—and requested that he transfer the fellowship which he had offered her for the 1948–49 school term to her former classmate and friend Clyde McLeod.[6] Living in New York after she left Yaddo, O'Connor wrote to Jean Wylder that she had seen Engle while he was in New York.[7] Later, in April 1949, during her troubles with

Rinehart Publishers, she wrote to Engle to protest what she perceived to be Rinehart's desire to direct her talent to a quickly publishable medium: "Now I am sure that no one will understand my need to work this novel out in my own way better than you" (14).

When *Wise Blood* was published in 1952, Engle, however, apparently felt insulted that O'Connor had given too little credit to him and the workshop. Commenting on Engle's criticism, she wrote to Robie Macauley in October 1952 that he didn't like the title of the novel or the fact that she hadn't mentioned the workshop on the book cover. She also wrote that she had assured Engle that this information would be added to the "drugstore reprint that has been sold to the New American Library" (*HB* 45).

The Engle file at the University of Iowa Library includes another letter (not published in *The Habit of Being*) that O'Connor wrote to Engle in 1955 after he and Hansford Martin chose "The Life You Save May Be Your Own" for inclusion in *Prize Stories for 1954: The O. Henry Awards*. She thanked them for the award and snidely related how she had been trying to convince her "kin" about the seriousness of her vocation as writer. She asserted that receiving the award had both enhanced her local reputation and helped her receive public recognition; she mentioned being invited to a meeting of the Atlanta Branch of the Penwomen and to participate on a panel at North Carolina Women's College in Greensboro.[8] One further positive reference to Engle occurs in a letter O'Connor wrote to Betty Hester in December 1956, when she offered to lend her friend two books—*The Craft of Fiction* and *Understanding Fiction*—that she believed would help Hester improve her own writing. Of the Brooks and Warren text, O'Connor wrote, "It is pure textbook and very uninviting and part of the value of it for me was that I had it in conjunction with Paul Engle who was able to breathe some life into it" (*HB* 192).

The connection described above had, of course, only begun to develop when O'Connor joined the workshop in the fall of 1945 as one of only three women in her class: the others were Kay Burford and Mary Mudge Wiatt, neither of whom knew O'Connor well. Burford remembers that, though O'Connor's work was "well thought of," it was not as highly praised as that of the men, mostly World War II veterans, who collectively approved each other's war stories. Though she doesn't remember which work O'Connor presented, Burford recalls at least one incident when an O'Connor story got "less attention than it deserved." Overall, she remembers O'Connor's quietness in the workshop sessions and her lack of interest in other people's writing: "You felt she was exceptionally quiet, but somebody you wished you had known better."[9]

Mary Mudge Wiatt also regrets not having known O'Connor better outside the workshop: "In class she seemed nice but very quiet and a trifle uncomfortable when reading aloud to the group." Wiatt also remembers one specific occasion when an O'Connor story strongly displeased the male members of the group: "I thought some people were being supercilious about her approach to blacks in something she read—that is, they considered that she was exhibiting 'the Southern attitude.' Even though I can't now clearly recall the piece itself, I remember being impressed with it and feeling that their response was wrong and mostly reflexive."[10] Men dominated the workshop through O'Connor's three years at Iowa, but no male writer of her stature emerged, though several of them later published both fiction and poetry and pursued successful careers in teaching and publishing. Andrew Lytle, for example, designated James B. Hall, now Professor Emeritus at the University of California, Santa Cruz, as probably second to O'Connor among his students at Iowa.[11]

Hall holds vivid memories of O'Connor in the workshop, recalling her as "an extremely guarded, most private person. She talked very little, in or out of class."[12] He has analyzed reasons for her reserve, beginning with the vast gulf which separated her as a young, innocent woman from the older veterans, who often drank heavily, had fervent interest in "bop jazz," and possessed little religious interest or faith: "I think of no person who had any religious conviction save Flannery and [William] Stafford, and he kept it pretty quiet." Hall believes that O'Connor was also alienated by her Southernness. He remembers her "heavy Southern accent" and her casual reference to "niggers; [she] once said to me, 'We [she and her mother] got us a nigger to drive our car.' Even then, that diction was uncomfortable, even on a racist, public campus." To support his description of the Iowa campus as racist, Hall tells of having served unsuccessfully on a committee that tried "to force the University barbershops to cut the hair of black, male students. The President (Hancher) wouldn't order it, so some of my friends had to go to Cedar Rapids." In his informal memoir of his years at Iowa, Walter Sullivan remembers the same episode, and Herbert Nipson, the only African American member of the workshop during this era, also recalls the racial atmosphere at Iowa in the late 1940s. He says that Hall "is right about racism on the campus. At that time no Blacks (including star athletes) were allowed to live in the dormitories, no barbers on or off campus cut Black students' hair and married Black students had difficulty finding housing in the town."[13]

Like Burford and Wiatt, Hall remembers O'Connor in the workshop as being generally quiet. She sat "at the end of a row, usually in the back." She was not, however, "entirely silent." He recalls that the points she made were "highly intelligent, but she tended to observe others, and if she had opinions (which I imagine she did have) she tended to keep those to herself in the classroom." O'Connor also left strong impressions on other male members of the workshop. Herbert Nipson came to Iowa in June 1946 and remained there until June 1949. He received his M.F.A. in creative writing and started work on a Ph.D., but left in 1949, when he decided to make journalism his career. He joined the staff of *Ebony,* ultimately becoming its editor, a position he held until his retirement in the fall of 1987. Nipson recalls the membership of the workshop and O'Connor's position in it; he remembers the many older veterans there and that, in comparison with them, "Flannery seemed much younger, was not too articulate and, to my memory, seldom took part in lengthy discussions"; however, he also remembers group reactions to her stories:

> When Flannery read, there was little criticism of her writing. I think that everyone in the workshop recognized her talent. She had a way with words. Discussions usually centered on what she had to say. Other listeners read more into her stories than she would admit to. I remember her reading one of her short stories set in a small Georgia town. After the reading one of the members complimented her on how she had treated one of the characters, a Black servant. The member felt that the servant had been treated in a dignified, human way and asked if she had done this to make a point. As I remember, Flannery's answer went something like this, "No. That was just the way he was."

Hank Messick, another contemporary of O'Connor's in the workshop, who later published several books—novels and nonfiction—recalled how Paul Engle seemed to favor her over him:

The only fellow student I remember was Flannery O'Connor. My wife and Flannery had gone to school together in Georgia and so we became friends. We argued a lot about writing and the purpose of writing. She, of course, was a genius and was so recognized by Engle, whereas I was scarcely tolerated. Consequently she was a bit arrogant, perhaps, but we got along nicely nevertheless. [. . .] She had, of course, a morbid, obviously Catholic point of view, and disagreed angrily at my optimistic suggestions that man might improve himself by his own efforts.[14]

Another workshop member, who joined the group in February 1946, also remembers O'Connor's shyness in the workshop and his being asked, because he too had a Southern accent, to read some of her stories for her: "Flannery turned to me because my colloquial speaking style fit her material. [. . .] We also shared a certain literary manner which might be described as metaphorical in form, metaphysical in theme, and Gothic in tone."[15]

One of O'Connor's most enduring connections established among the faculty at Iowa was with fellow Southerner Andrew Lytle, who first became her teacher during the spring 1947 semester, just before she was awarded an M.F.A. Engle had brought Lytle to Iowa that semester as a guest teacher; he also arranged for Lytle to replace him in the spring 1948 semester while he (Engle) was on leave. A letter from Engle to then Dean Earl J. McGrath explained this arrangement: "Andrew Lytle, my associate in the second semester this spring will come to replace me if it can be arranged. He knows our system and is a fine teacher; he was formerly editor of the Sewanee Review and has a new novel out this month. May I, through Mr. [Baldwin] Maxwell [then head of the English department] (who is in accord with me on wishing Mr. Lytle to come) offer him what I received last year? I doubt if he would move his family up here for less."[16] At considerable expense and worry for himself and his family—Lytle recalled, for example, that he had to buy a new automobile to make the long drive to Iowa City—he did replace Engle as director of the workshop during the spring 1948 semester. Of his total experience at Iowa, Lytle said, "It [Iowa] was a very strange world but a rather nice world." Despite his problems with weather, housing, and lack of servants, he was still glad he went, primarily because at Iowa he developed methods of helping students to write better, which he took with him to the University of Florida, where he founded the program in creative writing.

Several of Lytle's students and colleagues at Iowa attested to his positive performance as director of the workshop in fiction. Hank Messick, who felt slighted by Engle, wrote, "Luckily for me, he [Engle] went away on leave or something and Andrew Lytle replaced him. Lytle and I got along fine, and it was he who approved my thesis and restored my faith."[17] Hansford Martin, in a letter to Engle in Florida, described both Lytle's social success and his traditional views of fiction: "He, incidentally, I like fine; being a wondrously charming person; but his criticism seems to be deeply grounded in a strong naturalistic (or at least realistic) basis, so that something like [Warren] Miller's novel—which is Kafka like—leaves him groping."[18]

James B. Hall retains significant memories of the positive interaction between O'Connor and Andrew Lytle, whom he remembers as "'a demanding affectionate man, [who] saw no contradiction in his own career of farmer and one-time professional actor'" (Dinger 14). Hall believes that Lytle exerted pivotal influence on O'Connor's fiction, working "more closely with Flannery O'Connor than any staff member at Iowa." He elaborates: "He [also] sometimes talked to me about how talented she was and how quickly she learned. For example, he said, 'You only have to tell her something once. And she's got it. The same mistake won't show up again.' He liked, and encouraged the visual aspects of fiction, including hers." Hall also recalls the pride Lytle took in O'Connor's early success: when the manuscript of *Wise Blood* won the Rinehart-Iowa prize for fiction, Lytle told him about it: "He was very, very proud of this—understandably; he saw it as recognition for a[nother] Southern writer."

Andrew Lytle himself remembered O'Connor's special ability, declaring her the "only student there of exceptional talent." He particularly recalled their private conferences together: "We met and we had successful talks," during which O'Connor was open and talkative. She possessed, he discerned, a talent so great that "she scared the boys. They felt that she could cut them to pieces." In a tribute he wrote for O'Connor in *Esprit* in 1963, Lytle described their first encounter:

> Years ago at Iowa City in a rather informal class meeting I read
> aloud a story by one of the students. I was told later that it was
> understood that I would know how to pronounce in good

country idiom the word chitling which appeared in the story. At once it was obvious that the author of the story was herself not only Southern but exceptionally gifted. The idiom of her characters rang with all the truth of the real thing, but the real thing heightened. It resembled in tone and choice of words all country speech I had ever heard, but I couldn't quite place it. And then I realized that what she had done was what any first rate artist always does—she made something more essential than life but resembling it. [. . .]

This of course was Flannery O'Connor. (Lytle, "Flannery O'Connor—A Tribute" 33)

Lytle also recalled one conference he and O'Connor had over a section of *Wise Blood*. Like Engle, he felt that O'Connor had somehow not handled the seduction scene between Haze and Leora Watts right; he disagreed with her having Hazel get "in bed with a hat on his head." Overall, he said that in their meetings he "told her things she couldn't do, that didn't work," but he added, "She was wonderful, of course; you couldn't teach her anything much." He did believe, however, that O'Connor "finally, I think, looked to me as a person who could teach her. [. . .] I say that with hesitancy."

Robie Macauley, who was at Iowa during O'Connor's last year there, recalled that even as he helped her, Lytle had reservations about her work: "As I recall Andrew liked Flannery but thought her fiction rather uncouth, while acknowledging her talent. Andrew [was] a sophisticated stylist and fiction about rednecks turned him off, I believe." In a letter to Thomas Carter, a student at Washington and Lee in the early 1950s and editor of *Shenandoah,* Lytle both prophesied O'Connor's future greatness and expressed reservations about her power during the time she was working on *Wise Blood* at Iowa: "[I]f people quite [*sic*] tampering with Flannery, and she shows up with critical sense, the basic technical sense which guides you and lets you know what you've got and where you're going, she'll make the best writer of sardonic irony, if such a thing can be, that I know. When I read her mss. and advised her at Iowa, she hadn't this sense; and whoever advised her to cut that book, cut it to the bone and left out, or rather made it an allegory almost."[19] Another interesting side issue concerning Lytle and *Wise Blood* involves his unwillingness to review the book for *Shenandoah*. When Thomas

Carter wrote to him in June 1952 to solicit a review, Lytle excused himself from writing it, claiming that he had his own work to do—both literary and agrarian. He also argued,

> Then Flannery was a student of mine at Iowa, and I advised with her in the process of getting the right form for her material. I couldn't approach it without much care, and I don't know now what I think about it. I think she has left out too much circumstance of sardonic humor; and it would require more time than I've got now to go into this. It's a good book and she's a fine talent. There is a move towards the Old Church on the part of some of my friends, and I'm afraid an extraneous zeal is confusing their artistry.
>
> But thank you anyway.[20]

O'Connor, apparently was unaware of Lytle's reservations about her early work, for she continued to place strong value on his critical opinions after she left Iowa. Though only two letters from O'Connor to Lytle appear in *The Habit of Being,* O'Connor referred to him many times in letters to other correspondents. In 1952, for example, she included Lytle on a list of critics from whom "a good word [about *Wise Blood*] might be squeezed out." In 1955 she wrote to thank Lytle for a letter (regarding *A Good Man Is Hard to Find*) he had sent to Harcourt Brace in her behalf: "What you said in it is what I see in the stories myself but what nobody who reviews them cares to see." She went on to explain both the spiritual and the Southern emphases of her work: "To my way of thinking, the only thing that keeps me from being a regional writer is being a Catholic and the only thing that keeps me from being a Catholic writer (in the narrow sense) is being a Southerner" (*HB* 104). O'Connor also read Lytle's *The Velvet Horn* when it appeared in 1959, writing to John Hawkes that she "was entirely taken with it. I didn't follow all the intricacies of the symbolism but it had its effect without working it all out" (351). When she published *The Violent Bear It Away* in 1960, she wrote to Lytle, again thanking him for understanding her work: "I feel better about the book, knowing you think it works. I expect it to get trounced but that won't make any difference if it really does work. There are not many people whose opinion on this I set story by" (373).

Though she and Lytle disagreed about the humanity of the grandmother in "A Good Man Is Hard to Find"—"Andrew insists that she is a witch, even down to the cat" (*HB* 389)—their literary relationship continued until her death. As editor of the *Sewanee Review* in the early 1960s, Lytle planned and published an issue (summer 1962) partly devoted to her work with essays by John Hawkes and Robert Fitzgerald and her long story, "The Lame Shall Enter First." Finally, early in 1964, O'Connor submitted "Revelation" to Lytle at the *Sewanee Review,* writing to Betty Hester: "I could get $1500 for it from *Esquire* but I emulate my better characters and feel like Mr. Shiftlet that there should be some folks that some things mean more to them than money" (563). Published in the spring 1964 issue of the journal, "Revelation" was the last story O'Connor saw in print before her death. Of the two stories he published, Lytle said, "They're both magnificent things, very fine, both of them." Commenting in the summer of 1993 on O'Connor's ultimate reputation, Lytle said, "She was one of the best and she will live, I think. It's the real thing."

In addition to Engle and Lytle, writer Paul Horgan, who replaced Engle as director of the workshop in the fall 1946 semester, was also one of her instructors in the workshop: "At Iowa, I was only a student and Horgan never knew I was in the room, I am sure—though once he noted forty things wrong with a story of mine and I thought him a fine teacher" (*HB* 237). Paul Engle also remembered her interaction with Robert Penn Warren, a visiting lecturer at Iowa during O'Connor's time there. Warren read and criticized a scene in one of her stories that included both black and white characters. According to Engle, she changed the passage on Warren's advice because she "always had a flexible and objective view of her own writing, constantly revising, and in every case improving" (Giroux viii). Still another visiting lecturer at Iowa, Allen Tate, admitted his own early misreading of O'Connor's work. He said that he read a fragment of *Wise Blood* and only later realized that his remarks about the manuscript were generally "irrelevant": "I hadn't the vaguest idea of what she was up to; I offered to correct her grammar; I even told her that the style was dull, the sentences being flat and simple declarative. No doubt what I said was true; but it was irrelevant. The flat style, the cranky grammar, the monotonous sentence-structure were necessary vehicles of her vision of man. It was a narrow vision, but deep; unworldly, but aware of human depravity as only a good Jansenist can be" (Tate, "Flannery O'Connor—A Tribute" 48).

These memories of both students and faculty, then, provide glimpses of O'Connor in the workshop during her first two years at Iowa. After earning her M.F.A. degree in June 1947, O'Connor stayed on in Iowa City for an additional year, financially supported by the Rinehart-Iowa Fellowship in fiction. O'Connor's award, based on her partially completed manuscript of *Wise Blood,* allowed her to continue to work on her novel and to attend meetings of the workshop. An article that appeared in the university paper gave O'Connor's reaction to the award. She said, "'I was surprised and gratified when I heard about the award. You see, this will give me enough money to finish the novel here at the university next year.'" When pressed by the interviewer for more information about the source of her novel, O'Connor replied that she could not tell where she got the idea for her novel: "'It was not one idea but a creative process and a combination of many things. [. . .] I wish I could be more definite, but a novel in the process is not a very definite thing.'"[21] The photograph of O'Connor that accompanies the article shows her wearing glasses, a necklace, lipstick, styled hair, and a pleasant expression.

During her last year in Iowa, then, O'Connor became both much more confident of her potential success as a writer and socially less self-conscious. Among the aspiring young writers who joined the workshop in the fall of 1947 were Jean Williams (later Wylder) from Iowa, Walter Sullivan from Tennessee, Clyde McLeod (later Hoffman) from North Carolina, and Robie Macauley, a recently discharged veteran from the Midwest, who came in the dual role of student and instructor. These people became her friends or, at least, fairly close acquaintances.

Of them, only Jean Williams Wylder published an account of their year together at Iowa. Wylder, who died in 1989, recounted her first impression of O'Connor: "On the opening day of class, Flannery was sitting alone in the front row, over against the wall. She was wearing what I was soon to think of as her "uniform" for that year: plain gray skirt and neatly ironed silkish blouse, nylon stockings and penny brown loafers. Her only makeup was a trace of lipstick" (58). Revealing that she, O'Connor, and McLeod were the only women in the workshop that fall, Wylder thought that O'Connor, especially, seemed "out of place" in this group of men. The women felt alienated by the greater age and experience of the men as well as by their interest in "New Criticism theories; many sensitive young writers got shot down by the heavy onslaught of their critical fire. Stories were dissected like so many literary specimens: few stood up under the minute probing" (58). According to Wylder, O'Connor seldom contributed to workshop discussion, though she did remember one exception:

> The only comment I ever heard her make in class was the next spring. Andrew Lytle was in charge that semester [. . .] and he asked her what she thought of the story we were discussing that day. By then, most of the students knew she was already a published writer; everyone in the room wanted to hear what she would say. In a perfectly dead-pan voice, addressing herself to the general emptiness at the front of the room, came her laconic reply: "I'd say the description of that crocodile in there was real good." The irony of Flannery's statement lay in the fact that the crocodile *was* the best thing in the story but it had absolutely no meaning in the texture of the story itself. She had said all there was to say but she would have never offered that much if Mr. Lytle hadn't asked her. (58)

Several workshop members, including Wylder, remember that during the spring 1948 semester O'Connor read one of her own stories at a meeting. Writing to Wylder on 26 December 1972, workshop member Gene Brzenk recalled: "Flannery's deadpan reading in her flat, nasal drawl was exactly right for the material, and this was one of the rare times when members of the Workshop relaxed completely and laughed appreciatively. There was a Zasu Pitts quality to her reading, yet she never looked up and acknowledged her audience only when the laughter drowned out her voice. When she finished reading we all applauded and the meeting broke up in high good humor."[22]

In her memoir, Wylder, too, described the reading, particularly emphasizing the positive reaction of O'Connor's audience; she recalled that after O'Connor read, the group remained silent until "Andrew Lytle gave meaning to our silence by saying Workshop was over for the day." The silence, Wylder wrote, "was a tribute to her genius." She also recalled that she and Clyde McLeod, wanting to give O'Connor even more recognition, "went around Iowa City on that late spring afternoon, walking into people's yards as if they were public domain, to gather arms full of flowering branches—taking only the most beautiful—and we carried them up to Flannery" (62). In a letter to

Paul Engle—on leave that spring in Florida—Hansford Martin, then an instructor in the workshop, also recalled the occasion. His comment about her appropriately summarizes O'Connor's last months in the workshop: "Among the elderly, Flannery seems happiest of all, blossoming like a rose, packing for Yaddo, and even reading Out Loud in class."[23]

O'Connor's interaction with and learning from professors and fellow students in the workshop represent the real importance of her years at Iowa; for example, in letters to several correspondents, she admitted that only when she came to Iowa did she begin to read modern fiction. She told Betty Hester that after discovering these writers she "began to read everything at once" (*HB* 98). O'Connor did, however, have a life outside her graduate work. As a young woman (only twenty when she entered the workshop) away from home (and the protection of her mother) for the first time, she also developed at Iowa social friendships—some brief, others enduring.

In her first two years in Iowa City as a graduate student, O'Connor lived at 32 East Bloomington Street in a house (no longer standing) that served as an annex to Currier Dormitory for Women. It housed eight graduate students. During her years in the Annex, she apparently roomed with whatever student the housing office assigned to share the room. O'Connor's last roommate at the Currier Annex was Martha Bell (later Spreiser), who joined her there in January 1947; they lived together, according to Spreiser, "in a first-floor northeast room" that was "not large, but adequate." Both roommates earned M.A. degrees on 7 June 1947. O'Connor's, of course, was an M.F.A., while Martha Bell earned an M.A. in business education.[24] Spreiser describes how they became coincidental roommates, asserting that when she heard about a vacancy in the Currier Graduate House, she "'jumped at the chance' and thereby acquired Flannery as a room-mate in January 1947."

Both young women were so "deeply involved in thesis-writing and fulfilling other academic requirements that there was *very little* time for socializing or getting acquainted." Spreiser, however, does recall O'Connor "as a quiet, unassuming girl, very much introverted, with a deep religious conviction and a delightful sense of humor." She also remembers that O'Connor's writing "totally consumed her attention; *nothing* could distract her. Flannery insisted on having the shades pulled, even in day-time, no doubt to prevent distractions. Our artificial light was one unshaded bulb hanging by a long cord from the center of the ceiling."

Spreiser, who kept a diary throughout her years at Iowa, has found a reference to only one social jaunt with O'Connor. On 29 May, after they had completed their written and oral examinations, she, O'Connor, and Sarah Dawson—their housemother, who was actually about their age—drove to Cedar Rapids (twenty miles from Iowa City) to celebrate: "We had dinner there, did some window-shopping and then went to see *The Egg and I*." Spreiser also found a notation in her diary (27 May 1947) that she had "read Flannery's thesis." She does not, however, recall her reaction to the stories. After they graduated, O'Connor and Spreiser wrote to each other occasionally; in an 25 April 1952 letter to Bell, O'Connor revealed a sense of humor about attention her work was receiving in the *Iowa Alumnae Review*. She told Spreiser that she thought only football players received such notice. She wryly suggested that maybe they had confused her with a short stop. She ended by proudly announcing that her book *(Wise Blood)* would go on sale 15 May.[25] O'Connor later invited Martha Bell to the book-signing party held for her at the GSCW library after the publication of the novel. Spreiser today regrets that she was unable to attend.

Walter Sullivan describes the overall situation in housing at Iowa during O'Connor's last year there, 1947–48, remembering that "it was hard to find a place to live" because so many returning veterans had arrived at Iowa that fall. They were, he says "a pretty riotous bunch, very hard-living people, which wouldn't have fit Flannery's life style at all." O'Connor, however, did find a convenient—and, apparently, suitable though chilly—place to live in a boardinghouse at 115 East Bloomington Street, not far from the Currier Annex. In a 1952 letter to Jean Wylder, she wrote of her difficulty finding this room and how physically cold it was; her landlady, she felt, didn't like her staying home and requiring the heat to be on.[26]

When Rosalyn Barnes, a GSCW graduate and a friend of O'Connor, went to Iowa herself in September 1960, O'Connor wrote to her that she knew where Barnes was living because she had lived nearby "at 115 East Bloomington, a big grey house owned then by a Mrs. Guzeman. Some time ask your landlord about Mrs. Guzeman. She was most a hundred then so I suppose she is in the cemetery now" (*HB* 410). In a later letter to Barnes in December 1960, O'Connor revealed that Barnes had indeed found both the boardinghouse and Mrs. Guzeman. Since 1960, however, the boardinghouse has been razed—a Delta Delta Pi building now occupies the space where it sat. Still, the street appears similar to the way it was when O'Connor lived there. Although the houses that remain are certainly no longer boarding-houses, they obviously house students. Generally clapboard in construction and comfortable in appearance, some of them were surely there when O'Connor lived on the street. In 1986, James O. Freedman wrote of the fame of O'Connor's boardinghouse and of the myths that grew to surround it. He recalled that Gail Godwin (a later workshop participant) had said "that if every apartment claimed by the landlords to have been lived in by Flannery O'Connor were genuine, she would have had to move every few weeks to live in them all."[27]

Jean Williams Wylder learned to know O'Connor after she had moved into Mrs. Guzeman's boardinghouse. Though they met in the workshop, Wylder's longest conversation with O'Connor occurred before Christmas 1947 when they traveled by train together from Iowa City to Chicago; she recalled that O'Connor talked of Milledgeville, her family, and her interest in exotic fowl. After their trip together, Wilder asserted that she came to consider herself O'Connor's closest friend on campus even though they seldom met outside the workshop: "I would have liked to have gone to the movies with her or had a Coke with her, but it simply didn't occur to me that things like that could ever be part of her life" (60).

In her memoir, Wylder described the simplicity of O'Connor's private life. One day she met O'Connor outside the local Woolworth's store; noticing that O'Connor had bought only a single cake of Palmolive soap, she went on to recall the "monastic simplicity" of O'Connor's room at Mrs. Guzeman's, where the only extravagance Wylder noticed was "a box of vanilla wafers beside the typewriter. She nibbled on cookies while she wrote, she said, because she didn't smoke" (59). Wylder, who worked at the Mad Hatter Tea Room as a "salad girl," also remembered that since Mrs. Guzeman didn't serve meals on Sundays, O'Connor sometimes had lunch at the Tea Room above Bremer's Clothing Store in Iowa City.

O'Connor's religious practice was no doubt as simple, regular, and private as the rest of her life in Iowa. Wylder, for example, wrote that it wasn't until several years after O'Connor left Iowa that she learned of O'Connor's Catholicism. The church O'Connor attended, St. Mary's, still sits on East Jefferson Street, within easy walking distance of both the Currier House Annex and Mrs. Guzeman's boardinghouse. Of her attendance at mass, O'Connor wrote to Roslyn Barnes in December 1960 that she went to St. Mary's "practically every morning [. . . for] three years and never knew a soul in that congregation or any of the priests, but it was not necessary. As soon as I went in the door I was home" (*HB* 422). Robie Macauley was not aware that O'Connor attended mass every day, but felt that her religious faith was the most serious thing in her life: "She was interested in theology and knew much more about it than I did. At Kenyon, I'd had an intensive course in *The Divine Comedy,* which encompassed a lot of reading in theology and history as well as reading Dante in Italian. That was about the extent of my knowledge of Catholicism. I remember some very interesting talks we had about Dante and how knowledgeable she was." Walter Sullivan recalls that in class and out O'Connor was generally reticent about expressing opinions about religion but provided commentary when required: "She and I were in a [Henry] James and [James] Joyce seminar and Austin Warren decided that she would have to be the Catholic authority in the class when we were looking at *The Portrait of the Artist as a Young Man.* She never volunteered anything, but he would say, "Now Miss O'Connor, what are we talking about here?" And she would not seem at all reluctant to answer. She would give him the answer and we would go on from there until we came onto some other point and she'd give the answer." Of the overall importance of religion to O'Connor, Sullivan says, "She had this wonderful experience of never losing her faith. This was wonderful for her."

Though several of O'Connor's classmates at Iowa mistakenly believe that she was already suffering from lupus at Iowa, she was actually apparently quite healthy during those years. Her former GSCW professor, Helen I. Greene, for example, recalls that during those years O'Connor's health was very good: "She never was sick." Her chief exercise, apparently, was walking. According to Wylder, O'Connor's favorite place to walk in Iowa City was the city park: "Once, I walked out there with her on an especially bleak February Sunday afternoon to look at the two sad and mangy bears, the raccoons, and the special foreign chickens they had. It seemed a particularly desultory thing to be doing, and I was puzzled at how completely absorbed and interested Flannery was that day looking at these things which I knew she'd looked at many times before" (60). Obviously the area provided O'Connor details she used to create the Taulkinham park in *Wise Blood.* After O'Connor left Iowa in June 1948, she and Jean Wylder never again met, but they continued a sporadic correspondence until O'Connor died. In her memoir, Wylder published excerpts from the seven letters O'Connor wrote to her, but they have yet to be published in their entirety. After 1952, the correspondence between Wylder and O'Connor lapsed until Christmas 1961, when Wylder wrote to her suggesting that the climate in Albuquerque, where the Wylders were then living, might improve O'Connor's health. O'Connor's tersely replied that climate was not a issue with her illness. O'Connor wrote a final letter to Wylder on 5 March 1962, after she had received Wylder's gift of a ceramic peacock; she expressed enthusiastic appreciation and went on to describe how her actual peacocks, with their large feet, either trampled flowers or ate them. She told Wylder that, with the gift, she would now have peacocks both outside and in.[28] Though the correspondence between the two ended after this letter, their friendship at Iowa, as Wylder's memoir shows, helped reveal O'Connor's social place and creative stature in Iowa City during her last year there.

According to Walter Sullivan, James B. Hall, and other returning veterans who entered the workshop in that the era, the overall social atmosphere at Iowa during O'Connor's years was fairly energetic with many wild parties and much social drinking. Walter Sullivan cannot recall whether O'Connor attended any of these events: "I don't remember her much around at night any time except when she was with Robie [Macauley] and at our house. She was not a swinger." Another workshop participant remembers that in the spring of 1947, Paul Engle hosted a party "for the Workshop members and their spouses at his country house in Stone City. [. . .] I had just acquired an old 1936 Ford coupe—cars were in short supply in those days following the war—and I used it to drive Flannery and myself to the party." He doesn't remember much about their conversation, but he does recall her refusal to "participate in the group photo that was taken of the rest of us. My memory is supported by a copy of the photograph, which was sent to me by Engle, in 1966, and which I still have. Flannery is conspicuous by her absence." James B. Hall remembers still another photograph of workshop members taken "in the stone quarry at Stone City; Flannery is standing off to one side, alone. This catches her in a typical stance."

Other documented evidence of O'Connor's involvement in social activity at Iowa occurs in letters two instructors in the workshop wrote to Paul

Engle in Florida during the spring 1948 semester. Both Paul Griffith and Hansford "Mike" Martin told of Sunday evening sessions at Austin Warren's home. Andrew Lytle also remembered these gatherings, asserting: "These were where the people got their education. It was extravagantly strange at times." Paul Griffith's detailed description, in a letter dated 16 February 1948, gave a clear and vital précis of these meetings:

> There are of course, Sunday evenings, at Mr. Warren's. [. . .]
> I haven't been able to decide whether they are great fun or the most fantastic social predicament I've ever gotten myself into. Charter Members: AW, Mr. Lytle, Macauley, [Warren] Miller, [Hansford] Martin, O'Connor, [Clyde] McLeod and Griffith. The point: to be literary with one's equals. What has happened: selections read from the works of three authors on as many evenings, namely chapters out of novels by Griffith, O'Connor, Miller. Next week: the last novel of Mr. Martin. The difficulty: how to be honestly literary while staying loyal to one's friends, nay, to the only people whose company is bearable and certainly not to be lost, at least until spring comes and one can commune with nature. Question: does AW, whose intellect and charm I have the most genuine respect and liking for, does he *enjoy* seeing all six of us squirm while, to please him, we stab at honesty and, to keep our friendships, we try not to stab each other? Otherwise, we have a good time: we drink (but not enough), listen to Mr. Lytle's marvelous stories (he's a virtuoso [. . .]), and invariably end up with Clyde singing, quite beautifully and with true hill-billy ornamentations, voice-cracking and so forth, southern ballads. And always, until the next soiree comes around, there's a lot of talk about, lots of feelings to patch up, lots of extracurricular literary decisions to be made. [. . .] Flannery's novel is surely going to be beautiful: her chapter at AW's was polished and colored to perfection.[29]

Martin wrote his letter, dated 22 February 1948, after he had read from his own work: "[M]y turn came last week, and everybody liked it, which I interpret as the sign of relief which goes up when People realize Well that boy ain't gonna be no threat to our fame."[30]

Despite evidence that O'Connor maintained an image as a social outsider, she clearly was involved in the Austin Warren meetings; in addition,
several of her classmates claim that O'Connor did her share of social drinking at Iowa. The most interesting occurs in a letter Hank Messick wrote to
Stephen Wilbers in 1976:

> As to Flannery, I remember only that she liked to talk
> about writing, and that, with home folks like us, she was a pretty
> heavy drinker. She enjoyed tossing the empties into the river
> next to our trailer.
>
> [. . .] For Christmas that year, we asked my folks back in
> the Blue Ridge to send us a gallon of pure spring water which
> we kept in the icebox and served as you might serve a rare wine
> or brandy. Flannery took it straight and probably drank more of
> that gallon than anyone else. When it was gone, she returned to
> her mixed drinks, claiming a lot of Scotch was necessary to
> make the water drinkable.[31]

For shock effect, Messick may have been exaggerating the tale of O'Connor's
drinking alcohol, but his anecdote about her affection for the Blue Ridge
spring water rings with authenticity.

Andrew Lytle told an amusing anecdote about his one attempt to enlarge
O'Connor's social circle. After he and his wife, Edna, had come to know both
O'Connor and another young student named Henry Himmelwhite, they
decided to plan a double date to bring the two younger people together: "[S]he
was a nice-looking woman then and I had a young man there a New Yorker,
Himmelwhite, a young Jew that was charming and I arranged a date and
Edna and I—we felt silly—we went out and he did the best he could and she
did the best she could, but nothing came of it, and I never tried that again."
Other than on this one occasion, Lytle said that he never saw O'Connor in any
other social situation: "I remember that she scared those boys. She didn't have
any dates. The only date she had we arranged with this boy Himmelwhite."

Despite Lytle's direct assertion of her lack of success with men, Flannery
O'Connor did form, in her last year at Iowa, a close friendship with Robie
Macauley, who, in a letter to Stephen Wilbers, admitted that he "used to date"
O'Connor at Iowa.[32] As late as 1993 (two years before he died), Macauley
used the same phrase in an interview with Thomas E. Kennedy.[33] But in his

interview with me, Macauley clarified his comment: "'dating'—this means a few movies, perhaps and some Sunday dinners in Amana, no more." Sally Fitzgerald, however, believed that the relationship was serious from O'Connor's point of view, that she fell in love with Macauley and was deeply hurt when her love for him remained unrequited (S. Fitzgerald, "Flannery O'Connor" 413). Whether Fitzgerald's theory is valid remains questionable; for one thing, Macauley was already engaged to be married when he came to Iowa in the fall of 1947. He explained, "Flannery and I had no 'romantic' relationship. When I knew Flannery in Iowa, I was engaged to Anne Draper (who was in New York) and Flannery was well aware of it." It is probable, then, that the *friendship* between them developed so fully because it lacked a romantic component, which might have interfered with their ability to share intellectual interests. Macauley said, "We did spend a lot of time talking and reading manuscripts aloud."

Of the closeness between Macauley and O'Connor, Walter Sullivan asserts that "Robie took care of Flannery" and that he knew her better than anybody else at Iowa: "He and Flannery were really sort of soul-mates and they had the same kind of humor. They appreciated the same sort of things. [. . . but] there was never any question of a romantic attachment between them and he sort of escorted her around because he [. . .] wasn't much of a party man either." Sullivan also believes that Macauley helped O'Connor adjust to the "sharp edge" that characterized many relationships among workshop participants: "He had a gift of making her relax."

Macauley knew O'Connor's writing before he met her at Iowa. In 1946, he, Robert Giroux, and Robert Penn Warren served on a panel of judges at the Women's College of the University of North Carolina, where they were to select winners in a college fiction contest. They chose a story by O'Connor, which they praised before a WCNC audience. Though he did not recall the exact occasion when he and O'Connor first met at Iowa, he believed that it was at one of the workshop sessions in the early fall. He said that he admired "Flannery's writing (which, as I recall, was somewhat disdained by other people in the Workshop) and we got to be friends. She was working on *Wise Blood* at the time."

Robie Macauley initiated the friendship between O'Connor and Walter Sullivan and his wife, Jane, when he brought O'Connor to a small party at their home, after telling them earlier that "'there's a little Georgia girl here you've got to meet.'" They both recall her as being "perfectly charming," under Macauley's influence. Jane Sullivan reveals more about O'Connor's ability as a raconteur: "Flannery would get strung out and start telling stories about the South—funny stories and it was hysterical, but this required a small group for conversation; it wasn't party stuff." Sullivan remembers that one of the first stories she heard O'Connor tell was of her pet chicken in Savannah that possessed the unique ability to walk backward. A new detail that Jane Sullivan adds is O'Connor's revelation that the chicken had its own wool snowsuit!

Admitting that he "saw quite a bit of her," Macauley told of their going "to Amana (an Amish-like colony) for Sunday dinner and sometimes Paul Griffith and his girlfriend would go along. We ate in a big-barnlike dining hall with everybody seated together at long tables. Flannery liked that." More significantly, however, Macauley recalled that O'Connor shared her manuscript of *Wise Blood* with him: "I heard Flannery read *Wise Blood* aloud, chapter after chapter in the evenings we sat out on the porch of the rooming house where she lived. I thought it was marvelous: wild, funny, chilling and completely original." In her memoir, Jean Wylder revealed that Macauley stimulated O'Connor to read new books; she said that once she met O'Connor when she was on her way to the library to check out Gogol's *Dead Souls:* "She said Robie Macauley recommended that as one every writer should read, 'so I reckon I'd better do it'" (Wylder 59). Macauley himself remembered that he and O'Connor read Flanders Dunbar's *Mind and Body: Psychosomatic Medicine,* a book that he said was "intellectually fashionable" that year. They then spent "a lot of time discussing psychosomatic medicine." In retrospect, he wondered whether O'Connor had "an intimation about her own disease then."

Macauley provided one other written memory of a conversation he and O'Connor had on the porch of her boardinghouse:

> One afternoon [. . .], we were sitting in the swing on the porch of Flannery's boarding house in Iowa City. We talked about the problem of Negroes and Whites in the South and wondered when and how the racial question would ever be settled. Flannery told an anecdote. She said that when John Crowe Ransom had been asked to read one of her stories before a writing class, he had

suddenly come across the word "nigger." He refused to say it—
all through the story he substituted "Negro" for "nigger." "It did
spoil the story," Flannery said, "the people I was writing about
would never use any other word. And Mr. Ransom knew that
quite well. But he did the only thing a good man could do." It was
a small incident, but I think that Flannery always knew, in her
writing, that Christ is inward and, finally, inexpressible. The anti-
Christ is present, visible, articulate; he walks around in the light
of the sun. Her stories are mostly about him. And, she was saying,
one must first know him before one can have a whole knowledge
of Him. (Macauley, "Flannery O'Connor—A Tribute" 34)

Even after Macauley's marriage, O'Connor maintained a warm friendship with him for many years. Only six letters from O'Connor to Macauley
are in *The Habit of Being;* however, O'Connor often mentioned him in letters to other correspondents, usually recommending his fiction to them or
talking of his general expertise as a writer and editor. As any friend would,
O'Connor also took pleasure in Macauley's other successes, like his replacing John Crowe Ransom as editor of the *Kenyon Review* in 1958: "I hope he
livens it up a little instead of it dulling him down some" (*HB* 277). Part of
the suggested livening up certainly came with Macauley's publication of
O'Connor's story "The Comforts of Home" in the fall 1960 issue; she did,
however, object to the illustrations he selected for her story as she revealed
in an unpublished letter to Cecil Dawkins; she called these drawings "lewd"
and revealed that she had written to Macauley to object, asserting that such
illustrations might undercut the *Kenyon Review*'s reputation for dullness but
make it "vulgar" in the process.[34]

Friendships, good instruction, reading, writing, maturation: all charac-
terize O'Connor's active years at Iowa. After she left the workshop, however,
Paul Engle apparently felt that O'Connor gave too little credit to it for launch-
ing her success. It was not, however, part of O'Connor's nature to be effusive
about any influence on her development. Because she viewed her writing as
an adjunct to her Roman Catholic faith, she would have been more likely to
attribute her success to the grace of God than to Paul Engle. Still, in her infrequent interviews, O'Connor, when asked, invariably gave the workshop
credit for helping her to get started. In a 1960 interview with Margaret

Turner, O'Connor explained that her instruction at Iowa "'wasn't training to write as such; it was training to read with critical attention—my own work and other people's'" (*Con* 43). On the other hand, O'Connor also expressed strong reservations about the workshop method in remarks that she made at Emory University in Atlanta, remarks later published in *Mystery and Manners* in the essay "The Nature and Aim of Fiction": "I don't believe in classes where students criticize each other's manuscripts. Such criticism is generally composed in equal part of ignorance, flattery, and spite. It's the blind leading the blind, and it can be dangerous. A teacher who tries to impose a way of writing on you can be dangerous too. Fortunately, most teachers I've known were too lazy to do this. In any case, you should beware of those who appear overenergetic" (*MM* 86).

O'Connor's strongest—and most immediate—statement concerning the value of her experience at Iowa occurred in an article she published in 1948, just after she left Iowa City. She stated her strong reservations about any graduate work in English for the incipient writer, asserting that "scratching" to complete Ph.D. requirements certainly inhibits some "nascent writers" from producing "fine poetry or fiction." She went on, however, to applaud universities like Iowa that have added the M.F.A. degree to their programs. She believed that such schools help young writers in a number of ways:

> [They] can put him in the way of experienced writers and literary critics, people who are usually able to tell him after not too long a time whether he should go on writing or enroll immediately in the school of Dentistry. It is much easier to loose one's early mistakes on a critic paid to stand up under them and give counsel than on a critic paid to announce them to the public. No one can be taught to write, but a writing ability can be more quickly developed when it is concentrated upon and encouraged by competent literary people than when it is left to wander.
>
> A graduate program for writers should give the writer time and credit for writing and for wide reading, and if his writing and reading are of high enough quality, it should offer him a degree.

Realistically, O'Connor asserted that most creative writers cannot expect to make a living from their writing alone so that an advanced degree will allow them to support themselves by teaching. Of her workshop experience, she said directly: "The only writing program I am familiar with—there are many considered to be adequate—is that at the University of Iowa. The program there is designed to cover the writer's technical needs as mentioned above, and to provide him with a literary atmosphere which he would not be able to find elsewhere. The writer can expect very little else" (O'Connor, "The Writer and the Graduate School" 4). In 1960, when O'Connor traveled to the College of St. Teresa in Winona, Minnesota, students asked her directly whether she thought her work at Iowa helped her. She answered: "Yes, I do. When I went there I didn't know a short story from an ad in a newspaper. I won't say that they taught me how to write, but they gave me that initial push that a writer needs to discover that he can write and that he wants to write" (*Con* 59).

O'Connor's own writing at Iowa proves that her experience there made her realize that she could indeed write for publication. Though she wrote mainly fiction at Iowa—the stories which she presented to the workshop—the O'Connor Collection at GCSU holds two examples of writing that she did for classroom assignments. One is the brief autobiography she produced for Magazine Writing during her first semester at Iowa. The autobiography obviously shows O'Connor writing in the same satirical mode she used in her essays for the *Corinthian* at GSCW. She continues to deprecate her own importance and to condemn the "watered-down" progressive education she had experienced at Peabody and GSCW. Also interesting is her obvious distaste for the possibility of being forced to teach English in rural Georgia for the miserable salaries then paid public school teachers. Another example of O'Connor's classroom writing at Iowa is an examination she wrote for Paul Engle in his course, Understanding Fiction. Dated 28 November 1945, the essay is a thorough and intelligent analysis of a short story. Her efforts earned her a grade of A+ and the single comment "*Admirable.*"

Of the stories she wrote and submitted for possible publication while at Iowa, O'Connor, in her 1955 television interview with Harvey Breit on "Galley Proof," asserted, "Then I began to write short stories, publicly" (*Con* 6).

During her first year in Iowa City, O'Connor submitted two stories, "The Geranium" and "The Crop," to *Accent* on 7 February 1946, "mailing them from Currier Graduate House, State University of Iowa at Iowa City" (Giroux 551). *Accent* accepted "The Geranium," publishing it in its summer 1946 issue. After becoming the lead story in O'Connor's M.F.A. thesis, the story was also the only story from the thesis that she returned to later, working on an intermediate version titled "An Exile in the East" and publishing a final version as "Judgement Day" in *Everything That Rises Must Converge*.

During her first year at Iowa, O'Connor also submitted her stories "Wildcat" and "The Coat" to Allen Maxwell, editor of the *Southwest Review*. In two letters, dated 25 June 1946 and 16 July 1946—both addressed to *Mr. Flannery O'Connor*—he rejected the stories. Though Maxwell praised her handling of suspense in both stories, he told her that her writing was marred by technical difficulties.[35] "Wildcat," one of the stories in O'Connor's M.F.A. thesis, was not published until after O'Connor's death, appearing in the *North American Review* in the spring 1970 issue and in *The Complete Stories* the next year.

"The Coat," not published until the summer of 1996 in *Doubletake,* concerns a black couple in rural Georgia. The wife, Rosa, is strong, the husband rather stereotypical: he drinks alcohol and resorts to violence. Coming home one day, he finds a coat on the path, exchanges it for cheap wine, and gets drunk. Meanwhile, Rosa, having discovered the coatless corpse of a white man, assumes, when her drunken husband comes home, that he has killed the man for his coat; she forces him to bury the corpse. While at it, he is discovered by a gang of white hunters; when he panics, they kill him. Later the wife learns that the coat her husband found was that of one of her white customers. The story is better than most apprenticeship fiction, but, in light of O'Connor's later assertion that she was unable to get inside the minds of black people, it seems strange that O'Connor wrote early fiction peopled by primarily black characters. In this story, in which she uses a third-person limited perspective, O'Connor is definitely inside the black woman's head.

O'Connor published "The Turkey," another of her M.F.A. stories in *Mademoiselle* in November 1948 under the title "The Capture." It remained uncollected until Robert Giroux published *The Complete Stories* in 1971. Two other autonomous stories in O'Connor's M.F.A. thesis, "The Barber" and "The Crop," remained unpublished until after O'Connor's death. Robert

Fitzgerald, then O'Connor's literary executor, published "The Barber" in *Atlantic* in October 1970 and "The Crop" in *Mademoiselle* in April 1971. In his note to "The Barber," Fitzgerald wrote, "'I have consented to this publication with a note making clear [. . .] the earliness of the story and its apparent standing in the estimation of the author'" (qtd. in Giroux 551). In a second note to "The Crop," Fitzgerald explained: "Although it is obviously far from her best work, 'The Crop' would never be mistaken for anyone else's production. [. . .] We enjoy a small caricature of that shady type, the imaginative artist. [. . .] The exacting art, the stringent spirit, and the sheer kick of her mature works are promised here" (qtd. in Giroux 551).

The sixth story is her M.F.A. thesis, "The Train," actually an early version of the first chapter of *Wise Blood,* which she had begun to write during her second year at Iowa. Under the title "Train," it appeared in the *Sewanee Review* in April 1948 before O'Connor left Iowa. In 1949, after she left Iowa and was living in New York and Connecticut, O'Connor published in *Partisan Review* two more early versions of episodes that would appear in *Wise Blood:* "The Heart of the Park" in February and "The Peeler" in December. One other story that O'Connor *may* have written at Iowa, "A Stroke of Good Fortune," which appeared in *A Good Man Is Hard to Find and Other Stories,* was first published as "A Woman on the Stairs" in *Tomorrow* in August 1949. Little wonder, then, that with all of her success in publishing, the men in the workshop were intimidated by her. When he introduced her in 1959 at Vanderbilt, Walter Sullivan, for example, recalled the awe her fame as a published writer inspired in her workshop colleagues: he said she was already "a kind of legend."[36]

The University of Iowa itself was somewhat slow to recognize O'Connor's genius. When she published *Wise Blood* in 1952, the university newspaper, the *Daily Iowan,* contained a brief account, mentioning only that O'Connor "was a student in the university writer's workshop and received her M.A. in 1947."[37] In 1957, when Paul Engle declared O'Connor's "Greenleaf" the first prize winner in the O. Henry Prize Stories competition for 1957, the *Daily Iowan* published a slightly longer article, but most of it concerned R. V. Cassill "the one native Iowan represented in the new collection."[38] Later that same year, the newspaper again mentioned O'Connor as a contributor to Granville Hicks's *The Living Novel: A Symposium.* It was not, however, until 1986 that the University of Iowa established the Flannery O'Connor Chair in her honor. Writing in the *Des Moines Sunday Register* in September 1986, James O. Freedman recalled that "many years ago" Jean Wylder had

> suggested that the City Park zoo dedicate a pair of birds to her memory.
>
> The time has now come when the University of Iowa is able to create a living memorial to Flannery O'Connor and her art, a memorial more lasting than anything in Iowa City's bedraggled and now defunct little menagerie could have been. The Flannery O'Connor Professorship in Letters pays tribute to the genius of one of this country's most important writers and one of the most gifted students in the workshop.[39]

Nearly forty years earlier, however, O'Connor—this "most gifted student"— quietly left Iowa City, without much fanfare or recognition, to pursue her craft at Yaddo in Saratoga Springs, New York.

CHAPTER FIVE

YADDO, NEW YORK CITY, AND
CONNECTICUT, 1948~1950

During her last year at Iowa, O'Connor applied for admission to Yaddo, the famous artists' colony in Saratoga Springs, New York, under the urging of Paul Griffith, one of her instructors in the workshop. Paul Engle and Andrew Lytle also supported her application (*CW* 1242). Having been accepted by director Elizabeth Ames and the Yaddo board, O'Connor arrived there in June 1948, intent on continuing work on her novel *Wise Blood*. The artists' colony, formerly the private estate of New York millionaires Spencer and Katrina Nichols Trask, contrasted sharply with O'Connor's final home in Iowa City: Mrs. Guzeman's drafty boardinghouse on Bloomington Street.

Yaddo was and is an elaborate estate of more than forty acres with a fifty-five-room central mansion and a number of studios, all of which house the artists—writers, painters, and musicians—invited to the colony. Constructed of gray stone, the main house features a number of cupolas, porches, and bay windows on the outside and stained glass, oiled wood floors, and marble statues on the inside. The Trasks bought the estate in 1881 as a retreat from New York City, where Spencer Trask, a banker and philanthropist born in 1844, pursued many financial and charitable activities. An original backer of Thomas Edison, Trask supported railroads and helped finance Adolph Ochs after Ochs bought the faltering *New York Times;* Trask also founded a home for orphan girls and was an active opponent of legalized gambling (Furman 75).

During her lifetime, his wife, Katrina Trask, an intense advocate of the arts, entertained and promoted such luminaries as Ellen Terry, Booker T. Washington, and Jacob Epstein. Mrs. Trask also wrote popular plays and novels. Laura Furman writes that, although Trask "was religious and mystical," she also possessed "undeniable vision: [. . .] She believed that 'beauty and possibility lie in our hands.' Her nephew described her as a 'peculiar blend of idealism, romanticism, and pretentiousness'" (75). Though financially prosperous, the Trasks were unable to produce surviving progeny: they had four children, all of whom died in either infancy or childhood; one of them, however, gave Yaddo its name when she mispronounced *shadow*. Even before the Trasks bought the estate, it had achieved cultural and literary fame. During the late eighteenth century a German immigrant and Revolutionary soldier, Jacobus Barhyte, lived on the site and kept a tavern widely reputed for its excellent food. Barhyte's grandson James told Katrina Trask's youngest brother, Acosta Nichols, of an Edgar Allan Poe connection with the tavern. Poe, he said, while visiting the inn in the early 1840s, began to compose "The Raven" during his jaunts through the countryside (Waite 20). The Poe connection with Yaddo seems singularly appropriate for O'Connor: throughout her life, she acknowledged her debt to Poe and his "humerous" [*sic*] tales.

In the twenty-two years before Flannery O'Connor arrived there, Elizabeth Ames, who became the first director of Yaddo in 1926, had welcomed a number of famous writers and artists: James T. Farrell, John Cheever, Dorothy Parker, Jean Stafford, Katherine Anne Porter, Eudora Welty, Carson McCullers, Granville Hicks, Malcolm Cowley, and Alfred Kazin were among them. In a brief memoir of the time she later spent at Yaddo—20 June–20 August 1972—Gail Godwin wrote of the artistic richness of the Yaddo environment: "[T]he forty or so acres on which the principal buildings of Yaddo stand have seen more distinguished activity in the arts than any other piece of ground in the English-speaking community or perhaps in the entire world" (Godwin 3).

O'Connor arrived at Yaddo in the summer of 1948, feeling self-confident and vastly relieved to have found a place to write other than Iowa City—which she was ready to leave after three years—or Milledgeville, where she would have returned somewhat unwillingly to the bosom of the Cline family, who, including her mother Regina Cline O'Connor, had little understanding of or sympathy for aspiring genius. Living and writing at Yaddo gave O'Connor both financial and artistic security, providing her with a sanctuary where she could avoid the distractions of either the academic and social life of Iowa or the social and family affairs of Milledgeville. O'Connor spent her first months at Yaddo immersed in *Wise Blood;* in fact, she liked the atmosphere so well that she asked Elizabeth Ames for permission to stay on: first through the fall of 1948 and later until the summer of 1949. She also began to identify herself as a professional writer and to act like one.

In June 1948, advised by Paul Moor, another Yaddo resident, O'Connor successfully contacted and retained her lifelong literary agent, Elizabeth McKee. In her first letter to McKee, O'Connor reviewed her recent and forthcoming publications—"The Train" in the *Sewanee Review* and "The Peeler" in *American Letters*—before explaining that the Rinehart-Iowa Fellowship, which she was awarded in 1947, gave Rinehart "the option but nothing else" to publish the novel on which she was currently working. Eager to support herself with her fiction, she wrote, "I am writing you in my vague and slack season and mainly because I am being impressed just now with the money I am not making by having stories in such places as *American Letters* [a new quarterly]" (*HB* 5). She called herself "a very slow worker" whose total focus was on the novel she was trying to complete. She hoped that she was the "type of writer" whose work would interest McKee. Almost immediately, McKee agreed to accept her as a client. Replying on 23 June she told O'Connor that she (McKee) was not concerned about the amount the young writer produced. McKee, applauding O'Connor for being committed to her craft, told her that a serious dedication was the main influence on her choice of whom to represent.[1] McKee began to place O'Connor's stories and to assist her as she tried to negotiate a contract with John Selby, then editor in chief at Rinehart. In her early correspondence with McKee, O'Connor, carefully and repeatedly, emphasized her method as a writer: "I don't have my novel outlined and I have to write to discover what I am doing. Like the old lady, I don't know so well what I think until I see what I say; then I have to say it over again" (5). In the same letter, she told McKee that she had probably written 50,000 words—twelve chapters—of the first draft of the novel but also asserted that most of the chapters would need to be rewritten.

At the end of July 1948, O'Connor left Yaddo for about six weeks to visit her mother in Milledgeville but returned to the writer's colony by 18 September. By then, O'Connor had decided to apply for a Guggenheim Foundation Grant and solicited McKee's advice in choosing people to support her; she had already chosen Robert Penn Warren and Paul Engle.[2] Even though Engle, Robert Lowell, Robert Penn Warren, and Philip Rahv wrote letters for her, the Guggenheim Foundation did not award O'Connor a fellowship (Giroux xi).

In her early letters to McKee, O'Connor sounded happy, content to be in the North, busy writing and trying to support herself with her fiction; however, she felt somewhat uncomfortable in the social and political environment at Yaddo. When she arrived at Yaddo, she joined a number of other guests already in residence, among them Alfred Kazin, Elizabeth Fenwick, Paul Moor, Edward Maisel, and Elizabeth Hardwick. Robert Lowell, who would become her friend there, did not arrive until November 1948. Of guests who were at Yaddo during the summer of 1948, O'Connor maintained the closest—and most enduring—friendship with Elizabeth Fenwick (later Way), who early in 1949 helped O'Connor find a place to live in New York City and corresponded with her for the rest of O'Connor's life. Sally Fitzgerald also asserted that at Yaddo she established a special bond with the musician Edward Maisel: "He sought her company as much as possible, arranging long walks around the grounds and boating expeditions on the little lake nearby. He took her into Saratoga Springs to meet some of the townspeople he found amusing. His interest proved invaluable to Flannery" (S. Fitzgerald, "Flannery O'Connor" 414).

O'Connor apparently disliked the pseudo-sophistication of some of the other guests, most of whom were totally secular in their interests and beliefs. Many also held leftist political opinions; some even were admittedly communist sympathizers. O'Connor expressed her reservations about these people both early and late in her life: first to Helen Greene in Milledgeville and later (1959) to her friend Cecil Dawkins, who was applying to Yaddo herself. Greene recalls: "She said it was a beautiful place and everything was provided for thinking and writing and talking and she met some poets she thought were gifted but she said they are just not themselves. They are afraid not to be stylish. With her it was very disappointing." Greene also remembers O'Connor's concern about both the outspoken atheism of some of the guests who made Communism their substitute religion; Greene writes, "She was really shocked to find that many of these gifted fellows appointed to do creative work at Yaddo were unwilling or unable to believe in God. Their main reason, perhaps, was the appeal of Communism—whatever it meant to them. She had no patience with such attitudes and left" (Greene, "Mary Flannery O'Connor" 46).

In a letter to Dawkins in late 1959, O'Connor described the overall moral atmosphere of Yaddo in 1948, asserting that "the help" was "morally superior to the guests" (*HB* 483); in fact, as evidence of her respect for the workers at Yaddo, O'Connor, in a later letter to Dawkins when Dawkins was at Yaddo in 1962, asked her to give her greetings to two Yaddo employees, Jim and Nellie Shannon (483). In her 1959 letter to Dawkins, O'Connor wrote of the drinking that went on among the guests, admitting that she had attended "one or two" parties but "always left before they began to break things." She also alluded to the casual sex prevalent at Yaddo during her stay, writing "if you don't sleep with the opposite sex it is assumed that you sleep with your own." She also remembered that Yaddo guests discussed "Seconal" and "barbiturates" at breakfast. She advised Dawkins that the best way to survive in "this atmosphere" was by "minding your own business and by having plenty of your own business to mind; and by not being afraid to be different from the rest of them" (363–64). In other letters to Dawkins, O'Connor further described the people at Yaddo as too "arty" and "so much all the same kind that it gets depressing."

Alfred Kazin was surely one of the sophisticated Northern writers to whom O'Connor was referring. He first visited Yaddo in 1940 and continued to return to the colony through the decade, spending a few weeks there during the summer of 1948. In one of his autobiographical memoirs, Kazin wrote: "Yaddo had once been my greatest refuge and release on earth. It was the perfect escape for writers who needed solitude. [. . .] There was nothing to do all day but to write, after writing to walk in the woods, to walk down Union Avenue, which Henry James had thought the most beautiful street in

America. [. . .] If you responded gratefully to the Victoriana hovering over your writer's prison, a few winter weeks of solitude put you chapters ahead, gave you back to yourself" (Kazin, *New York Jew* 203–4). Though he did not establish a personal relationship with O'Connor at Yaddo, he was impressed with her reserved dedication to her faith and to her writing. Of her devout Catholicism, he said: "This is so rare in America that it makes her stand out in every possible way. To me she is one of the few writers of that post-war generation who will live for a very long time."[3]

Like Kazin, O'Connor felt that Yaddo provided a genuine refuge for writers. When she urged Cecil Dawkins to apply, O'Connor strongly praised the physical facilities: "The food is very good. The quarters are elegant. The servants are very nice. The scenery is magnificent. Mrs. A. runs it efficiently. Skidmore College is down the road and has a good library, or anyway, good enough" (*HB* 362). After Dawkins was actually living at Yaddo, O'Connor recalled where she had lived on the estate and some of her activities. She had lived both "upstairs in the big house during the summer and on the first floor of West House in the fall and winter." She had a studio outside the house during the summer but a separate studio room in the West House during the fall and winter. Walks both on the Yaddo grounds and into Saratoga Springs occupied her during her free time; she also enjoyed the wildlife on the estate—"the studio squirrel," chipmunks, and "a large important-looking woodchuck" (483). When Dawkins decided to remain at Yaddo during the fall of 1962, O'Connor wrote that Dawkins would enjoy being there then because "it is beautiful in the fall and winter and most of the creepy characters take off at the end of the summer" (490). Besides enjoying the physical comforts and beauty of Yaddo, O'Connor also apparently listened to music at Yaddo as she recalled in a 1964 letter to Thomas Stritch, who had sent her a number of phonograph recordings. She told him that she hadn't listened to music since her time at Yaddo (564).

O'Connor no doubt adapted easily to the rules of Yaddo, rules still mandated, as outlined in a recent brochure: "Traditionally, Yaddo has reserved the periods between 9 A.M. and 4 P.M. and after 10 P.M. as 'quiet hours,' for artists to work without interruption. During this period there should be no interference with the working time of fellow guests and no studio visits without direct invitation. The same policy applies to outside visitors, who may come after 4 P.M. (though they cannot be accommodated at dinner), and stay until 10 P.M., when they must leave."[4] That such a regimen correlated well with O'Connor's disciplined writing life is certainly borne out by her asking Mrs. Ames to allow her to stay through the winter. Had not what Malcolm Cowley facetiously designated the "great Yaddo scandal" intervened, O'Connor might have indeed remained at Yaddo through the winter of 1949.

Early in 1949, however, O'Connor, in spite of her dedication to her writing, did become involved in this farcical imbroglio, fomented in equal parts by the anti-Communist frenzy of the postwar era, the actual Communist connections of Agnes Smedley, the suspicions of Elizabeth Hardwick, Edward Maisel, and O'Connor herself, and the egotistical, messianic fervor of Robert Lowell. With Lowell as its leader, this group of four set out to remove Elizabeth Ames from her directorship at Yaddo. Lowell already had a reputation for taking individualistic stands: he had refused induction into military service during World War II and been jailed for his resistance; at the same time, he was staunchly anti-Communist. Alfred Kazin recalled the tension he felt at Yaddo during his weeks there: "I was not there when anything erupted but I could see that things were getting very tense because there were very few people at Yaddo. [I was made] very uncomfortable by what I felt to be already the sort of hysterical McCarthyism of Cal Lowell." In addition to his anti-Communist stance, Lowell, at this point in his life, had just achieved phenomenal literary success with the publication of *Lord Weary's Castle.*

After its appearance in December 1946, Lowell, who already had the support and friendship of the Fugitive poets—particularly John Crowe Ransom, Allen Tate, and Robert Penn Warren—won the Pulitzer Prize, a Guggenheim fellowship of $2,500, and an award of $1,000 from the American Academy of Arts and Letters. Had he accepted, he could have taught at Chapel Hill or Iowa; on the basis of his success, he also received an invitation to Yaddo, where he was first in residence the summer of 1947. From there he went to Washington, D.C., where he accepted the prestigious post of Consultant in Poetry to the Library of Congress, which paid him $5,000 for the year (Hamilton 124). Alfred Kazin described the effect of this sudden and great success on Lowell:

He was at the top of a psychic crest down which he would slide the next season; but at this peak he talked in tongues; he was of the great company, with Milton and Hardy and Eliot; he was wonderful and frightening. He was not just damned good, suddenly famous and deserving his fame; he was in a state of grandeur not negotiable with lesser beings. He was Lowell; he was handsome, magnetic, rich, wild with excitement about his powers, wild over the many tributes to him from Pound, Santayana, his old friends Tate, Jarrell and Warren. Flannery O'Connor who was also at Yaddo seemed to be attending Lowell with rapture. (*New York Jew* 204)

Kazin believed that O'Connor's rigorous Catholicism kept her from developing a sexual interest in Lowell, but he did assert that "she was certainly terribly attracted by Cal. He was a Lowell, he was an American patrician of a very famous family; he was a very gifted man." In addition to his family background, literary genius, and personal magnetism, Lowell's then ambivalent impulse toward Catholicism certainly added to his appeal to O'Connor. Kazin asserted, "There is no question in my mind that part of the attraction that Lowell exuded for Flannery was the fact that he had adopted, even so briefly, the Catholic faith." When Lowell married Jean Stafford in 1940 after his graduation from Kenyon, she was already a Catholic; a year later while doing graduate work at Louisiana State University, he began to read Catholic theologians, particularly Etienne Gilson, Newman, Maritain, E. I. Watkins, Hopkins, and Pascal. In the spring of 1941, he became a communicant in the Roman Catholic Church (Hamilton 78). By 1947, however, Lowell had left both his marriage to Stafford and the Church. But at Yaddo in the summer of 1948, he experienced a temporary resurgence of faith. In a letter to Betty Hester in 1956, O'Connor recounted that episode: "I watched him that winter come back into the Church. I had nothing to do with it but of course it was a great joy to me. I was only 23 and didn't have much sense. He was terribly excited about it and got more and more excited and in about two weeks had a complete mental breakdown. That second conversion went with it, of course" (*HB* 152).

Robert Fitzgerald, who during the Yaddo confusion sent an open letter to twenty prominent writers—all of whom were friends and supporters of

Lowell—asserted that on 26 February 1949 the day of the pivotal meeting between the four conspirators and the Yaddo board, Lowell went to mass with O'Connor "for the first time in over a year." The next day (27 February), Lowell and O'Connor visited the Fitzgeralds in New York, where Lowell announced that "'he had returned to the Church that morning after receiving an incredible outpouring of grace.'" Just after his reconversion, Lowell, according to Fitzgerald, "visited a priest for absolution and then went off to make a week's retreat for absolution and counsel with the Trappists in Rhode Island."[5] O'Connor's only problem with Lowell's reconversion was that, somehow in the process, Lowell began to identify her with St. Thérèse of Lisieux (Hamilton 149).[6] In his biography of Lowell, Ian Hamilton quoted from a passage in Fitzgerald's journal from 4 March 1949, in which he recorded details of a telephone conversation with Lowell; Lowell had asserted that 3 March

> "is the day of Flannery O'Connor, whose patron saint is St. Thérèse of Lisieux." That morning [3 March], he said afterward, he filled his bathtub with cold water and went in first on his hands and knees, then arching on his back, and prayed thus to Thérèse of Lisieux in gasps. All his motions that morning were "lapidary," and he felt a steel coming into him that made him walk very erect. He went to the Guild bookshop [in the Church of St Francis] to get Flannery a book on St. Thérèse of Lisieux but instead before he knew it bought a book on a Canadian girl who was many times stigmatized. (Hamilton 150)

Years later (1960), Betty Hester somehow heard the story of Lowell's mad attempt to canonize O'Connor and asked O'Connor about it. O'Connor reacted with uncharacteristic anger, telling Hester that the story was "revolting"; she advised Hester to "impress on him [the source of the story] the impropriety of repeating this kind of slop" (*HB* 395). She wrote: "At the time it was happening, poor Cal was about three steps from the asylum. He had the delusion that he had been called on some kind of mission of purification and he was canonizing everybody that had anything to do with his situation then. I was very close to him and so was Robert [Fitzgerald]. I was too inexperienced to know he was mad, I just thought that was the way poets acted. Even Robert didn't know it, or at least didn't know how near collapse he was" (395). Certainly, however, it was Lowell's yearning toward Catholicism that drew O'Connor, first, into a close friendship with him during the fall of 1948 and a bit later into the attempt to remove Elizabeth Ames from her longtime post as director of Yaddo.

During her many years as director, Ames had served, with the help of the Yaddo board, as a fairly competent administrator, although her attitude toward Yaddo residents was, apparently, more personal than professional. Alfred Kazin asserted that though her administrative skills were not good because she was "a terribly personal administrator. [. . .] She was a very dear friend to me and many writers." The Yaddo membership committee, in conjunction with Ames, chose Yaddo guests, but Ames apparently had considerable control over the length of their tenures. Cecil Dawkins, for example, recalled that when she went to Yaddo in 1959, Mrs. Ames immediately told her she could stay as long as she wished because she liked her writing.[7]

A frequent visitor at Yaddo between 1943 and 1948 was a woman named Agnes Smedley, whose associations with the Communist Party helped involve Yaddo and Flannery O'Connor in the controversy. In testimony before the Yaddo board, Edward Maisel described what he perceived to be the special relationship between Elizabeth Ames and Smedley: "I can only speak of my own impressions. [. . .] Miss Smedley's status was unique, privileged. [. . .] I do not think anyone else, any of the other guests felt privileged in the way Miss Smedley was, and her status was quite different. I believe the impression prevailed at first that she was co-directoress."[8]

The trouble began at Yaddo on 10 February 1949 when a story, supplied by Gen. Douglas MacArthur, appeared in the *New York Times*. It asserted that in 1942 a Russian spy ring had operated out of Japan and that Agnes Smedley had organized the group of spies in Shanghai (Minutes 17). Though the *Times* retracted its original story about Smedley's involvement on 19 February the FBI, which later testimony revealed had been interested in Yaddo since 1942, immediately sent agents to Saratoga Springs to question Yaddo residents about Agnes Smedley's activities there. When they arrived, only five guests remained: Robert Lowell, Elizabeth Hardwick, Flannery O'Connor, Edward Maisel, and James Ross (Peter Taylor's brother-in-law). Not wanting to get involved, Ross, who only recently had come to Yaddo, left.

FBI agents questioned Elizabeth Hardwick and Edward Maisel at some length. In testimony before the board, Hardwick described how nervous she became during the interrogation because she felt such questioning was a serious mistake (Minutes 46). Reacting, then, to the FBI interrogation, the four remaining Yaddo guests panicked. At the 26 February 1949 meeting of the board, Chairman John A. Slade speculated that their reaction was brought on partly by the "excitement, hysteria, perhaps, which seems to be part of the post-war period in American history" (5). In their panic, the four consulted the most immediately available board member, Dr. Everett V. Stonequist, a professor at Skidmore College. He told the board how Edward Maisel called, asking for a private meeting to discuss confidential matters. Lowell, Maisel, O'Connor, and Hardwick then visited Stonequist, who described them as being "quite excited, and talk[ing] two or three at the same time" (7). This first meeting lasted "at least three hours" and resulted in still another meeting with additional members of the board. By the time the four met again on 21 February with Stonequist and other board members, including Newton Arvin, Granville Hicks, Kathryn M. Starbuck, and Thomas F. Luther, they had narrowed their concerns to two basic issues summarized by board chairman John A. Slade during the full board meeting held on 26 February: "One was the alleged presence of a Communistic organization doing business from Yaddo; however, the large emphasis was upon the personality and methods of the Executive Director, with a great deal of criticism and a statement [. . .] that unless Mrs. Ames was removed from her position, this group intended to leave [Yaddo]" (8).

When the four appeared before the full board meeting on 26 February, Robert Lowell served as their spokesman. In remarks recorded in the minutes of the meeting, Lowell excitedly and aggressively urged the board to take direct action against Mrs. Ames: "I am speaking as a delegate for Yaddo guests who are present, Miss Hardwick, Miss O'Connor and Mr. Maisel. [. . .] We petition the Board: that Mrs. Elizabeth Ames, the executive director, be fired; that this action be absolute, final and prompt; that pending discussion she be immediately suspended from all administrative function" (Minutes 11). During the meeting, Lowell, Hardwick, and Maisel also testified about Ames's reaction to the FBI investigation and her defense of Smedley. Lowell recalled, for example, that at dinner on 10 February—the day the Smedley story broke—Ames referred to "Miss Smedley as an 'old-fashioned Jeffersonian democrat'" (18). Edward Maisel reviewed Smedley's Communist connections, emphasizing, particularly, her proselytizing at Skidmore College.

Though Flannery O'Connor said very little during the board meeting, at one point Lowell did question her directly about Elizabeth Ames. O'Connor described her relations with Ames as being "very pleasant" during her first two months at Yaddo; however, she called their more recent connection as "precariously cordial," elaborating that she felt free to speak only with Ames "when agreeing with her, because I felt more like Mrs. Ames' personal guest than a guest of the Corporation" (Minutes 31). O'Connor also admitted that Ames's personal regard for herself and her writing allowed her to stay on at Yaddo after her original tenure ended. She explained, "I asked to stay through July, largely through economic pressure, which has not improved, but *I am leaving next Tuesday*" (31; emphasis mine). When Lowell asked her about Mrs. Ames's attitude toward Agnes Smedley, O'Connor replied, "Miss Ames said that Agnes Smedley had been living in fear for a long time [. . .]. [T]hat [. . .] did not seem to fit in with an impression of her as an old-fashioned Jeffersonian Democrat" (31).

As the board meeting continued, both Elizabeth Ames and her secretary, Mary Townsend, testified. Townsend verified that Ames's treatment of guests was more personal than professional: "I would say that Mrs. Ames' displeasure should not be taken lightly" (Minutes 39). Townsend, who had been Mrs. Ames's secretary for three years, also admitted that from the time she began to work for Ames, she had been sending data ("between twenty and thirty notes") about suspected Communist activity to the FBI (39). Under sharp questioning by the board, Ames herself repeatedly declared her innocence of any Communist connection. She admitted that she felt a personal obligation to Smedley, who had helped nurse her sister, Marjorie Peabody Waite, during the last months of her life. She called Smedley a personal friend and insisted that they seldom talked about politics. She also revealed her own distress and shock when she realized that the FBI had questioned Hardwick and Maisel (57).

In later testimony, Ames tried to explain Elizabeth Hardwick's "hysteria" by recalling that "Miss Hardwick had some experience with Communism in her early years; she is disillusioned and bitter" (Minutes 58). The minutes of the board meeting clearly show that Elizabeth Ames was certainly not guilty of any political wrongdoing; several board members, however, did see the charges as giving them the opportunity to remove Ames from her longstanding directorship. Most members, including Malcolm Cowley, believed that the charges were both spurious and outrageous—not to be taken seriously. On 1 March 1949, he wrote to Granville Hicks: "Elizabeth can't be made a scapegoat, certainly not for difficulties that arise from the system followed at Yaddo and from the changing political climate" (MC Papers).

The immediate result of the board meeting was that the "Yaddo Four" delivered on their ultimatum: when the board refused to fire Ames, they left Yaddo as a group on 1 March. Lowell also made good his threat to spread word of a "communist conspiracy" to high-placed literary friends in New York City. On 16 March, Cowley wrote to board member C. Everett Bacon that "their talk has started a counter movement in defense of Yaddo, which promises to be more popular than the attack" (MC Papers). Among writers who came to the aid of Yaddo were Alfred Kazin, Eleanor Clark, Arna Bontemps, Carson McCullers, Robert Fitzgerald, Katherine Anne Porter, Harvey Breit, and John Cheever. On 21 March 1949, a petition signed by forty-four supporters reached the Yaddo board: "We reject as preposterous the political charge now being brought against Elizabeth Ames. We reject any insinuation that at any time she deliberately used the facilities of Yaddo for any purpose other than the furthering of the Arts in America."[9] In a second meeting of the Yaddo board on 26 March 1949, members voted to ignore charges "brought by the former Yaddo guests as unsupported by the evidence they introduced."[10] The board also passed a motion expressing appreciation to Ames for twenty-five years of service.

By the second meeting, Flannery O'Connor was no longer actively involved in the case against Ames, though she was staying with Elizabeth Hardwick in her apartment at 28 East 10th Street in New York City. According to Malcolm Cowley, only Lowell, Hardwick, and Maisel continued to object to both the board's handling of the affair and to the countermovement among Ames's supporters; however, O'Connor revealed that she strongly believed in the validity of the original charges in letters she wrote from New York City to her friend from GSCW, Betty Boyd. As late as 1974, when Boyd was writing a memoir of her friendship with O'Connor, Regina Cline O'Connor expressed hesitancy about allowing her to quote from the letters O'Connor wrote to her about Yaddo, declaring that Boyd was almost the only friend that O'Connor had written to concerning the Yaddo episode.[11]

In a still unpublished letter to Boyd, written on 8 June 1949, O'Connor wrote of her political motivation for entering the cause; she expressed her belief that there had been "collusion" between Elizabeth Ames and Communists visitors to Yaddo, particularly Agnes Smedley, who had lived at Yaddo for five years. According to O'Connor, Smedley was "an active communist."[12] O'Connor seemed disgusted that Ames remained as head. In another letter to Boyd on 22 June, O'Connor called the Yaddo board corrupt and speculated that they had probably voted to support Ames in order to cover their own "negligence." In a third unpublished letter to Boyd in November 1949, O'Connor had heard that Ames might leave Yaddo and felt that, if she did leave, their attempt to remove her would then be justified. Mrs. Ames, however, did not resign; in fact, she remained director of Yaddo until 1969; she died in 1977 at ninety-two (Bongartz 33).

Another Milledgeville acquaintance with whom O'Connor discussed Yaddo was Helen Greene, who remembers a visit from O'Connor after she left Yaddo in March 1949. In her November 1949 letter to Boyd, O'Connor herself recalled their conversation, telling Boyd that during her last visit home, she had discussed the Yaddo "deal" with Greene. According to Greene, O'Connor seemed shocked about the "Communists at Yaddo." When she visited Greene, O'Connor asked her why she hadn't studied Communism in college (Greene, "Mary Flannery O'Connor," 46). Greene says she reminded O'Connor that she *had* studied the subject but speculates that real exposure to Communist influence was far more appalling to O'Connor than a textbook introduction. Greene recalls that during their visit, O'Connor told her, "'I'm the only one up there that believes in God. I'm sure they do but they're ashamed of it. They think they're intellectuals with a capital I.'" O'Connor believed that Yaddo intellectuals had substituted a belief in Communism for belief in God. Greene also remembers O'Connor's assertion that Mrs. Ames herself "hoped" to join the Communist party. O'Connor maintained a conservative attitude toward Communism throughout her life as evidenced by her reluctance to have her fiction published in Communist countries. In April 1956, she wrote to Elizabeth McKee that she didn't want her work published in "Russian-occupied" countries because she feared that they might use it to promote "anti-American propaganda." She recalled Jack London's popularity in Russia.[13]

Though O'Connor seemed to be in complete—though somewhat passive—support of the uprising against Ames and the so-called Communist influence, the episode left no strong or enduring impression on her life, either personal or professional. Letters to Betty Boyd and the visit home that allowed her to discuss the episode with Helen Greene helped dispel her excitement about being part of the uprising. O'Connor did not harbor long-term hostilities against Yaddo or Mrs. Ames. Writing to John Hawkes in September 1963, she declared herself "a veteran of Yaddo" (*HB* 538). She also strongly supported Cecil Dawkins's plans to visit Yaddo and, though she had all the rural isolation she needed at Andalusia to produce her own fiction, she seemed a bit pleased when Elizabeth Ames invited her to consider returning to Yaddo herself in 1958.

One Yaddo board member, who did not attend either of the board meetings but read the minutes from both was Acosta Nichols, Katrina Trask's brother and a teacher at Groton. On 16 April 1949 he wrote to Malcolm Cowley: "Frankly, as I had read the proceedings, I had felt that Lowell was almost unbalanced, Miss Hardwick somewhat unstable, and the others merely scared."[14] Nichols's remark about the fear that motivated O'Connor to join the others seems accurate. Young, naive, virtually uneducated about the world outside her craft, influenced by the power, charisma, and Catholic longings of Robert Lowell, Flannery O'Connor fell, temporarily, into the hysteria of her era.

O'Connor left Yaddo on 1 March with Elizabeth Hardwick and Robert Lowell and stayed briefly with Hardwick in her apartment at 28 East 10th Street. She revealed her positive feelings toward Hardwick and her work in a letter to Betty Hester in 1957. She told Hester that Hardwick was from Kentucky and "is a lot better writer than she gets credit for being"; she said, "I used to go up to Elizabeth's apartment to see her when I lived in New York and the elevator man always thought I was her sister. There was a slight resemblance" (*HB* 196). Hardwick herself has commented on this perceived resemblance: "Perhaps it was the accent—although mine is a good deal lighter than F.'s since I'm from the upper South."[15]

In February 1949, shortly before the four dissidents left Yaddo, Robert Lowell also introduced O'Connor to the man who became both her lifelong friend and her final publisher, Robert Giroux. In his introduction to *The Complete Stories* (1971), Giroux gave his first impressions of the young Georgian transplanted to New York City: "Behind her soft-spoken speech, clear-eyed gaze and shy manner, I sensed a tremendous strength. This was the rarest kind of young writer, one who was prepared to work her utmost and knew exactly what she must do with her talent" (viii).

Elizabeth Hardwick and Robert Lowell also introduced O'Connor to Mary McCarthy. Certainly one of the most interesting episodes in O'Connor's life in New York concerns her famous interaction with this former Catholic and literary success. O'Connor spent one particularly memorable evening at McCarthy's apartment, as she described in a 1955 letter to Betty Hester:

> The people who took me [to McCarthy's apartment] were Robert Lowell and his now wife, Elizabeth Hardwick. Having me there was like having a dog present who has been trained to say a few words but overcome with inadequacy had forgotten them. Well, toward morning the conversation turned on the Eucharist, which I, being the Catholic, was obviously supposed to defend. Mrs. Broadwater said when she was a child and received the Host, she thought of it as the Holy Ghost. He being the "most portable" person of the Trinity; now she thought of it as a symbol and implied that it was a pretty good one. I then said, in a very shaky voice, "Well, if it's a symbol, to hell with it." That was all the defense I was capable of but I realize now that this is all I will ever be able to say about it, outside of a story, except that is the center of existence for me; all the rest of life is expendable. (*HB* 125)

Of the episode, Hardwick said, "I don't remember this, but I read about it later. I don't think the memory (Flannery's) is particularly damning to Mary McC., the 'Real Presence' is indeed a matter of some perplexity. F. C. clearly believed in it with the ardor she expresses." In an unpublished 1959 letter at Duke to Father James McCown, O'Connor again recounted the occasion, recalling that she said nothing the entire evening because of the "powerful intellecchul" conversation that surrounded her.[16] She then retold the rest of the story in words identical to those in her letter to Hester. In both accounts, O'Connor's strong defense of her faith clearly shows how little she had in common with the literati of New York City in the late 1940s. The strength of Catholic faith that marked her personal sensibility was clearly out of place in the spiritually empty metropolis; in fact, she had even expressed her devotion to Catholicism by joining the Catholic Unity League while she lived in New York.[17]

Toward the end of February 1949, in a letter to Elizabeth McKee, O'Connor asserted that once in New York, she would "be looking for a place to stay"; she asked McKee for suggestions and told her that she will be "staying at something called Tatum House but I want to get out of there as soon as possible" (*HB* 11). While living at the "horrible" YWCA for a few weeks, she wrote Jean Wylder that her room had the smell of "an unopened Bible."[18] At the end of March she visited Milledgeville briefly and then returned to New York for the summer, living at 255 West 108th Street in the apartment that Elizabeth Fenwick helped her find (*CW* 1244). She wrote letters to Betty Boyd—8 June and 17 August 1949—and to Jean Wylder from this address, letters which show how little O'Connor became assimilated into New York City life. In a humorous last paragraph of a 22 June letter to Boyd, O'Connor wrote that most elderly women in New York City were wearing "sun back" dresses that summer. In October from Connecticut, she compared New York City with Los Angeles, where Boyd was about to move. She declared her disgust with both New York's "culture fog" and its approval of "fornication." Early in November, after a two-day trip into the city, O'Connor facetiously wrote to Boyd that she was glad not to know the huge populace of New York City.

One brief acquaintanceship that O'Connor established in New York City was with Dr. Lyman Fulton, a native of Johnson City, Tennessee, who was doing his residency in medicine at New York Hospital–Cornell Medical Center in the summer of 1949. He met O'Connor through her first cousin Louise Florencourt, whom he had earlier come to know through Mary Virginia Harrison, O'Connor's girlhood friend in Milledgeville. Having seen O'Connor "3 or 4 times, always with Louise" in her apartment in New York City, he recalls how uncomfortable she seemed about living in the city and how dedicated she was to her writing: "I decided she was reclusive, probably a book worm."[19] He also remembers that her feelings about Yaddo were "disapproving": "As I recall, she had found the place to be not what it was cracked up to be. [. . .] I [. . .] remember that she had a definitely negative opinion of Truman Capote, who had been at Yaddo." When interviewer Virginia Wray asked Fulton to give his most "striking recollection" of O'Connor in New York, he replied: "One of my most enduring memories of Flannery is of her fondness for goat milk cheese, which I think she was eating when I first met her. It appeared to be an important part of her diet at the time, which I thought was amusing. And so goat milk cheese became a kind of running joke between us, probably because of my kidding her about it."

In late February of 1949 Robert Lowell introduced O'Connor to Sally and Robert Fitzgerald. Sally Fitzgerald described that first meeting and her initial impressions of O'Connor:

> "She was 24 years old, a slender, fine-boned girl about 5 feet 5 inches tall—an average height—with sandy blonde hair and a long smooth white neck which she tended to thrust forward. This was obviously something she noticed about herself because in one or two of her stories there is a character whose neck thrusts forward. She was attractive, but not a beauty, but she had astonishing blue eyes which everyone noticed, quite shining blue eyes, large and very attentive; a gaze so penetrating I always wondered how anyone dared to speak out openly around her, [. . .] but the first impression was one of an appealing, likeable young girl." (Bassett 18)

O'Connor's friendship with the Fitzgeralds was one of the most important in her life, for they soon provided her a sanctuary in Connecticut in which she could work toward completion of *Wise Blood;* Robert Fitzgerald also introduced her to the plays of Sophocles—O'Connor first read *Oedipus Rex* while living with the them; they also became literate and sympathetic correspondents through the rest of her life. When she died, Robert Fitzgerald became her literary executor; his introduction to her posthumous collection of short stories, *Everything That Rises Must Converge,* remains an important biographical essay. In 1969 the Fitzgeralds, after studying manuscripts of O'Connor's lectures and magazine articles, published *Mystery and Manners.* After Robert Fitzgerald died, Sally selected, edited, and published many of O'Connor's letters in *The Habit of Being* (1979); and she selected and edited material for O'Connor's *Collected Works* in the Library of America series (1989). Before her death in June 2000, Sally Fitzgerald, O'Connor's only authorized biographer, traveled widely giving talks and opinions concerning O'Connor's life and work.

In his biographical introduction to *Everything That Rises Must Converge,* Robert Fitzgerald gave impressions of his first meeting with Flannery

O'Connor: "We saw a shy Georgia girl, her face heart-shaped and pale and glum, with fine eyes that could stop frowning and open brilliant upon everything. [. . .] Before she left that day we had a glimpse of her penetration and her scornful humor, and during the spring we saw her again and saw the furnished room where she lived and worked in a drab apartment hotel on the upper West Side" (R. Fitzgerald, "Introduction" xii–xiii).

The friendship between O'Connor and the Fitzgeralds quickly grew so strong that late in the summer of 1948, they invited her to move into a garage apartment at their new home in Connecticut. Robert Fitzgerald revealed the circumstances of that invitation: "Having two small children and the promise of more, we were looking for a house in the country, and in July we found and bought one, a stone and timber house that lay back in the wilderness of laurel and second-growth oak on a hilltop in Connecticut. Over the garage part of the house was a separate bedroom and bathroom with a stairway of its own, suitable for a boarder. We badly needed a boarder, and Flannery volunteered" (xiii). Fitzgerald described O'Connor's apartment as "austere. The only piece of furniture I distinctly remember was a Sears Roebuck dresser that my wife and I had painted a bright sky blue." He remembered that the walls of the apartment were of a "beaverboard" so thin that O'Connor could hear field mice running inside them as winter approached: "Our boarder's device against them [the mice] was to push in pins on which they might hurt their feet, as she said" (xiii).

Since the Fitzgeralds then practiced Catholicism with a devotion at least equal to that of O'Connor, Robert Fitzgerald recalled that the family's day began with early mass in Georgetown, a town four miles from their home. He and Sally alternated driving with O'Connor to mass, while the other stayed home with the children and to get breakfast (xiv). In a letter to Betty Hester in June 1956, O'Connor described the Fitzgeralds as "very intense Catholics and their religion covers everything they do. When I lived with them, they said the Benedictine grace before meals in Latin every day while the dinner got cold" (*HB* 161). She added that *she* preferred warm food to their prayers.

After breakfast the family unit dissolved: Robert was off to Sarah Lawrence College, where he was then teaching; O'Connor went to her apartment to write; and Sally looked to the needs of her children. Robert Fitzgerald wrote that O'Connor "would reappear about noon in her sweater, blue jeans and loafers, looking slender and almost tall, and would take her

daily walk, a half mile or so down the hill to the mailbox and back"
(R. Fitzgerald, "Introduction" xiv) to post her daily letter to her mother and
to pick up the one that Regina had written to her. After she, Sally, and the
Fitzgerald children had lunch, O'Connor babysat one of them for an hour as
she had previously arranged with the Fitzgeralds. Sally Fitzgerald described
O'Connor's method: "'Her idea of baby-sitting was to lie back on the bed
and look at the child. After her baby-sitting stint she started to write again,
and she wrote the rest of the afternoon'" (Bassett 18).

In the evenings after the children were in bed, O'Connor and the
Fitzgeralds enjoyed more adult pleasures, including "a small pitcher of mar-
tinis" and "long and lighthearted" talks at the dinner table: "[T]hey were
our movies, our concerts, and our theatre" (R. Fitzgerald, "Introduction"
xiv). Sally Fitzgerald wrote, too, that conversation was their chief diversion
in Connecticut. They discussed books, ranging from Catholic philosophy
and theology to current fiction. Robert Fitzgerald recalled that O'Connor
recommended *Miss Lonelyhearts* and *As I Lay Dying* to him and that she
also liked Ring Lardner and Andrew Lytle's essay on Caroline Gordon.
Together, they read Newman and Acton and Father Hughes's history of the
Church. Robert Fitzgerald lent O'Connor a copy of the *Divine Comedy,*
which he was teaching at Sarah Lawrence. She also read some early French
literature (in French) and Eliot's *The Family Reunion* (xv). Discussion about
writing also filled their time together—O'Connor was working on *Wise
Blood,* Robert Fitzgerald was translating the Oedipus plays, and Sally had
begun to write book reviews. O'Connor also talked about her mother and
her friends, telling the same sort of regional stories that she had so enjoyed
relating in Iowa City (Bassett 18). Robert Fitzgerald recalled that O'Connor
said "comparatively little about Iowa City" (Introduction xiv) but that she
did talk about her friendship with Robie Macauley.

Sally Fitzgerald clearly described O'Connor's personality and role within
the family:

> "She was not a sour, reclusive figure. She didn't have a lot of
> small talk, but she always had plenty to say those evenings and
> she was a good listener, much interested in everything my hus-
> band had to say.
>
> [. . .] Ours was really a family situation, as though she was
> a younger sister who lived with us, and she lost her shyness and

became very chatty with us. Often we talked until midnight, and then when we finally got around to the dishes, she and I would slosh around in the dishpan for sometimes an hour or so, still talking even after all the earlier conversation." (Bassett 18–19)

Robert Fitzgerald, too, recalled how much a part of the family O'Connor had become: "She was now one of the family, and no doubt the coolest and funniest one. She often entertained a child in her room or took one for a walk, and she introduced me to the idea and the Southern expression of cutting a switch to meet infant provocation—a useful recourse then and later. She was sure that we grown-ups were known to the children in private as 'he,' 'she,' and 'the other one'" ("Introduction" xvi). So close was O'Connor's relationship with the Fitzgeralds that they asked her to stand as godmother when their daughter Marie Juliana was baptized in May 1950; Robert Giroux served as godfather to the daughter, who became Sister Mary Julian in 1970 (Giroux xi).

O'Connor's letters to Betty Boyd during the summer of 1949 describe her relationship with the Fitzgeralds as well as focusing on her continued efforts at completing *Wise Blood* and working out details of a contract for its publication. In a letter to Boyd, dated 17 August 1949, O'Connor described the planned move with the Fitzgeralds and gave her address after 1 September as being R. D., Ridgefield, Connecticut. She revealed that their nearest neighbor was Mrs. Alger Hiss's first husband. She also said that she had no special reason for leaving New York but that she could economize by making the move; she was also worried about her publishing problems with Rinehart and told her she was trying to move her book to Harcourt Brace.

The snare that O'Connor referred to involved her increasingly poor relations with John Selby at Rinehart. By mid-January 1949, O'Connor had completed and polished nine chapters of *Wise Blood* and sent them to Elizabeth McKee, who was to submit them to Selby. By that time, Robert Giroux, then an editor at Harcourt Brace, had expressed a strong interest in the novel—offering her a $1,500 advance. O'Connor waited to hear from John Selby, who did not react to her manuscript until 16 February. Both his opening remark in which he called the young writer a "straight shooter" and his reservations about the manuscript upset O'Connor. Admitting that he believed she had "an astonishing gift," he went on to criticize the manuscript rather sharply:

[. . .] the chapters we have now don't seem to have the directness and direction that you probably feel yourself, and [. . .] there are probably some aspects of the book that have been obscured by your habit of rewriting over and over again.

Do you want us to be specific and work with you the way we do with most of the writers on our list, or do you prefer to go it alone? To be honest, most of us have sensed a kind of aloneness in the book, as if you were writing out of the small world of your own experience, and as if you were consciously limiting this experience.[20]

The next day (17 February), O'Connor wrote to Elizabeth McKee expressing her disgust with Selby's approach; she called his criticism "vague" and asserted that his objections to the book were what she considered its virtues: "The letter is addressed to a slightly dim-witted Camp Fire girl, and I cannot look with composure on getting a lifetime of others like them" (*HB* 9). On 18 February, O'Connor wrote to Selby himself, both defending herself and agreeing to see him in New York City the next week. She told him that she preferred to work alone rather than in a cooperative arrangement with him:

I am not writing a conventional novel, and I think that the quality of the novel I write will derive precisely from the peculiarity or aloneness, if you will, of the experience I write from. I do not think there is any lack of objectivity in the writing, however, if this is what your criticism implies; and also I do not feel that rewriting has obscured the direction. I feel that it has given whatever direction is now present.

In short, I am amenable to criticism but only within the sphere of what I am trying to do; I will not be persuaded to do otherwise. The finished book, though I hope less angular, will be just as odd if not odder than the nine chapters you have now. The question is: is Rinehart interested in publishing this kind of a novel? (*HB* 10)

During her visit to Milledgeville that spring, O'Connor wrote to Paul Engle to report her difficulties with Selby and to assert her individualism as a beginning writer. She told him that she had "to develope [*sic*] in my own way" and that she refused "to be hurried or directed by Rinehart." She felt that the company was interested only in the "conventional" and that she had "no indication that they are very bright" (*HB* 14). Engle wrote back to her on 16 May 1949, urging her "to send Selby some reassurance so that he won't take an overdose of sleeping pills some night."[21] He asked her to send him some sort of outline of the "rest of the novel" so that he could assure Selby that she was completing the novel. Engle seemed worried about the $750 that Rinehart had awarded her at Iowa and even suggested that she repay part of it if she signed with another publisher. Engle's letter could not have done much to reassure O'Connor. As he wrote in the letter, he seemed to be "blowing from Rinehart's point of the compass."

In a letter to Paul Engle early in May 1949, Selby himself revealed that he was upset by the forthright confidence of the young writer: "I am genuinely disturbed about this business—not because of her slowness but because of the hardening of the arteries of her cooperative sense. It seems most unbecoming in a writer so young."[22] The result was that Rinehart finally gave O'Connor a provisional release her from her obligation to them in November 1949. The terms of the release disturbed O'Connor because in it Selby had described her as "'stiff-necked, uncooperative and unethical'" (*HB* 17). In a letter written to Mavis McIntosh, Elizabeth McKee's partner, on 31 October 1949, O'Connor showed her resentment of Selby's charge but wondered whether she should show him more of the manuscript before signing a contract with Harcourt Brace. The result of her worry and confusion over her dealings with Selby was, according to Robert Giroux, that it was not until the fall of 1950 that O'Connor obtained her final release from Selby at Rinehart: "[I]n October, [. . .] I offered and she signed a contract [at Harcourt Brace] for *Wise Blood*" (Giroux xi).

In spite of her problems with Selby, O'Connor, during the summer and fall of 1949, steadfastly worked toward completion of the novel. By this time, O'Connor—a perfectionist from the beginning—had written and rejected hundreds of pages of manuscript. From the novel that she had begun at Iowa, she gradually pared the stark narrative of Hazel Motes's journey from self-proclaimed nihilism toward salvation. This pivotal—and ambivalent—struggle toward Grace became the central concern of most of her fiction. Her wide reading at Iowa impelled her to begin with a large canvass and many characters in imitation of writers like Balzac and Flaubert, Henry

James and Faulkner. Learning her craft and realizing the limits of her own genius, O'Connor whittled Haze and his story from the mass of material she had created at Iowa, Yaddo, and in New York City. Of her progress on the novel in Connecticut, Robert Fitzgerald revealed that there she wrote the "central episodes with Enoch Emery and Hoover Shoates (a name we all celebrated)" (xvi). He also wrote that in the summer of 1950, O'Connor "had reached an impasse with Haze and didn't know how to finish him off [until] she read for the first time the Oedipus plays. She went on then to end her story with the self-blinding of Motes, and she had to rework the body of the novel to prepare for it" (xvi).

Though O'Connor successfully resolved the publishing problems with Selby at Rinehart and continued to make progress in writing *Wise Blood,* her health also began to deteriorate during her time with the Fitzgeralds. Dr. Lyman Fulton describes her problems: "Shortly after she left New York [for Milledgeville], she wrote to me about having had a so-called Dietl's Crisis. This is a condition, often very painful, in which a kidney slips out of place so as to cause a kinking and obstruction of the ureter. Surgery is often necessary." When O'Connor went home to Milledgeville for Christmas at the end of 1949, she had the kidney surgery, describing it to Elizabeth McKee as "having a kidney tacked up."[23] She spent most of January 1950 in the Baldwin County Hospital in Milledgeville before returning to Connecticut in March; on 13 February 1950 she had written to McKee that she hoped "to be back in Connecticut by March 20th" (*HB* 20). Between March and December 1950, O'Connor continued to polish the novel and to type the first complete version, a task she had apparently completed ahead of her planned 1950 Christmas trip to Milledgeville.

Of the onset of O'Connor's illness that early in the next year doctors would diagnose as lupus erythematosus, Robert Fitzgerald wrote that, after she finished typing her first complete draft of the novel, "Flannery told us with amusement of a heaviness in her typing arms. When this got worse, we took her to the doctor at Wilton Corners, Rheumatoid arthritis, he was afraid it was, but he advised her to have a hospital check-up in Georgia when she went home for Christmas. On the train going south she became desperately ill. She did not have arthritis but a related disease, lupus, the disease that killed her father" (Giroux xvi–xvii). When she arrived in Milledgeville, O'Connor had become so ill that her uncle who met her described her as looking "'like a shriveled old woman'" (*HB* 22). On her arrival in Georgia, O'Connor went almost immediately to the local hospital; Regina O'Connor called the Fitzgeralds two weeks later to tell them that Flannery was dying; however, Sally Fitzgerald explained, "'She was finally saved by an Atlanta doctor [Dr. Arthur J. Merrill] who was a lupus specialist and who diagnosed the disease over the phone. Then when he saw her there was no doubt that she indeed had disseminated lupus. [. . .] The doctor was the one who pulled her through that crisis and took care of her the rest of her life'" (Bassett 21).

This disease that struck O'Connor in late 1950, as it had her father about ten years earlier, would dramatically transform her life. Though she was then unaware of the seriousness of her illness, she would never leave Milledgeville permanently again. She would publish all her books from the town and fall into a lifelong mutual dependency with her mother.

Systemic lupus erythematosus, usually simply termed *lupus,* remains still somewhat mysterious. A chronic systemic immune disease that can cause inflammation in virtually nearly every part of the body, it is relatively common, more prevalent than leukemia, muscular dystrophy, and cerebral palsy. Doctors term the disease *chronic* because once diagnosed, the patient will suffer from the disease throughout life. Lupus is systemic because it can affect so many different parts of the body; the disease is autoimmune because, in a person suffering from lupus, the body's immune system becomes confused: antibodies that normally fight off harmful organisms and diseased cells instead attack the body's normal cells. In confusion, then, the immune system produces "antibodies to the self, called autoantibodies, which trigger a chain reaction of defense tactics."[24] Inflammation occurs wherever the immune complexes settle and, without treatment, causes major damage to organ systems and tissues. Since symptoms of the disease vary so greatly from person to person, it is hard to diagnose; because Edward O'Connor died from lupus, Dr. Merrill no doubt based his final diagnosis of O'Connor's illness on his knowledge of her father's medical history. Her earlier kidney problem also must have provided clues.

No known cause of lupus has ever been isolated, but most researchers now believe that a combination of genetic and environmental factors cause the disease. Far more women than men suffer from lupus, and it usually attacks them during childbearing age (fourteen to forty-five) (Horowitz and Brill 15). Studies have shown that estrogen may make women more susceptible to immune system problems, including lupus (Eichelbaum 7). More recent research has also shown a genetic or hereditary connection: "about 20% of lupus patients have a first-degree relative (parent, child, or sibling) with some autoimmune disorder. [. . .] [A]n additional 15 to 20% of lupus patients' close relatives have signs of immunological aberration, such as anti-nuclear antibodies, although they have (and will have) no auto-immune disease" (Blau and Schultz 29). Environmental factors also play a part in the onset of lupus: drugs, chemicals, sun exposure, viruses, and stress may trigger the disease.

In 1950, when O'Connor fell victim to lupus, not even this sort of basic information about the disease was available. Only recently had doctors begun to treat it with steroids, and their knowledge of how to control dosages was incomplete. Reports in medical journals during the late 1950s describe experimental treatments but offer few positive results from their use. Most of the research conducted in the early to mid-1950s centered on establishing chemical similarities between lupus erythematosus and other chronic illnesses. Experimenters tried applying to the skin of lupus sufferers drugs used in treating other skin problems. In 1956, one doctor at the UCLA Medical School suggested that injecting white blood cells might help control the damage to organs that lupus causes.[25] In 1958, another study at the University of Southern California demonstrated that a new steroid, triamcinolone, was producing a positive response in some lupus patients, but not without negative side effects.[26] This enigmatic disease that struck Flannery O'Connor was so severe in its initial attack that the outcome for her was at first problematic. During the next year her recovery was so slow that the prospects for both her nearly completed novel and her life were uncertain. When she did partially recover from this first attack, she had to make decisions that would clearly influence the way she would live and write for the rest of her life.

Cathedral of St. John the Baptist, Lafayette Square, Savannah, 1992.
Courtesy of Dr. William C. Harris, who took the photograph.

O'Connor home at 207 East Charlton Street, Lafayette Square, Savannah.
Courtesy of the photographer, Cynthia Gilliatt.

Regina Cline O'Connor circa 1930. Courtesy of the Flannery O'Connor Collection, Ina Dillard Russell Library, Georgia College and State University, Milledgeville.

Edward F. O'Connor, circa 1930. Courtesy of the Flannery O'Connor Collection, Ina Dillard Russell Library, Georgia College and State University, Milledgeville.

Mary Flannery O'Connor, age three. Courtesy of the Flannery O'Connor Collection,
Ina Dillard Russell Library, Georgia College and State University, Milledgeville.

Gordon-Ward-Beal-Cline-O'Connor mansion, Milledgeville. Photograph by the author.

Mary Flannery O'Connor (*standing center*) and friends at a birthday party in Milledgeville, circa 1939. Courtesy of the Flannery O'Connor Collection, Ina Dillard Russell Library, Georgia College and State University, Milledgeville.

Mary Flannery O'Connor, age twelve. Courtesy of the Flannery O'Connor Collection, Ina Dillard Russell Library, Georgia College and State University, Milledgeville.

Mary Flannery O'Connor, Peabody graduate, 1942. Courtesy of the Flannery O'Connor Collection, Ina Dillard Russell Library, Georgia College and State University, Milledgeville.

(Above) O'Connor as editor of
The Corinthian, Georgia State
College for Women, 1945.
Courtesy of the Flannery
O'Connor Collection, Ina
Dillard Russell Library,
Georgia College and State
University, Milledgeville.

(Left) O'Connor outside
Currier Graduate Dormitory,
Iowa City, 1947. Courtesy of
the photographer, Martha
Belle Spreiser.

Flannery O'Connor, emerging author, circa 1948. Courtesy of the Flannery O'Connor
Collection, Ina Dillard Russell Library, Georgia College and State University, Milledgeville.

Andalusia, Milledgeville, where O'Connor spent the last twelve years of her life.
Courtesy of the photographer, Joe McTyre.

O'Connor at the book-signing party for *Wise Blood,* Georgia State College for Women, 1952. Courtesy of the Flannery O'Connor Collection, Ina Dillard Russell Library, Georgia College and State University, Milledgeville.

O'Connor with Frances and Brainard Cheney at their home in Smyrna, Tennessee, 1953.
Courtesy of Roy M. Neel, literary executor of the Cheneys.

O'Connor with Katherine Anne Porter, Andalusia, 1958.
Courtesy of Thomas and Louise Gossett.

O'Connor and one of her peacocks at Andalusia, 1962.
Courtesy of the photographer, Joe McTyre.

CHAPTER SIX

RETURN TO MILLEDGEVILLE
AND A PIVOTAL DECISION

W hen Flannery O'Connor, suffering from the disease that would finally kill her, returned permanently to Milledgeville early in 1951, she returned most unwillingly. Having chosen to leave the insularity of small-town Milledgeville first to enter the writers' workshop at the University of Iowa and later to live in New York and Connecticut, O'Connor had made a decision like those of her Southern literary contemporaries—most notably and permanently, William Styron—to leave the South in order to write about both its mysteries and manners. She had decided that she needed distance from the South in order to use it as a setting for universal concerns; however, the lupus that struck her while she was living with the Fitzgeralds in Connecticut left her no choice but to return to Milledgeville.

That return, however, which O'Connor so dreaded, enhanced rather than stifled her creativity. When her friend, Maryat Lee, contemplated a similar return to the South, O'Connor wrote to her in June of 1957: "So it may be the South! You get no condolences from me. This is a Return I have faced and when I faced it I was roped and tied and resigned the way it is necessary to be resigned to death, and largely because I thought it would be the end of any creation, any writing, any WORK from me. And as I told you by the fence, it was only the beginning" (*HB* 224).

Since O'Connor—alienated by both her individuality and genius—had never been particularly comfortable in Milledgeville, she, on her return, had to make compromises and adjustments that would enable her to continue to develop and use her unique talents. She had to accept the limitations imposed on her by lupus erythematosus, restrictions that partly influenced her writing schedule and certainly controlled her travel away from Milledgeville. The disease also forced her to make a basic decision about the role of sexuality in her life; too physically weak to maintain both a marriage and a writer's vocation, she chose to remain unmarried.[1] O'Connor also had to accommodate to the demands and eccentricities of the Cline family and to her mother's overly protective nature. By leaving Milledgeville, she had temporarily escaped the almost compulsive control of a family dominant in the town and of Regina Cline O'Connor, who, from her daughter's early childhood, had guided and partly curbed her interests and behavior; returning to Milledgeville forced O'Connor to accommodate her interests with those of her mother.

Resolving the role of love and sexuality in her life became a major issue that O'Connor faced after her return to Milledgeville. Having read O'Connor's fiction and learned a bit about her life, contemporary readers invariably ask, Was she married? Did she *ever* have a heterosexual love relationship? Was she a latent lesbian who formed close friendships with women based on sexual attraction? All of these questions are intrusive and irrelevant: what matters most in the life of Flannery O'Connor is her enduring fiction; however, because the questions continue to be asked, it becomes necessary to speculate and form conclusions about O'Connor's sex life or lack thereof.

This rather prurient curiosity has emerged as an outgrowth of our sexually obsessed era. Most younger people today find it hard to believe that a young adult in the late 1940s and early 1950s might have chosen celibacy over other options. O'Connor's friend in Milledgeville, Elizabeth Horne, recalled a visit from a priest [in the 1980s] whose first questions concerned the author's "dating life." When Horne told him that in her opinion O'Connor had experienced "no such life," he replied that "that could just not be." Horne says that at this point, she got up and left the interview. Even if O'Connor did have a few heterosexual dates in Milledgeville and elsewhere, her intense devotion to writing, her desire to achieve recognition as a woman writer in an era when the literary work of women was just beginning to gain serious attention, and her being struck down by lupus while still a young woman, all contributed to her conscious decision to renounce sexuality.

In early life, Mary Flannery O'Connor clearly showed little interest in her contemporaries, either male or female. Brought up in a clearly matriarchal family, surrounded by overly protective, elderly female relatives, and interested in matters of the intellect, she cultivated her inner life. Reading and writing precociously, she produced juvenilia like the self-revealing story in which her protagonist tries to confuse her neighbors by passionately kissing her pet chicken. Even later, O'Connor apparently preferred to remain the perennial twelve-year-old who could dress as casually as she wished and love exotic fowl rather than boys; thus she avoided the perils of social activities like dancing and dating.

As a teenager in Milledgeville, Mary Flannery O'Connor attended only single-sex schools: Peabody High School and the Georgia State College for Women. Although opportunities for interaction with males were certainly possible for her more extroverted classmates, she, as a teenager, developed little if any such interest. Having finished high school at sixteen and college at nineteen, she was a decided exception to the Southern belle stereotype. Part of Flannery's hesitation about entering into the social activities of Milledgeville must have been a conscious rebellion against this stereotype. Evidence proves that with few exceptions, Flannery O'Connor left Milledgeville for Iowa with only limited sexual interest or experience. O'Connor, in a letter to Betty Hester in 1956, made a specific assertion about her inability to think in terms of differences in gender: "I just never think [. . .] of qualities which are specifically feminine or masculine. I suppose I divide people into two classes: the Irksome and the Non-Irksome without regard to sex. Yes and there are the Medium Irksome and the Rare Irksome" (*HB* 176). In another letter to Hester, O'Connor made her most telling statement about her inability to establish warm personal relationships. She wrote that she wanted relationships but had little success in forming them; however, in still another letter to Hester in 1955, while they were discussing Joy-Hulga's lack of romantic experience, O'Connor reacted rather sharply to Hester's biographical interpretation of the character: "That my stories scream to you that I have never consented to being in love with anybody is merely to prove that they are screaming an historical inaccuracy. I have God help me consented to this frequently" (170–71).

Supporting the above declaration, Sally Fitzgerald in a paper first delivered at "The Habit of Art" conference at Georgia College in Milledgeville in 1994 and published in a revised version in 1998, offered an unusual interpretation of O'Connor's problems in establishing enduring heterosexual relationships (S. Fitzgerald, "Flannery O'Connor" 407–25). She theorized that beginning with her years at GSCW, O'Connor became a lifelong victim of unrequited love. Fitzgerald asserted that O'Connor's first failed relationship occurred while she was an undergraduate. John Sullivan, a Marine sergeant stationed at the naval base at GSCW, and O'Connor met when her aunt, Katie Cline, invited the young soldier to Sunday dinner. Fitzgerald wrote "that an immediate rapport appears to have developed between them—not, in his description, a romance, but a close comradeship enjoyed by both" (410). Fitzgerald claimed that Sullivan and O'Connor attended one dance at GSCW, explored the town together, went to the movies, and traded anecdotes about their Catholic families. Sullivan also encouraged O'Connor's writing. Their friendship continued through correspondence after he transferred to another naval base and while he was stationed in the Pacific, with O'Connor carefully drafting and revising her letters to him. The letters between them stopped when he entered a seminary to become a priest; however, Sullivan eventually left the seminary, married, and went into business, leaving, according to Fitzgerald, O'Connor behind, the victim of unrequited love (410).

Once at Iowa, O'Connor's interest in men remained somewhat neutral, though Fitzgerald asserted that her thwarted relationship there was with Robie Macauley. O'Connor did develop a strong and enduring friendship with Macauley; they spent considerable time together during the 1947–48 school term, though he was already engaged to the woman he married in the summer of 1948; in addition, he asserted that Fitzgerald never asked him about a probable romantic interest between O'Connor and himself. Fitzgerald believed, however, that while Macauley considered their friendship only platonic, O'Connor fell in love with him and was so distressed by his marriage that she chose not to attend his wedding (S. Fitzgerald, "Flannery O'Connor" 413).

Andrew Lytle's anecdote about the date he arranged for O'Connor and a fellow student shows how little success she apparently had in social dating.

Lytle's belief that the young men in the workshop were frightened of O'Connor's obvious talent reveals much about her failure to form an enduring relationship with any of the men she met there or later. In the mid-twentieth century, intellectually and artistically talented women were still the exception and thus frightening to many men. Remember, too, her male classmates' comments about her social isolation. Both James B. Hall and Walter Sullivan emphasize how uncomfortable she was socially, though the Sullivans recalled her warm friendship with Macauley. Clearly, O'Connor was not husband hunting at Iowa.

To support further her theory of O'Connor as the victim of unrequited love, Fitzgerald offered one other unsuccessful relationship that O'Connor established in Milledgeville, after she had fallen ill with lupus. In her detailed chronology in *Collected Works,* Fitzgerald asserted that in 1953 O'Connor met and "fell in love" with Erik Langkjaer from Denmark, then a textbook salesman for Harcourt Brace (*CW* 1247). Mary Barbara Tate, who knew O'Connor fairly well in Milledgeville in the late 1950s, remembers nothing about the relationship firsthand but has discussed it with Sally Fitzgerald: "Sally had told me that she had found [. . .] that she [O'Connor] had really been in love [with Langkjaer] and that he had not responded and it had been very painful for her, and Sally felt that that was quite a significant event in Flannery's life and she was glad to have discovered that" (M. B. Tate, interview 1989).

O'Connor's former history professor, Helen Greene, introduced Langkjaer to O'Connor. Calling him "the nicest young man," Greene remembers that his mother worked at the United Nations and that he was studying for a degree at Columbia University. A summer job, selling college textbooks, brought him to Milledgeville. Greene recalls how she brought Flannery and Erik together: "I said, 'Wouldn't you like to meet an author that your company publishes?' 'Oh,' he said, 'yes.'" Greene says that she then called Andalusia, and Regina welcomed the visit. Greene and Langkjaer visited the O'Connors and the young book salesman stayed over in Milledgeville for a day or two afterward; during that time Flannery "took him all over the county. I think she really liked him a lot." Greene also hoped that the friendship might develop into a genuine romance, but "he wasn't Roman Catholic."

O'Connor herself revealed that she and Langkjaer were indeed involved in a relationship when she wrote to Betty Hester about her knowledge of his

aunt Helene Iswolsky, who in the 1950s taught at Fordham College and published a magazine called *The Third Hour.* In describing the magazine to
Hester, she said directly, "I used to go with her nephew so I heard considerable about it" (*HB* 97). In a later letter to Hester, O'Connor asserted that
Langkjaer "used to tell me that she was the ugliest woman in the world and
that I reminded him of her which was why he liked me" (226). Fitzgerald
believed that the relationship between O'Connor and Langkjaer "represents
a profoundly important event in her life—the last, and most seriously painful, instance in which the old pattern of unrequited love was to reappear"
(S. Fitzgerald, "Flannery O'Connor" 420). She reported that Langkjaer visited O'Connor fairly often in Milledgeville, but when he began to realize that
O'Connor had fallen in love with him, he pulled away. When he decided to
return to Denmark, their correspondence continued until their final letters
crossed: Fitzgerald asserted that in her last letter to him, O'Connor wrote
openly of her longing for their companionship, telling him that "'if you were
here, we could talk for a million years'" (421). His letter told her that he was
about to marry someone else. Fitzgerald speculated that Langkjaer was cautious about forming a permanent relationship with O'Connor because of her
health and because he felt intellectually inferior to her: "[H]e didn't want to
be just someone's husband" (420).

In the late 1950s, evidence of other heterosexual relationships O'Connor
might have formed is thin. Her friendships with two slightly younger college teachers from the area, William Sessions and Ted Spivey, were based
more on shared intellectual interest (Spivey) or a sincere interest in friendship (Sessions) than on romance. One other documented fact that seems to
indicate O'Connor's deliberate decision to eschew marital love exists in a
note Alta Haynes made in a journal she kept of O'Connor's visit to Lansing,
Michigan, in 1955. She noted that during their visit together, O'Connor confided to her that she would never marry because of the lupus.[2] O'Connor
was, by this time, clearly aware of the limitations that her illness placed on
her. Under a virtual death sentence, it seems realistic that she made the choice
to pursue her vocation single-mindedly rather than to dissipate her energies
with the burdens of marriage and family.

Aside from speculation about O'Connor's heterosexual interests,
rumors about O'Connor's possible lesbianism have long circulated in
Milledgeville, fueled by jealousy and a desire to spice small-town lives with

salacious gossip. Using the fallacy of guilt by association, some assert that, because several of her closest correspondents were lesbian, she certainly must have been lesbian herself. One story in Milledgeville reports that when the makers of the TV version of *The Displaced Person* filmed the adaptation at Andalusia in 1978—both exterior and interior shots—they found a shelf of books about lesbianism hidden on top of one of the tall bookcases which were then still at Andalusia.[3] Such gossip is virtually unverifiable; however, stronger speculations about O'Connor's possible lesbianism evolve from her close friendships with women, particularly with Maryat Lee.

When her college friend Betty Boyd revealed her plans to marry late in 1949 (four years after their graduation from GSCW while O'Connor was living with the Fitzgeralds in Connecticut), O'Connor seemed a bit stunned:

> In honor of my nuptial blessing I am writing on white paper, 6 pound bond, suitable [& left over from] 2nd & 3rd copies of theses. The following are violets [She drew three flowers in a line into the manuscript] or at least I would have you think of them as such.
>
> Marriage is always a shock to me.
>
> Will you live in Los Angeles & take a Los Angeles paper?
>
> I would like to send you a teaspoon. What kind would you like me to send? [. . .]
>
> I am leaving a large space at the bottom to make this look more nuptial.
>
> An abundance of peace. (*HB* 19)[4]

Two sentences in the letter are of particular interest. "Marriage is always a shock to me" indicates quite clearly how little Flannery O'Connor thought about the possibility of marriage for herself. The institution did not appear to be an option for the young, ambitious writer whose chief focus at this time was on completing *Wise Blood*.

In another sentence, excised from the letter by Sally Fitzgerald when she included it in *The Habit of Being*, O'Connor made a statement of even greater interest. She commented that a GSCW friend of her and Boyd should be relieved by the announcement of Boyd's forthcoming marriage. This woman, at one point, had embarrassed O'Connor by asking her whether she (O'Connor) was interested in being married.[5] O'Connor made several unflattering comments about this classmate in other letters to Betty Boyd, but the excised sentence seems particularly relevant to the question of O'Connor's sexual identity. Her sentence implies that their friend was suspicious of the relationship between O'Connor and Betty Boyd during their years at GSCW. Homosexual attachments between women in schools for women were fairly common during this time period, although they were generally closeted. O'Connor's comment to the newly engaged Betty Boyd suggests that the other young woman must have somehow suspected or hinted that the friendship between O'Connor and Betty Boyd had a sexual component. O'Connor's caustic statement, along with Betty Boyd's marriage, suggests that the friend's speculations had no basis in fact.

O'Connor's friendship with Maryat Lee, formed during the late 1950s in Milledgeville, provides stronger fuel for those who have tried to identify O'Connor's sexual orientation as lesbian. O'Connor met Lee, the sister of Robert E. "Buzz" Lee, president of GSCW from 1956 to 1967, late in 1956, when Maryat was spending the holidays with him and his family. Maryat Lee was admittedly bisexual. Though she married an Australian David Foulkes-Taylor on 19 July 1957 in Japan, Maryat lived with him only briefly.

Any reader of *The Habit of Being* knows of the strong friendship between Lee and O'Connor. According to Maryat's brother, their friendship was mutually rich and creative. Lee says that his sister "had not only a gift for friendship" but also "a passion for deep friendship" and that, despite Maryat's tendency to dominate her friends, her relationship with O'Connor was that of equals and, therefore, unique. He maintains that O'Connor was, in fact, "one of the very few people who would not be overpowered by Maryat." Their friendship, he believes, was based on "mutual respect," without any "sense of [O'Connor's] being overpowered" by Maryat.[6]

Study of the letters between the two women and examination of the journal Maryat Lee kept throughout her friendship with O'Connor gives clear evidence that the relationship between the two women was free of any sexual component, though Maryat Lee may have desired such an attachment.[7] In a journal entry of 28 December 1956, Lee, back in New York City, recorded her first impressions of O'Connor: "So much has happened! [. . .] I called to see Flannery O'Connor, who is a fiction writer 31 years old—two novels [*sic*] published. She had already asked to see me—she heard [about Lee's visit to Milledgeville] from a Wesleyan girl who was in the class I attended [Lee gave a guest lecture at GSCW]. Flannery is very young, very unpretentious, crippled & I like her almost without reservation—except her metaphysical interests. She's Catholic."[8] Lee also described O'Connor's "proper mother under foot" and "her [Flannery's] glowing face, once or twice."

As early as March of the next year (1957), Maryat noted in her journal that she had had a "daydream about getting Flannery up here. Strong hunch it would be a good thing for her but more than that I'd like to have her here." By May 1957, Maryat was considering marrying David Foulkes-Taylor; O'Connor's advice to Maryat again showed how skeptical she remained about marriage: "Well, you have a decision in front of you if you have to decide whether to live your whole life with a man. I am sure it requires a metamorphosis for anybody and cannot be done without grace" (*HB* 220). On 31 May 1957, in a shipboard letter to O'Connor as she was traveling to the Orient with Foulkes-Taylor and another man (Donald Ritchie) she had met on shipboard, Maryat talked of her love for both Foulkes-Taylor and Ritchie; she then also declared her feelings for O'Connor: "Oh, Flannery, I love you too. Did you know that? I almost said it when we were standing by the fence, but I was just too depressed and low and desperate, about work and family and etc. What would you have done if I had come up with it? Gone flippity flapping away on your crutches I bet."[9]

O'Connor's reaction to Maryat's declaration of this love came in her return letter of 9 June 1957, in which she told Lee that her capacity for love needed "to be diluted with time and with matter," and that its real source lay in grace: "it is the blood of Christ and I thought, after I had seen you once, that you were full of it and didn't know what to do with it or perhaps even what it was" (*HB* 224–25). In her journal on 14 June 1957, Maryat reacted to the letter: "Fascinating letter from Flannery [. . .] re loving her which she *did* manage to bypass by calling it a mystical thing I was filled with and [. . .] She *did* go flopping away on her crutches!" Ten days later, she also reacted in a return letter: "I take you with or without the blood of the lamb, and still it is you I love and it is I that love you, and my heart leaps. Oh Flannery, your reply falls pitifully short, a ruse of bones, a chill breeze, inadequate, obfuscating, limp, full of clichés, the quaver of a solitary voice in the airless eternities and fog drifting over in sheets."

O'Connor's reply to this letter is also interesting, because in it she both apologized, in rather intellectualized terms, for rejecting Maryat's offer of love and defended her own theologically influenced conception: "You are of course entirely right that the reply was inadequate and cliché-ridden. It always will be" (*HB* 227). She wrote that she hated "pious language," but then explained that, to her, genuine love involves a belief "in the resurrection of the body. I also believe in it before it gets that way, dear girl, so don't put me down in yr Associate Reformed Presbyterian black books. It's my own & your own but also the Essential" (227). In a letter dated 8 October 1957, O'Connor again apologized to Maryat for her failure to react to her declarations, telling her that she herself didn't "have a highly developed sensibility and I don't know when I hurt people until they tell me. To have caused you any pain is very painful to me and is the last thing I would have wanted to do" (245).

On 15 July 1957, while in Japan, Maryat reacted in her journal to O'Connor's second letter: "My dear girl, I am not attacking your *religion*—but your use of it. Surely you can't find in xten [manuscript is illegible, but Lee probably means Christian] dogma the argument that when someone says simply & clearly they love you that you are called upon to elaborate (needlessly) upon the ultimate significance of same. You may be a Catholic but you're acting like a damn Puritan or, just as bad, cautious intellectual." After this interchange, Maryat apparently relinquished her love interest in Flannery. From this time forward their friendship continued, but on more neutral grounds. On several occasions in her journal, however, Maryat commented on what she perceived to be O'Connor's lack of physical feeling, including her most extended comment in June 1959:

> Flannery only person no need feeling with. But it is a little sterile—no its only limited—her limits are set—so far as relationships go—Religion tends to this [,] rather you set on religion to do it—cement your limits the stronger it is—the stronger the impulse and wish to break limits—Her deep blush when I embraced her—No—She's not dead—just jailed. And my once enormous determination to free people is greatly reduced. This hard sad face as she shut me out for supposed meanness. I had no impulse to make her see her mistake.

O'Connor's rejection of Maryat's overtures seem to indicate fairly clearly both her lack of lesbian orientation and her conscious decision to keep herself free of entangling love relationships. O'Connor's only documented comments on lesbianism occur in two letters, one to Beverly Brunson in September 1954: "As for lesbianism I regard that as any other form of uncleanness. Purity is the twentieth centuries dirty word but it the most mysterious of the virtues and not be to discussed in a light fashion even with ones own and surely not with strangers" (*CW* 925). In another letter, this one to Betty Hester in 1957, O'Connor gave her reaction to another correspondent who has confided that she has "'lost her homosexuality.' As to her homosexuality I don't know if that is really a trouble of hers or if she is just like the rest of those arty people in the Village, who feel that all kinds of experimentation is necessary to discovering life and whatnot" (*HB* 202). In a memoir of their friendship, Fr. James McCown wrote derisively of rumors about O'Connor's homosexuality: "[I]f anybody suspects that she had deviant sexual leanings, let them put that idea to rest. How such sophistication could co-exist with such innocence and delicacy of conscious is still a marvel to me" (McCown, "Flannery O'Connor" 18).

Thus, it seems clear that despite some minor interest in men during her young adulthood, O'Connor never actively pursued either a heterosexual or a homosexual relationship. Though her friendship with Maryat Lee evoked strong feelings in Maryat, O'Connor did not reciprocate them, though she valued Maryat as a highly entertaining friend. O'Connor clearly knew that her most enduring interests were in practicing her religion and writing as vocation. In order to function as a successful female artist, she eschewed the ordinary in order to attain the eternal. Fr. James McCown wrote another cogent anecdote concerning O'Connor's celibacy:

> Ralph McGill [. . .] once had me to dinner with an Atlanta novelist, Margaret Long. Margaret said, "Flannery certainly is a great writer, but, you know there is no *love* in her writing." I confronted Flannery with this. "She's right," she said. "You can't write about love when you haven't had it, leastwise the kind she is talking about. I never had any." The early onset of her terrible illness ruled out the normal activities of youth that lead to love and marriage. She was incapable of being anything but herself, and the self she was would probably have frightened away any save a suitor of singular discernment. (McCown, "Remembering Flannery O'Connor" 87)

Another important comment O'Connor made relevant to such a decision came in a letter she wrote to Betty Hester in 1956: "There is a great deal that has to either be given up or be taken away from you if you are going to succeed in writing a body of work. There seems to be other conditions in life that demand celibacy besides the priesthood" (*HB* 176). Her forced return to Milledgeville, then, drastically changed the course of O'Connor's life as an artist and as a woman. Had she remained well and in New York, she might have pursued a quite different direction in her fiction after *Wise Blood,* possibly even incorporating within it stronger insights into urban existence. Had she not fallen ill, she might have entered a heterosexual love relationship that could have somewhat shifted her focus from art as vocation. Finally, had she not returned to Milledgeville, she would have retained the physical distance from her mother. Flannery O'Connor had made a deliberate decision to leave Milledgeville and to return only for regular visits; illness, however, forced O'Connor to accept the realities of a circumscribed existence including a renewed personal—and permanent—relationship with both the town and her mother, Regina Cline O'Connor.

CHAPTER SEVEN

REGINA AND FLANNERY

After she had returned to Milledgeville early in 1951 and made a temporary recovery from lupus, O'Connor faced the pivotal adjustment of living again under the loving but dictatorial care of her mother, Regina Cline O'Connor. Since Mrs. O'Connor had exerted such major influence on her daughter's life during her early years, it is interesting to speculate about her response to Flannery's forced return. That she was much concerned about the seriousness of Flannery's illness goes without saying, but she also must have felt a sense of personal relief to have her talented but difficult daughter back under her protection and control. Regina Cline O'Connor may secretly have rejoiced in regaining a prominent role in her daughter's future.

Soon after her health stabilized, O'Connor and her mother left the Cline home on Greene Street and moved to a farm, Andalusia, then four miles from Milledgeville. Mrs. O'Connor's unmarried brothers Louis and Bernard Cline owned the place. The traditional reason given for the move has been that Mrs. O'Connor decided the farmhouse there was architecturally more suited to Flannery's needs than the Cline mansion with its many stairs and convoluted floor plan. Kitty Smith Kellam believes that they also moved to get away from Regina's much older sisters, Mary and Katie; isolation from these two individualistic women provided O'Connor the freedom to write as she wanted to write and to live as she wanted to live. Kellam also recalls that Katie, who was in a wheelchair during this period, occupied the only downstairs bedroom in the Greene Street house.

In a letter to the Fitzgeralds shortly after the move, O'Connor wrote of her mother's early enthusiasm for the farm: "She is nuts about it out here, surrounded by the lowing herd and other details, and considers it beneficial to my health" (*HB* 26). Mrs. O'Connor and Flannery lived together at Andalusia from 1951 until O'Connor's death in 1964. Their relationship was—on the surface, at least—strong, loving, and peaceful, despite considerable differences in their personalities, outlooks, and values. Clearly Regina Cline O'Connor was a shrewd women with a fully developed business sense. She was well ahead of her time in operating first a dairy farm and later raising beef cattle at Andalusia. After visiting the O'Connors at the farm in 1960, Richard Gilman wrote of his impressions of Regina Cline O'Connor: "The writer's mother [. . .] struck me as an amazingly competent woman, of a pioneer-like stamina and courage. Though she employs a Polish refugee family and several Negro laborers to run the place, it was clear that the reins of the complex operation were in her hands" (*Con* 49).

Without directly asserting her mother's pioneering role as a female farmer, O'Connor, in the letters of *The Habit of Being,* often mentioned Regina's brave assumption of male roles; for example, writing to Betty Hester in October 1956, O'Connor told of accompanying her mother to a cattle auction: "Yesterday, Regina [. . .] and I went to a cattle auction down near Dublin. R. is an old hand at cattle auctions but it was my first. [. . .] The cows went cheap and Regina bought ten. She's usually the only lady present at these things and gets treated in highstyle by the auctioneer" (*HB* 177). Numerous other references in the letters show how dedicated and innovative a farm manager Mrs. O'Connor was. Despite her physical limitations as a woman and her status as a member of Milledgeville's "social elite," Regina actually worked with her employees; in a letter to William Sessions in May 1963, O'Connor wrote, "My mama did appreciate the card and directs me to tell you so. She is in the field, haying. She has recently been bit by two wasps and caught her hand in the car door but is still in command" (521).

Because of her leadership skills, Mrs. O'Connor also dealt effectively with farm help—black, white, or foreign. To her many correspondents, O'Connor detailed the various difficulties her mother faced in handling the constant flow of itinerant white laborers; shortly after their move to Andalusia, O'Connor wrote to the Fitzgeralds of the arrival of a new hand and his family: "My mama has never read *Tobacco Road* but she thinks it's moved in. I don't know how long they will be with us but I am enjoying it while it lasts, and I aim to give my gret reading audiance a shot of some of the details sometime. Every time Regina brings in some new information, our educ. is broadened considerably" (*HB* 41). Several years later, in March 1957, O'Connor told Betty Hester of the arrival of a new farm worker, describing him as "doing fine. He is the kind who isn't happy unless he is working, and as my mother is the kind who isn't happy unless he is working, they get along just fine" (211). By August of the same year, however, Regina had to dismiss this man because he "was selling the milk out of the cans between here and Eatonton and proving himself in general more trouble than the cows" (232).

This continuing parade of white farm workers and their families functioned at two levels in Flannery O'Connor's life at Andalusia. On the personal level, their various antics provided her with considerable entertainment, as anecdotes in letters to her friends clearly show. In one of the most interesting, a letter to Frances and Brainard Cheney, she described the marriage of their dairyman's daughter and the reception Regina held for her at Andalusia: "We have survived high ceremonies here. The Stevens' (dairyman's) daughter, age 16, 9th grade, got married and my mother let them have the reception here. It was quite a wedding with the bridesmaids in six flavors, children with dripping candles, and a cadaverous preacher in white pants, blue coat, and black and yellow striped tie. My mother always prepares for the wrong accident—she was expecting a hole to be burned in her tablecloth. But somebody set a wet punch cup on her Bible" (*CC* 16–17).

On the level of her art, these farm families provided O'Connor models for parallel figures in her fiction. Mrs. Freeman and her daughters Glynese and Carramae in "Good Country People," the Shortleys in "The Displaced Person," and the Greenleafs are composite evocations of real employees at Andalusia. Because O'Connor observed her mother's farm workers so closely, with so much interest in the details of their personalities, characters, and lives, she was able to re-create them with both humor and her sympathy.

The permanent employees at Andalusia, however, were the African Americans with whom Regina Cline O'Connor struggled through the years. Her treatment of them shows how deeply she remained entrenched in the paternalistic racial attitudes of the nineteenth century. She saw blacks as innately inferior, always in need of direct supervision. Her comments on them as related in her daughter's letters reveal supremacist attitudes; for example, in a 1953 letter to the Fitzgerald's, O'Connor quoted her mother as asserting that blacks "are smart as tacks when it comes to looking out for No. 1" (*HB* 65), a statement revealing Regina's distrust of the race. In a letter to the Robert Lowells a year later, O'Connor reported her mother's assertion that "every nigger she knows has a better-looking car than she does" (65), a comment that shows her jealousy of the material progress of the blacks around her. O'Connor included one of Regina's most startling comments concerning speech and race in a letter to Betty Hester in 1956: "My mother says, 'You talk just like a nigger and someday you are going away from home and do it and people are going to wonder WHERE YOU CAME FROM'" (148). Regina O'Connor was announcing that she would consider her daughter's being identified as a member of the black race an ultimate indignity.

Despite such unsettling comments, Regina Cline O'Connor also cared for and loved the blacks who worked for her at Andalusia. O'Connor frequently mentioned Louise and her husband Shot, both of whom lived and worked at Andalusia during all the years Flannery spent there. Louise was cook and housekeeper and Shot a general farm worker. O'Connor told many "amusing" stories about them, often centering on their behavior under the influence of alcohol; still, both O'Connor and her mother accepted the couple as permanent members of the Andalusia establishment. Regina took Shot to the dentist, taught him to drive, and helped him pass the examination for his license. When an elderly dependent of the couple died on the farm, Regina made arrangements for his funeral and burial. When Louise and Shot got drunk and fought, Regina acted as mediator and Flannery as entertained observer. More dramatically, when Shot had a potentially fatal accident with the hay baler, Mrs. O'Connor rescued him: "It was some time before he could be got out and he is pretty badly damaged but lucky to be alive. It didn't break any of his bones, but tore out some big gaps of flesh and gave him several third-degree belt burns. Regina and Lon Cheney, who was here at the time, stayed with him until the mechanic could come to get him out of the machine and the doctor could come. Then they took him to the hospital in her car and the doctor says he will be there for some time" (*HB* 442).

Overall, Regina O'Connor's attitude toward her workers was not too unlike that of benevolent but supercilious slaveholders in the antebellum South. She consistently remarked on their intellectual, social, and moral inferiority; at the same time she depended on them for the work they performed at Andalusia, and she was intimately concerned about their well-being as O'Connor's narrative above proves.

Flannery O'Connor herself was a white Southerner only a generation removed from her mother's rather unsavory attitude toward blacks, yet as Ralph Wood has suggested, when she left Milledgeville in 1945, she had already begun to develop a more liberal outlook on race (Wood 98). Although, as an adult writer, she asserted her inability to get inside the heads of black characters, at Iowa she was quite interested in creating them. She peopled two of her early stories, "Wildcat" and "The Coat," with only black characters—and handled them with sympathy. Other members of the Iowa Writers' Workshop recall these stories, some with approval; Herbert Nipson remembers her unassuming reaction to having been praised for her realistic creation of a black character.

After her forced return to the South, however, O'Connor, like any resident of the Deep South in the 1950s, had to experience the constant racial tension that developed in the aftermath of the 1954 *Brown* vs. *Board of Education* decision. She found the issue of Civil Rights infinitely fascinating as revealed in her seven-year dialogue on the subject with Maryat Lee. A number of readers of their correspondence—most arrestingly, Ralph Wood—have interpreted this intriguing debate as clear evidence of O'Connor's racism (Wood 90). If the exchanges, in which Maryat seems to emerge as the racial liberal and Flannery as the racist reactionary, are read too literally, the charge seems valid; however, a closer reading of the correspondence reveals that the racial content of many of O'Connor's letters to Lee must be read with caution.

Maryat Lee, herself, in her 1976 memoir of O'Connor described their racial dialogue, which actually began in their first exchange of letters: "The racial anomaly was to be a constant motif in her letters, and it is worth noting the difference in tone that took place between the first and second of her letters, because it was here that Flannery permanently became devil's advocate with me in matters of race, as I was to do with her in matters of religion. Underneath the often ugly caricatures of herself in which she slid in and out of the role of red-neck, I could only believe that she shared with me the sense of frustration and betrayal and impotency over the dilemma of the white South" (M. Lee, "O'Connor, 1957" 45). Lee's reference in the first sentence above was to the content of O'Connor's first letter to Maryat in which they discussed Maryat's having arranged to ride to the Atlanta airport with Emmett Jones, who worked as a gardener at the Old Governor's Mansion, where her brother, GSCW president, lived. In that letter, O'Connor seemed to distance herself clearly from the town's negative view of Maryat's liberalism concerning race:

> A few days after you left, my mother and I saw E. [Emmett Jones] rolling down the street. [. . .] When you left, my mother said to me, "Don't tell a soul that she is going in E.'s car. Don't you even tell Sister. If that got out, it would ruin Dr. Lee." [. . .]
>
> It is often so funny that you forget it is so terrible. Once about ten years ago while Dr. Wells was president, there was an education meeting held here at which two Negro teachers or superintendents or something attended. The story goes that everything was as separate and equal as possible, even down to two Coca-Cola machines, white and colored; but that night a cross was burned on Dr. Wells' side lawn. And those times weren't as troubled as these. The people who burned the cross couldn't have gone past the fourth grade but, for the time, they were mighty interested in education. (*HB* 194–95)

O'Connor's story of the disturbance at GSCW, shows that her sympathies lay with the voice of reason. Both the separate but equal Coca-Cola machines and the cross burning were, in her word, "terrible."

As the Civil Rights movement gained momentum, however, and Maryat Lee became personally involved in it, O'Connor enjoyed portraying herself as a racial conservative against Lee as Civil Rights activist. Throughout their correspondence, O'Connor chided Lee for her racial liberalism, ridiculing her participation in Civil Rights events. What seemed to be one of her most damning comments to Lee, however, came late in their correspondence on

3 May 1964. Maryat had apparently written to Flannery suggesting that she write a letter to a local newspaper favoring the integration of Milledgeville schools. O'Connor replied that, because she lived in Milledgeville, writing such a letter would be utterly impossible. Even if she wrote the letter, she claimed her opinion would carry no weight. She also clearly stated her position on race, calling herself publicly in favor of integration but privately favoring segregation. Finally, she declared her strong dislike of current Civil Rights activists.[1] Maryat must have reacted to the above letter by asking O'Connor to explain her generalizations, for in a letter to Lee on 21 May 1964, O'Connor elaborated her position:

> About the Negroes, the kind I don't like is the philosophizing, prophesying, pontificating kind, the James Baldwin kind. Very ignorant but never silent. Baldwin can tell us what it feels like to be a Negro in Harlem but he tries to tell us everything else too.
>
> [Martin Luther] King I don't think is the age's great saint but at least doing what he can do & has to do. Don't know anything about Ossie Davis except you like him but you probably like them all. My question is usually would this person be endurable if white. If Baldwin were white nobody could stand him a minute. I prefer Cassius Clay. [. . .] Cassius is too good for the Moslems. (*HB* 580)[2]

To our own era, O'Connor's comments and rather obvious role-playing do not seem amusing, but it is certain from the content of their letters that Maryat and Flannery amused each other with their stereotypical positions, neither of which should be taken with absolute seriousness.

Besides examining her dialogue with Lee, however, any seeker of biographical truth about Flannery O'Connor's position on race must consider it from both private and public perspectives. First, because her bad health forced it, she lived in Milledgeville, Georgia, with a mother whose attitudes about race were little advanced from those of her nineteenth-century forebears. Certainly, in her own racial outlook, O'Connor was, to a considerable extent, her mother's daughter. As long as she lived in the town, she felt that she had to remain true to the mores of Milledgeville. The best evidence of her attitude here occurs in her unwillingness to entertain James Baldwin in Milledgeville. When Maryat Lee, acting as a go-between, asked O'Connor to meet Baldwin at Andalusia, O'Connor replied: "No I can't see James Baldwin in Georgia. It would cause the greatest trouble and disturbance and disunion. In New York it would be nice to meet him; here it would not. I observe the traditions of the society I feed on—it's only fair. Might as well expect a mule to fly as me to see James Baldwin in Georgia. I have read one of his stories and it was a good one" (*HB* 329). O'Connor's most intriguing sentence in this letter is the third one in which she specifically admitted her artistic dependence on the town; the sentence implies more than coexistence. When she admitted that she "feeds" on the traditions of Milledgeville society, she was acknowledging the source of the subject matter of her fiction. Since she had to live in Milledgeville and draw her art from her surroundings, she could not, quite literally, "bite the hand that fed her."

Ralph Wood, a theologian by training and profession, has had some difficulty balancing O'Connor's often abrupt comments about blacks with her intense spiritual faith; he seems to forget that O'Connor, besides being devoutly religious and almost obsessively committed to her artistry, was also a human being whose sense of humor embraced all of her day-to-day concerns. She ridiculed her mother for *her* obsessive attention to managerial details; she ridiculed herself for her clumsiness, her lack of social graces; she ridiculed Maryat Lee for her deliberately outlandish behavior and style; she ridiculed the town of Milledgeville for its too scrupulous attitude toward segregation of the races; and she ridiculed the blacks at Andalusia for their moral lapses—particularly their excessive consumption of alcohol that often resulted in violence. All features of her surroundings were fair game for O'Connor's barbed wit.

O'Connor's public pronouncements on the race issue and her treatment of both black characters and themes in her fiction present a much more liberal and intellectual view than her facetiously rendered private comments, which have to be taken for what they are—attempts to entertain her correspondents or to pique their outraged reactions, as was certainly true in her dialogue with Maryat Lee. Her treatment of black characters and themes in her fiction is balanced. If certain of her characters, like Ruby Turpin in "Revelation," spout racist garbage, they do so because they are realistic representatives of the Deep South mentality that O'Connor so carefully depicted.

O'Connor's most sympathetic treatment of a black character occurs in "The Geranium," one of the stories that comprised her M.F.A. thesis at Iowa.

Ralph Wood termed this story, in which the elderly, displaced white character, Dudley, holds a stereotypically racist attitude and the black character a
sympathetic and open outlook, the "work of a young racial liberal" (Wood 99).
When she rewrote "The Geranium" as "Judgment Day" for inclusion in
Everything That Rises Must Converge, she made a major change in her Northern black character, whom she now draws as an angry Civil Rights activist,
one who refuses to be patronized by the racist Southerner, renamed Tanner.
Angry at Tanner's refusal to see him as a human being, the black man reacts
inhumanely, virtually—if not literally—killing Tanner by putting him in the
"stocks" of the stairway's banisters. In "Judgment Day," O'Connor asserts
that anger and violence are no antidote to white racial prejudice.

When black characters inhabit O'Connor's other mature stories, they
appear in somewhat stereotypical roles like that of the delivery "boy" in "Revelation," or the farm workers, Astor and Sulk, being "displaced" by Guizac
in "The Displaced Person." Only in "Everything That Rises Must Converge"
and the "The Geranium" does race occupy a central position. O'Connor
admittedly wrote "Everything That Rises Must Converge" as her fictionalized contribution to Civil Rights literature, albeit unwillingly. In the spring
of 1961, as she was writing the story, she told several of her correspondents—
Maryat Lee, Roslyn Barnes, and Brainard Cheney—that she was using
Teilhard's "proposition" to "comment on a certain topical issue in these
parts" (*HB* 436). She wrote Fr. James McCown that she would "like to write
a whole bunch of stories like this, but once you've said it, you've said it, and
that [the story] about expresses what I have to say on That Issue" (468).

Her most revealing comments on "Everything That Rises Must Converge," however, came in a letter to Betty Hester in September 1963 when she
was reacting to Eudora Welty's Civil Rights story, "Where Is That Voice
Coming From?" She felt that Welty's story, based on the assassination of
Medgar Evers and published in the *New Yorker,* would promote a negative
view of the South, leaving "all the stupid Yankee liberals smacking their lips
over typical life in the dear old dirty Southland. The topical is poison. I got
away with it in 'Everything That Rises Must Converge' but only because I
say a plague on everybody's house as far as the race business goes" (*HB* 537).
O'Connor's comments are important both for what they reveal about her
intentions in "Everything That Rises Must Converge" and about her public
positions regarding race. In relation to the story, she clearly asserted what

most readers find in it: that both wearers of "the Hat" are equally culpable in their attitudes. Julian's mother remains so immersed in the past that when she is dying, she calls for the long dead black servant of her childhood. Before that final moment, however, she expresses intense anger about the changes in the world around her, asserting that the "bottom rail is on the top" and "They should rise, yes, but on their own side of the fence" (*CW* 487–88). Her patronizing attitude toward the black child on the bus displays her nineteenth-century sensibility, not O'Connor's. On the other hand, O'Connor finds the uncontrollable rage of the black woman equally objectionable. The sort of anger she displays toward Julian's mother's patronizing kindness can only damage the already fragile racial balance in the South; she is guilty of a breach of manners. Finally, O'Connor also finds Julian's pseudo-liberalism offensive, for his real sympathies lie clearly with those of his mother, a reality he is unwilling to admit. Hence, as O'Connor asserts, a plague on both houses, both races for their inability to compromise and see each other as human.

In the early 1960s, when O'Connor was most active as a lecturer and reader of her stories, she occasionally faced questions from reporters and interviewers who were eager to solicit her opinions on the race issue. Their constant questioning so disturbed O'Connor that, in letters she wrote to Maryat Lee in 1963, certain comments, if taken out of context, again damn her as a blatant racist. After having visited Washington to lecture and read at Georgetown, she angrily reacted to the constant questions of reporters. Feeling inept and cornered, she wrote to Lee that she could hardly keep from telling them that her "solution" to the race problem was to deport all blacks to Africa. O'Connor's statement seems both hateful and hurtful, but the comment clearly evolved from her frustration with being labeled an expert in an area in which she claimed little or no expertise. Since she seldom suffered fools gladly, the strident voices of reporters clearly irritated her.

O'Connor's most public and seriously articulated comments on the problems of race in the South occur in two pivotal interviews O'Connor granted in 1963. Though she seemed reticent about expressing her opinions, she obviously advocated a moderate but optimistic attitude toward integration. When Gerard E. Sherry (in the spring of 1963) asked her what "integration is doing to the culture of your native South," she replied: "I don't think it's doing anything to it. White people and colored people are used to milling around together in the South, and this integration only means that they are going to be milling around together in a few more places. No basic attitudes are being changed. Industrialism is what changed the culture of the South, not integration" (*Con* 102). Sherry also asked her about the role of Southern manners in dealing with racial turmoil; she replied that "[m]anners are the next best thing to Christian charity," and "I have confidence that the manners of both races will show through in the long run" (102). In the second interview (June 1963), O'Connor further elaborated the role of manners in achieving racial harmony:

> It requires considerable grace for two races to live together, particularly when the population is divided about fifty-fifty between them and when they have our particular history. It can't be done without a code of manners based on mutual charity. [. . . and] when the charity fails—as it is going to do constantly—you've got those manners there to preserve each race from small intrusions upon the other. The uneducated Southern Negro is not the clown he's made out to be. He's a man of very elaborate manners and great formality which he uses superbly for his own protection and to insure his own privacy. All this may not be ideal, but the Southerner has enough sense not to ask for the ideal but only for the possible, the workable. (103–4)

Overall, O'Connor's attitude toward the racial problems of the late 1950s and early 1960s clearly reflected those of other intelligent Southerners of the era. She was uncertain about its immediacy, but she knew that integration was inevitable and that with mutual charity and forbearance it could occur without violent repercussion.

Besides the blacks at Andalusia, Regina brought one other group of farm workers to Andalusia—the Polish refugee family, the Matisiacks, who came to Andalusia in 1952. In a letter to the Fitzgeralds just before Christmas 1951, O'Connor described her mother's preparations for their arrival. Regina was refurbishing and furnishing a house for the family who would arrive on Christmas night. She and her dairyman's wife were making curtains for the house "out of flowered chicken-feed sacks" and worrying about the colors not matching: "Mrs. P. (who has no teeth on one side of her mouth) says in a very superior voice "'Do you think they'll know what colors even is?'"

(*HB* 30). Early in 1952, the refugees had not yet reached Andalusia, but Regina remained concerned about their welfare and had been encouraging Flannery to teach them English: "I say well I ain't able to and she says well *she* could if she wanted to and I say how and she says CAT: C—A—T. And you draw a picture of one. I don't doubt but what she could do it" (31).

Regina's recruitment of the Matisiacks provided the obvious background subject matter for O'Connor's short story "The Displaced Person," which also features an energetic farm owner, Mrs. McIntyre, who, under the aegis of the Roman Catholic Church, brings the Guizacs to her farm. The outcome for the fictional Guizacs, however, was far different from that of the Matisiacks, whose descendants still live in Milledgeville. Through the Guizacs, O'Connor ponders the then topical issue of human responsibility in the wake of the Holocaust. At the same time, she uses the family to show the results of cultural displacement, for they enter a Southern culture that Mr. Guizac is certainly not able to understand. His plan to bring a cousin to Georgia to marry the black farmhand Sulk shows his complete ignorance of the society he has entered. Finally, O'Connor uses the Guizacs to condemn Mrs. McIntyre's boundless greed and utter secularity. Her motives for bringing them to her farm are entirely selfish—they will enable her to make even more money. Mrs. McIntyre's limited perspective will not allow her to consider the negative results of her decision. Regina Cline O'Connor, quite unlike Mrs. McIntyre, thrived at Andalusia, developing considerable talent as farm manager, cattle grower, and personnel director. Because of her business acumen, she raised herself above her position as a member of polite Milledgeville society. She evolved as a business woman, capable of caring for and supervising her ailing daughter, handling white farm hands, black employees, and "displaced persons" while "making a living" and developing autonomy as an independent human being.

Though she disliked being called a farmer, Flannery O'Connor, at Andalusia, clearly participated in her mother's activities with admiring vicariousness. In 1955, when she went to New York City to appear with Harvey Breit on his television show *Gallery Proof,* he asked her in an interview whether she worked on the farm. Her terse reply—"No, I'm a writer"— clearly shows how she separated herself from either farm work or farm management (*Con* 11). The first sentence in an article Betsy Lochridge wrote for the *Atlanta Journal-Constitution* also illustrates O'Connor's desire to separate herself from farm life: "'Don't make me out a farm girl. All I know about the land is, it's underneath me'" (37). O'Connor, however, was not wholly immune to the allure of the farm setting. As she wrote in "King of the Birds," first published in *Holiday* magazine in September 1961, moving to Andalusia enabled her to pursue her fascination with exotic fowl, which she had developed years earlier during her Savannah girlhood. O'Connor's interest in raising unusual poultry shows both her own agrarian bent and her desire to witness the births and growth of surrogate offspring. She also used her peacocks to create a telling symbol for spiritual transcendence.

By September of 1951, she was writing to the Fitzgeralds about her twenty-one brown ducks, her five geese, and her fifteen turkeys that "all have sorehead and the cure for that is liquid black shoe polish—so we have about fifteen turkeys running around in blackface. They look like domesticated vultures" (*HB* 28). By May of 1952, she had added pheasants to her flock, writing to Robert Lowell that "[t]he pheasant cock has horns and looks like some of those devilish people and dogs in Rousseau's paintings" (35). One of the pheasants appears in the striking self-portrait O'Connor painted in the mid-1950s. In late summer of 1952, she turned to peacocks:

> My quest, whatever it was actually for, ended with peacocks. Instinct, not knowledge, led me to them. I had never seen or heard one. Although I had a pen of pheasants and a pen of quail, a flock of turkeys, seventeen geese, a tribe of mallard ducks, three Japanese silky bantams, two Polish Crested ones, and several chickens of a cross between these last and the Rhode Island Red, I felt a lack. I knew that the peacock had been the bird of Hera, the wife of Zeus, but since that time it had probably come down in the world—the Florida *Market Bulletin* advertised three-year-old peafowl at sixty-five dollars a pair. I had been quietly reading these ads for some years when one day, seized, I circled an ad in the *Bulletin* and passed it to my mother. The ad was for a peacock and hen with four seven-week-old peabiddies. "I'm going to order me those," I said.
>
> My mother read the ad, "Don't those things eat flowers?" she asked.
>
> "They'll eat Startena like the rest of them," I said. (*MM* 4–5)

Through the rest of her life, O'Connor increased both the size of her flock and her knowledge of peacocks. She wrote to the Lowells in March 1953 that she sat "on the back steps a good deal studying them. I am going to be the World Authority on Peafowl, and hope to be offered a chair some day at the Chicken College" (*HB* 57).[3] By July 1955, with a total of sixteen peachickens, she wrote to Catherine Carver that she hoped by the next year "to have them all over the place, hope to be stepping on them" (91). By the time she wrote her article for *Holiday*, she admitted that she had "forty beaks to feed" (*MM* 7). Benjamin Griffith, who visited O'Connor at Andalusia several times during the 1950s and early 1960s remembered her affinity for her exotic fowl: "All the visits ended with a stroll among her peacocks, black swans and other fowl. Her Muscovy ducks who waddled in single file, were called Merrill, Lynch, Pierce, Fenner and Bean. One of the Chinese geese was named Clair Booth Luce Goose. Once when 15 turkeys, bizarre in blackface—appeared, she explained they were treated for 'sorehead' with a liquid shoepolish, making them look like 'domesticated vultures'" (Griffith, "Ten Years" M4).

In the *Holiday* article O'Connor wrote of the cosmic appeal the peacock exerts on those able to appreciate its splendor, its astounding good looks, and its piercing call, which a good many visitors to Andalusia remember. Pat Persse, for example, describes the shrieks that kept her awake during a visit she made to Milledgeville in the 1950s: "The peacocks were squawking like mad—you couldn't see them, but you could surely hear them in the trees, making all this noise." To avoid any charge of sentimentality regarding her attitude toward her peafowl, O'Connor, in the *Holiday* article, follows her own advice about the use of exact sensory detail, giving both positive and negative features of her birds. That the O'Connors were not unduly sentimental about their poultry is also evident in their using some of them for food. Mary Barbara Tate recalls this seeming contradiction, and O'Connor herself wrote of a particular goose that ended up in their Deepfreeze: "My Canada goose got so mean we had to wring his neck and he is now in the deepfreeze waiting on us to have the proper company to serve him. He nearly broke my wrist and I said: This rascal has bit me for the last time" (*HB* 184). Regina did, indeed, cook the goose and they ate it on Thanksgiving Day in 1957.

In spite of her ability to eat her own goose, O'Connor certainly placed transcendent, even theological, value on her peacocks. In her *Holiday* essay, she described a peacock's spread tail as a "galaxy of gazing, haloed suns" and the "unfurled map of the universe" (*MM* 10). She admitted, however, that not all people are susceptible to the meaning of this spectacular beauty; the telephone repairman, so eager to have the peacock spread its tail, sees not the universe in its display but only its "'long ugly legs'"; on the other end of the spectrum are the responses of the old black woman who cried "'Amen! Amen!'" when she witnessed an unfurling, and the wonder of an old countryman, at Andalusia to buy a calf, who tells his children: "Churren, that's the king of the birds!" (*MM* 12–13). This speaker clearly serves as O'Connor's surrogate; the peacock as an exotic example of God's gifts became an important symbol in her work, particularly in her short story "The Displaced Person."

In this story—one of her finest—O'Connor uses Mrs. McIntyre's three remaining peacocks as symbols for the spiritual dimension of existence, which Mrs. McIntyre has lost altogether. Hers is a world of control, of pride in material accomplishment, and a hubristic secular belief in social rigidity. Her utter disdain for any meaning in life beyond the routine of work and control impels her to disregard both the Roman Catholicism the priest offers and the peacocks he correctly identifies as emblems of God's grace. O'Connor begins "The Displaced Person" with a description of the peacock following Mrs. Shortley, the farm hand's wife, who is also uncomprehendingly secular: "Moving one behind the other, they looked like a complete procession." Mrs. Shortley ignores the "white afternoon sun which was creeping behind a ragged wall of cloud as if it pretended to be an intruder and cast her gaze down the red clay road that turned off the highway." The peacock, on the other hand holds it head "drawn back as if his attention were fixed in the distance on something no one else could see" (*CW* 285). Immediately, then, O'Connor establishes a contrast between the utterly physical and repulsive Mrs. Shortley and the transcendently beautiful peacock.

When Father Flynn arrives at the farm with the Guizacs, O'Connor uses a conversation between him and Mrs. McIntyre to illustrate the essential secular/spiritual contrast between them:

> "What a beauti-ful birdrrrd!" the priest murmured.
>
> "Another mouth to feed," Mrs. McIntyre said, glancing in the peafowl's direction.
>
> "And when does he raise his splendid tail?" asked the priest.

"Just when it suits him," she said. "There used to be twenty or thirty of those things on the place but I've let them die off. I don't like to hear them scream in the middle of the night."

"So beauti-ful," the priest said. "A tail full of suns," and he crept forward on tiptoe and looked down on the bird's back where the polished gold and green design began. The peacock stood still as if he had just come down from some sun-drenched height to be a vision for them all. The priest's homely red face hung over him, glowing with pleasure. (*CW* 289)

In a still later conversation between the priest and Mrs. McIntyre, O'Connor reiterates both how clearly the priest understands the peacock's symbolic meaning and how utterly oblivious Mrs. McIntyre is to it. During the episode when Mrs. McIntyre tries, unsuccessfully, to explain to the priest why she must get rid of the Guizacs, he remains concerned with the beauty of the peacocks:

The priest stood transfixed, his jaw slack. Mrs. McIntyre wondered where she had ever seen such an idiotic old man. "Christ will come like that!" he said in a loud gay voice and wiped his hand over his mouth and stood there, gaping.

Mrs. McIntyre's face assumed a set puritanical expression and she reddened. Christ in the conversation embarrassed her the way sex had her mother. (*CW* 317)

The old priest, still caught in this moment of spiritual insight, murmurs "The Transfiguration," as the peacock spreads it tail, but Mrs. McIntyre has "no idea of what he was talking about"; the bird cannot work its magic on those like Mrs. McIntyre, who are too secular to accept its message. Though Regina O'Connor, like Mrs. McIntyre, may have felt that the upkeep of the peacocks was a nuisance when the flock reached thirty and beyond, she allowed them to live on at Andalusia long after O'Connor's death. In late 1966, she wrote to Alta Haynes about the pleasure she still felt in keeping her daughter's much-loved collection of fowl.[4]

Mrs. MycIntyre's interest in money, however, surely reflects that of Regina Cline O'Connor, who, throughout her life, put great emphasis on financial security. She possessed a keen business sense, a bottom-line mentality. Though she came from a family with local prestige and considerable financial success, she was one of many children; thus, she apparently felt that her early inheritance from her father was not sufficient to allow her to live securely. Her spartan years in Savannah with Edward O'Connor also contributed to Mrs. O'Connor's obsession with money. She apparently found those early years in Savannah, when she was financially dependent on her wealthy cousin, Kate Flannery Semmes, hard to forget. Regina O'Connor saw little value in any activity—her daughter's writing included—that did not bring in money. O'Connor's most succinct statement concerning her mother's mercenary sensibility occurred in a letter she wrote to the Fitzgeralds in 1952 just after she had received a Kenyon Fellowship: "My mamma is getting a big bang out of notifying all the kin who didn't like the book [*Wise Blood*] [. . . about] the Rockerfeller Foundation. [. . .] Money talks, she says, and the name of Rockerfeller don't hurt a bit" (*HB* 49).

O'Connor's acquaintances also recalled her mother's materialistic interests and attitudes. Helen Greene remembers Regina's "genuine understanding of economic problems and the ability and spirit to tackle them" (Greene, "Mary Flannery O'Connor" 48). Another member of the GSCW faculty, the late Rosa Lee Walston, became O'Connor's friend after her forced return to Milledgeville. Through the years, she also came to know Regina Cline O'Connor well. Her strongest impression of Mrs. O'Connor was that she, like the rest of her family, "was oriented toward making money." Walston once asked Regina why Flannery chose writing over cartooning: "Regina said, 'Well, of course, she knew she had to make a living.' Now, that's ridiculous because [. . .] Regina was a millionaire and Flannery was an only child. She certainly did not have to make a living."[5] O'Connor's Persse cousins in Savannah, however, do not believe that Regina was as wealthy as Walston assumed; in fact, they assert that O'Connor's income was essential to the survival of the family. Certainly, Regina O'Connor thought her daughter needed to contribute to the financial upkeep of the household, an idea clearly substantiated by Richard Gilman, who visited the O'Connor's at Andalusia after the publication of *The Violent Bear It Away*:

> One evening at dinner she [Regina] said to me, while Flannery stared at her food in embarrassment, "Now I want you to tell me what's wrong with those publishers up there in New York. Do you know how many copies of Mary Flannery's

novel have been sold? Three thousand two hundred and seventy eight, that's how many copies of Mary Flannery's novel have been sold, and there is something very wrong with that, they are not doing right by her." I said that Farrar, Straus was a fine publisher and that *The Violent Bear It Away* wasn't the kind of novel likely to have a big sale. And then I added that Flannery's reputation was more and more secure and that was the important thing. "Important thing!" she snorted, "reputations don't buy groceries." (*Con* 56–57)

Walston also recalled another social-literary occasion when she found Regina O'Connor's excessive interest in money embarrassing. The historian Allen Nevins had come to GSCW and when he asked to meet Flannery O'Connor, Walston arranged for him to have dinner at Andalusia: "Regina happened to get seated next to him. Flannery was [not able to talk with him] until I effected a change in the seating arrangement. [. . .] Regina was talking [to him] about the price of cattle!"

Having lived in Milledgeville until the late 1980s, Walston was able to record Regina's continued obsession with money long after Flannery died. She suggested that the reason Regina let the Cline mansion decline so dramatically during her last years was the expense of having it refurbished. At Regina's death in May 1995, the house, because of her thriftiness, was in a deplorable condition; yet, she could still, on the occasion of the 1994 "The Habit of Art" conference, hire Pinkerton guards to surround the mansion in order to ensure her privacy.

In her short stories, O'Connor makes certain use of her mother's obsession with financial success. Ann E. Reuman goes so far as to assert that the negative businesswomen of O'Connor's stories demonstrate O'Connor's revenge against her mother's mercenary nature. Alluding to Kafka's hostile letter to his father, Reuman says that the negative fictional protagonists of O'Connor's farm stories clearly target Regina Cline O'Connor as an evil villainess who crippled her daughter's existence: "Bottled up by Southern codes of silence and Catholic respect for elders and aggravated by dependence on her mother without hope of change in her status, O'Connor's adolescent resentment carried into adulthood, building in intensity and exploding into her fiction" (Reuman 202–3).

Given her intense spiritual belief and her obvious love for her mother in spite of her weaknesses, Flannery O'Connor would not have been likely to base (either consciously or subconsciously) the negative women of her stories—particularly Mrs. May of "Greenleaf," Mrs. McIntyre of "The Displaced Person," and Mrs. Hopewell of "Good Country People"—entirely on Regina O'Connor. Rather O'Connor picks and chooses among Regina's negative traits in order to create allegorical women whose destinies hinge on a single trait; for example, avarice and greed completely control both Mrs. May and Mrs. McIntyre. Money mattered to Regina Cline O'Connor but so did the Church, her community, and her daughter. Of particular interest is the contrast between Regina's obvious love and pride in Flannery and Mrs. May's inability to love either of her sons. Wesley is correct when he tells Scofield, "'You ain't her boy, Son'" (*CW* 517). To the end of her life, Regina O'Connor cherished her remarkable daughter. In a recent article, Sally Fitzgerald, who knew both O'Connor and her mother well, defended Regina O'Connor against critics like Reuman and, earlier, Caroline Gordon, who asserted that O'Connor deliberately targeted her mother in her stories: "Certainly there are recurring figures who have some of her mother's qualities, personality, and character, even her style. And not always the best of these. But exaggeration was an essential characteristic of this writer's art" (Fitzgerald, "The Invisible Father" 8).

Rather than utterly disdaining her mother's interest in money, Flannery O'Connor, in spite of her dedication to religion and writing, possessed a considerable interest in money herself. She inherited Regina's desire to make her own financial way in the world, as evidenced by her attempts to gain fellowships while at Iowa (and later in New York and Milledgeville) and her desire to stay on at Yaddo after her first summer there in 1948. Even though her fiction had critical approval, her stories and novels lacked the popular readership that might have made O'Connor wealthy; therefore, while she lived in Milledgeville with her mother, she tried to increase her rather meager income by selling at least one story to television, by giving paid lectures, and earning grants and prizes. When she sold "The Life You Save May Be Your Own" to CBS television in 1956, she told many of her friends that the sale enabled her to buy a state-of-the-art refrigerator for her mother.

As early as the summer of 1948, O'Connor was worried about the money she was not making by publishing her stories in academic journals rather than popular magazines. That summer, she also tried, unsuccessfully, to win a Guggenheim fellowship. When Elizabeth McKee sold the paperback rights to *Wise Blood* for $4,000 early in 1952, O'Connor fumed about getting her $2,000: "I never believe nothing until I get the money. However, they advanced me $500 against the guarantee of $4,000, but I still suspicion the whole thing, as my mama's dairyman's wife says" (*HB* 33).

That same year, when John Crowe Ransom suggested that she apply for a Kenyon Review Fellowship, O'Connor wrote Sally Fitzgerald that she had "applied before the envelope was opened good" (*HB* 46). When she was awarded the two-thousand-dollar fellowship and received it again the next year, she confided to the Fitzgeralds that she would use most of the money to pay medical bills and to buy books; however, after the renewal she considered investing some of the money in either the stock market or in "colored rental property" (66). In 1957, O'Connor did buy rental property: "a very cheap, yellow, four-room house on the way to the waterworks—this being the fruit of my savings from literary earnings over the last ten years. I feel I have took on stature being a property owner" (223). A year later she reported to Thomas Stritch that she was earning fifty-five dollars a month rent from the house. By this time, she had also inherited the house in Savannah, which was also providing her with rental income; however, she experienced problems with both properties, as she described in a letter to Maryat Lee in April 1959; the house in Savannah needed a new roof and she "had to buy a $129 hot-water heater for the other tenant [in the Milledgeville house] who, bless his heart, isn't but two months behind in his rent" (329–30).

O'Connor took a great deal of pride in the money she earned from two sales unrelated to the regular sale of her fiction. In 1957 she sold "The Life You Save May Be Your Own" to television. She wrote of her first reactions to the deal in a letter to Betty Hester in September 1956, revealing that the General Electric Playhouse was to dramatize the story; she facetiously wondered whether Ronald Reagan, who then introduced the dramatizations, would take on the role of Mr. Shiftlet, describing the possibility as "[a] staggering thought." She mentioned the refrigerator that she planned to buy for her mother: "While they make hash of my story, she and me will make ice in the new refrigerator" (*HB* 174). Later in her short life, O'Connor made another extra-literary sale when she sold *Holiday* magazine her personal essay on peacocks. She wrote Hester: "*Holiday* took the peacock bait.

$750—more than I have ever got for any piece of writing, by about half. Crime pays" (411).

Other prizes and awards contributed to O'Connor's personal income. In December 1954, she earned two hundred dollars as the second-prize winner in that year's O. Henry contest. Three years later she won first prize in the competition for "Greenleaf," earning "$300 untaxable dollars" (*HB* 182); in 1964 just before her death, she learned that "Revelation" had again taken first place in the 1964 O. Henry competition. In 1957, the National Institute of Arts and Letters awarded O'Connor a grant of $1,000; she reacted that "any honor sent through the mail and cashable is about the only kind I got any great respect for" (218). The largest amount of money O'Connor earned from fellowships was the Ford Foundation award in 1958: $8,000, which she told the Fitzgeralds she intended "to live on for ten years" (218). In March 1959, O'Connor again wrote to the Fitzgeralds concerning the award: "People are very respectful of me these days, thinking that $150,000 of Mr. Ford's money has been divided eleven ways. I even got an advertisement from an investment broker this morning" (323).

O'Connor also earned money from her lectures and readings; in 1956, she told Elizabeth Fenwick Way that the standard fee for lectures was only $50, "but as I now have 25 peachickens to support, I cannot scorn it. Scratch-feed is going up" (*HB* 181). When she traveled to Notre Dame in April 1957, she wrote Hester that "those Jesuits are paying me a hundred bucks and my plane fare" (207). She earned $350 at Vanderbilt in 1959 and $500, "the hard way," at Sweet Briar in 1963. Her extended lecture tour to Hollins, Notre Dame of Maryland, and Georgetown in the fall of 1963 earned her "enough money to float me through the next six or eight months" (543). By the fall of 1963, O'Connor was humorously lamenting her financial success:

> I am in terrible shape with the govermint. I made more money than usual one year on the Sisters' book and the next year I had to talk at a lot of places to pay my income tax, which made me make more money again so I had to talk at a lot of places which made me make more etc. etc. I'm as poor as they come and getting poorer and my income tax is getting higher every year and I think this must end somewhere short of the penitentiary or the poor house. (*HB* 540)

O'Connor, like her mother, then, was not averse to making money; however, the great difference between them was that Regina Cline O'Connor's interest was of major importance in her life. Though enjoying the financial fruits of her labors, O'Connor's attitude toward money was self-deprecating, as her above humorous statement about income tax shows. For her, money-making provided a comic diversion from the real focuses of her life.

Regina Cline O'Connor and her daughter also held contrasting attitudes toward social obligations and conversation. Nearly everybody who visited O'Connor at Andalusia remembers Regina as loquacious and Flannery as taciturn. Because her mother was so talkative, Flannery must often have felt stifled in holding her own on these social occasions. In one of her first letters to Maryat Lee, O'Connor lamented her lack of privacy for open conversation: "[T]he parental presence never contributes to my articulateness, and I might have done better at answering some of your questions had I entertained you in the hen house. That's a place I would like to keep two cane-bottomed chair in if there were any way to keep the chickens from sitting on them in my absence. My ambition is to have a private office out there complete with a refrigerator" (*HB* 195). Other visitors to Andalusia also recall how Regina seemed to take charge of entertaining them in a social way. She did not seem to realize that many of them had come to see Flannery O'Connor, the writer, not Regina Cline O'Connor, the socialite and farmer.

Pat Persse remembers that when she visited Andalusia in the early 1960s, Regina's loquacity entertained her visitors through the evening. She says that Flannery "was funny when she said something, but the mother carried the evening. The mother dominated the conversation." Other guests at Andalusia also recall both Regina's social grace and her intrusiveness. People who were part of the book review group that formed around O'Connor in the late 1950s remember that Regina politely left the room when serious discussion started, appearing again only at the end of the evening to offer refreshments. Milledgeville friends of Regina describe her as a "charming" and "delightful" hostess who tried very hard to draw Mary Flannery into the social life of the town after her enforced returned to Milledgeville. Elizabeth Horne recalls the polite struggle between Regina and Flannery over their social activities in the early 1950s: "When she came back after she got lupus, [. . .] she wouldn't take any phone calls and that sort of thing and [Regina] finally understood that. In other words, in the beginning it was strange to her; being a typical

Southern lady, she would never think of refusing a phone call or visitors." Horne also remembers that a bit later, to monitor their visits, Regina gave Flannery's acquaintances the "rules" that Flannery observed in her workday. Another friend recalls that Flannery often used Regina to help her entertain social guests, but also that when Regina had visitors during her (Flannery's) working hours, Regina had to entertain them out of Flannery's hearing.

Granville Hicks, who visited the O'Connor's in the 1950s, later wrote of his impressions of their social life together: "Her mother, a woman of great energy, not only managed the plantation efficiently but also, as a member of one of Milledgeville's leading families, took her place in its social activities. Flannery not only mingled with her mother's friends but, to my surprise and amusement, talked to them as if she were any little old Southern girl" (Hicks 30). Other, more negative comments about Regina's presence in Flannery's social life occur in two statements by Fr. James McCown, who visited Andalusia frequently in the late 1950s. In his memoir of their friendship, published in *America* in 1979, he wrote: "I visited her [O'Connor] often. And always, Regina, her bright-eyed little mother [. . .] sat in dead center of every conversation and steered it insistently to such topics as the modification of the Communion fast, nuns doffing their habits, what did I think of priests running around in gray suits and so on and on. Occasionally, she would remember a pot on the stove and excuse herself for a moment, but the respite were not long" (McCown, "Remembering Flannery O'Connor" 86).

In a letter Father McCown wrote to Tom Gossett in 1973, when Regina had begun to become difficult in her dealings with scholars of O'Connor and her work, he recalled:

> About Mrs. O'Connor let me add my 2-cents' worth. As you say, she was really attractive in a folksy way. But when you wanted to visit Flannery she was a nuisance. She sat in on each conversation and invariably side-tracked it into something about the scandalous new things happening in the Church. She loved to talk, and she considered her subjects as engrossing and important as anything Flannery talked about. Yet, Flannery never showed the least impatience, or rolled her eyes in despair, or anything like that. Once she told me that although she had to use her mother and all the rest of her limited milieu for her

stories, her mother knew this and understood it, and that by and large, she was deeply grateful to her mother for her love and care through the years.

[. . .] I do remember [. . . once] that we [Father McCown and a friend] invited her out to dinner somewhere with us. [. . .] Mrs. O. immediately declined for Flannery before her daughter had a chance to decline for herself. An irritation to me, but Flannery seemed unperturbed.[6]

Two statements are of particular interest in this letter; one concerns Flannery O'Connor's obvious tolerance of her mother's social pushiness, her intrusiveness, and her takeover attitude. If McCown is to be believed—and he was, after all, a priest—little tension existed between the mother and daughter in their regular social milieu. McCown's assertion that Regina O'Connor was aware of her daughter's use of her immediate surroundings in her fiction is also important. O'Connor admitted what any astute reader knows: that her mother knew and accepted her role as a partial satirical target in the farm stories.

The O'Connor story that most clearly targets her mother's garrulousness is "Good Country People," in which Joy/Hulga's mother is a virtual encyclopedia of empty clichés. Being totally conventional, Mrs. Hopewell has no understanding of her daughter's intellectual genius. She prefers the sexually precocious daughters of her farm hand to her own daughter, who has earned a Ph.D. in philosophy. Ann Reuman interprets O'Connor's creation of Mrs. Hopewell as an obvious version of Regina Cline's insipidity and the author's reaction to it: "As 'Good Country People' and other stories written after 1951 suggest, O'Connor's sense of entrapment, impotence, and frustration in the face of her mother's willful blindness and infuriating dominance precipitated a fierce and boiling rage which precluded any chance of sustained and unconflicted love" (Reuman 214). Though Regina clearly shared some of Mrs. Hopewell's emptiness, her daughter again simply drew on *one* of her characteristics to produce her satirical portrait of Joy/Hulga's vacuous mother. Obviously the quality in Regina provided O'Connor with the idea for Mrs. Hopewell, but Regina Cline O'Connor was an authentic human being, who, more fully than Mrs. Hopewell, understood both her daughter and the world around them.

One final area of intense difference, however, between mother and daughter was in the quality of their intellects. Despite her creation of negative fictional intellectuals like Rayber in *The Violent Bear It Away,* Shepherd in "The Lame Shall Enter First," and Asbury Fox in "The Enduring Chill," Flannery O'Connor was herself an intellectual. Though, under the impetus of Caroline Gordon she often deprecated her incomplete education, O'Connor was a brilliant woman whose understanding of literature and theology was unequaled by that of most of her contemporaries. Though she grounded her stories in the sensory world, as she asserted that all successful writers of fiction must do, she was also so intellectually and spiritually aware that she daunted not only her workshop colleagues at Iowa but also correspondents like Elizabeth Bishop, who wrote to Robert Giroux that although O'Connor once invited her to visit at Andalusia, she did not accept the invitation because O'Connor's intellect frightened her (Bishop 630). O'Connor's many reviews in *The Bulletin* offer immediate proof (besides her fiction) of her powers of intellect, for she wrote astute criticism of books by some of the best minds of her era.

Regina Cline O'Connor, on the other hand, was a literate woman with outstanding business acumen, but she was neither particularly educated nor particularly intellectual. O'Connor's comments in *The Habit of Being* about her mother's attempts to read her work show how little she understood it. Regina tried to read *Wise Blood* in 1951, but O'Connor reports that "she went off with it and I found her a half hour later on page 9 and sound asleep" (*HB* 27). Years later in an interview with Margaret Shannon, Regina O'Connor revealed only limited knowledge of the novel: "I think she worked on it five years. I read that somewhere. But I do know she was a long time doing it. She never submitted anything until she was absolutely satisfied. That's the reason it took her so long, I reckon" (Shannon 8).

When nearly ready to publish *The Violent Bear It Away* in 1959, O'Connor described Regina's problems with the novel in a letter to Cecil Dawkins: "The current ordeal is that my mother is now in the process of reading it. She reads about two pages, gets up and goes to the back door for a conference with Shot, comes back, reads two more pages, gets up and goes to the barn. Yesterday she read a whole chapter. There are twelve chapters. All the time she is reading, I know she would like to be in the yard digging. I think the reason I am a short-story writer is so my mother can read my work in one sitting" (*HB* 340). Regina, however, had difficulty even with the short stories, as O'Connor tersely reported in a letter to Maryat Lee, who had written her to applaud "Everything That Rises Must Converge": "I'm cheered you like the converging one. I guess my mama liked it all right. My stories usually put her to sleep" (489). Realistically, the one piece of writing by O'Connor that received Regina's unqualified approval was the nonfictional introduction to Mary Ann: "[E]ven Regina likes it which means something" (419).

Though Regina was apparently incapable of reading her daughter's tersely constructed and difficult fiction with much enjoyment, she did read. Early, O'Connor described her taste in fiction to the Fitzgeralds, "She likes books with Frank Buck and a lot of wild animals" (*HB* 27). In many references in the letters of *The Habit of Being,* O'Connor mentioned other books that met with Regina's approval, including Elizabeth Fenwick Way's mystery novels. Regina also reacted favorably to an unpublished travelogue by Father James McGown: "Regina said to tell you it was her kind of literature—places and folks" (468).

Still, under the influence of her brilliant daughter, Regina became interested, theoretically at least, in the writers Flannery was reading, asking "Who is Kafka?" or "Who is this Evalin Wow?" (*HB* 33). Her questions were no doubt aimed more at *seeming* interested in her daughter's intellectual pursuits than exploring them herself. In a letter to the Fitzgeralds, O'Connor re-created a comic interchange between Regina and herself, a conversation that, as Loxley Nichols (20) has suggested, sounds almost like a stand-up comedy routine with Regina in the straight role:

> My mamma and I have interesting literary discussions like the following which took place over some Modern Library books that I had just ordered:
>
> SHE: "*Mobby Dick.* I've always heard about that."
> ME: "*Mow-by Dick.*"
> SHE: "*Mow-by Dick. The Idiot.* You would get something called Idiot. What's it about?"
> ME: "An idiot." (*HB* 55–56)

In another letter to the Fitzgeralds, O'Connor again showed her mother's lack of even basic literary knowledge when she told them that Regina had asked her whether she knew Shakespeare was Irish, after reading the error published as fact in the Savannah newspaper. O'Connor told her mother that the man who made the assertion was wrong: "I say well it's just him that says it, you better not go around saying it and she said listen she didn't care whether he was an Irishman or a Chinaman" (59).

The strongest evidence, however, of Regina's lack of understanding of O'Connor's fiction lies in an angry comment O'Connor included in a letter to Cecil Dawkins in April 1959 after Dawkins had sold a story to the *Saturday Evening Post;* she described how "impressed" Regina was with that acceptance and recounted a recent conversation between them: "The other day she asked me why I didn't try to write something that people liked instead of the kind of thing I do write. Do you think, she said, that you are really using the talent God gave you when you don't write something that a lot, a *lot*, of people like? This always leaves me shaking and speechless, raises my blood pressure 140 degrees, etc. All I can ever say is, if you have to ask, you'll never know" (*HB* 326). Robie Macauley also recalled O'Connor's frustration with her mother: "With me, Flannery tended to be a bit joking and sarcastic about her mother. But the idea that Regina was a tyrant—though a beloved one—also came through."

Regina's ignorance of her daughter's serious fictional intentions surely must have influenced O'Connor's creation of similar fictional mothers, even more ignorant than she of their children's intellectual precocity and talent. Mrs. Hopewell in "Good Country People" has no understanding of Joy/Hulga's education; she is able only to question the value of a Ph.D. in philosophy: "You could say, 'My daughter is a nurse,' or 'My daughter is a school teacher,' or even, 'My daughter in a chemical engineer.' You could not say, 'My daughter is a philosopher.' That was something that had ended with the Greeks and Romans" (*CW* 260). Mrs. Hopewell's confusion about Joy/Hulga's Ph.D. suggests that Regina O'Connor may have held the same outlook on her daughter's M.F.A. Even closer to Regina's lack of appreciation for her daughter's fiction is Mrs. Hopewell's inability to comprehend the books her daughter studies. When she reads the nihilistic passage from Malebranche, she is utterly stunned, closing the book quickly to get back to her "real world." Mrs. Hopewell, so clearly secular and earthbound, like so many of O'Connor's mothers, cannot conceive of the life of the mind and, rather than try, she ignores it. When Joy/Hulga shouts across the table at her mother,

"'Woman! do you ever look inside? Do you ever look inside and see what you are *not?*'" (268), O'Connor is partly dramatizing her own frustration with her mother's similar lack of understanding.

More related to Regina's impassioned argument for fiction that appeals to a wide audience is Asbury Fox's mother's attitude in "The Enduring Chill." This mother, too, seems to share qualities with Regina Cline O'Connor. She is a proud, forceful, and successful farmer who relishes her agrarian life. When illness forces her son, like Flannery, to seek refuge in a the sanctuary of the home that he despises, his mother urges him to write in the popular vein: "'When you get well,' she said, 'I think it would be nice if you wrote a book about down here. We need another good book like *Gone with the Wind*'" (*CW* 560). Mrs. Fox's words allow O'Connor a dual surrogate pleasure. She is pillorying her mother for similar suggestions at the same time that she is undercutting the artistic value of Mitchell's novel.

Overall, then, the relationship between the artist, Flannery O'Connor, and her mother, Regina Cline O'Connor, was a complex one. Because they lived together through all but five years of the novelist's life, Regina probably influenced Flannery more even than the novelist would have wanted to admit. Both Regina and Flannery possessed a native resourcefulness, a desire to fulfill themselves as dynamic women, and an intense devotion to Roman Catholicism, though Regina's practice was more conventional than her daughter's. The most negative traits that O'Connor inherited from her mother are those concerned with race and money; Regina's nineteenth-century attitude toward the black race and her obsessive concern with money were qualities so outstanding in her sensibility that her daughter could not avoid their influence.

When Flannery O'Connor, who had clearly tried to make her break from Milledgeville and Regina's influence, had to return to the town, she had no choice but to accept her mother for both her good and bad qualities. It is certain that Regina O'Connor was fully dedicated to prolonging her daughter's life and to providing her with an environment in which she could use the talent for writing she had already proved through publication. Regina may have preferred that her daughter write for a mass audience, producing popular fiction in the style of *Gone with the Wind,* but she had to accept the reality that her daughter was not the writer of best sellers.

Regina loved her talented but difficult daughter, cared for her, guarded her health, and created an environment in which she could produce *The*

Violent Bear It Away and write and publish the short stories, collected in *A Good Man Is Hard to Find* and *Everything That Rises Must Converge*. She also encouraged her daughter's literary friendships and the visits of scholars and friends to Andalusia; when O'Connor was able to leave the town to lecture and read from her work, Regina arranged for or provided transportation. With limitations of intellect and personality over which she had little control, Regina Cline O'Connor still contributed significantly to the ultimate success of her brilliant daughter. Not the least of that contribution is in the fictional benefit that Flannery O'Connor derived from her mother's character and life. Louise Abbot, who became a friend of both Flannery O'Connor and her mother in the late 1950s, visited Andalusia fairly regularly and observed the relationship between Regina and Flannery; she says

> No better portrayal of Regina O'Connor could be given than the one that emerges from her daughter's writing. [. . .] The letters in *The Habit of Being* depict a rich and complicated relationship full of comedy, irony, difficulty and devotion. [. . .]
>
> Neither mother nor daughter would ever have expected to live together as adults, but when they had it to do, they did it well. They did a very difficult thing well.[7]

CHAPTER EIGHT

MILLEDGEVILLE~
EARLY FRIENDSHIPS

A fter returning to Milledgeville permanently, making the personal decisions that guided the rest of her life, and readjusting
to life with her mother, Flannery O'Connor also had to reas-
similate herself into a middle-classed, Southern atmosphere that
she found somewhat stifling. Although her mother often invited townspeople to Andalusia, O'Connor was not completely comfortable with those
Milledgevillians who continued to identify her mainly as "Miss Regina's"
daughter. Katherine Anne Porter, who visited O'Connor at Andalusia in
1958 and again in 1960, related an anecdote that clearly shows the position
(or lack of one) that Flannery O'Connor held in Milledgeville:

> Ladies in Society there—in that particular society, I
> mean—were nearly always known [. . .] to their dying day by
> their maiden names. They were called "Miss Mary" or whoever
> it was. And so, Flannery's mother, too; her maiden name was
> Regina Cline and so she was still known as "Miss Regina Cline"

and one evening at a party when I was there after the Conference, someone mentioned Flannery's name and another—a neighbor, mind you, who had probably been around there all her life—said, "Who is Flannery O'Connor? I keep hearing about her." The other one said, "Oh, you know! Why that's Regina Cline's daughter: that little girl who writes." (Porter 52)

Fr. James McCown also wrote of a similar experience with a resident of Milledgeville; on his first visit to O'Connor, he stopped in town to get directions from a woman who described O'Connor as "a sweet girl [. . . who] comes to mass every Sunday. But those stories she writes! They are terrible. Everybody says so. I'm afraid to go near her. She might put me in one of her stories" (qtd. in McCown, "Remembering Flannery" 86). As a virtual nonentity in a town that refused to recognize her genius, O'Connor had to find a niche for herself and to establish relationships with people who transcended the immediate and ordinary pattern of life in Milledgeville.

O'Connor's connections with professors at GSCW, Helen I. Greene and Rosa Lee Walston—who had recently joined the faculty—helped both to insulate O'Connor from annoying social trivialities and to fill emotional and intellectual voids in her life. Another of her earliest close friendships from outside Milledgeville was with Fr. James McCown, whom she identified as the first Roman Catholic priest to respond warmly to her work. She also formed new friendships with other people who lived near Milledgeville, including Ben Griffith and Tom and Louise Gossett, who taught at colleges in nearby towns. Louise Abbot from Louisville, Georgia, also became her friend. Another group of area residents whom O'Connor welcomed to Andalusia between 1957 and 1960 were those who participated in what O'Connor herself termed "pseudo-literary and theological gatherings" (*HB* 271–72).

After her health had improved enough so that she could, quite literally, carry on conversations outside the family, Flannery O'Connor, in spite of her own social reluctance, began to reconnect with life in Milledgeville. Her first major literary project after she gained some control over the lupus was the completion of *Wise Blood,* which Harcourt, Brace & Company published in May 1952. On 15 May, the day the novel went on sale, O'Connor's friend Betty Ferguson—a librarian at GSCW—and other members of the staff at

Ina Dillard Russell Library, organized and held a book-signing party for O'Connor in its Beeson Reading Room. *The Union-Recorder,* the Milledgeville newspaper, carried two stories on the event, one on the day it was held, another on 22 May. An article in the Georgia College *Alumnae Journal* for summer 1952 also described the event: "Throngs of guests [more than three hundred] were in the library for the occasion, and many were fortunate to be able to purchase autographed copies of the novel, a few of which were on hand that morning" ("Autograph Party" 7). Regina Cline O'Connor and her sister Mary, as well as other relatives and friends, received the guests. O'Connor recorded her candid reaction to the party to her GSCW friend Betty Boyd Love, who by this time had married and was living in California. She ignored the cocktails and concentrated, she said, on signing a number of books, including one for Betty herself. She also speculated on how "relics like Alice Napier" would react to the *Wise Blood* once they "toted" it home. O'Connor also told Betty that "Miss Mary Boyd" had attended the party: "She is still violently interested in finding herself a husband and still asks personal questions without any preparation and at the most inconvenient times. I do wish somebody would marry the child and shut her up. I am touched by her but you know what a long way a little goes" (*HB* 36).

Photographs of O'Connor, taken at the event, show a seemingly recovered, attractive young woman (she is not wearing glasses), who seems to be taking the party in stride. Milledgeville native Jay Lewis, who "happened to be home for a visit and went to that autograph party," remembers that O'Connor was dressed up for the event but appeared to be "very uncomfortable." Lewis also recalls the negative attitude that most residents of Milledgeville held toward *Wise Blood:* "Oh, they hated it; they were horrified by it. They couldn't imagine why a nice Southern girl would write such a book. [. . .] The average Milledgeville person would have seen them [O'Connor's characters] and would have thought this is how she sees us." Two days after the party for *Wise Blood,* O'Connor wrote a thank-you note to the library staff at GSCW; she told them they were "most brave" to plan and carry out the party. She even admitted that she had "enjoyed" the event.[1]

Two GSCW faculty members who attended the book signing were Helen I. Greene and Rosa Lee Walston. During her time away from Milledgeville, O'Connor had maintained her correspondence with Greene and had seen her during visits home. After her return to Milledgeville,

O'Connor rekindled her friendship with her former history teacher, who says that she "went to see them many afternoons and took a lot of students out there to meet her. She was always friendly and glad to see them." In her reminiscence of O'Connor, Greene writes of taking a "special group of people to Andalusia," who included men and women with political and social connections like the well-known Russell family of Georgia (Greene, "Mary Flannery O'Connor" 47). Greene reveals that, in spite of her reluctance to behave in a traditionally social way, O'Connor in Milledgeville did accommodate to the fabric of the conventional Southern community.

The friendship between Greene and O'Connor also developed on a more intimate level: they sometimes shared meals at Andalusia. Greene recalls, "The only thing I can cook is chicken and rice and so every now and then I would take some out there. They were always nice about it." On one occasion, Helen Greene even gave Flannery one of her "outgrown" dresses; to their mutual friend Roslyn Barnes, who had also been one of Greene's favorite students, O'Connor wrote in November 1960: "Dr. Green [*sic*] has supper with us every now and then, but I have not seen her since school began. The last time she came out she appeared with one of her dresses in a brown paper bag and gave it to me as it was too small for her and I had admired it. She has two requirements for any dress she buys she says: it must be reduced and it must be navy blue" (*HB* 420). Greene herself recalls the episode, including Regina's remark that "'Mary Flannery wanted that dress more than anything and it was not reduced.'"

Rosa Lee Walston joined the English faculty at GSCW in 1946, the year after O'Connor graduated. They met when O'Connor, still at Iowa, returned to Milledgeville for a visit. According to Walston, "her contemporaries brought her around to my office and with great pride introduced her. Our friendship began at that point." Walston subsequently became, if not one of O'Connor's closest personal friends, certainly one of her closest connections at GSCW. In one of her memoirs of their friendship, Walston wrote of her relief at not having been one of O'Connor's teachers at GSCW: "I have always said I was glad I never taught Flannery as it would have been devastating had I failed to recognize her potential" (Walston, "An Affectionate Recollection" 43).

Walston related, however, that their friendship developed "effortlessly because we found that we could take our agreement on so many basic assumptions for granted" (43). She also said that she never asked O'Connor about her works-in-progress or visited her too frequently because she knew both of O'Connor's dedication to her work and of her fragile health. When they were together, however, Walston said they "met and chatted just as any two people would do. It might be about books sometimes, but mostly we laughed about the absurdities of things." She described the adult O'Connor as invariably "courteous" and "reserved" but capable of enjoying social visits. O'Connor also sometimes invited Walston to help her entertain "difficult" guests: "[S]he thought [. . .] I could sort of diffuse the conversation. Mostly, when she asked me to come specifically, it was [to deal with] kooks. She liked to have somebody there to chat with her. She had a great sense of humor;" Walston recalled that once O'Connor received a letter from some-one in Florida who had sent a pulled tooth mounted in silver for her to examine; but the correspondent had also asked her to return it! Walston remembered that O'Connor humorously "suggested that if I had any spare teeth around, I'd better have them mounted in silver right away."

Walston also sometimes brought visiting scholars or writers to GSCW to meet O'Connor at Andalusia. Among those she introduced to O'Connor were Mary Olive Thomas, a professor at Georgia State, and Caroline Ivey, a writer from Alabama. She recalled that initially these two visitors felt that they were too important to meet O'Connor, but once the two were at Andalusia, O'Connor and Ivey formed an immediate bond; O'Connor sub-sequently invited her to spend a week at Andalusia and the two became "very good friends." Walston also helped continue O'Connor's connection with GSCW by getting her involved with the Literary Guild, an organiza-tion of English majors at the college. Walston recalled that it was at a meet-ing of the Guild that O'Connor made one of her most quoted statements: "It was at the Guild that she replied to the question, 'Why do you write' with the matter-of-fact statement, 'Because I am good at it.' Flannery knew pre-cisely what kind of bomb she had dropped. Without one flicker of an eye-lash to help them, she left the students to resolve the paradox of this to them ultimate in conceit with what they had already come to recognize as her genuine modesty" (44).

O'Connor also gave talks to the group nearly every year and, Walston recalled, "We got in the habit of going out to Andalusia every spring for a picnic." When the students visited, however, O'Connor did not act as hostess:

We took our own lunch, but the kids would just scatter over the farm. Flannery sat there on the front porch and talked and she watched the different ones as they came around and she picked somebody to ask me about. She had an uncanny eye for picking the person who was unusual. I think she must have done a little bit of showing them [the unusual ones] a special attention because several of them got in the habit of going out to see her and I wouldn't have thought of taking Flannery's time like these kids did. One or two of them were writing.

One of these students was a former science major named Roslyn Barnes, with whom O'Connor maintained a correspondence and friendship while Barnes attended the University of Iowa and later when she became a missionary in Brazil.

Rosa Lee Walston also helped to organize O'Connor's more formal presentations at GSCW. In 1960, after O'Connor was invited to present a lecture in a series the college held every year, Walston introduced her presentation, "Some Aspects of the Grotesque in Southern Fiction." Walston's remarks clearly show both the esteem that she felt for O'Connor's works and her clear understanding of them.[2]

Walston's friendship with O'Connor continued until shortly before the writer's death, though Walston was in England when O'Connor died in August 1964. Walston did, however, make a final visit to O'Connor in the hospital in Milledgeville. She recalled that O'Connor's name was never posted as Flannery, only Mary O'Connor: "I had gone to visit a friend who happened to have the room across the hall from hers. [O'Connor was not allowed visitors.] Regina came out and said, 'Flannery heard your voice and she wants you to come in.' We just had a delightful time. I remember that she was chuckling over the fact that her doctor had told her that he did not want her to do any work and she said, 'Well, I had hoped that I could write.' 'Oh,' he said, 'That's all right.'"

Besides her friendships with members of the GSCW faculty, one of the first Georgia professors O'Connor met after her return to Milledgeville was Benjamin Griffith, a recent Ph.D. from Northwestern University who was teaching at the Baptist, Bessie Tift Women's College in Forsyth, Georgia, a town about fifty miles from Milledgeville. Within two years, he had moved to Mercer University in Macon. In a letter to Betty Hester, written two years after Griffith first wrote to O'Connor, she explained that their friendship began when Griffith found a paperback copy of *Wise Blood* in a drugstore, read it, and later wrote her "a very intelligent letter about it" (*HB* 118). O'Connor's letters to Griffith show that in him she found a sympathetic and knowledgeable reader. His was also the first writing that she read and criticized. In her second letter to Griffith (3 March 1954), she gave her often quoted statement about the relationship between her Catholicism and the content of *Wise Blood*: "Let me assure you that no one but a Catholic could have written *Wise Blood* even though it is a book about a kind of Protestant saint. It reduces Protestantism to the twin absurdities of The Church Without Christ or The Holy Church Without Christ, which no pious Protestant would do. And of course no unbeliever or agnostic could have written it because it is entirely Redemption-centered in thought" (69–70).

By June of 1955, Griffith had visited O'Connor at Andalusia and brought with him a review he had done of *A Good Man Is Hard to Find* that he was hoping to publish and a short story that he was working on. Regarding his fiction, she advised him to read two stories in *Understanding Fiction*, Chekhov's "The Lament" and Pirandello's "War." Sounding like her own advisor Caroline Gordon, she directed him to avoid authorial intrusion: "Let the old man go through his motions without any comment from you as author and let the things he sees make the pathetic effects." She also warned him against relying on "local effects" because his is "not the kind of story that gets its effects from local things, but from universal feeling of grief that old age and unwantedness call up" (*HB* 83–84).

Later that year, in a letter to Betty Hester, she called Griffith a nice man; he, too, formed a positive impression of her: "As we talked and sipped iced tea on the front porch, she projected an intellectual's mind in a flat Middle Georgia drawl. A gifted mimic, she told hilarious—never hateful—stories about the farm workers, black and white. This slender, graceful, affable woman always seemed to present her true self, completely without artistic temperament. She listened well, focusing her blue eyes with bird-like intensity as I spoke. We had real conversations, not separate monologues" (B. Griffith, "Ten Years" M4). Griffith visited O'Connor formally in May 1956 when he and the Gossetts brought Alfred Kazin to Andalusia and again in 1962 with a class of Mercer students; he tells how she showed them around the farm and patiently answered their questions: "[S]he made something important of even the simplest question" (M4).

In 1989 Griffith reviewed O'Connor's *Collected Works* for the *Sewanee Review;* his introductory comments in the essay provide a brief commentary on his early relationship with O'Connor and his comprehension of her work: "Wherein lies O'Connor's uniqueness? I think it is in her compelling distinctive voice, pervading stories that are both spiritually profound and excruciatingly funny. Knowing its etymology, O'Connor would have approved my choice of the word *excruciatingly,* rooted in the Latin for *cross* and *crucify:* her works are deeply religious, and the humor makes them deceptively so for readers" (B. Griffith, "After the Canonization" 575–76).

In the mid-1950s, O'Connor also established a strong friendship with a Jesuit priest, Fr. James McCown. It seems particularly fitting that she should have formed one of her earliest close friendships with this jolly, affable priest, apparently so different from the then resident priest in Milledgeville. In a letter to Father McCown in the O'Connor collection at Duke, O'Connor wrote about the excessive Irishness of this priest who decorated the church with green carnations and a statue of St. Patrick and objected to Roman Catholic girls at GSCW attending the baccalaureate sermon at the college.[3]

McCown was a native Southerner who had come to Macon, Georgia, in the early 1950s as assistant priest at St. Joseph's Catholic Church. Part of his responsibility was also to do mission work in the rural area outside Macon where only "about 20 people" attended "our little mission church" (McCown, "Flannery O'Connor" 2). At his home church in Macon, McCown felt impelled to heighten the "cultural level" of his congregation, particularly after one of his "literary" parishioners mentioned Flannery O'Connor: "I decided to get on the O'Connor trail. I read her two books and their reviews. Like the rest, I thought *Wise Blood* gripping but too concerned with bizarre, freakish people. *A Good Man Is Hard to Find* was more to my tastes" (McCown, "Remembering Flannery O'Connor" 86).

When Father McCown decided to visit O'Connor, he had to hitch a ride to Milledgeville (priests did not own automobiles in the 1950s) with "Horace Ridley, a fat, big-hearted unacademic whiskey salesman" (86). McCown recounted their arrival at Andalusia and his first impressions of Flannery O'Connor. She greeted him with a terse "Howdy," and "she looked at me for a disquieting few seconds, and I looked at her. What I saw was not the smart-looking, independent-acting lady author that her name somehow promised. She was dressed in old jeans, long before they became modish, and a brown blouse, and she leaned on a pair of aluminum crutches. Sharp blue eyes looked at me from a face that was roundish, puffy and a little blotchy—the results of her strong medication" (86).

O'Connor described McCown's first visit in a letter (22 January 1956) to Sally and Robert Fitzgerald and again a few days later to Betty Hester; she was impressed with the "white Cadillack" in which he arrived, but also, more important, with his approval of her fiction. For O'Connor the result of this visit was a strong and enduring relationship; this sympathetic priest served her as both friend and spiritual advisor. He became, in effect, her "personal priest." Their friendship, however, began with their shared interest in literature; in her first letter to him, she described her enthusiastic reading in contemporary Catholic fiction—the works of Bloy, Bernanos, Mauriac, and Greene; however, she wrote about their limitations: "at some point reading them reaches the place of diminishing return and you get more benefit from reading someone like Hemingway where there is apparently a hunger for a Catholic completeness in life, or Joyce who can't get rid of it no matter what he does" (*HB* 130). A few months later, O'Connor described to Father McCown another contemporary Catholic novel she was reading. She called the book "propaganda and its being propaganda for the side of the angels only makes it worse. The novel is an art form and when you use it for anything other than art, you pervert it" (157).

Through the years, O'Connor recommended many works of fiction to Father McCown, including Bernard Malamud's *The Magic Barrel* in 1958, which she felt illustrated the superiority of the Jewish brain (*HB* 288). In November 1958, she advised him to read two other books: Martin Buber's *The Eclipse of God* and *Doctor Zhivago,* which she described as a great novel.[4] The next year she recommended Romain Gary's *The Roots of Heaven* to him and also began to write to him about the work of Teilhard de Chardin. In December 1960, she even recommended Updike's *Rabbit, Run,* though "the sex is laid on too heavy [. . .]; but the fact is that the book is the product of a real religious consciousness" (420). When she sent Father McCown a copy of Percy's *The Moviegoer* in 1961, she declared it not as good as its newly made critical reputation but extremely well written.[5]

After their first visit, Father McCown was so impressed with O'Connor's literary acumen that he recommended her to Harold Gardiner, S.J., then literary editor of *America,* who immediately asked O'Connor to write an article for the Catholic journal. The result was "The Church and the Fiction Writer," published in the magazine on 30 March 1957, with one sentence edited by Father Gardiner. McCown recalled her reaction as "furious. Flannery, bless her heart, thought boldly and straight, and was not intimidated by the rigorist-neurotic cast of much Catholic moral theology of the time" (McCown, "Remembering Flannery O'Connor" 87). Through the years Father McCown also served, he said, as a sort of "moral guide and dogmatic advisor" to O'Connor. When the literary group that she hosted at Andalusia between 1957 and 1960 wanted to read Gide, whose works were on the Catholic Index of forbidden books, she asked Father McCown to help her; he expeditiously solved her dilemma. Father McCown also recalled his position as her private priest: "She [. . .] wrote me about problems in her spiritual life. I can only go so far as to say they were of the scope and seriousness found in a convent-bred high school girl" (McCown, "Flannery O'Connor" 18). In September 1959, she wrote to him about inadvertently breaking the Catholic dietary law that forbade eating meat on Fridays. She was worried about having eaten vegetables at the Sanford House that she suspected had been cooked in ham stock.[6] To undercut her excessive concern, however, O'Connor also wrote in the letter that she knew she wouldn't go to hell because of having eaten the butter beans. O'Connor clearly valued Father McCown's friendship as indicated by the rich content of her letters to him and her comments about him to other correspondents; their admiration was mutual. Father McCown wrote, "It was my unutterable good fortune to have known [Flannery O'Connor] as a person"; he called her "the most honest person [and] one of the most interesting characters I ever knew" ("Flannery O'Connor" 1, 2, 19).

Father McCown also helped initiate the friendship O'Connor formed with two colleges professors who also lived in Macon, Tom and Louise Gossett, who, from 1954 until 1958, when they took jobs in San Antonio, taught in Macon colleges—he at Wesleyan, she at Mercer. Tom Gossett met Father McCown as a direct result of a lecture series Gossett ran at Wesleyan. Father McCown, who enthusiastically attended these lectures, asked Tom Gossett whether he had heard of Flannery O'Connor. At that time, Gossett hadn't, but he soon went with Father McCown and another priest to Milledgeville to meet the young writer. Gossett recalled that Father McCown and Regina O'Connor always teased each other a great deal and that on this first trip to Andalusia, McCown told Regina that he had brought a "real priest [. . .] this time [referring to the other priest who had accompanied them.] Mrs. O'Connor replied, 'It's so nice you brought a real priest because you meet so many of the other kind!' Father McCown said, 'Touché!'" For the next twenty minutes, Mrs. O'Connor addressed Tom Gossett as Mr. Touché. Gossett remembers, "I noticed that Flannery O'Connor, standing on crutches behind her mother, was laughing heartily because her mother had got my name wrong. Later, Mrs. O'Connor realized she had made a mistake. While the other members of the group were talking to each other, she said to me: 'You mustn't mind me; I'm ignorant.'"[7]

Louise Gossett recalls that her first contact with O'Connor came as a result of a note she wrote to her after she (Gossett) had read somewhere that O'Connor was a convert to Catholicism rather than "cradle-Catholic." O'Connor wrote back, suggesting that with a name like hers could there be any question that she was not a born Catholic. From these rather humorous beginnings, a genuine friendship developed between the warm, academic couple and the brilliant, young writer. Theirs was a relationship based more on mutual congeniality than on any desire the professors might have had to probe O'Connor's intellectual depths. Tom Gossett said that O'Connor "liked to work in the morning but she loved to have company so Louise and I used to go to see her and that's how we got to know her." Louise recalls that "[s]he was very generous with her time. We also took students over occasionally." When Tom Gossett asked her whether seeing students was a nuisance to her, she replied, "Oh, I am delighted to have them come. I don't like them to come in the morning, but in the afternoon, I am very happy to see them." He also remembered one specific visit that occurred after she had read "A Good Man Is Hard to Find" at Wesleyan:

> She invited my class at Wesleyan to come to her house. She had read "A Good Man Is Hard to Find" at the college and the students wanted her to read another of the stories. She said, "I hesitate to read any except 'A Good Man' because the other stories strike me as humorous and I can't keep myself from laughing. 'A Good Man' is so obviously grim that I can read it in public

without difficulty." When the students asked her if she would choose another of her stories to read to them, she chose "Good Country People." It was true that Flannery could not prevent herself from laughing while reading the story. When she got to the part in which Manly says that he has been believing in nothing all his life, she laughed so much that the book fell off her lap and a student had to retrieve it.

Both Gossetts recall their many visits to Andalusia and their conversations, which usually did not deal with O'Connor's fiction. Tom Gossett says, "I think you found out there were certain things she didn't like you to ask her [about her work]." Once, when he, influenced by the symbol-mongering attitude of the time, asked her whether she meant to place symbolic value on Father Vogel's name in "The Enduring Chill," because *Vogel* meant *bird* in German, she caustically replied that she didn't even know what *Vogel* meant in German.

Louise Gossett elaborates further on the restraints that governed their friendship with O'Connor: "[W]e always stood in such awe of her as such an accomplished person that we never wanted to intrude on her life and her way of living. Lots of time the visits were very casual, very simple. We sat on the porch and drank a daiquiri and chatted about the world around us. Maybe one of the reasons she enjoyed our company was that we weren't making demands that she perform in a great manner."

The friendship between the Gossetts and O'Connor continued after they left Macon to assume positions at colleges in San Antonio; they then spent summers at a farm near Lewisburg, West Virginia, which had been in Louise Gossett's family for several generations. Louise Gossett recalls, "Driving back and forth, we would go through Milledgeville on the way up and through Milledgeville on the way back to see Flannery." They also remember that O'Connor had planned to give a presentation in San Antonio in the summer of 1964; however, her surgery in February that reactivated the lupus forced her to cancel her plans. As late as April 1964, however, O'Connor wrote to Tom Gossett that she was reading and enjoying his book *Race: The History of an Idea in America,* published in 1963. The Gossetts' admiration for O'Connor has continued. In 1985, Louise Gossett contributed the essay on O'Connor to Louis Rubin's authoritative *The History of Southern Literature.*

As a result of her friendship with the Gossetts, O'Connor was able to interact with several literary guests who lectured at Wesleyan. One of the first of these visitors was Alfred Kazin, whom O'Connor had met at Yaddo. In a letter (7 May 1956) to Ben Griffith, she wrote, "I would love to have you and Mr. Gossett come over Friday and bring Alfred Kazin. I met him a good many years ago and he is very pleasant but I don't know him well" (*HB* 156). Kazin, the Gossetts, and Fr. McCown remembered the visit but from somewhat different perspectives. Kazin recalled:

> I was giving a lecture [. . .] somewhere near Milledgeville and [Fr. James McCown], who went to my lecture, said, "Why don't you come and visit Flannery?" [. . .] I had been a great admirer of her work, but because of the incident at Yaddo, where she knew I had been very troubled by Lowell's behavior, I was reluctant. But the chance to see her [. . .] was irresistible so the priest drove me to her house; as he was driving, it was a very hot Georgia day and he took off his shirt and his clerical collar and was driving in his undershirt. We got to Flannery's house and to my astonishment he said, "Well, here it is; I'll see you later." I said, "Aren't you coming in?" He said, "Certainly not. I'm scared to death of her." [Tom Gossett suggests that Father McCown "must have been teasing" Kazin when he made this remark since McCown's relationship with Flannery was "very friendly"] [. . .] The meeting itself was insignificant. She was very stiff with me. I think I figured in her mind as one of those New York "interleckchuls."

Father McCown described the trip to Milledgeville a bit differently: "It was good, good talk the whole trip. Smart people are so interesting. I felt no inclination to tell any of my good jokes. Kazin encouraged me (sizing me up, I guess, as an authentic Southerner) to talk, and he listened as intently and humbly as if I were somebody" (McCown, "Remembering Flannery O'Connor" 87).

The Gossetts' memories of the visit offer a third perspective: they feel that Kazin was a bit condescending toward O'Connor; Tom Gossett says, "I thought he made a terrible mistake. He seemed to think he was the celebrity [. . . and] that he could do something for her rather than she might be able to do something for him." Gossett even recalls that Kazin appeared bored and drowsy during their conversation, though Louise Gossett feels that Kazin's behavior was motivated more by Northern manners than genuine rudeness.

O'Connor's only documented reaction to the visit occurred in a letter (20 May 1956) to Father McCown: "It was good to see you turn up with that crowd from Macon. It reminded me slightly of one of those early books of Waugh's that had Fr. Rothschild, S.J. in it. He is always appearing in unlikely company, usually in disguise" (*HB* 160). After his visit, O'Connor continued to respect Kazin's literary judgment: in October 1959, she asked Robert Giroux to send Kazin an advance copy of *The Violent Bear It Away.* As Tom Gossett recalls, Kazin "wrote very favorably of her" later, and Kazin himself said, "Flannery was a great favorite of mine and I admired her very much [and] I think her work will live much longer than [Robert Lowell's] because I think she is a wonderful writer." In his *Bright Book of Life* (1973), Kazin elaborated: "She is one of the few Catholic writers of fiction in our day [. . .] who managed to fuse a thorough orthodoxy with the great possible independence and sophistication as a writer" (Kazin, *Bright Book of Life* 57).

In November 1957, the Gossetts took another important visitor to Andalusia: Maire MacEntee, an Irish delegate to the United Nations. Tom Gossett recalls that O'Connor and MacEntee "had a quite interesting discussion about Irish writers." O'Connor herself wrote to Betty Hester on 11 January 1958, that her "opinion of the Irish" had "gone up" as a result of MacEntee's visit: "I asked her what they had in Ireland to correspond with the angry young men in England. She said they had some angry young men but that they didn't have the class business to be angry over. Anti-clerical? I asked her. Yes and anti-religious too. Most of them go the way of Joyce, she said, but it is very painful to them because when they cut themselves off from the religion they cut themselves off from what they have grown up with—as the religion is so bound in with the rest of life" (*HB* 262). From this comment it is easy to infer how much the Gossetts contributed to O'Connor's life in Milledgeville. Forced by her lupus to remain, geographically, outside the cultural and intellectual world she otherwise would have inhabited, O'Connor benefited richly from contacts with this world that the Gossetts instigated.

The most famous Southern writer whom the Gossetts brought to Andalusia was Katherine Anne Porter, whom they arranged to bring to lunch at Andalusia the day after Porter participated in a conference at Wesleyan on 28 March 1958. O'Connor had first read Porter's fiction at Iowa and like many others was interested in this rather vain artist who, throughout her life, placed as high a value on her personal life as on her writing. On December 1957, ahead of Porter's visit to Georgia, O'Connor wrote to Cecil Dawkins of her hypothetical impressions of the woman based on the gossip she had heard about Porter's particular attractiveness to men. She wrote, "So many catty remarks circulate and people always suppose that there is some rivalry between women writers. If so, I always figure they are not the best writers" (*HB* 260).

By February 1958, O'Connor was aware of Porter's impending visit as she related in a letter to Maryat Lee. In early March she also wrote to Fr. McCown about the upcoming visit and invited him to come to lunch with "Miss Katherine Anne Porter," whom she described as both an excellent "lady-writer" and "a lapsed Catholic."[8] Louise Gossett vividly recalls the occasion and the visit to O'Connor:

> We took Porter over [to Andalusia with Arlin Turner and Hugh Holman]. Katherine Anne, a very elegant person, was beautifully dressed in a black suit and a big gray hat—and gloves and high heels. She emerged from our Chevrolet as Flannery was coming down the steps in a skirt and sweater and on crutches. They met and Katherine Anne Porter turned and looked out across the farm land to the woods and exclaimed, "What a lovely prospect!" Flannery looked. Then she turned back to Katherine Anne and said, "Looks like a field to me." We had some apprehension about what these two women would make of one another; [. . . but] they were very quickly, on good terms and admired one another. At that time, I remember, Katherine Anne Porter was working on *Ship of Fools* and was groaning about how slowly it was going and the difficulty of doing it, and they talked about that problem. They talked very easily and had a happy lunch together. That was certainly one of the occasions when Mrs. O'Connor was hostess, but she did not in any way dominate the scene. Later in the afternoon, we strolled around looking at peacocks and talking about peacocks.

The Gossetts made a permanent visual record of that visit in photographs taken of O'Connor and Porter together; these snapshots are today part of the O'Connor Collection at Duke University Library.

In a letter to Betty Hester on 4 April 1958, O'Connor herself described a part of the conversation at the luncheon that concerned O'Connor's upcoming trip to Lourdes: "She said that she had always wanted to go to Lourdes, perhaps she would get there some day and make a novena that she would finish her novel—she's been on it 27 years." The subject of conversation then turned to death, "the way that death is discussed at dinner tables, as if it were a funny subject. She said she thought it was very nice to believe that we would all meet in heaven and she rather hoped we would but she didn't really know. She wished she knew who exactly was in charge of the universe, and where she was going. She would be glad to go where she was expected if she knew. All this accompanied by much banter from the gentlemen. It was a little coy and a little wistful but there was a terrible need evident underneath it" (*HB* 276). Porter herself recalled the postcard she received from O'Connor from Lourdes in which O'Connor commented on the unique correlation there between "[f]aith and affliction" ("Gracious Greatness" 56). O'Connor gave further details of her reactions to Porter's visit in an April letter to Cecil Dawkins, describing the writer as "very nice indeed, very pleasant and agreeable, crazy about my peacocks; plowed all over the yard behind me in her spike-heeled shoes to see my various kinds of chickens" (*HB* 276). In several letters, including the one just cited, O'Connor expressed concern about the twenty-seven years Porter has been working on *Ship of Fools;* she worried about her own completion of *The Violent Bear It Away.*

Though Porter and O'Connor seldom communicated after this first visit, Porter did send her appreciative note about *The Violent Bear It Away* in 1960 and asked her to sign a card for enclosure in her copy of the novel. Two years later, on 28 October 1960, O'Connor appeared with Porter, Caroline Gordon, Madison Jones, and Louis Rubin at an arts festival at Wesleyan titled "Recent Southern Fiction: A Panel Discussion." The O'Connors gave a dinner party for the participants at Andalusia the next evening. In a letter to Cecil Dawkins, O'Connor wrote appreciatively of Porter's second visit to Milledgeville; she was especially impressed with Porter's inquiring "about a chicken of mine that she had met here two years before. I call that really having a talent for winning friends and influencing people when you remember to inquire for a chicken that you met two years before" (*HB* 416). When Porter's novel, *Ship of Fools,* came out in 1962, O'Connor read it with considerable enthusiasm, writing to Betty Hester in July: "It has a sculptured quality. I admire the bulldog in it the same way I would admire a bulldog carved to perfection. Essence of bulldog" (484).

Porter made her most extended critical comments on O'Connor in a short article she wrote for the issue of *Esprit,* devoted to O'Connor in 1964. Her assessment of Flannery O'Connor's special position in American literature seems particularly apt: "Now and again there hovers on the margin of the future a presence that one feels as imminent—if I may use stylish vocabulary. She came up among us like a presence, a carrier of a gift not to be disputed but welcomed. She lived among us like a presence and went away early, leaving her harvest perhaps not yet all together gathered, though, like so many geniuses who have small time in this world, I think she had her warning and accepted it and did her work even if we all would have liked to have her stay on forever and do more" ("Gracious Greatness" 50).

In addition to the professors and the celebrities they brought to Andalusia, O'Connor's connections soon included an aspiring writer, Louise Abbot, a warm and sensitive woman who wrote a vivid memoir of her friendship with O'Connor, in which she documents the growth and quality of a friendship that began because of the enthusiasm Abbot developed first for O'Connor's fiction, then for the person. Abbot has said:

> *A Good Man Is Hard to Find* intensified my interest [in O'Connor]. These stories made me aware of her theological concern but I failed to discern her intentions. Laughing my way through the stories of this first collection, gasping at their shocking turns, recognizing my own southern territory, marveling at their brilliance, I still misunderstood the writer's point of view. With hindsight, it seems incredible, but my "speed-reading" had me convinced that Flannery O'Connor was an intellectual skeptic casting a comic, ironic, deeply informed, rueful, if not ruthless eye, upon the "good country people" of Georgia. [. . .] During our first visit, Flannery corrected my mistake as she caught it by making her faith as a person and her intentions as a writer clear. I returned to her fiction somewhat chastened, but also with a sharper plow and a slower gait.[9]

Abbot and O'Connor met early in 1957 after Abbot had written to her, asking permission to visit. A graduate of the University of North Carolina, Chapel Hill, Abbot was married to a lawyer from Louisville, Georgia, and the mother of two young children. Most important to her future friendship with O'Connor, she herself was a published writer; in fact, when she wrote to O'Connor, she had first thought of pretending to be a journalist requesting an interview, but changed her mind and even told O'Connor about her abortive ruse. In her first letter to Abbot, written on 27 February 1957, O'Connor invited her to visit but cautioned her "to drop a card the week before" or telephone ahead of time. O'Connor also thanked Abbot for abandoning her plan to arrive under the guise of a journalist: "I am very glad that you have decided not to be a lady-journalist because I am deathly afraid of the tribe" (*HB* 205).

In her published memoir of their friendship, Abbot describes her April 1957 arrival at Andalusia during a heavy rainstorm. O'Connor's first words to her were, "Did you get caught in that big rain?" Abbot was so nervous that she replied "No." When readying herself for the visit, Abbot had dressed casually in a blue shirtwaist dress and brown loafers, prompting her husband to ask her whether she was properly "got up" for the occasion. When she met O'Connor, however, Abbot was herself a bit surprised to find the writer dressed in loafers, blue jeans, and "a long tailed plaid shirt" (Abbot, "Remembering Flannery" 63). Abbot believes O'Connor had deliberately dressed so casually. She speculates that, by wearing this outfit, O'Connor was testing to see whether Abbot would be appalled by the young author's casualness: "Perhaps she figured that, if I were a lady who belonged to one of the other tribes of which she was 'deathly afraid,' I might be offended and not return, saving her the necessity of dismissing me" (63).

Abbot describes the conversational content of that first meeting. One topic was writing—both O'Connor's and Abbot's; when Regina made a remark about Abbot's literary efforts that Flannery found condescending, she flattered her new acquaintance by informing her mother, "She's had a story published. She's a *professional* writer" (63). They also talked about religion, particularly Abbot's membership in the Associate Reformed Presbyterian Church, of which O'Connor had never heard: "'What in the wurld-d is that?' she asked, delighting in the name" (66). O'Connor and Abbot also discussed their similar backgrounds: both came from families who had lived in Georgia for more than a hundred years and both had spent part of their early years in Savannah. Abbot soon learned, too, that they shared the "same kind of sense of humor, shyness in certain situations, some detachment from the life around us and the loneliness that goes with it."

Beginning with that first meeting and the shared interests it uncovered, the two, in Abbot's own words, "became friends." Abbot saw O'Connor fairly often in Milledgeville and, after that first visit, usually came for lunch, either at Andalusia or at the Sanford House in Milledgeville, where she was able to observe the townspeople's attitude toward the writer. According to Abbot, older residents viewed O'Connor's skill as a writer of fiction as being simply incidental to her social standing as Regina Cline's daughter. Anybody from the college, however, knew who O'Connor was and accorded her "affectionate respect." Because Abbot visited regularly at Andalusia, she was able to give unique details of the setting in which O'Connor lived and wrote (71–72).[10] Abbot's description helps us to see O'Connor in her own locale, surrounded by books, her own writing station, and her paintings with which she decorated her walls.

As soon as Abbot realized how deeply spiritual O'Connor was, the issue of religious faith became central to their friendship. Abbot recalls their conversations on spiritual issues and the disquiet that O'Connor stimulated in her own sensibility, compelling her "to question my agnosticism and to reexamine the claims of Christian faith" (70). On an undated Saturday in 1959, after Abbot had apparently confided some of this spiritual questioning to her friend, O'Connor wrote her a sympathetic letter in which she asserted her understanding of how deeply religious doubters suffer:

> What people don't realize is how much religion costs. They think faith is a big electric blanket, when of course it is the cross. It is much harder to believe than not to believe. If you feel you can't believe, you must at least do this: keep an open mind. Keep it open toward faith, keep wanting it, keep asking for it, and leave the rest to God.
>
> Whatever you do anyway, remember that these things are mysteries and that if they were such that we could understand them, they wouldn't be worth understanding. A God you understood would be less than yourself. (*HB* 353–54)

This letter clearly proves Abbot's belief in O'Connor's "robust spiritual health." Only a woman, certain in her own faith, would have been able to confront her friend's doubts so directly and so sympathetically. She understood the suffering that comes from doubt; there was nothing holier-than-thou in her advice. O'Connor's mature attitude about the cost of religious faith was also comforting; her use of the "electric blanket" image to describe the born-again concept of religion was highly realistic. She almost mirrored an idea of Paul Tillich when she advised Abbot to "keep an open mind" even when she found herself unable to believe. In "Symbols of Faith," Tillich asserted that true atheism lies in utter indifference.

During the last year of O'Connor's life, she and Louise Abbot both faced ovarian surgery, but O'Connor's came first. Though they did not see each other at Andalusia during the last months of O'Connor's life, they continued to correspond and Abbot visited her in the hospital in Atlanta. Louise Abbot made a final visit to Andalusia in the spring of 1965; she sat in O'Connor's room feeling "her presence [. . .] all around me" (Abbot, "Remembering Flannery" 70). To avoid becoming excessively sentimental, Abbot turned from the room to gaze out one of the long windows: "Directly below me, facing me, on a line with the corner of the sofa, is a peacock—one of the many I failed to see while I was busy seeing her. While I watch, he raises his flags of glory in salute" (81).

Overall, then, the friendship between these two middle-Georgia women was warm and cordial, one based on similar backgrounds and shared interests. As Abbot described their friendship, it developed naturally and seemed singularly free of any unstated agenda. The two women shared mutual affection and respect. Indeed, their connection shows O'Connor's ability to form an almost ordinary friendship. Abbot's reminiscence does much to humanize the brilliant writer whom many felt incapable of personal warmth. She revealed her compassion and caring to Louise Abbot, who, through her memoir, helps us understand the writer's ability to combine friendship with artistry.

Besides her friendships with the GSCW professors, Ben Griffith, Father McCown, the Gossetts, and Louise Abbot, O'Connor between 1957 and 1960 also became involved with another group of Milledgeville residents through a book discussion group that she allowed to hold its meetings at Andalusia. These people met regularly under O'Connor's guidance to discuss philosophy and fiction. Realizing that Flannery O'Connor had already gained a national, even international, reputation as the author of *Wise Blood* and *A Good Man Is Hard to Find and Other Stories,* members of this group were eager to know her better and to benefit from her genius. The benefit, however, was not exclusively theirs; O'Connor, through this interaction, gained a closer intellectual connection with the hometown that she had hoped to abandon.

Former Episcopal priest in Milledgeville, William Kirkland, who retired to Scott Depot, West Virginia, modestly admits that he originated the idea of the gatherings at Andalusia. Kirkland says that, though he had not even heard of Flannery O'Connor before his arrival in Milledgeville, he soon realized that she was an intellectual force to be reckoned with. He remembers that, when they met in 1954 or early 1955, he was particularly impressed by "the breadth of this woman's knowledge."[11] She had done, he soon discovered, a great deal of reading, "especially on the Catholic philosophers." Only a few years out of seminary, where he had developed a special appreciation for the German Roman Catholic philosopher, Baron Friedrich von Hügel, the Episcopal minister had tried for five years to find a Catholic priest who had read von Hügel's essays. Kirkland was pleased to discover in O'Connor a Catholic with whom he could discuss the Baron's work.

Recognizing O'Connor's intellectual strength, Kirkland therefore decided that he and a few other people in Milledgeville would benefit from meeting with her to talk about philosophy and theology. He explained, "I had sense enough to know as time went on, after two or three years, that this woman was going somewhere [. . .] so that is why the group [was formed]." Louise Abbot has written that Kirkland "inaugurated the project as 'an extension of charity' toward a lonely, bored man," but Kirkland himself emphasizes the benefit that all participants gained (Abbot, "Remembering Flannery" 68). He also suggests that O'Connor welcomed the meetings, too: "Most of the time when I was there, I had the feeling that she did not have a great number of visitors. [. . .] Both [O'Connor and her mother] were genuinely pleased to have guests." Mary Barbara Tate verifies that Kirkland started the group, though she did not recall his later participation in it. She also believes that Kirkland, concerned that a representative sampling of Milledgeville intellectuals be invited to join, selected the original members (M. B. Tate, interview 1989).

O'Connor herself first mentioned the group in a letter to Fr. James McCown on 20 December 1957:

> Two or three things have come up on which I need some expert SOS spiritual advice. Not long ago the Episcopal minister came out and wanted me to get up a group with him of people who were interested in talking about theology in modern literature. This suited me all right so about six or seven of them are coming out here every Monday night—a couple of Presbyterians, the rest Episcopalians of one stripe or another (scratch an Episcopalian and you're liable to find most anything) and me as the representative of the Holy Roman Catholic & Apostolic Church. The strain is telling on me. Anyway this minister is equipped with a list of what he would like us to read and upon the list is naturally Gide also listed on the Index. I despise Gide but if they read him I want to be able to put in my two cents worth. [. . .] You said once you would see if you had the faculties to get me permission to read such as this. Do you and will you? All these Protestants will be shocked if I say I can't get permission to read Gide. (*HB* 259)

In his published memoir of O'Connor, McCown described how he solved the problem posed by the "terrible Catholic Index of Forbidden Books": "I wrote my old morals professor, Gerald Kelly, S. J. His satisfactory response was that a Catholic has an obligation to obey church law, yes. But she has an even higher obligation to protect the church from ridicule. He suggested that she use an *epeikia,* a reasonable interpretation of a law here and now patently inapplicable" (McCown, "Remembering Flannery" 88). O'Connor reacted enthusiastically to the loophole McCown created: "I am very much obliged for your taking the time to find out about the permissions etc. I will use the *epeikia* and also invoke that word, which is very fancy" (*HB* 263).

The people who assembled at Andalusia for weekly, at first, and later biweekly meetings were a heterogeneous group. In addition to Kirkland, with his particular interest in theology and philosophy, the group numbered, as O'Connor herself asserted, fewer than ten. Except for O'Connor and her mother, the membership apparently was not absolutely concrete.

Participants—some regular, some occasional—included Dr. George Beiswanger, professor of humanities and philosophy at GSCW; James Tate, a career officer in the air force, stationed near Milledgeville; his wife, Mary Barbara Tate, a recent graduate of GSCW and a local high school English teacher; Mary Phillips, assistant professor of English at GSCW; Lance Phillips, her husband, a freelance writer; Elizabeth Ferguson, reference librarian at GSCW; Paul Cresap, an English teacher at Georgia Military College in Milledgeville; Stephen Kramer, a psychiatrist at the nearby mental hospital; Mary Sallee, O'Connor's near contemporary and neighbor who earlier had been a reporter for the *Atlanta Journal-Constitution;* Maryat Lee, O'Connor's close friend, a would-be dramatist and the sister of Dr. Robert E. Lee, president of GSCW; and Russell Green, a resident of nearby Gray, Georgia. Tom Gossett also recalls that he attended one of the gatherings. William Kirkland asserts that he himself did not attend all meetings but was "there as much as anybody."

He sees his prime role as the instigator of the meetings. His interest in theology and philosophy helped form the original reading list for the discussion, including Kierkegaard, whom he had studied as a seminarian: "We started with existentialism. [. . .] I was curious to get her reaction to [. . .] the subject." Kirkland doubts that when they began their discussion O'Connor had read any of the work of Kierkegaard, or that she even knew him, but she was, indeed, aware of the philosopher's work. In a letter to Betty Hester, dated March 1958, she wrote: "Did I lend you a copy of *Thought* with a piece in it on Kierkegaard and St. Thomas? You may have sent it back and I lent it to somebody else but for the moment I can't lay my hand on it. The Pseudo Theol. Society has started reading Kierkegaard and when I resurrect that copy I want to lend it to the minister" (*HB* 273).

George Beiswanger, the GSCW professor who guided O'Connor to Iowa, attended the gatherings irregularly. He explained, "I don't remember doing much talking myself, though engaged in thinking all the time, following the thought." Beiswanger remembered the leaders of the group being "simply those with the most assertive manner of conversing on serious matters, as a personal habit—I would say—rather than egotist pressuring." Kirkland recalls that Mary Phillips and O'Connor herself took the most active roles while Mary Barbara Tate retains the impression that the leadership role "was fairly evenly divided between James [her husband] and

Lance and Mary [Phillips]. She [O'Connor] would talk a lot when the subject interested her specifically [but] she didn't dominate the conversation. She talked but not as much as they [James Tate and the Phillipses]" (M. B. Tate, interview 1989).

James and Mary Barbara Tate were the only members who later wrote memoirs of the gatherings. James Tate, who died in March 1985, wrote his account in 1966 at the request of Rosa Lee Walston, then head of the Department of English at Georgia College. In an intracollege memo, attached to the manuscript of Tate's article in the O'Connor Collection at Georgia College and State University, dated 24 April 1967, Walston wrote that she had asked "eight people who had close association with Flannery to write informal accounts to be included in our [the college's] files for anyone who might be interested. Though all promised only one has sent in his material." James Tate's memoir with an introduction by his son J. O. Tate appeared in *The Flannery O'Connor Bulletin* in 1988. Mary Barbara Tate has written and published two articles concerning O'Connor, the first in a Georgia College publication, *Columns,* in the fall of 1964; her later article appeared in the special O'Connor issue of *Studies in the Literary Imagination* in 1987.

Elizabeth Ferguson, who had been responsible for the autograph party that the GSCW library held when O'Connor published *Wise Blood,* attended some of the gatherings. Mary Barbara Tate asserts that "from the beginning she [Ferguson] knew that Flannery would be someone we would want to have information on" (M. B. Tate, interview 1989). With genuine prescience, Ferguson started collecting O'Connor material for the library in the early 1950s. In addition, she also tried to promote O'Connor's work throughout the state. Writing in January 1954 to Ralph McGill at the *Atlanta Journal-Constitution,* she asked him to help publicize O'Connor's fiction. In a letter to Ferguson in the O'Connor Collection, McGill promised to write an editorial on O'Connor and added: "The truth is that very few people know her, and unless someone like you lets us know about her, she remains unnoted. I am very grateful to you for writing me."[12] Beiswanger described Ferguson at the gatherings as "softspoken, highly informed, courteous, helpful, with important 'if modest' contributions to every conversation." Kirkland remembers that Ferguson was so close to both Flannery and Regina O'Connor that when she died in May 1960, mother and daughter "held a private memorial service for her in Miss Betty's home."

Regina Cline O'Connor was present at Andalusia during the gatherings at her home but took no active role in the discussions. Kirkland, Tate, and Beiswanger all remembered that she came to greet visitors as they arrived, then retired to another part of the house. Mary Barbara and James Tate recalled that she often reappeared at the end of the meetings to serve light refreshments. In her article, "Flannery O'Connor at Home in Milledgeville," Mary Barbara Tate writes, "Mrs. O'Connor served decaffeinated coffee and thin store-bought cookies to our group [. . .] and sometimes we brought a special dessert. Once we had a celebration when Flannery won an award for one of her stories" (M. B. Tate, "Mary Flannery O'Connor" 32).

Flannery O'Connor was, of course, the central member of the group. As Kirkland asserts, he may have been the instigator "at the outset, but the group soon began to rely on O'Connor for guidance on what to read as well as for insights." In his 1965 published reminiscence of O'Connor, Kirkland tells of her effect on him:

> Remembering her conversations (and I vividly remember the regular visits some of us made to her home over a period of several months), I would say just two things about her. First, she felt called to hurl protests, as loud and vehement as she could make them, against the two-fold assumption that "God is Dead," and "Man is God." [. . .]
>
> My second observation is obvious to anyone who knows anything about Flannery O'Connor. She was steeped in the traditions, the lore, and the language of middle Georgia. (Kirkland, "Flannery O'Connor" 160)

Of O'Connor's role in the meetings, Mary Barbara Tate writes: "She didn't dominate conversation, but joined in when her attention was seriously engaged. She expressed her opinions firmly when she had strong convictions" (M. B. Tate, "Mary Flannery O'Connor" 33). Tate also reveals that after Kirkland's list of philosophers and theologians had been exhausted, O'Connor usually chose the books to be read and even ordered them for the participants; however, the group did not always agree with O'Connor's selections. Tate further recalls that O'Connor wanted them to read Dickens's *Hard Times,* for example, but the group voted her down (32). O'Connor herself seemed a bit relieved when the subject of discussion turned from theology to fiction. Late in February 1958, she wrote to Betty Hester: "Tonight I cope with the Rev. Kirkland's little group. Fortunately they've forgotten all about theology and we talk about Ring Lardner and Stephen Potter and any old thing" (*HB* 270).

Beiswanger eloquently summarized O'Connor's role in the meetings as

> [t]hat of host, in the simplest, most open, cordial, welcoming way. She was present without making herself present: writer, thinker, friend, person. Her role included, at the same time, that of being what the scholastics used to call *the sufficient cause or reason* (their term) for the gatherings. She was the central explanation for our being there, engaged in conversing about what concerned all of us mutually in connection with writing, fiction, letters, culture, perspective, outlook. [. . .] Though host and basic reason for the "gatherings," Flannery did not plan the meetings or dictate the direction in which the conversation should go.

Format and content of the discussions evolved during the first few months of the gatherings. Though none of the participants remembered exactly when the initial gathering occurred, O'Connor first mentioned the meetings in December 1957. They started at Monday night sessions but were soon shifted to Wednesdays. James Tate wrote that at first the group met every Wednesday night but soon changed to every other Wednesday because "Flannery's stamina" wasn't up to weekly meetings. He also remembered that the group disbanded by 10:00 to 10:30 P.M. (J. Tate 67). Though beginning with theology, the discussions gradually moved to fiction. According to Kirkland, there was no deliberate decision to "leave theology behind; Flannery didn't want to do that." O'Connor, however, seemed relieved to escape discussion of what she termed "pseudo-theology."

Soon fiction replaced theology; the group made selections in advance of meetings so that they could order books and make adequate preparation. Among the novels the group read and discussed were Melville's *Billy Budd,* Dostoyevsky's *Notes from the Underground,* Camus's *The Stranger,* Hawthorne's *The Marble Faun,* and Henry James's *What Maisie Knew.* All surviving participants remember O'Connor's enthusiasm for James. Kirkland asserts that she admired James both for his craftsmanship and his concern with the deep undercurrent of evil that lies beneath social facades. Abbot remembers that in *What Maisie Knew,* O'Connor "was much impressed with the manner in which James had handled the child in the story, making her entirely credible without sentimentality" (Abbot, "Remembering Flannery" 69). James Tate, however, wrote that O'Connor was "somewhat incredulous about the tediousness" of this story and that she was "ambivalent" about Henry James (J. Tate 67).

Another of O'Connor's favorite works that the group read and discussed was George Bernanos's *Diary of a Country Priest.* One contemporary non-Catholic novel that the participants discussed was William Styron's *Lie Down in Darkness.* Tate, Kirkland, and Beiswanger did not remember reading the novel, but O'Connor made two cogent comments about it in her letters. Early in October 1958, she wrote to Cecil Dawkins: "We are reading *Lie Down in Darkness* for our Wednesday night gathering and I find it very impressive so far" (*HB* 297). By October of the next year, again writing to Dawkins, she had revised her opinion of the book: "I have read Styron's *Lie Down in Darkness.* To my way of thinking, it was too much the long tedious Freudian case history, though the boy can write and there were overtones of better things in it" (356). Though O'Connor and Styron never met to discuss their varying outlooks on religion, it seems logical that she would have had strong reservations about her contemporary's spiritual ambiguity.

Because the participants knew each other at least fairly well, discussion of the works was generally informal. Mary Barbara Tate explains, "What people would do would be maybe read a paragraph or an introduction or just say, 'Well, I thought that this part [. . .] made me think so and so. [. . .]' But it was informal." After a time, she says, the group found that a novel "was very hard to cover in an evening [. . .] so that was when we shifted to short stories and read them there and discussed them immediately. Sometimes we would know the story but sometimes we wouldn't." Tate remembers that when two people brought stories, the group selected one, reserving the second for reading and discussion at the next meeting. Overall, she describes the format of discussion as "free-wheeling" (M. B. Tate, interview 1989).

Among the stories members brought to the group were works by Stephen Crane, Franz Kafka, Ring Lardner, Peter Taylor, Eudora Welty, Katherine Anne Porter, James Purdy, Stephen Potter, and Robie Macaulay. In her 1987 article, Mary Barbara Tate wrote that "Flannery always asked one of the men to read the selected story" (M. B. Tate, "Mary Flannery

O'Connor" 32). In a letter to Betty Hester in March 1958, O'Connor herself wrote about reading and discussing one of Robie Macauley's stories: "The last time the pseudo-literary & theological gathering gathered, we read 'The Chevigny Man' aloud and they seemed to like it. A very nice boy does the reading" (*HB* 271–72). O'Connor did not identify the "very nice boy," but he was probably either Paul Cresap or James Tate, who recalled O'Connor's reaction to the Lardner story: "Once Ring Lardner's 'The Golden Honeymoon' was read aloud and she laughed and laughed—as much, really, as I'd ever heard her laugh" (J. Tate 67). Mary Barbara Tate also remembers that individual group members sometimes brought criticism of a story just read and discussed at the preceding session.

On only one occasion was an O'Connor story presented for discussion. James Tate recalled asking her to allow him to read one of her stories aloud: "She refused permission but agreed to read one herself. It was a magnificent event. The story was 'The Enduring Chill,' a work in progress. She brought out all the comic flavor and her intonation and inflection were perfect. It was by far my most enjoyable time" (J. Tate 65). Kirkland also recalls her performance: "She really bore down in her reading with special emphasis on [Asbury's comment] 'What's wrong with me goes *way* beyond Block.'"

Again, a comment by Beiswanger on the overall mood and atmosphere of the gatherings gives clear insight into what it must have been like to have been a participant:

> [The tone was] genuinely conversational—good talk—not lecturing or posturing (in the sense of attitudinizing) however strongly someone might state an opinion. No pressure, as if the talk might die down and would need some social commonplace to keep going. There was (I feel) an essential ease about it, due in part to the getting together (without exception, I believe) of people who knew (or should easily take to knowing) each other, because inhabited by interests of a genuinely serious sort connected with the field of writing.
>
> [. . .] Plus their *first* reason for being there, *Flannery,* who, by her person and manner, prevented *that* reason from becoming too important or even apparent. She took it for granted, and so did we, without feeling any need to make gestures about it. There was no gush!

The meetings, then, continued nearly three years, giving, according to Kirkland, Tate, and Beiswanger, intellectual sustenance to the participants; however, near the end of 1960, the group disbanded. Kirkland by this time was involved in the Civil Rights movement as it moved into middle Georgia. Beiswanger thought that O'Connor's declining health might have been a factor in bringing the gatherings to an end, but Mary Barbara Tate believes that they stopped for a much more dramatic reason, clearly described in her husband's memoir:

> [O]ne of our "characters" [Lance Phillips] introduced a play to be read aloud. He declined to read it himself and persuaded one of our more diffident members [Paul Cresap] to read; of course, the reader had no idea what he was in for. It was a play, by a Frenchman of absurd (Kierkegaardian sense) and "Chatterley" persuasion, and a more prurient, lascivious mess has never been heard. Four-letter words and anatomical explication abounded. We were all stunned but endured in utter silence. The reader, reddened throughout, felt, perhaps through some existential sense, that he was honor bound to finish it. Finish it he did. Afterward, the ladies, especially, pounced on the "character" for perpetrating such a contretemps. He allowed as how he wanted to see our reactions and was utterly unfazed. (J. Tate 66)

According to Mary Barbara Tate, O'Connor, totally outraged by Phillips's tasteless joke, left the room after the reading; Mary Barbara followed her into the kitchen, where she found O'Connor seething with anger (M. B. Tate, interview 1989). After the episode, Mary Barbara recalls other, more informal visits she and James made to Andalusia to talk about literature, but the more formal gatherings ended with Lance Phillips's tactless prank.

Though the gatherings ended more than three years before O'Connor's death, they added considerable variety to her life between 1957 and 1960. O'Connor benefited from these regular contacts with other Milledgeville people who enjoyed talking about philosophy and literature. In a 1958 letter to Betty Hester, however, she showed her typical biting humor in a comment about them: "The chief result of the Monday night affairs is that we have to air the room all the next day to get the stinking cigaret smell out of it" (*HB* 262); still, her notes to Russell Green in 1960 show that O'Connor both enjoyed and looked forward to the meetings. She kept track of the dates for them and was obviously careful to alert participants to any change of plans. In one of the notes to Green, she commented, a bit ruefully, that nobody had turned up for the previous meeting. These gatherings, then, were important to both the other participants and to O'Connor: they helped intelligent Milledgevillians to understand and appreciate O'Connor as a serious writer, and they provided her with a semipublic forum at which to discuss works and ideas relevant to her own fiction. Along with the early friendships that she developed with people in Milledgeville and those who lived within a few miles of the town, these gatherings helped enable O'Connor to survive in Milledgeville and to continue to practice her art.

CHAPTER NINE

LATER FRIENDSHIPS

In a letter to Betty Hester, Flannery O'Connor wrote about both her desire for close friendships and her inability to establish them; she expressed, rather poignantly, how she turned to writing as compensation. By the time she made this confession, however, O'Connor had already formed a number of friendships both in Milledgeville and away from the town. After a rather lonely adolescence, she had left Milledgeville and had begun to establish her literary reputation with stories and sections of *Wise Blood,* published in a number of journals. She had also formed strong friendships—many based on a shared interest in writing—that clearly helped her sustain her emotional and intellectual health once lupus forced her return to Milledgeville.

Correspondence with literary friends and acquaintances she had made at Iowa and in New York and Connecticut (Robie Macauley, the Robert Lowells, Elizabeth Fenwick Way, and Sally and Robert Fitzgerald) provided outlets for both intellectual and emotional interaction. Her friendships with Robie Macauley and Andrew Lytle, initiated at Iowa, continued to enrich her life. The importance of her relationship with Sally and Robert Fitzgerald also cannot be minimized: she considered them part of her immediate, emotionally connected family. Their exchange of news, gifts, and gossip certainly helped nourish O'Connor's emotional life in Milledgeville. Though Elizabeth Hardwick and Robert Lowell remained often in her thoughts through her years in Milledgeville, her correspondence with them was somewhat sporadic, probably influenced both by their living in the North and by the mental problems Lowell experienced intermittently through the 1950s and 1960s. Still, knowing the Lowells provided O'Connor with another link to the literary world that her illness had forced her to relinquish; it was also Robert Lowell who suggested that his friend Elizabeth Bishop write to O'Connor in 1957. Though Bishop and O'Connor never met, they shared a correspondence based on mutual interests in writing and religion. They came closest to meeting when Bishop telephoned O'Connor from Savannah, where the freighter she was traveling on to Brazil docked in October 1957.

One other outside connection, forged just after her return to Milledgeville, had a strong effect on O'Connor's writing. That relationship was with Southern novelist and teacher Caroline Gordon. O'Connor certainly knew about Gordon and her work before the Fitzgeralds, who had come to know Gordon in New York City, suggested to O'Connor that the brilliant writer, teacher, and editor might be willing to read the manuscript of *Wise Blood* before she sent a final version to Harcourt Brace. Despite her marriage to the more famous fugitive-agrarian Allen Tate, Caroline Gordon was a talented writer herself who wrote novels, taught students in writing classes all over the United States, and served, informally, as a willing mentor to younger, aspiring authors like O'Connor and Walker Percy.

In his biography of Percy, Jay Tolson comments on Gordon's editorial generosity:

> The amount of time and care she gave to the novices who came to her, particularly those with real talent, was something quite remarkable. It is hard to see how she had any time left over for her own work, much less for her busy life. [. . .] Caroline Gordon gave her students a full and rigorous course in the craft of fiction. Her standards were derived from Aristotle's *Poetics* and the examples of the best Modernist writers: Flaubert, Joyce, Conrad, James, and Ford. Control, objectivity,

a sustained point of view, exactness of detail, and concern for presenting things and people so that they were seen—these were the principles that she insisted on. She also expected her charges to read and understand Aristotle's reflections on the primacy of plot. (Tolson 219)

Any study of Flannery O'Connor's statements about the writing process—the most succinct statement of these ideas occurs in "The Nature and Aim of Fiction" in *Mystery and Manners*—shows how clearly she followed Gordon's advice in all the areas Tolson describes.

In a 1979 article Sally Fitzgerald explained in detail how Gordon became involved with O'Connor's manuscript: "Robert Fitzgerald, who was, as she [O'Connor] said, satisfied that her book was good, had decided that such a new and arresting work was likely to be of interest to a friend for whose taste and artistry he had the highest regard, the novelist Caroline Gordon. With Flannery's permission, he sent the manuscript to her for a reading" (S. Fitzgerald, "A Master Class" 828). After Gordon read the manuscript early in 1951, she reported to Robert Fitzgerald her immediate enthusiasm for the novel: "This girl is a real novelist. (I wish I had had as firm a grasp on my subject matter when I was her age!) At any rate, she is already a phenomenon: a Catholic novelist with a real dramatic sense, one who relies more on her technique than her piety" (qtd. in "A Master Class" 828).

Despite her enthusiasm, however, Gordon had "'a few suggestions'" for improving the book that she shared both with Fitzgerald and Flannery O'Connor, who followed these suggestions in producing yet another draft which she again asked Gordon to read. Gordon readily agreed to a second reading and also offered to review the novel upon its publication; in her correspondence with O'Connor, she also mentioned Walker Percy; she had recently read the manuscript of his still unpublished novel "The Charterhouse" and set out to make O'Connor aware of his work: "'I don't know that your paths are likely to cross, but if they ever should I imagine that you'd find it interesting to know each other. He has been in the Church about five years'" (qtd. in "A Master Class" 830). That Gordon discovered and read novels by these two major representatives of the second wave of the Southern Literary Renascence at so nearly the same time seems somehow to be part of a grand design for Southern Letters.

Having lived in Tennessee in the 1920s and 1930s with her husband, Allen Tate, Gordon had come to know everybody of literary or academic importance in Nashville. One of these people was Brainard Cheney, a minor Nashville writer and political journalist who was also to become a close friend of O'Connor and an advocate of her work. In a letter to Cheney in late 1951, Gordon wrote of her enthusiasm for both Percy and O'Connor:

> Speaking of books, the best first novel I ever read has just come my way and from the most unlikely place. Walker Percy, Will Percy's nephew, wrote me several months ago asking if I'd criticize a novel he's just finished. [. . .] It is [. . .] a sample of what the next development in the novel will be, according to me! And it *will* be something new. At least something we had not had before. Novel[s] written by people who are *consciously* rooted and grounded in the faith. [. . .] It is no accident, I'm sure, that in the last two months the two best first novels I've ever read have been by Catholic writers. The other novel is by Flannery O'Connor. Harcourt, Brace say it is the most shocking book they have ever read but have finally agreed to publish it.[1]

After her second reading of O'Connor's novel, Gordon responded with, in O'Connor's words, "some nine pages of comments and she certainly increased my education thereby. So I am doing some more things to it and then I mean to send it off for the LAST time" (*HB* 28). In her article on Gordon and O'Connor, Sally Fitzgerald included the complete text of Gordon's critical commentary on the novel, which ranged from what she perceived to be problems in point of view to criticism of O'Connor's diction and mechanics. Gordon's close reading of *Wise Blood* shows how carefully she read and criticized all of O'Connor's later fiction. To the end of her life, the younger writer continued to send each of her works to the older, experienced editor and teacher before submitting them for publication. Of Gordon's importance to O'Connor, Brainard Cheney's wife, Frances, asserted, "Caroline Tate probably knew Flannery better than any of us; she knew her work better because she read it before it was published."[2]

O'Connor proved the importance of Gordon in her life in the dozens of comments she made about her "mentor" to other correspondents.[3] Often, in counseling aspiring writers, O'Connor even sounded like Gordon. At the same time, O'Connor apparently saw little contradiction between her enthusiasm for Gordon's advice and her hesitation about assigning the highest literary value to Gordon's own fiction. Walter Sullivan asserts, "She [O'Connor] was a better writer than Caroline [. . .] and she must have known it." When Gordon became her editor, O'Connor had apparently read little of the older writer's work. Later, when Betty Hester was reading Gordon's collection *The Forest of the South,* O'Connor admitted that the only story she had read from it was "Old Red"; after getting the volume herself and reading "Summer Dust," she worried about her use of scriptural references similar to those in Gordon's story. She was "in a quandary as to whether to change that in 'A View of the Woods'" (*HB* 187). Fortunately, for the success of her own story, O'Connor did not delete the scriptural reference.

When Gordon published her Catholic novel, *The Malefactors,* in 1956, O'Connor read it, but with mixed views of its artistry. She privately berated the reviewer in *Time* magazine for his unfavorable notice and urged *The Bulletin* to allow her to review it; however, she felt free to comment on Gordon's failures in characterization, calling her depiction of Dorothy Day "a little *bodiless* and I can't decide if this was intentional or not" (*HB* 133). To Alta Haynes, to whom she had recommended the novel, she stated her reservations even more frankly; however, she also expressed her gratitude for Gordon's positive influence on her own work.[4]

O'Connor's appreciation of Gordon and her reliance on the older writer's expertise continued until she died, although toward the end she probably sent her work more out of habit than necessity. After Gordon read the manuscript of *The Violent Bear It Away,* O'Connor's reaction to her enthusiasm is interesting. To Betty Hester, she wrote: "It would have done your heart good to see all the marks on the copy, everything commented upon, doodles, exclamation points, cheers, growls" (*HB* 321), but she was also worried that Gordon was *too* enthusiastic about the novel and afterward asked her former official editor at Harcourt Brace, Catharine Carver, to read the manuscript, explaining: "Caroline Gordon has seen it and she likes it but she shares my point of view on some things and I want somebody to read it who doesn't necessarily" (319). O'Connor wrote her last story, "Parker's Back," while she was literally dying. She sent even that story to Gordon, who replied with her usual copious suggestions, which O'Connor rather resented; she wrote to Betty Hester, "I did well to write it at all" (594).

Through the years, O'Connor and Gordon also developed a personal friendship; the first result was O'Connor's spending a weekend with Gordon and her friends in Connecticut in June 1955. In a letter to the Fitzgeralds, O'Connor described the visit: "They had a party at which the chief guests were dear old Malcolm Cowley and dear old Van Wyke Brooks [*sic*]. Dear old Van Wyke insisted that I read a story at which horror-stricken looks appeared on the faces of both Caroline and Sue. 'Read the shorter one!' they both screamed. I read "A Good Man Is Hard to Find," and Mr. Brooks later remarked to Miss Jenkins that it was a shame someone with so much talent should look upon life as a horror story. Malcolm was very polite and asked me if I had a wooden leg" (*HB* 85).

Gordon also visited O'Connor several times in Milledgeville, either alone or in the company of their mutual friend Ashley Brown, an enthusiast of Gordon's work who wrote his doctoral dissertation at Vanderbilt on her fiction. O'Connor enjoyed these visits but remarked in several of her letters that she found the occasions "strenuous," probably because of Gordon's boundless energy, her neuroticism brought on by alcohol, her marital problems with Tate, and her constant editorial advice: in a letter to Cecil Dawkins in October 1959, O'Connor described how Gordon during one visit "gave me several hours' lecture on my prose" (*HB* 356).

Shortly before O'Connor died, Caroline Gordon visited her at the Baldwin County Hospital in Milledgeville; she recalled that last visit and O'Connor's continued dedication to her vocation even when deathly ill. O'Connor kept a notebook under her pillow and "wrote in it 'whenever they aren't doing something to me'" (Gordon, "Heresy in Dixie" 266). Gordon's interest in O'Connor and her work did not end when O'Connor died. During the next fifteen years, Gordon promoted her protégée's work, trying both to advance its readership and to enhance O'Connor's literary reputation. In her *Esprit* tribute to O'Connor in 1964, Gordon praised her for having wed a "revolutionary technique to its appropriate subject matter[, . . .] the operation of supernatural grace in the lives of natural men and women" (Gordon, "Flannery O'Connor" 28). In "An American Girl," Gordon rated O'Connor as the "most talented—and the most professional" of the young writers of her generation and compared O'Connor's approach to that of Henry James. Both writers, she asserted, were dedicated to the writing of fiction as a "sacred calling" (Gordon, "An American Girl" 130).

When Georgia College held its first O'Connor symposium on 6 and 7 April 1974 to mark the tenth anniversary of O'Connor's death, Caroline Gordon delivered the Flannery O'Connor Memorial Lecture, "Rebels and Revolutionaries: The New American Scene." In that presentation, Gordon continued her comparison of O'Connor with James, emphasizing that both writers were concerned with the spiritual health of their characters. Gordon's insistence on this connection between O'Connor and James says much about her enthusiasm for the work of both writers; her advocacy of the fiction of Flannery O'Connor was, however, forever steadfast as her final comment in the address proves: "Her place in the history of American literature is, I believe, secure, and it is no small niche, either" (Gordon, "Rebels and Revolutionaries" 56).

Partly through the influence of Gordon and partly through that of Ashley Brown, with whom O'Connor first corresponded when he was an instructor at Washington and Lee University, O'Connor, in 1953, established another significant literary and personal friendship—that with Brainard and Frances Cheney who lived and worked in Nashville, Tennessee. In her correspondence with them and others, O'Connor always called the two by nicknames: Lon and Fannie. Her connection with the Cheneys also helped O'Connor establish stronger friendships with both Ashley Brown and Thomas Stritch, close friends of the Cheneys. In 1956 and 1957, O'Connor formed vital friendships with two other women: Elizabeth "Betty" Hester from Atlanta became a friend to whom O'Connor exposed more of her personal history and feelings than to any other; Maryat Lee, whose brother was president of GSCW, provided her a vibrant connection with the cultural and social life of New York City.

Brainard and Frances Cheney came to occupy a significant position in O'Connor's life after he reviewed *Wise Blood* in the autumn 1952 issue of *Shenandoah,* a highly successful student publication of Washington and Lee University. Cheney's understanding of her intentions in the novel drew him and his wife Frances into a correspondence with O'Connor that developed into friendship. Theirs was the only home outside Milledgeville that O'Connor visited socially in the late 1950s and early 1960s. The Cheneys also saw her fairly regularly at Andalusia, and Brainard Cheney and O'Connor read and criticized each other's fiction.

Their long acquaintance began when Ashley Brown urged Tom Carter, student editor of the journal, to ask Cheney to write a review of *Wise Blood* after Andrew Lytle had refused Carter's offer. Cheney knew about O'Connor before he read her novel because Caroline Gordon had praised *Wise Blood* in the letter to him in late 1951. Shortly after he published the review, Cheney wrote of his own enthusiasm for the novel to Tom Stritch: "I have recently read an important first novel, I should like to commend to you: *Wise Blood* by Flannery O'Connor—I reviewed it for *Shenandoah*. She really makes use of the hysterical religions. It is allegory and, while there is no similarity in their style or technique, her effect is somewhat like Kafka. [. . .] I might add that this 26-year-old girl gives me some of the wryest and fiercest humor I ever read."[5] Having read Cheney's review in *Shenandoah,* O'Connor wrote to Gordon asking about Cheney; Gordon immediately wrote to him on 2 February 1953 expressing her hope that the Cheneys would meet O'Connor:

> I think you'd both like her. Cal Lowell says she is a saint, but then he is given to extravagance. She may be, though, at that. She is a cradle Catholic, raised in Milledgeville where there are so few other Catholics; [. . .] she sure is a powerful Catholic. No nonsense about her! She has some dire disease—some form of arthritis—and is kept going only by huge doses of something called ACTH. We are expected to adore all the Lord's doing, but it does give you pause when you reflect that this gifted girl will probably not be with us long whereas Truman Capote will live to a ripe old age, laden down with honours.[6]

It seems logical, then, that O'Connor, encouraged by Gordon, would have wanted to communicate with Cheney. Her February letter to him was uncharacteristically warm and communicative. She thanked him not just for the review but also for insights into the novel that helped increase her own awareness of its meaning. In his return letter to her, written in March 1953, Cheney wrote of the recent conversion of his wife and himself to Roman Catholicism. He also told O'Connor of his long friendship with Caroline Gordon Tate and suggested that he and O'Connor should meet: "There are not so many of us [Catholics] that we should set the common bent at naught" (*CC* 5). Because the Cheneys owned property at St. Simon's, a resort area in southeast Georgia, he asked if they might visit her en route to their home there. Subsequently, their first visit to Andalusia occurred on 6 June 1953. In separate letters to others, both Brainard Cheney and O'Connor reacted to that meeting. O'Connor wrote to the Fitzgeralds the next day, "The Cheneys stopped by yesterday on their way to South, Ga. and we liked them very much. [. . .] Mrs. C. is a liberry science teacher at Peabody but she is very nice in spite of that" (*HB* 58). On 28 June Cheney wrote to Robert Penn Warren, "Incidentally, I dropped by to see Flannery O'Connor the other day on my way down to the Georgia coast—I had never met her—and was delighted with her. I think she is a very talented girl."[7]

After this first visit, O'Connor and the Cheneys maintained not only a constant flow of written correspondence but also a number of visits back and forth until O'Connor's death. Frances Cheney recalled their immediate enthusiasm for each other:

> We just hit it off. It was just as if we had known her all our lives and our backgrounds were exactly the same and we had a lot in common, too. And we liked to read the same things and we laughed at the same things. Flannery had a kind of Gothic humor.
>
> She used to come see us right often. Her mother always made her buy a new dress. [As a house guest] she was marvelous. We put her back in the junk room and I'd go in there— she spent a good deal of time there—and she would be saying her prayers.

O'Connor first visited the Cheneys—along with Ashley Brown—in late July 1953 as a letter to the Fitzgeralds revealed. She also described the content of their conversations in an October letter to Robie Macauley: "I heard a lot of Tennessee politics and more literary talk, most of it over my head, then since I left Iowa" (*HB* 64). Brainard Cheney described O'Connor's first visit to Cold Chimneys in a letter to Robert Fitzgerald on 14 August 1953: "Flannery O'Connor was up to see us for a week-end last month and we enjoyed her so much—she seems a very solid sort and salty. She appeared almost simultaneously with her story, THE RIVER, in the Sewanee Review, and she read it for us in her good Georgia drawl; the exact tone of voice for the story, which I believe is her finest, perhaps."[8]

From this promising beginning, the friendship between the Cheneys and O'Connor flourished through the next eleven years. As early as 1955, they invited O'Connor to accompany them on a planned trip to Europe. O'Connor turned down the invitation because she was still getting accustomed to the crutches her deteriorating hip joints had forced her to use. Still, she visited them two or three times a year and they—sometimes together, sometimes Brainard Cheney alone—stayed at Andalusia on a number of occasions, though during the late 1950s and early 1960s both Cheneys were much occupied with their busy lives. Brainard Cheney, a fairly liberal Southern Democrat, was a political journalist and campaigner intimately involved with Tennessee politics at the highest levels, and Frances was head librarian at George Peabody College in Nashville. She taught classes both in winter and summer sessions. Active in the American Library Association, she also attended meetings all over the country.

One of O'Connor's visits to the Cheneys occurred simultaneously with that of noted conservative Russell Kirk. In October 1955, he came to Vanderbilt to lecture and stayed with the Cheneys at Cold Chimneys. Because of their mutual reserve, he and O'Connor had little to say to each other. Fannie Cheney recalled O'Connor's inability to talk with Kirk, and, in letters to Betty Hester, O'Connor herself wrote of both her desire to hear him lecture—that didn't happen because he lectured on Monday instead of Saturday, as she had expected—and their failure to communicate: "He is about 37, looks like Humpty Dumpty (intact) with constant cigar and (outside) porkpie hat. He is nonconversational and so am I, and the times we were left alone together our attempts to make talk were like the efforts of two midgets to cut down a California redwood" (*HB* 112).

Their only real dialogue occurred, she remembered, in their mutual condemnation of liberal educational reformers William Heard Kilpatrick and John Dewey. Kirk himself published a brief memoir of their meeting in *The Flannery O'Connor Bulletin* in 1979 (Kirk, "Memoir by Humpty Dumpty" 14–17). He admitted that he knew nothing of O'Connor's work ahead of their meeting, but was immediately fascinated when she read "A Good Man Is Hard to Find" aloud; he was, in fact, so impressed that he began to read her stories on his return trip from Tennessee to Michigan; he also recommended her fiction to T. S. Eliot, who wrote to him "that he had seen a book of her stories when he had been in New York, 'and was quite horrified by those I read. She has certainly an uncanny talent of a high order but my nerves are just not strong enough to take much of a disturbance'" (16). Kirk treasured his memory of their one meeting despite their inability to communicate well with each other: "We seemed to agree on everything." He called that meeting "one of Eliot's Timeless moments" and commented on O'Connor's ability to understand transcendent truths: "[A]t the age of sixty I begin to understand truths which Flannery discerned at the age of thirty;" he declared, "She was made for eternity" (15–16). O'Connor proved her respect and admiration for Kirk when, on 21 July 1956, she reviewed Kirk's collection of essays, *Beyond the Dreams of Avarice,* for *The Bulletin;* quoting Romano Guardini's comment that "when a man accepts divine truth in the obedience of faith, he is forced to rethink human truth," O'Connor applauded Kirk's ability to follow Guardini's advice: "Mr. Kirk has managed in a succession of books which have proved both scholarly and popular to do both and to make the voice of an intelligent and vigorous and conservative thought respected in this country" (*PG* 23).

On their visits to Andalusia, the Cheneys formed strong impressions of the O'Connors' lives there and the quality of the relationship between O'Connor and her mother. Frances Cheney believed that the impression that Regina and Flannery didn't get along is "completely untrue, completely false. They were just as companionable as they could possibly be. [. . .] Flannery wouldn't have lived as long as she did if it hadn't been for the tender, loving care of her mother." She did recall, however, that Regina had a tendency to intrude on literary conversations with Flannery: "She wanted her presence felt."

Brainard Cheney visited the O'Connor's alone several times and reported his reactions to these visits in letters to his wife. One letter in particular, written 3 December 1956, offers considerable insight into the lives of Regina and Flannery at Andalusia:

> Most pleasant week-end with Flannery and Regina. F. and I got in a lot of literary talk—I might say, despite R. God bless her! I read a new short story of F.'s about which she is uncertain and she read the first-draft of my first chapter [of a novel he was currently trying to write. . . .]

Brother (or Uncle [Louis Cline], as you will) was there with a young lady, whom he had just taken horseback riding, when I arrived. But they soon disappeared. We went in to town (since I was there to drive at night) to confession Saturday evening—and to bed by 10:30 P.M. And to Mass the following morning at 7:15 (which is really 6:15) in N[ashville].) and I might say, drove in that four miles, in the pink dawn at somewhere close to zero—at least the frost was so heavy it looked like snow!

Brother was out as the morning warmed up. He, rather freely, confided in me that the place was not doing what it ought to do, but that R. wouldn't take any advice from him! Only a moment later, she well demonstrated this when he made a suggestion about the water pump—a more embattled sister I never saw! The only difference between me and Lee [his sister] is that *he* never answered her back. Just let it go.

I asked her if she made a profit. Heavens no! If she broke even! Not on the books, but then it furnishes brother an ideal way to save on his income tax. After being conducted on a tour Sunday afternoon by Regina (I may say it's a big place: I'd guess 3 to 4 hundred acres) I am convinced that the chief value of the farm is to furnish locus and characters and situations for F.'s short stories! And I can't think of a more valuable use to put a farm to.

R., also, took me on a tour of the town, including the family mansion, which, I may say, is very handsome and has charm. It back[s] up, at right angles, to the one-time Governor's Mansion (which is impressive). A splendid diningroom [in the Cline mansion]![9]

The friendship between O'Connor and the Cheneys was especially important to her because it provided her, along with their warm cordiality, constant literary stimulation. She knew that when she visited the Cheneys in Nashville she could become part of a much more sophisticated environment than that of Milledgeville. She could stop being Regina Cline's daughter who wrote and become, at least on occasion, part of a literary elite composed of people who recognized her genius. Cold Chimneys also gave her the opportunity to read her stories to an appreciative audience that sometimes included Ashley Brown and Tom Stritch, both of whom became close friends.

Ashley Brown, whom one of his literary acquaintances called the "Jimmy Fiddler" of contemporary literature, has made a full life of establishing acquaintances with some of the major literary figures of the twentieth century, including, among many others, Ezra Pound, Caroline Gordon, Elizabeth Bishop, and Flannery O'Connor. Brown is also addicted to travel, so much so that in 1960 O'Connor wrote to Andrew Lytle: "That boy is on the road more than Kerouac, though in a more elegant manner" (*HB* 373). To Betty Hester, O'Connor described him as "the original air plant" (481). After earning a Ph.D. at Vanderbilt, Brown joined the English faculty at the University of South Carolina, where he remained until his retirement in 1996.

O'Connor first became acquainted with Brown when he was an instructor at Washington and Lee. Because he then read all the important literary journals, he was aware of her work from around 1948, but at first he "wasn't quite sure whether she was male or female."[10] He particularly recalls her early stories in *Accent*. As faculty advisor to *Shenandoah,* Brown wrote to O'Connor about publishing one of her stories in the journal. O'Connor and Brown actually met for the first time during her late July 1953 visit to Cold Chimneys, which Brown describes as "a kind of literary center for some of the so-called Southern Renascence. [. . .] It was an absolutely wonderful place." The friendship between O'Connor and Brown flourished afterward, with his making frequent visits to Andalusia, especially after he settled at South Carolina in 1959. Brown describes the nature and basis of his friendship with both Flannery and her mother:

> We already had all this correspondence in connection with *Shenandoah* and then it developed that we had a number of friends in common. She was a very easy person to know. [. . .]
>
> It was a very easygoing friendship. Let's put it this way: I was the kind of friend who visited Andalusia [. . .] and help[ed] do the dishes after dinner. [. . .] My typical visit there would be a few days, a kind of extended weekend, so they knew perfectly well that I did not have to be entertained in any way.
>
> I [was] always on easy terms with her mother, too. Some people, I think, were not, and she put them off, but I had no

trouble at all because Regina O'Connor [was] a typical woman of her time and place. [. . .] Actually, as Flannery grew older, during the years in which I knew her, let's say the last eleven years of her life, I think mother and daughter grew much closer than they might have seemed at first. I noticed Flannery increasingly would use "we" rather than "I" in speaking of things at home. At first [her living at home with her mother] might have seemed a slightly forced situation, that is to say, Flannery *had* to fall back on Milledgeville and specifically on her mother.

In letters in *The Habit of Being,* O'Connor showed her considerable affection for Brown in references to his interest in contemporary fiction, his extensive foreign travel, and his "strenuous" visits to Andalusia. At one point, in 1957, Betty Hester must have asked O'Connor whether her connection with Brown had a "romantic" component; her reply clearly stated the boundaries of their friendship: "Don't however refer to him as 'your' A.; there are no claims there and none desired. He is very dry and very intelligent and it is always good to have somebody like that to talk to" (*HB* 236–37).

A particular interest shared by Brown and O'Connor was their enthusiasm for contemporary literature. Because of her self-perceived lack of education, which she certainly compensated for by wide reading, O'Connor capitalized on friendships with those whom she immediately learned were more widely read than she. Brown emphasizes that O'Connor's high regard for Robie Macauley, also a friend of his, was partly based in her admiration for the depth and breadth of Macauley's knowledge. Brown's own expertise in contemporary literature helped kindle *their* friendship; for example, he says that he introduced her to the work of both Iris Murdoch and William Golding. In March 1960, O'Connor wrote to Betty Hester of Brown's enthusiasm for Golding: "The last time Ashley was here he brought me the *Lord of the Flies.* Good old Ashley is a fan of people like Golding usually ten years before anyone else knows they exist" (*HB* 384). When Brown chose to write his doctoral dissertation on Caroline Gordon's fiction, his relationship with O'Connor became even stronger. In May 1959 at the Cheneys', she read his chapter on *The Malefactors* and reported to Gordon: "I think it's the best thing I've read on *The Malefactors*" (332). Overall, like other of Ashley Brown's contemporaries, O'Connor liked him in spite of his eccentricities.

Their shared friendships, his personal warmth, his literary interests, and his gadfly addiction to travel all appealed to her. In 1962 she wrote to Betty Hester, who must have made a critical comment about him: "That about Ashley is right. He knows nothing much beyond the rational about literature, but in other ways I have had glimpses of a good deal of tenderness and even some charity in him" (503).

Thomas Stritch, a native Tennessean, was still another friend of the Cheneys who also became a closely acquainted with O'Connor. What must have drawn them together more than anything else was their mutual family history as Roman Catholics in the South. Of that connection, Stritch himself has written, "Flannery and I were both cradle Catholics, rare in the South" (Stritch 175–76). Though O'Connor's Cline ancestors were pivotal in establishing the Roman Catholic Church in Milledgeville, Stritch's family history in the Church was even more illustrious. His uncle, Cardinal Samuel Alphonsus Stritch (1887–1958), was both a cardinal and archbishop of Chicago (Stephens 120). In 1963 O'Connor, in fact, offered Stritch advice about the memoir he was trying to write about this uncle: "I have some advice for you about the Cardinal's portrait. My advice is free, excellent, unsought after but given without stint. If you have only written it three times, it is still supposed to be no good. You have a defect of patience, not a defect of energy. But even if you have both you ought to keep on with it" (*HB* 524).

Sally Fitzgerald, also a longtime friend of Stritch, wrote of the friendship between O'Connor and him: "Thomas Stritch was one of Flannery O'Connor's most cherished friends. [. . .] Flannery greatly enjoyed his company."[11] O'Connor and Stritch apparently met in June 1957 when she lectured at Notre Dame, where he was a professor; she afterward reported to Brainard Cheney: "I liked Tom Stritch very much." Afterward the two corresponded frequently and Stritch visited her several times at Andalusia. The content of her letters to him show that she regarded him as both a personal friend and a literary correspondent; in her first letter to him, she wrote of her disgust at the current literary establishment, representatives of whom she had just experienced at Southern Writers' Workshop at the University of Georgia:

> They are all writing television plays in television language and they are all nuts; and so was I after three hours. [. . .] However I was one of the lesser features. The big attractions were The New

York Agent Who Sold *Gone with the Wind* to the Movies, and two giant-sized poetesses from South Georgia who conducted a panel on "The Religious Market." One old sister said she wrote true-confession stories with one hand and Sunday-school stories with the other—which sounds right to me as I always suspected the same mind produced both. (*HB* 231)

O'Connor showed how strongly she valued Stritch's opinion of her work when she wrote to him after he had read *The Violent Bear It Away*: "I am real pleased you liked the book. Some folks I don't care whether they like it or not but it adds a certain glint to it for me that you do" (*HB* 388). Through the years, O'Connor often invited Stritch to visit her in Milledgeville, telling him in the letter above, "We are real cheered you're coming to see us & suit yourself about the time. We'll take you when we can get you" (524).

Stritch spent most of a week in late August 1963 at Andalusia, and O'Connor's most revealing comment about her strong feelings for him came in a letter she wrote to Betty Hester soon after in September 1963: "About dedicating books. You know I've been writing 18 years and have only published three. You sound like I had one a month at least on the presses. Maybe someday there will be one for Thos. but the next is slated for Louis I Cline, who is 70½ while Thos. is only 50½. I don't want them to die before I get around to them, though that may happen" (*HB* 541). The sad irony is, of course, that O'Connor herself died before either Louis Cline or Stritch; *Everything That Rises Must Converge,* published posthumously, has Robert Fitzgerald's introduction but no dedication.

O'Connor began what was one of the major friendship-correspondences in her life on 20 July 1955, when she answered a letter from an admirer in Atlanta who had written to her with an intelligent and appreciative reading of *Wise Blood* and *A Good Man Is Hard to Find.* That correspondent, to whom O'Connor ultimately wrote approximately 150 letters, was the young woman —a near contemporary of O'Connor—whom Sally Fitzgerald in *The Habit of Being* identified only as "A." After Elizabeth Hester committed suicide on the day after Christmas in 1998, Atlanta newspapers immediately revealed her identity as O'Connor's "correspondent" and "obscure penpal." In an obituary in the *Macon Telegraph,* Fitzgerald asserted that she had protected Hester's identity because "'[s]he was quite unstable emotionally. She didn't want to risk being overstimulated by the academics, the students and the reporters that would have been calling on her.'"[12]

Hester, a woman with a somewhat limited formal education, was, however, an inveterate reader and aspiring writer with a strong interest in Catholicism. In an unpublished paragraph in a letter O'Connor wrote to Cecil Dawkins in April 1960, O'Connor described her friend as a "Credit Reporter" and an inveterate reader and writer who came from a harsh family background, including the suicide of one parent and being "shipped off" to a remote private school when she was quite young. At the end of the paragraph, O'Connor cautioned Dawkins against spreading this information.[13]

Of the immediate attraction between the two, Sally Fitzgerald wrote in *The Habit of Being*: "Flannery was obviously hungry for conversation on matters of primary interest to her, and she found with her new correspondent exactly the kind of exchange she needed" (89). Louise Westling also asserts that O'Connor's letters to Hester "document an intense, dynamic friendship which relieved O'Connor's intellectual and emotional isolation on the Georgia farm and probed the central questions of her identity and her purposes as a writer, as well as religious issues important to them both" (Westling, "Flannery O'Connor's Revelations" 15).

Hester's appreciation for O'Connor's work, her intelligence and interest in writing, her acquaintance with Louis Cline, her having an aunt who had known Edward O'Connor, and her striving toward Roman Catholicism all help explain her appeal to Flannery O'Connor. Though she visited O'Connor at Andalusia three or four times during the years of their friendship, the fact that they didn't visit often also helps account for the richness of the numerous letters between them. Had they met more frequently, they would have talked about rather than written of their shared interests. Ashley Brown also suggests that because O'Connor had no sibling, Hester, in addition, may have filled this role in her life: "The correspondence with Betty Hester is, of course, very important. [. . .] Betty was in some ways, a difficult person, but I see what the relationship was more clearly now. Flannery had no sibling; in a way, Betty [. . .] filled a psychological need. [. . .] She was a kind of sister [to Flannery]." Whether surrogate sister or intellectual soul mate, Betty Hester was certainly a major figure in O'Connor's life, particularly during the first two years of their correspondence. A rich flow of letters passed between O'Connor and Hester between July 1955 and July 1957; fifty-five from

O'Connor appear in *The Habit of Being*. Copies of Hester's letters to O'Connor, now at Emory University, will not be available to scholars until 2007.[14]

O'Connor's letters to Hester during these two years are longer than those to most other correspondents and cover a greater variety of subjects. She wrote of family, of gender issues, of books they had read or were reading, of their writing, and of religion. One practical benefit to O'Connor of her friendship with Hester was that the Atlanta resident had immediate access to bookstores and libraries that far surpassed the number and variety of those in Milledgeville. As early as September 1955, O'Connor wrote to her, "You are very good to offer to get me books from the Atlanta library and if there is something I especially need and can't get here, I will not hesitate to ask you" (*HB* 107).

What is first quite certain from exploring the letters between the two women is that, in corresponding with Hester, O'Connor revealed herself personally to a greater degree than in letters to other correspondents. Theirs seemed clearly a "marriage of true minds." It was to Hester that O'Connor wrote of her father; no other published letters contain references to him. That Hester's aunt had known Edward O'Connor certainly influenced O'Connor to talk about him, but Hester must also have given O'Connor the emotional security she needed to talk about the father whom she had lost so early. Of O'Connor's revelations about her father, Louise Westling has written, "O'Connor wrote movingly to [Hester] about him, describing her relationship to him without any of the irony or comic detachment she used in remarks about her mother" (Westling, "Flannery O'Connor's Revelations" 19).

Other highly significant and personal revelations occur in a letter she wrote to Hester in July 1956, in which she made her most telling statements about the effects of her illness or her life, on how success affected her, and on her inherited inability to express much emotional warmth. Nowhere else in her correspondence did O'Connor so candidly reveal her attitude toward her illness; again, most of her friends—among them the Gossetts, who had to ask Regina if they wanted to know about O'Connor's health—never heard her refer to her illness, even when she was obviously suffering. Her usual attitude toward celebrity was also often deprecating rather than moralistic; even with Hester, on another occasion, she derided being thought of as a "somebody." Finally, it is only to Hester that she admitted the paucity of emotional expression in her family; at the same time, however, it is only to this correspondent that she admitted having fallen in love several times in her life.

Another important phase of their friendship evolved around their mutual interest in writing. In a June 1956 letter, O'Connor gave Hester a detailed description of her writing station: "I have a large ugly brown desk, one of those that the typewriter sits in a depression in the middle of and on either side are drawers. In front I have a stained mahogany orange crate with the bottom knocked out and a cartridge shell box that I have sat up there to lend height and hold papers and whatnot and all my paraphernalia is somewhere around this vital center and a little rooting produces it" (*HB* 161).

Hester often read O'Connor's works in progress and made suggestions which O'Connor sometimes followed; for example, when she was writing "A View of the Woods," she wrote Hester explaining how she had followed several of them: "Well I have now acted on yr three suggestions with much profit to the story. The business about traveling too close to the embankment is meant to show the old man's concern for her safety at all times but seeing it doesn't give that impression, I have extended it with a sentence to the effect that Mr. Fortune was always careful to see that she avoided dangers. 'He would not let her sit in snakey places or put her hand in bushes that might hide hornets'" (*HB* 177).

Hester, apparently, also asked O'Connor directly whether she had based Hulga in "Good Country People" on herself. She offered Hester a reasoned reply on 24 September 1955, calling Hester's identification "a little too sweeping for me." She admitted that "something of oneself gets through," but asserted that the real job of the artistic writer is to see that such an identification "does not happen" (*HB* 105).

O'Connor refined some of her ideas about writing by reading and commenting on the fiction that Hester was trying to write. She also soon realized both how hard it was to advise other writers when she herself found the process as arduous as that of Camus's Sisyphus: "I am convinced that anybody who gives anybody else any advice ought to spend forty days in the desert both before and after. Anyway, when I told you to write what was easy for you, what I should have said was what *possible* for you. Now none of it is easy, none of it really *comes* easy except in a few rare cases on a few rare occasions. In my whole time of writing the only parts that have come easy for me were Enoch Emery and Hulga; the rest has been pushing stone uphill with my nose" (*HB* 241).

In a November 1956 letter to Hester, O'Connor wrote that she did not criticize "other people's manuscripts" very severely because in reading them she didn't "concern myself overly with meaning" (*HB* 183). O'Connor also scolded Hester for trying to produce formulaic writing exercises; in the process of explaining how to begin to write fiction, she revealed much about her own approach to writing:

> Don't do anything that you're are not interested in and that don't have a promise of being whole. This doesn't mean you have to have a plot in mind. You would probably do just as well to get that plot business out of your head and start simply with a character or anything that you can make come alive. When you have a character he will create his own situation and his situation will suggest some kind of resolution as you get into it. Wouldn't it be better for you to discover a meaning in what you write than to impose one? Nothing you write will lack meaning because the meaning is in you. Once you have done a first draft then read it and see what it says and then see how you can bring out better what it says. (*HB* 188)

Hester sent much of her own fiction to O'Connor for her expert reading. She wrote a number of never-published short stories and at least two novels during the years of their friendship. O'Connor helped Hester with this fiction in spite of her reluctance about giving editorial advice. O'Connor, patient and scrupulous in advising her friend, went so far as to suggest journals that might take certain stories and even offered to submit a story for her. *New World Writing,* which had published O'Connor's early fiction, apparently held one of Hester's stories for further consideration and O'Connor tried to interest her own editor, Elizabeth McKee, in Hester's work. Despite O'Connor's help, however, Hester's only publications during their friendship were several reviews in the Georgia diocesan publication *The Bulletin.* In unpublished letters to Cecil Dawkins written during the early 1960s, O'Connor commented sympathetically on Hester's problems. She described

Hester's feeling discouraged about not publishing any of her writing and asked Dawkins to write to Hester to offer encouragement. In a later letter to Dawkins, O'Connor wrote of Hester's failure to write steadily; she felt that Hester was too emotional and insufficiently disciplined.

O'Connor also told Dawkins of Hester's enthusiasm for Iris Murdoch and her work; in fact, Hester had begun a correspondence with Murdoch that continued until the British novelist fell victim to Alzheimer's disease in the mid-1990s. As early as 1961, O'Connor seemed to have been a bit suspicious of Hester's rabid devotion to Murdoch, writing to Dawkins about the Murdoch "kick" Hester was on. When Hester planned to visit O'Connor in May 1962, O'Connor wrote to Dawkins that she hoped Hester would not bring her obsession with Iris Murdoch to Milledgeville. O'Connor worried that this infatuation affected both Hester's own writing and her faith in God. The end of Hester's long-term correspondence with Murdoch, who died early in 1999, may indeed have contributed to her own death.

Aside from the literary and personal, the most salient feature of the early correspondence between Flannery O'Connor and Betty Hester was their discussion of spiritual issues. Peter S. Hawkins has written of O'Connor's role as spiritual advisor to Hester:

> The Defender of the Faith in O'Connor clearly had her work cut out; in fact, the correspondence produced an outpouring of theological reflection and spiritual wisdom not only outstanding in the context of O'Connor's collected letters, but on par with anything in Baron von Hügel or C. S. Lewis. It was also an outpouring that would change directions several times in response to "A"'s move from an initial wariness toward Catholicism (Summer 1955), to her decision to be baptized (Winter, 1956) and confirmed (Spring, 1956), to the announcement of her leaving the Church (Autumn, 1961). (99)

Writing to Hester, who at the beginning of their friendship was already intrigued by Roman Catholicism, helped O'Connor to clarify for herself certain theological issues. Her comments influenced Hester to ask even more questions and, as a result, made O'Connor think about her own faith in a more intellectual way. In an early letter, she reacted to a questioning statement that Hester had apparently made about church dogma: "Dogma can in no way limit a limitless God. [. . .] For me a dogma is only a gateway to contemplation and is an instrument of freedom and not restriction" (*HB* 92). In the same letter, O'Connor also analyzed the role of the individual communicant in the Church. She asserted that any member, "no matter how worthless himself, [is] a part of the Body of Christ and a participator in the Redemption. There is no blueprint the Church gives for understanding this. It is a matter of Faith and the Church can force no one to believe it" (92). Later, O'Connor also explained her ideas about any supposed emotional content of religion: "I must say that the thought of everyone lolling about in an emotionally satisfying faith is repugnant to me. I believe that we are ultimately directed Godward but that this journey is often impeded by emotion" (100). In these early letters, O'Connor also clearly delineated her Belief as being entirely different from that of a pantheist who worships God in nature, asserting that "[f]or me the visible universe is a reflection of the invisible universe. Somewhere St. Augustine says that the things of the world poured forth from God in a double way: intellectually into the minds of the angels and physically into the world of things" (128). Through their discussion of "A Temple of the Holy Ghost," O'Connor and Hester also began a dialogue on the meaning of sexual purity within the Church. O'Connor explained her own feelings on the issue: "Purity strikes me as the most mysterious of the virtues and the more I think about it the less I know about it. 'A Temple of the Holy Ghost all revolves around what is purity'" (117).

Through this sort of discussion, O'Connor, apparently without even being aware of it, was leading her friend toward conversion. When she learned that Betty Hester was about to enter the Church, O'Connor admitted to her correspondent that she had been sounding like "a besieged defender of the faith" (*HB* 131); however, she quickly added that the defense she had launched was "not a defense of the faith, which don't need it, but a defense of myself who does. The Church becomes a part of your ego and gets messed in with your own impurity. [. . .] Smugness is the Great Catholic Sin. I find it in myself and don't dislike it any less" (131). As Hester was about to become a communicant, O'Connor expressed her great pleasure in her friend's decision and offered to send her books in Catholic theology which she hoped would help Hester strengthen her faith. She wrote that she had not offered them earlier "because I thought they were 'too Catholic' and I did not want you to think I was trying to stuff the Church down your throat" (134). At the same time, O'Connor was "really pleased to be your sponsor for Confirmation. [. . .] I have never been anybody's sponsor before" (154).

Though their friendship continued until O'Connor's death, it suffered a great shock when Hester left the Church in 1961. On hearing of Hester's decision, O'Connor wrote to her: "I don't know anything that could grieve us here like this news. I know that what you do you do because you think it is right, and I don't think any the less of you outside the Church than in it, but what is painful is the true realization that this means a narrowing of life for you and a lessening of the desire for life" (*HB* 452). She also told Hester that her "unbelief" would eventually wane as she had now lost faith. "Leaving the Church is not the solution," she asserted, and urged her to return when her desire for faith reasserted itself. With Hester, as with Robert Lowell, O'Connor never lost hope that she might reembrace the Church, but she also began to lose patience with her friend as she revealed in a letter to Cecil Dawkins:

> I'll tell you what's with Betty Hester, why all the exhilaration. She has left the Church. Those are the signs of release. She's high as a kite and all on pure air. This conversion was achieved by Miss Iris Murdoch, as you could doubtless see by that paper. [She] now sees through everything and loves everything and is a bundle of feelings of empathy for everything. She doesn't believe any longer that Christ is God and so she has found that he is "beautiful! beautiful!" Everything is in the eeeek eeek eureka stage. The effect of all this on me is pretty sick-making but I manage to keep my mouth shut. (*HB* 459)

O'Connor's annoyance with Hester's leaving the Church clearly demonstrated, as Peter Hawkins has written, how tightly Hester "had gotten under her skin [and had] become so painfully a part of her" (Hawkins 103). In her most angry statement to her friend in October 1963, O'Connor chastised her for believing that humans can love and understand each other fully: "Love and understanding are one and the same only in God. Who do you think you understand. If anybody, you delude yourself. I love a lot of people, understand none of them. This is not perfect love but as much as a finite creature can be capable of" (*HB* 543). Hawkins writes, "In these blunt remarks, O'Connor's love for [Hester] showed its compassion through confrontation. If she accepted [Hester], it was also clear that she did not accept her ideas; rather, she judged them, and judged by standards not of rationality but of revelation" (103).

Though Betty Hester did not return to the Church, in the few years left in O'Connor's life they continued to write to each other and O'Connor continued to worry about her friend's emotional health; she wrote to Cecil Dawkins in April 1963 that she was upset with Betty's "cosmic speculations." Still, that O'Connor wrote a last letter to Hester on 25 July 1964, only a few days before she died, shows how much she valued their friendship: Hester's questioning forced O'Connor to think through and formulate some of her most basic ideas about her life, her faith and her writing.

Another major friendship-correspondence in O'Connor's life began in 1956 when she met Maryat Lee. In 1960, Flannery O'Connor, at home in Milledgeville, sent Lee, who lived in New York, a copy of *The Violent Bear It Away,* inscribing the book "To Maryat from Flanneryat." The wordplay on her own name reflects the basic kinship O'Connor felt with Lee, who, although an infrequent visitor to Milledgeville, became her lifelong correspondent after they first met there in late 1956.

Judging purely on appearances an outsider could hardly imagine a more unlikely friendship than that between the self-controlled, almost ascetic novelist and the flamboyantly outgoing, emotional playwright, who long pursued a lesbian lifestyle; indeed, in 1965 in her journal, Lee described herself as the "direct antithesis" to O'Connor. Maryat Lee's brother, Robert E. Lee, reveals that he and Maryat were born in Covington, Kentucky, "to parents who were [. . .] college graduates [. . .] given to civic service." Maryat graduated from Wellesley and in the late 1940s immigrated to New York City, ambitious to make a name for herself in theater. She achieved success as early as 1951 when her play *Dope!,* a street drama first performed in Harlem, achieved immediate notoriety. *Life* covered the play, which appeared in *The Best Short Plays of 1952–53.*

By the time Lee and O'Connor met in December 1956, O'Connor had published her first novel, *Wise Blood* (1951), and her first collection of short stories, *A Good Man Is Hard to Find* (1955); thus, their mutual interest in writing helped draw them together. In her memoir of the first year of their friendship, Lee wrote that, just as she was about to appear at Andalusia unannounced, Flannery, at the suggestion of a mutual acquaintance, invited her to visit. The two women formed an immediate friendship despite quite obvious differences in their personalities and basic outlooks on life.

Lee can be described as dynamic, rebellious, and even, at times, outrageous: her brother calls her "a rebel *with* a cause." Lee's dedication to rebellion carried over into her attitude toward religion. Though she majored in Bible history at Wellesley, studied theology with Paul Tillich at the Union Theological Seminary, and took a master's degree in religious drama from Columbia, her chief interests were secular rather than spiritual. Though never denying God's existence, her chief focus in life was worldly, her main interest in self-fulfillment, her main social concern with the good that her writing could promote. *Dope!,* like Nelson Algren's *Man with the Golden Arm,* helped the rather stagnant society of the 1950s realize the existence of drug addiction. Her work with the Forest Memorial Theater in North Carolina in the 1960s helped promote the Civil Rights movement, and her last work with ECO Theater in West Virginia helped demonstrate the dramatic and artistic possibilities of life in rural isolation.

Flannery O'Connor, on the other hand, held an absolute religious faith that prompted her vocation as a writer. As she often asserted, her major impetus for writing was to undercut the secularity of her era, to guide the unbelieving toward belief; in addition, she was totally dedicated to the rules of Roman Catholicism. She attended mass regularly, complied with dietary restrictions imposed by her faith, and read theology with considerable enthusiasm. The religious differences between the two women, then, provide additional evidence of their antithesis. Lee was the very kind of secular humanist O'Connor derided in portrayals of characters like Rayber in *The Violent Bear It Away* and Sheppard in "The Lame Shall Enter First," while Flannery was the type of dogmatic Catholic Lee viewed with suspicion.

Another basic difference between the two women concerned their relative attitudes toward self-fulfillment. Despite her commitment to social reform, Lee was also, as her journals prove, an egocentric woman. She wrote many extended passages of introspective analysis as she set out to achieve a full personal development through forming close relationships with other people and participating in cultural activities, particularly music and art. She also loved travel—in the United States and abroad. Writing plays was important to her, but she needed other activities to complete her life.

Conversely, O'Connor, partly because of the onset of lupus and partly through choice, spent her most creative years in Milledgeville, a small town with its primary cultural activities offered by GSCW. Though in an early letter to Maryat, O'Connor revealed her initial anguish at being forced to return to the South, she, by building on inner resources of strength and spirituality, was able to achieve enormous creative success. She concentrated on her spiritual life, her writing, and friendships conducted both in Milledgeville and through wide correspondence with people elsewhere. She traveled only in order to visit colleges and universities to lecture on her work or to read from it. Overall, Lee quested for total experience: physical and existential while Flannery O'Connor, sustained by her religious faith and her creativity, used her talent—her extraordinary genius as a writer—not for self-aggrandizement but to lead other would-be Christians toward transcendent grace.

What, then, accounts for the warmth and depth of the relationship between these two opposites? Fundamental to answering this question must be an understanding of the special importance O'Connor placed on their friendship: Lee was, for her, a vital link to the exciting world of New York City, a world that she had briefly inhabited herself in the late 1940s. The gregarious Lee knew many people there from all parts of the world and pursued activities considered exotic in Flannery's small, Southern hometown. An especially forceful impetus to their friendship, then, evolved from O'Connor's isolation. Though she made a clearly satisfactory accommodation to her isolated life, she needed, both personally and professionally, the challenge of the world Lee inhabited.

Through her letters, Maryat shared with O'Connor her involvement in significant cultural activities in New York City. She wrote about the plays she attended, the concerts and lectures she heard; for example, in her journal in January 1962, Lee mentions having sent a recording of "Marcel's lecture down to Flannery and some of the Milledgeville folk," a lecture she had heard on WBAI in New York City in the fall of 1961. In an unpublished letter to Lee, O'Connor expressed appreciation for the lecture, calling herself a fan of his work. Early in February, when she, Dr. Rosa Lee Walston, and two other "Milledgeville folk" got together to hear the recording, O'Connor reported their joint enthusiasm to Maryat.[15]

In addition to the cultural stimulation that her friendship with Maryat provided, Lee's different way of life and her antithetical temperament enhanced the quality of O'Connor's rather quiet, secluded life in Milledge-ville. In another letter (omitted from *The Habit of Being*) from May 1960, she chides Maryat for having failed to answer specific questions she had recently asked:

> What gives with you? You do not keep me posted very good on your exciting activities, whereas me if I had exciting activities I would keep you posted on them. At least a dozen times I have asked you where that woman [unidentified] was raised up. Now I am asking you where the Thorington girl [unidentified] was raised up at. [. . .]
>
> What did the lady say to what you took out of the con-track? You are my soap serial without the soap. Do not leave me in suspense. I am a poor girl who lives on a farm, my only excite-ment a few chickens. (Cash, "Maryat and 'Flanneryat'" 61)

Despite the almost exotic appeal Maryat had to Flannery, the two also shared several outlooks and experiences. Both were Southerners, with the distinctive legacy of place, family, and tradition so thoroughly inculcated below the Mason-Dixon line. Though early in her life O'Connor briefly left the South, her illness forced the return that clearly enhanced her under-standing of the rural South that provides the setting for nearly all of her fiction. Maryat, on the other hand, held a clearly dichotomized outlook on the South; after a visit with her family (and Flannery) in Milledgeville in late 1962, she wrote in her journal: "I want to be cut off—I want to cut them [her family] off—to gain badly need reorientation with things and the world—to gain perspective, and get on my own. It is almost inconceivable in the south to be anonymous or cut off from an environment and make out on one's own the way I have for so long in the north." In at least two passages in her journal, Lee asserted her belief that O'Connor was "jailed" in Milledge-ville. Indeed, Flannery must have revealed that she shared some of Lee's dichotomized feeling about the South, for in April 1958, Maryat wrote in her journal: "[W]e were both repelled by the Southerner—under their smil-ing veneers like something so smelly."

Besides their Southern connection with place, both of these women were members of closely bonded families; in fact, both were named for relatives of distinction. Regina O'Connor, as previously discussed, gave her daughter the middle name "Flannery" in honor of her socially prominent Savannah cousin, Kate Flannery Semmes, while Lee was named for her great aunt, Mary Attaway, who, according to her nephew Robert Lee, lived to be ninety-nine. Both O'Connor and Lee eventually changed parts of their given names, though Mary Flannery, having dropped the "Mary" professionally, remained "Mary Flannery" within the confines of Milledgeville. Mary Attaway became Maryat during her twenties or thirties, when, as her brother explains "she became creative and realized how easy it was to change her name."

A keen sense of humor also drew the two women together. Though often troubled by personal doubts, Lee maintained an essentially optimistic outlook on life, an ability to accept the vicissitudes of human existence with humor and grace. Likewise, within the confines of a deeply religious sensibility, O'Connor nurtured a creatively wry humor. Despite an essentially grim outlook on life (she was always leery of optimistic secularism), she enriched her day-to-day existence, as well as that of others, with her quick wit. Nowhere does she better display it than in her letters to Maryat, especially in the names she created for Maryat and herself after the publication of *The Violent Bear It Away*. Of their exchange of names, Maryat wrote in an unpublished letter to Sally Fitzgerald:

> Our reference to these names is [. . .] complicated. It started—
> the names—when she was saying she had trouble liking Rayber.
> I said I liked him a great deal. No, she was partial to Tarwater
> and his ilk. Now this was/is very interesting to me. Herself a
> devotee of the Church which has had little toleration for schiz-
> matoids, which has insisted on apostolic succession, she
> identified emotionally with the self-ordained backwater type
> with no credentials whatsoever except his own passion and
> beliefs. [. . .] I believe I started calling her variations of Tarwater
> to which she responded with the Ray etceteras. (Cash, "Maryat
> and 'Flanneryat'" 62–63)

The remarkable range of O'Connor's humorous creativity is evident in the following list of these salutation-signature combinations: Raybucket-Waterbucket, May (?) 1960; Raybutter-Tarbutter, May 1960; Raybalm-Tarbilge, (late May?) 1960; Rayfish-Tarfeather, 22 August 1960; Rayverberator-Tarfaulkner, 6 September 1960; Mariattipus-Tartrot, 8 December 1960;

Maryhatrack-Tarbus, 24 January 1961; Maryankorite-Tarfunk, 14 February 1961; Maribennyfactor-Tarblender, 25 March 1961; Marywitchywater-Tarsot, 21 April 1961; Maryidiot-Tardoctor, 25 August 1961.

Another less amusing, but still quite significant, magnetic force between O'Connor and Lee evolved from their mutual concern with health. Confined to Milledgeville after her first bout with lupus in late 1949 and early 1950, O'Connor lived with what she facetiously termed in a letter to Lee her "dread disease" (*HB* 255). O'Connor was, however, decidedly neither an invalid nor a hypochondriac: her creative focus was too strong for that, but she was concerned about health—hers and that of Maryat from 1957 until her premature death in August 1964. She became quite knowledgeable about lupus and other medical problems and was more than willing to correspond with Lee concerning Lee's illnesses; for example, in August 1962, she advised Lee to have her thyroid checked out by a reliable physician. Maryat, motivated by an intense passion for life, was constantly vigilant about her own health; from her thirties on, she suffered from a variety of ills including allergies, eczema, hypoglycemia, depressions, headaches, tumors, and, finally, heart disease. Her brother says that, because of her concern with her own medical problems, Maryat assumed he had every illness she suffered from. He also reveals that in her last years, his sister "would have mortgaged her house [in Lewisburg] that was paid for to get a heart transplant to have another three or four years." Suffering from serious medical problems and sharing a concern with health must surely have contributed to the strength and durability of the friendship and correspondence between Lee and O'Connor.

Without a doubt, both Flannery and Maryat were also individualists. From her childhood in Savannah, people viewed O'Connor as unique. Though, as an adult in Milledgeville, she outwardly conformed to the Southern conventions, demurely dressed in public and ladylike in demeanor, O'Connor was different because of her artistic genius. No one else in Milledgeville had produced nationally and even internationally respected novels and stories; furthermore, at the time she was publishing, few people in Milledgeville appreciated or even read her work. Outwardly, Mary Flannery O'Connor conformed to Milledgeville standards; inwardly, she was a deeply religious woman with a literary talent that she fed and practiced with absolute ardor.

Maryat Lee was different, too, from conventional woman of the 1950s; as a pioneering and artistic feminist, she traveled the streets of Harlem and later the back roads of West Virginia to explore not only her own unique sensibility but also the natural drama in the sensibilities of simple people, the latter of which she captured in a style decidedly different from that of prevailing male playwrights like Tennessee Williams. Maryat Lee, a rebel, was well ahead of her time as an independent woman and avant-garde artist. Of Maryat's feminist concern in West Virginia, Robert Lee says: "When she moved to West Virginia, she established a farm house six miles outside of Hinton. It was known as 'The Woman's Farm,' a place for artists to go on retreat, particularly [those] in art, drama and music."

Maryat Lee's liberal outlook on the race issue also particularly fascinated O'Connor. After a Christmas visit to Milledgeville in 1960, Lee wrote in her Journal: "I was glad to leave—I was affected & guilt ridden again by the Negro sadness that hits you in the eye—It is the most pure bit of reality that strikes me while we were eating baby beef, porterhouse steaks 12 of them— & other very luxurious things & the 2 Negro women hearing & seeing it all— it is somehow untenable. I cannot go on visiting in the same way—but I know of no other except—belligerence or giving up my earthy possessions." To her family, as well as to O'Connor, Lee, a Southern liberal, was an anomaly. Flannery's interest in Lee's radicalism began as early as their first meeting, after which Maryat arranged to ride to the airport in Atlanta with Emmett Jones, the Black employee of GSCW who worked as a gardener at the Old Governor's Mansion. O'Connor's outlook on race was essentially that of a conservative, yet sympathetic, Southerner. Forced to live in rural Georgia and thus influenced by that cultural milieu, O'Connor, when the Civil Rights movement began to gain momentum, had some difficulty separating herself from prevailing attitudes. Because Maryat Lee was an integrationist by both principle and action, this area of difference was a continuing source of debate in their letters. O'Connor's sometimes outrageous comments were at least partly motivated by her desire to nettle her more liberal antagonist.

Finally of great significance to O'Connor and Lee's friendship and correspondence was their deep commitment to writing. Each woman wrote constantly; O'Connor's disciplined three-hour mornings at her typewriter are well known. Usually at work on one or more of her plays, Lee was, at the same time, one of the most inveterate journal keepers of the modern era, writing every day, apparently in at least two journals: one contains ideas for her writing projects; the other is her sensitively written, introspective diary. Though in her memoir of the first year of their friendship, Lee claimed that she and O'Connor discussed Flannery's illness when they first met in Milledgeville, a previously quoted entry (28 December 1956) from her journal shows that their main topic of conversation was writing, with Maryat obviously impressed by her friend's disciplined approach. In her published memoir, Lee wrote of their shared literary interest: "I began at this point [early 1957] to confide some of my own writing problems. I was getting discouraged with myself and the theater world. In spite of a big success in street theater six years before, there had been no future in it, nor was I able to adjust to the indoor theater, which seemed very lifeless to me. And I was toying with the idea of whether I should switch to prose, which scholastically I had always failed with, or even whether I could forget about writing altogether" (M. Lee, "Flannery, 1957" 48). During the first year of their correspondence, Maryat was struggling to write an autobiographical play, *Kairos*, set in the South. According to her journal (9 January 1957), she hoped to reveal the "confusion [of white people]. Their lack of real certainty and conviction." As she wrote the play, she asked O'Connor to help criticize it, usually receiving positive responses from her friend.

That O'Connor also sent Maryat her stories for reactions is evident in Maryat's intelligent evaluation (9 July 1958) of "The Enduring Chill":

> Looking it over now, I know it wasn't no fever that made me think so [that the story deserved a "paean"]. I genuflect. It's completely absorbing and in some ways more terrifying than Wise Blood because it has more deep exposures of those godawful human searches—not even that—growths. I went right along, and literally my hair crawled at the paragraph of his letter, with the huffy hawk. The communion with the two Niggers, the farce with the priest, the persistent overhand of his Knowledge— the whole thing is something beautiful to me, on so many levels. You really seem to have busted the ceiling. But—the last paragraph! This is the closest I have seen you come to your mind's passion. The first reading I didn't really know what was going on, and then thought maybe you didn't either. I mean this in

the simplest way—not the symbolic way. I wondered if you were leaving it mysterious and obscure—as to what happened—on purpose, but this seemed so out of character with the rest, that I couldn't think it of you. Now—*now*, on reading it, I begin to make out that moment when a man ordinary bitchy man can change into a saint. Am I right? That it happens to him, the descent of the Holy Icicle, despite himself.

O'Connor took Lee's criticism of this story seriously, often asserting her need to revise the conclusion before publishing it in a volume of stories.

O'Connor continued to advise Maryat about her writing throughout their friendship. In August 1959, after Maryat confessed that she has been writing as many as seven thousand words every day, O'Connor scolded her: "Did I understand you right that you are writing from 5000 to 7000 words of bad prose a day? By my calculations this is about 20 pages. Girl, it couldn't be anything else but bad. That is too much prose to write in one day. It must be automatic writing. Slow down for pity sake. Practice your mouth organ, do anything, but don't write 20 pages of prose a day. At that rate you would write a novel in two weeks" (Cash, "Maryat and 'Flanneryat'" 68). In December 1962, after consulting with Flannery about using her journal as the basis for fiction, Maryat wrote in her journal: "I talked with Flannery about the Journal becoming a piece of fiction—whether anyone had done this—the evolution as it happened—not looking back and reconstructing—the point of view itself in process of becoming—[. . . she] thought it could be done— I had a moment of excitement[,] popped up off the hard exercise board [and asked], Do you think so [. . . O'Connor replied, as Maryat paraphrases,] But it will become a piece of fiction separate also from just your journal by the process of selection and sometimes invention."

Until the end of her own life, Flannery continued to encourage Maryat's creative efforts; in May 1964, a few months before her death, O'Connor wrote to Lee: "Don't go pulling your horns in. Work a *little every* day and wait for the moment. It's given when the time comes. You got not too much to do with it" (Cash, "Maryat and 'Flanneryat'" 68). Maryat, too, reacted enthusiastically to the fiction Flannery was writing during the last year of her life. In her journal, she recorded an immediate, positive response to "Revelation":

Revelation by Flannery just came in Sewanee Review—& has knocked me over. Wellesley girl in doctor's office throwing a book at a typical O'Connor chatty lady smug & fat—& telling her to go back to hell that she was a wart hog—& then interesting the girls mad eyes drive the woman into a vision of her & her kind being *last* in the long line to the Kingdom. Just sent wire.

> "Flannery
> I'm floored with Revelation
> Love
> Raygrace" (16 April 1964)

Shortly thereafter O'Connor gave Lee half interest in Mary Grace, the "Wellesley girl."

The friendship and correspondence between the two endured until O'Connor's death on 3 August 1964. The last note Flannery wrote, dated 28 July 1964, was to Maryat; Regina O'Connor found it on Flannery's nightstand after her daughter had died. Published in *The Habit of Being;* it shows that among her last concerns was the welfare of her friend. Maryat apparently did not write about Flannery's death until early 1965, when she recorded an extended analysis in her journal:

> Flannery O'Connor upset some of my most precious themes. And took obvious delight in doing so. At the time of my first visit to my brother in M'ville, she came out of her customary routine ways enough to summons me—first out of simple Southern courtesy toward a visiting writer—& later, because I somewhat fascinated her, as she did me, as the direct antithesis of herself, yet someone she nevertheless seemed to care for—in the contrary way which is peculiarly dear to her. She summoned *me* from my brother's house each day—indeed she frequently summoned me to visit M'ville a bird Sanctuary.
>
> She upset my theories & I have often wondered if I caused any upset to her very tightly fashioned world. First of all, I have sought a free environment in order to be able to write. But Flannery wrote within limits which no one I know could endure for more than a week without blowing to pieces. I do not refer to the writing itself but to her personal lack of freedom so puzzling

to most of her guests. She was limited by her need for crutches —She finally got a license to drive—but only for emergency in case her mother became ill.

She never went out (nor did her mother) at night—no lectures, concerts, plays. (She saw only one professional play prod[uced] in her life.) They were not antisocial. Oh no. Most days at noon after the 3 hours of writing they drove into town & ate at Sanford House where they met friends (her mother's friends) & kin folk. They picked up mail and dropped by "Sister's" house, the eldest of Mrs. O'Connor's sisters & brothers, & then drove back to Andalusia—the whiteboard farm house on rolling hills—with pastures & pine forests. People have described this place in grand terms. It is a simple old but not early, farm house with a screen porch & glorified by dozens of pea fowl perched on the roof & around the yard. This was Flannery's day. She'd rest awhile & see folks—most often kin folks or some visiting admirers—At these times she seemed very wise. She could not bear cant. So she under-stated everything & it came out very wise.

I was startled & disturbed when I heard her address chapel at the College. This then was her second love—talking. She complained about speaking engagements & writing speeches—complained acidly, saying it was the money. But she *loved* talk-ing in front of people—she had a gift & most shocking to find it in her. Her passion was there & it warmed me deeply.

She was Catholic—no question. Yet all the overtones were Protestant to me. Protesting. This was her whole posture. I've found this same odd discrepancy in other fields. She fretted about a light being on unnecessarily—or about a long distance phone call, unable to enjoy it—She was almost comically penurious, yet this was antithesis to her nature. She wasn't really miserly [marked out] But her [marked out] caring. But her mother cared. And here is where I felt my theories weaken. She avoided oppos-ing her mother who could not be opposed—who was, she (the mother) told me, mayor, sheriff, judge, treasurer and boss of this little state—a feudal state where she was feudal queen. Regina was her name.

Maryat's assessment of her relationship with Flannery reveals both her admiration for the writer and her dismay that O'Connor led a life of isolated simplicity under what Lee perceived to be Regina O'Connor's control. That Lee, after deriding the geographic and cultural isolation that "jailed" O'Connor in Milledgeville, chose to spend the last fifteen years of her life in even greater rural isolation in West Virginia is a striking irony; in fact, it suggests that, as she matured, Maryat may have concluded that Flannery's relatively secluded life contributed greatly to her creative success. O'Connor, in turn, revealed in her numerous, humorously warm letters to Maryat that their friendship was vital to her. Just as O'Connor's passion for public speaking charmed Lee, so did Maryat's varied, adventurous life lend drama to Flannery's. Lee was, indeed, Flannery's "soap serial without the soap."

Friendships, then, that O'Connor formed either in her five years away from Milledgeville or shortly after her return to the town were of significant importance in helping her adjust to her enforced isolation in Milledgeville. These friends clearly demonstrate O'Connor's desire for people outside her family and outside the town; they provided the emotional support she needed to continue with her vocation as one of the outstanding writers of her generation.

CHAPTER TEN

LAST FRIENDSHIPS

D uring the late 1950s and early 1960s, Flannery O'Connor continued to develop her incredible capacity for friendship by establishing correspondences with even more enthusiasts of her work, some aspiring writers themselves or professors and students whom she met while visiting college campuses away from Milledgeville. Of the importance of these friendships to her life, O'Connor wrote (in an unpublished letter) to Cecil Dawkins in November 1959 that among her best friends were those whom she made through her writing.[1] Professors she met through her work included Ted Spivey, William Sessions, and Robert Drake. Among the most important of her writer-to-writer friendships were those with Cecil Dawkins, John Hawkes, and Alfred Corn. Writing to younger aspiring writers, such as Corn, O'Connor was the intelligent "older sister" who offered solid advice without sanctimonious didacticism. In these relationships, O'Connor displayed boundless generosity in reading and commenting on their works; she was more than willing, like her own literary advisor, Caroline Gordon, to guide them toward publication and literary success.

Cecil Dawkins heads the list of aspiring writers who wrote to O'Connor, first in admiration, later for advice about her own work. When she sent a letter to O'Connor in May 1957, Dawkins was teaching at Stephens College in Missouri and writing short stories in her spare time. In an interview with Kay Bonetti in 1983, Dawkins says that she came to know O'Connor and her work when a friend lent her a copy of *A Good Man Is Hard to Find:* "And I sat down with a six pack of beer one night and I started reading this book and I got increasingly excited, of course, and when I had finished, I wrote a note on just a yellow pad and said, 'You're really great. [. . .] You're terrific'; and I didn't know where to send it. I just sent it to Milledgeville and I didn't know if she'd ever get it. I'd had a lot of beer. But I got an answer by return mail and we wrote until she died."[2]

O'Connor developed an immediate rapport with Dawkins, a doctor's daughter from Alabama who came from a similar Roman Catholic background. Soon recognizing that Dawkins possessed a genuine talent for writing, O'Connor also helped her friend shape the stories she published in *The Quiet Enemy* in 1964. As early as September 1958, Dawkins had asked whether she might send one of her stories to O'Connor for her more expert reading. O'Connor replied that she was willing to read Dawkins's work in progress. She admitted that she didn't consider herself a genuine critic and was afraid of hurting a beginning writer, but she also said that she knew that an outside reader could give helpful advice. Of the essential connection between them, Dawkins has said, "She became my reader. Her reader was Caroline Gordon and Flannery read everything I wrote when I was finished with it" (B).

When Dawkins first wrote to O'Connor in May 1957, she apparently told O'Connor about teaching her stories to first-year students at Stephens. In her response, O'Connor expressed her delight that students in 1957 were being introduced to more modern writers than those she had read as an undergraduate. Thus began the correspondence between the two "literary pen pals." Dawkins has said that "even when I was here in Milledgeville, [she visited O'Connor twice] we didn't talk about very many personal things. We gossiped about other writers—not about their lives but about their work" (Dawkins, "Introduction to Reading").

Unpublished letters or sections of them not in *The Habit of Being* do contain considerable literary gossip. After contributing in 1957 to Granville

Hicks's collection *The Living Novel,* for example, O'Connor commented on some of the other contributors. She called Saul Bellow "the best," even though she hadn't read his novels, but she found Jessamyn West's stories too tame for her taste. In 1959, O'Connor also offered Dawkins her positive opinion of George Eliot's *Middlemarch;* she liked the novel except for its "silly ending." That same year, she expressed her dislike of James Agee's fiction, writing that after she had read an excerpt from *A Death in the Family,* she knew that she didn't want to read the rest of it. Commenting on Lillian Smith, whom she had met at a dinner in Atlanta, O'Connor declared her fellow Georgian a "nice" person but not her kind of writer. As she did elsewhere, O'Connor also expressed (in October 1961) her contempt for Carson McCullers's novel *Clock without Hands*, calling it the "worst novel" she had ever read.

In spite of Dawkins's assertion about the literary content of their correspondence, the two did frequently write to each other about personal and family matters. The complete file of 101 letters O'Connor wrote to Dawkins shows considerable emotional warmth. Since Cecil Dawkins was an avowed dog lover, while O'Connor and her mother hated them, there are a number of facetious references in O'Connor's letters to Dawkins's "hounds." When Dawkins visited O'Connor in Milledgeville, O'Connor arranged for the local veterinarian to board the dogs, and when Dawkins went to Yaddo, O'Connor inquired about the whereabouts of her pets. Another humanizing episode omitted from the letters in *The Habit of Being* concerns O'Connor's obsession with buying a vacuum cleaner with the money she earned from one of her appearances at Wesleyan in 1959. She wrote that she was planning to buy the appliance to clean up her "filthy" room. In May she had not yet bought the cleaner but still felt compelled to make the purchase. By June, she had indeed bought the vacuum and was impressed with both its efficiency and its self-winding cord that reminded her of an uncouth diner slurping up a "piece of spaghetti."

Another, more serious subject of their correspondence, particularly in the first year or so, was their mutual Catholicism. During this time, Dawkins was gradually retreating from the Church. In several letters O'Connor tried to encourage her friend to hold onto her faith. Realizing that Dawkins was a woman of intelligence, O'Connor suggested that Dawkins might solve her spiritual problems by reading modern Catholic novelists and theologians; she recommended those who had most affected her own religious life: Catholic novelists Bloy, Bernanos, and Mauriac, and philosophers Gilson, Maritain,

Marcel, Picard, Guardini, and Karl Adam (*HB* 231). A bit later O'Connor sent Dawkins one of Mauriac's books, hoping it would help her friend solve her "difficulties with the Church. Maybe time will settle this for you in a better way. I hope so" (264). Later, O'Connor also urged Dawkins to read Teilhard's *The Phenomenon of Man,* but her advice did not stop Dawkins from leaving the Church; however, O'Connor never felt alienated from Dawkins afterward, probably because she realized that Dawkins's decision was a reasoned one.

What mainly stimulated the long-term correspondence between the two writers was their writing. Betty Hester was never able to focus her life enough to produce anything publishable, but Cecil Dawkins was devoted to the craft of writing and determined to find acceptance for her fiction. Before O'Connor began to read or comment on Dawkins's fiction, she described her own patterns of writing. In a letter written on 16 July 1957 she talked about being a Southern writer who had tried to escape the South, but admitted: "The best of my writing has been done here" (*HB* 230). Much later (20 September 1962), after Dawkins had been at Yaddo and was applying for a job at the *New Yorker,* O'Connor urged Dawkins herself to return to the South: "I have thought you needed to come back for a long time. [. . .] You'd be better off in any town population under 5,000 in south Alabama than you would be in New York City. That's where reality goes out the window. That is, when it ain't your reality" (493).

Dawkins first sent one of her stories to O'Connor in June 1958; it was "Pop the Blue Balloon," which Dawkins had written five years earlier. O'Connor told Dawkins that she liked the story, primarily because it showed that the younger writer possessed "a very good ear." Dawkins subsequently sent a number of stories to O'Connor for reaction (she liked all of them) and advice; four of them—"The Mourners," "Hummers in the Larkspur," "Benny Ricco's Search for the Truth," and "The Quiet Enemy"— appeared in Dawkins's first published collection, *The Quiet Enemy.* O'Connor apparently did not send as many of her own works-in-progress to Dawkins as she did to Betty Hester, but one that she did send was "The Lame Shall Enter First," about which Dawkins was apparently somewhat skeptical. Having received Dawkins's response, O'Connor wrote to her, a bit miffed at her friend's Freudian reading: "[W]here do you get the idea that Sheppard represents Freud? Freud never entered my mind and looking back over it, I can't make him fit now. The story is about a man who thought he was good and thought he was doing good when he wasn't" (*HB* 490–91).

Dawkins appreciated O'Connor's fiction so much that in 1963 she asked O'Connor to allow her to write a dramatic adaptation of several of O'Connor's stories under the title "The Displaced Person":

> I wanted to do a play based on her stories because that mother's always the same mother with different names and those terrible kids—the intellectual and the artist—they're all the same kid and I wanted to put them together; and I wrote her and she wrote right back and said "Good idea." And so I did and we were in touch the whole time I was writing the play and then I was going down and read it with her in June of 1964 and I wasn't quite finished and she was sick and so we said, "We'll do it in August." And, of course, then I got the wire that she had died. And I just put the play away. (B)

Some months later, however, in 1965, Dawkins staged her play in New York at the American Place Theater and, more recently, at Georgia State College and University in the fall of 1997. When O'Connor died, Dawkins's stated reaction shows how much she valued their relationship: "I thought the only consciousness that ever saw from the same place in the universe that my consciousness saw from was gone. I had never felt so alone" (B). A final connection between the two writers was that in 1996–97 Cecil Dawkins occupied the Flannery O'Connor chair in creative writing at Georgia State College and University.

O'Connor's correspondence and friendship with novelist John Hawkes began in July 1958 when he and his wife stopped in Milledgeville to visit while on a trip to Florida. Her first letter to him shows that he apparently impressed her immediately, for she told him to "please stop again when you are down this way" (HB 292). They corresponded through the rest of her life, and Hawkes wrote a major early analysis of O'Connor and her work, "Flannery O'Connor's Devil," for the issue of *The Sewanee Review,* part of which Andrew Lytle devoted to O'Connor and her work in 1962.

Despite the highly experimental quality of Hawkes's work and the Christian vision of O'Connor's, a bit of research into the life and writing of Hawkes, who died in May 1998, reveals distinct similarities between them. They were almost exact contemporaries, born in 1925, though he was a Northerner from Greenwich, Connecticut. They were both only children whose lives were disrupted when their parents made pivotal moves while they were in middle childhood. His family moved to Juneau, Alaska, when he was ten, while hers moved from Savannah to Atlanta to Milledgeville when she was twelve; both their fathers were relatively unsuccessful as businessmen; as adolescents, both O'Connor and Hawkes were outsiders among their peers. Hawkes recalled his feeling of alienation when he and his mother returned to New York City at the beginning of World War II. Their outsider status, however, bothered neither O'Connor nor Hawkes: they took pride in their individualism. O'Connor clearly documented her aversion to dating and feminine finery and her affinity for reading and writing. Hawkes wrote of himself as a teenager: "I wanted to be a poet; I loved Poe; I was proud of a snapshot that was taken of me wearing a homburg, and a checked waistcoat, and carrying a copy of the Bible in one hand and a bottle of whiskey in the other."[3]

After academic failure at Harvard during his first year there, Hawkes became an ambulance driver for the American Field Service during World War II; he returned to Harvard in 1947 at the same time O'Connor was at Iowa surrounded by the returning veterans in the writers' workshop. Both began to write first novels during their years in writing programs; Hawkes published *The Cannibal,* which he had written at Harvard under the direction of Albert Guerard in 1950, while O'Connor published *Wise Blood,* which she had begun at Iowa under the instruction of Paul Engle and Andrew Lytle in 1952.

Their complete dedication to writing established the final and most vital connection between the two. O'Connor practiced cartooning and wrote nonfiction and even a bit of poetry before finding her voice in fiction, while Hawkes early wrote poetry. Her favorite answer when asked why she wrote was that "she was good at it." In 1950 when a *Harvard Advocate* interviewer asked Hawkes how it felt to be a writer, he answered, "it had never occurred to me to want to 'be' a writer [. . .] I was only interested in language and the work itself, and this has been my attitude from then to the present."[4]

Urged to read O'Connor's fiction by a granddaughter of Herman Melville, Hawkes immediately recognized her talent: "Flannery O'Connor to me suggested [. . .] guffawing peals of thunder (the figure is borrowed from 'The Life You Save May Be Your Own') above a dead landscape quite ready for new humor, new vision, new and more meaningful comic treatment of violence" (Hawkes, "Flannery O'Connor's Devil" 396). Such a strong reaction to her work motivated Hawkes's visit to O'Connor in Milledgeville. O'Connor probably had not read Hawkes's fiction before they met, but he gave her copies of his early novels, to which she reacted with enthusiasm in her first letter to him: "I am very much taken with your books and their wonderful imaginative energy. The more fantastic the action the more precise the writing and this is the way it ought to be" (*HB* 292). In that first letter, she also told him that James Dickey had recently visited her and that they had discussed Hawkes's fiction: "You may state without fear of contradiction that you now have two fans in Georgia."

As her correspondent, Hawkes set out to try "to persuade Flannery O'Connor that as a writer she's on the devil's side. Her answer is that my idea of the devil corresponds to her idea of God. I must admit that I resist this equation" (Hawkes, "An Interview" 146). Hawkes never convinced O'Connor that she was diabolic, but she did recognize a distinct similarity in their vision: "As you say, your vision, though it doesn't come by way of theology, is the same as mine. You arrive at it by your own perception and sensitivity, but I have had it given me whole by faith because I couldn't possibly have arrived at it by my own powers" (*HB* 352–53).

When Hawkes completed his third novel, *The Lime Twig,* in June 1960, O'Connor asked him to send her the galleys of the novel: "It sounds like a real exciting book. It will be to me. I think you have nothing to lose by making it more realistic than your others" (*HB* 399). When she had read *The Lime Twig,* she sent Hawkes an enthusiastic response:

> This is about how much I like *The Lime Twig.*
>
> [. . .] The action seems to take place at a point where dreams are lightest (and fastest?), just before you wake up. It seems to me that you have retained all the virtues of the other books in this one, but added something that will hold the reader to the reading.
>
> [. . .]

> You suffer this like a dream. It seems to be something that
> is happening to you, that you want to escape from but can't. It's
> quite remarkable. (*HB* 413)

Hawkes immediately asked O'Connor for permission to use part of this comment on the book jacket of the novel, though she had already sent what she called a more "jacketish" comment to Hawkes's editor at New Directions. He rightly preferred her comment about the dream-vision quality of *The Lime Twig*, which still exerts that effect on the reader.

When Andrew Lytle decided to dedicate a part of the summer 1962 issue of the *Sewanee Review* to O'Connor and her work, O'Connor was a bit shocked that he had solicited an analytical article from John Hawkes. The essay Hawkes wrote clearly set forth his theory of O'Connor's own diabolism: "My own feeling is that just as the creative process threatens the Holy throughout Flannery O'Connor's fiction by generating a paradoxical fusion of improbability and passion of the Protestant "do-it-yourself" evangelism of the South, and thereby raised the pitch of apocalyptic experience when it finally appears; so too, throughout this fiction, the creative process transforms the writer's objective Catholic knowledge of the devil into an authorial attitude in itself in some measure diabolic" ("Flannery O'Connor's Devil" 400–401). Hawkes sent O'Connor a copy of his article before submitting it to Lytle; she reacted to it positively, though she continued to disagree with his designation of her stance as diabolical; she also told him that she appreciated his pointing out that she disagreed with his analysis (*HB* 470).

In 1963 Hawkes asked O'Connor to read at Brown University, but her ill health kept her from fulfilling that request. She read the galley proofs of Hawkes's next novel, *Second Skin*, late in 1963 and reported her reactions to him: "I think this one has an added power to keep the reader right there with it and I had the thought that you're about 90% magician" (*HB* 553). In March 1964, as she lay seriously ill after the surgery that had reactivated her lupus, she wrote to Betty Hester, to whom she had sent the galleys of *Second Skin*, advising her "to hang them out of your fourth-story windows and let the birds tear them into strips for their nests" (569). Though she is being deliberately facetious here, it is also tempting to read her remarks as revealing unspoken envy of her contemporary, who, unhampered by either ill health or a writer's block, continued—as he did through the next thirty-five years—to produce his original, and extraordinary, fiction.

O'Connor's willingness to communicate with the writers of all serious letters she received is no better proved than in her brief but profound correspondence with Alfred Corn. Corn was a nineteen-year-old undergraduate at Emory University when she lectured there in 1962. She seems prescient in her ability to recognize both intelligence and talent in a person so young; Corn since has achieved success as a poet, reviewer, and fiction writer. His obvious need for reassurance about his Christian faith appealed to O'Connor, who held such strong faith herself.

O'Connor presented a lecture, "The South," at Emory on 20 May 1962. Alfred Corn was in the audience, but he reveals that "I hadn't so much as gone up to introduce myself at the end—after all, she was that awesome creature, a *famous writer.*" She had, however, made a "strong impression" on the young man, who soon "found [him]self writing a letter to her."[5] His chief reason for writing to O'Connor was to solicit her advice concerning his doubts about Christianity: "I had seen, the previous year, the Protestant fundamentalism of my upbringing crumble away from me under the flood of new ideas proposed in various undergraduate courses. [. . . In writing to her] [w]hat I wanted to know was how she, with her sharp and cultivated mind, had retained her faith."

O'Connor replied to Corn's letter, responding generously (both literally and figuratively) to his questions. She told him that his fear of losing his faith was actually evidence of the high value he placed on it and reminded him that St. Peter had prayed, "'Lord, I believe. Help my unbelief.' It is the most natural and most human and most agonizing prayer in the gospels, and I think it is the foundation proper of faith" (*HB* 476).

She encouraged Corn to realize that studying different religions does not require a Christian to justify them with his own belief: "Students get so bound up with difficulties such as reconciling the clashing of so many different faiths [. . .] that they cease to look for God in other ways" (*HB* 476). O'Connor even admitted to Corn that "[a]t one time the clash of the different world religions was a difficulty for me." She told him that the clash no longer bothered her "because I have got, over the years, a sense of the immense sweep of creation, of the evolutionary process in everything, of how incomprehensible God must necessarily be to be the God of heaven and earth" (477). She recommended that he read Pierre Teilhard de Chardin's *The Phenomenon of Man* (she later lent him her copy of the book) and admitted to him that what had kept her faith alive in college was her skepticism: "It always said: wait, don't bite on this, get a wider picture, continue to read." She also told him that he must work to maintain his faith: "It is a gift, but for very few of us is it a gift given without any demand for equal time devoted to its cultivation." Echoing a host of other Christians, she also urged him to realize that "in the life of a Christian, faith rises and falls like the tides of an invisible sea" (477).

Corn writes that what followed between them was a year of correspondence "that could be called theological, although neither Flannery O'Connor nor I really had any training in that discipline." Corn and O'Connor exchanged several letters and she later invited him to visit her at Andalusia. Though Corn never accepted O'Connor's invitation, more than thirty-five years later he continues to express gratitude for her generosity to him: "I admire her willingness to try to answer my questions, and I recognize now, if I didn't then, that her invocation of mystery is much more than a reflex brought on by a confrontation with what is difficult and apparently insoluble in human efforts to comprehend the divine."

William Sessions, Ted Spivey, and Robert Drake all met O'Connor because of their interest in her writing. Both Sessions and Spivey visited her fairly frequently at Andalusia, while Drake visited her there only once, in the summer of 1963. These three men have had long careers as academic scholars, Sessions and Spivey at Georgia State University and Robert Drake at the University of Tennessee. Each of them has written about his friendship with O'Connor, but Ted Spivey has remained fascinated with O'Connor throughout his life, presenting frequent conference papers and writing a number of articles about her and her work. At least one of his poems has O'Connor as its subject:

FLANNERY O'CONNOR

Her invisible touch
Wakened my soul
That final night,
The troubled spirit

Rising from agony's bed,
Remembering those words
Of the darkening age
She suffered to transcribe.

She who exorcised Satan,
Recalling at last his name,
Feeling his hot breath,
The hatred of anything human,
Suffered the soul's night,
Red roses withering to ash.

After twenty years,
Her spirit again,
Appearing with a kiss,
She affirming in heaven
The etheric Christ,
Approaching in light,
Transforming the world.

Woman of the one city,
I am true to your vision.[6]

In 1995 Spivey published a full-length study, *Flannery O'Connor, the Woman, the Thinker, the Visionary.*

Though Spivey and O'Connor possessed different personalities and interests, theirs was a strong literary friendship. The two (like Hawkes and O'Connor) were near contemporaries: he was born in 1927, she in 1925. Ted Spivey is a fine prose stylist, a prominent critic concerned with the connections between myth and literature, and a poet of considerable ability. He is, in addition, a secular visionary who has always placed strong value on the power of dreams. He continues to support the theories of Jung and Freud, both suspect to O'Connor. Further, he is clearly an outspoken extrovert, a man fascinated with language, the power of oral communication. Flannery O'Connor's social reticence is well documented though her range of intellectual interests was far-reaching. Suspicious of modern psychologists, O'Connor obviously placed her strongest faith in the Catholicism into which she was born. Spivey admits that he could never talk with O'Connor about Freud and Jung: "She was really afraid. [. . .] I guess I can't blame her—she was more interested in the theological approach."[7] Despite their differences, however, Spivey and O'Connor possessed a similar intellectual curiosity. Soon after they met, O'Connor wrote to Betty Hester her opinion that Spivey "has a very fine mind in spite of the apocalyptic tastes" (*HB* 302).

From the time that he began to read O'Connor's work, Spivey was convinced of her preeminence as a midcentury Southern writer; in fact, he has called her the "modern South's greatest writer after William Faulkner" (Spivey, "The Complex Gifts" 49). Intrigued by her fiction in the summer of 1958, Spivey wrote to her that he taught at Georgia State and that he was particularly interested in connections between literature, myth, and religion; he inquired about literary influences on her work, especially those of Evelyn Waugh and Graham Greene. He also asked whether he might visit her on one of his trips to Swainsboro, Georgia, where his parents lived. He says that she answered his letter immediately, declaring that her literary interests were more in Mauriac and Bernanos than Waugh or Greene. She also invited him to come by to visit at 2:00 P.M. on the day that he had suggested. Spivey declares that first visit an unqualified success: "When I knocked on her door, she appeared in a light-colored, rather conservative dress and suggested that we sit in rocking chairs on her porch. She asked me a few questions about myself, and within five minutes we were talking about writers and about their connection, when they had any, with religion. The talk lasted about two hours and it was intense" (Spivey, *Flannery O'Connor* 15). In that first conversation, O'Connor also learned that Spivey had taken a class with Allen Tate at the University of Minnesota, where Spivey had earned both an M.A. and Ph.D. This connection with Tate, Spivey asserts, helped solidify their early friendship. He recalls that O'Connor expressed "tremendous admiration" for Tate as a poet and admits, "I think O'Connor was attached to me intellectually because I could talk about Tate at great length, and nobody much, it seemed to me, that she ran into in Georgia talked about [him]."

Spivey feels that O'Connor was also particularly intrigued because his intellectual interests were so different from hers: "What I brought to her was not just a sounding board but somebody to argue with. She really did like to argue, I think, and [appreciated] somebody who would take a lot of her ideas seriously." He recalls that they had "many arguments. She was that way. She was irascible. There were many O'Connors; a very complex individual, she would say one thing to one person, another thing to another person. It would all be true; it was just what came out."

Spivey remembers that even though O'Connor did not much like to talk about her own work, she relished literary gossip; he is particularly interested in O'Connor's hatred for the fiction of Carson McCullers, speculating that O'Connor may have viewed McCullers as her literary competitor or secretly admired McCullers's outsider status. McCullers, after all, did spend most of her adult life away from the South, a move that O'Connor herself had early made. Spivey describes a dream of his in which he identified O'Connor with O'Connor: "I [. . .] dreamed that she had in her background—in the closet, another side to her. She was like Carson McCullers, dressed in blue jeans. I told her that dream and she didn't [. . .] dispute it. She smiled."

Letters between O'Connor and Spivey reveal the strong intellectual basis of their friendship. From the beginning they recommended to each other— and shared—works of religion and philosophy. Of O'Connor's interest in theology, Spivey has said, "I thought she had a better mind on theology and some aspects of psychology than just about anybody I had ever seen." In her first letter to him, O'Connor offered Spivey Eric Vogelin's *Israel and Revelation,* which she had just finished reading. In her second letter she listed her favorite Roman Catholic novelists and theologians: Bernanos, Guardini, Karl Adam, Marcel, and Baron von Hügel. She lent Spivey her copy of Bernanos's *The Country Priest,* and he loaned her Martin Buber's *The Eclipse of God,* which she found "readable," partly because Buber asserted that man cannot "participate in the Divine life" (*HB* 303). Spivey interprets O'Connor's interest in Teilhard de Chardin fairly late in her life as evidence of her movement away from absolute dogmatism toward a more modern outlook:

> Teihard represented for her a philosophy she could live with, a
> *new* Catholicism, it seemed to me. She didn't quite put it that
> way. [. . .] I finally decided it doesn't matter what she thought
> about the philosophy or theology in Teilhard. What she *did* like
> in any writer is to take some symbols; she, of course, said that

anything that rises must converge and that's a Teilhard idea. The problem with Teilhard [for her] theologically is that he tends in a very old-fashioned way to make God somebody Who is developing through evolution instead of the transcendent God.

Their continued discussion of religion and literature carried over into Spivey's unwillingness to understand O'Connor's work as she intended, particularly in *The Violent Bear It Away,* which Spivey has always read as the work of a visionary, whose ultimate vision is Christian. But in his view her vision also encompasses greater social meaning than O'Connor was willing to admit. As early as April 1960, O'Connor reacted to what she considered to be Spivey's misreading of her the novel: "You miss a great deal of what is in my book, my feeling for the old man particularly, because the Eucharist does not mean the same to you as it does to me. There are two main symbols in the book—water and the bread that Christ is. The whole action of the novel is Tarwater's selfish will against all that the little lake (the baptismal font) and the bread stand for. The book is a very minor hymn to the Eucharist" (*HB* 387).

Aside from discussion or argument about religious issues, O'Connor's friendship with Spivey helped her become interested in at least one group of writers whom she probably would have not known at all had it not been for Spivey's interest in them: the beatniks. Spivey says that at the time he met O'Connor he was not interested in producing a study of her works because his main interest then was in the beatnik writers. After Spivey called her attention to them, O'Connor wrote to him in June 1959: "reading about them and reading what they have to say about themselves makes me think there is a lot of ill-directed good in them. Certainly some revolt against our exaggerated materialism is long overdue. They seem to know a good many of the right things to run away from, but to lack any necessary discipline. They call themselves holy but holiness costs and so far as I can see they pay nothing" (*HB* 336–37). By introducing her to this movement—one so different from her life of creative isolation in Milledgeville—Spivey helped to fulfill O'Connor's need, as did Maryat Lee, for a connection with a "more exciting" literary and social world.

Spivey and O'Connor continued to write to each other and visit at Andalusia into the early 1960s. By this time O'Connor was fully aware of

Spivey's obsession with dreams and with his other eccentricities, as she revealed in a letter to Betty Hester in December 1961:

> Dr. Spivey arrived while Billy and Jenny [Sessions] were here and he was at his most hilarious, which entertained them and entertained him and kept me from having to entertain either of them. He was full of *La Dolce Vita,* which he went to see, taking someone with him to tell him what was going on, as he still suffers from psychosomatic blindness. The doctors have told him there is absolutely nothing wrong with his eyes, which delights him as it confirms all his theories. (*HB* 458–59)

Spivey did soon recover his eyesight and in a June 1962 visit told O'Connor of his plans to marry. She wrote to Hester that the marriage should thrive because "[s]he [fiancée Julia Douglass] too is interested in dreams and it seems that both their dreams prompted them to this action. He is as solemn as an owl about this" (*HB* 478). After his marriage, Spivey says that his relationship with O'Connor became more distant because O'Connor seemed to feel that his visits then became inappropriate. He quickly asserts, "I didn't think of her with romantic interest"; he does believe, however, that O'Connor herself should have married in order to "have someone look after her." He adds, though, that any husband of O'Connor would have had to move in with O'Connor and her mother because "I don't think she [Regina] would have ever let Flannery go!"

Almost forty years after her death, Spivey espouses an interesting theory of how O'Connor and her work might have evolved had she lived into the later part of the twentieth century. The popular notion that O'Connor lived as a sort of recluse in Milledgeville angers Spivey; he asserts, "She was not a recluse. The idea that she was like Emily Dickinson is just absurd. She could go in and make a bang-up speech, a presentation. She wanted to do it." He declares, unequivocally, that had she lived she would have become a woman of letters: "She would have written other things, and, even if she'd never written another piece of fiction, she could have been a great critic, a Woman of Letters. That's valuable—we need more of that sort of thing. She had a magisterial approach; she had an understanding approach; she was widely read."

William Sessions, who later earned a Ph.D. at Columbia and returned to Georgia and George State University, became another close friend of O'Connor and her mother two years before O'Connor met Ted Spivey. In 1956, Sessions was teaching at West Georgia College after having already earned an M. A. at Columbia. When O'Connor published *A Good Man Is Hard to Find,* Sessions wrote a review of it in the Catholic diocesan paper, *The Bulletin.* Interested in the review, O'Connor began a correspondence with him and soon asked him to visit at Andalusia. They met in 1956 on Ascension Thursday. The president of West Georgia College had won a state award and the presentation was held in Milledgeville; Sessions attended the ceremony and later visited O'Connor at Andalusia.

In a memoir he wrote of their friendship shortly after her death, Sessions describes his trips to Andalusia to visit O'Connor:

> I drove up it [the road to the farmhouse at Andalusia] in the summer when it was bone-dry and blazing hot, in winter when the rains churned it impassable. Rising on it toward the hill where the house at Andalusia sat, I always looked out at the landscape that Flannery saw from her front screened porch, as she used to every day, after two or three hours of writing every morning. The central Georgia hills rolled away, the bright reflection of a lake, and over all a starkness like a view from the walls of Avila in central Spain. ("Flannery O'Connor" 9)

One interesting intellectual argument between the two friends occurred after Sessions identified Freudian symbols in *The Violent Bear It Away* in 1960. O'Connor wrote him an immediate rebuff:

> I'm sorry the book didn't come off for you but I think it is no wonder it didn't since you see everything in terms of sex symbols, and in a way that would not enter my head—the lifted bough, the fork of the tree, the corkscrew. [. . .]
>
> In any case, your critique is too far from the spirit of the book to make me want to go into it with you in detail. I do hope, however, that you will get over the kind of thinking that sees in every door handle a phallic symbol. [. . .] My Lord, Billy, recover your simplicity. You ain't in Manhattan. (*HB* 407)

After this annoyed diatribe, however, O'Connor ends her letter with, "We'll look for you for Thanksgiving day."

As an aspiring writer himself, Sessions often asked O'Connor to read his fiction. By November 1956, she had read two of his stories and considered them ready to be "sent out": "I like the texture of both of them very much; the prose is relaxed and yet controlled and there is no feeling of strain" (*HB* 180). O'Connor gave Sessions detailed advice about minor revisions in both of the stories; of the second she said, "I have the feeling that the whole thing could have a little more dramatic unity" (181).

Like Ted Spivey (intellectually) and Maryat Lee (geographically), Sessions, who spent time in Europe soon after they began their friendship, also provided O'Connor with a connection with a more cosmopolitan world. Soon after they met, Sessions studied in Germany, a sojourn that apparently worried Regina O'Connor, who took a motherly interest in Sessions. In a letter to him on 1 September 1957, O'Connor wrote: "My mother keeps saying, 'Poor Billy, poor Billy, he can't talk over there, he can't talk, the poor boy, write him a letter, just think, he can't talk. Poor Billy,' etc. etc. etc. I tell her you doubtless ain't suffering but she is convinced you are" (*HB* 240). In a letter to him in late September 1957, O'Connor asked him whether he planned to visit her favorite modern theologians: "Are you going to see Heidegger on his mountain top? Are you going to see Msgr. Guardini, Karl Adam, or Max Picard, or is Max Picard still living? What about Marcel and what about that lady critic that is so good—Claude Edmond Magney?" (243–44). The list, which includes all those whom O'Connor had been reading and reviewing in *The Bulletin,* reveals her own desire to meet the people whose ideas she had found so stimulating.

Sessions was still in Europe in April 1958 when O'Connor and her mother made their pilgrimage to Lourdes during their only trip outside the United States. Sessions visited with them there and also remembered that while in Rome O'Connor had an audience with Pope Pius XII, Eugenio Pacelli. Later when he traveled in Greece, he sent O'Connor a postcard that featured an icon of Christ that may have influenced O'Connor's description of the Byzantine Christ O. E. Parker has tattooed on his back in "Parker's Back." While in Greece, Sessions also met the young woman who became his wife in August 1961. In a letter to Betty Hester on 19 August 1961, O'Connor gossiped about their two weddings, one civil, one Greek Orthodox:

"I can just see Billy glorying in this dramatic ceremony twice" (*HB* 448). By December of that year, Sessions and his wife had visited the O'Connors in Milledgeville: both O'Connor and her mother were impressed as O'Connor told Hester in another letter: "[T]his was a very fine girl and a very fine girl for Billy" (458). She went on to say that they can all be happy about "that marriage"; in fact, when the Sessions' son Andrew was born in 1962, they chose Regina O'Connor as his godmother. Sessions and O'Connor maintained their friendship until her death in August 1964. In his memoir of O'Connor, Sessions describes his last visit with her:

> I saw Flannery last in June [1964]. She was already in the hospital in Atlanta. Her hospital room was as barren as all those she must have known since the first appearance of *lupus* over ten years before. Only some manuscripts from hopeful writers (a perennial kind of service) and some books (of theology, I think) were near her bed. Her rather flat accents were as strong as ever, but her body had more bruises and skin-rashes than I had ever remembered. That peculiar humor of hers, more in her piercing eyes than in her voice, charged and volleyed and embraced as always. ("Flannery O'Connor" 9)

Sessions's connection with O'Connor continued long after her death through his friendship with Betty Hester. He has said that it was through his influence that Hester met Sally Fitzgerald and subsequently allowed her letters from O'Connor to be published in *The Habit of Being;* in addition, on the day she committed suicide Hester gave Sessions all of her unpublished manuscripts; later her nephew named Sessions Hester's literary executor and as a result his interest in the relationship between Hester and O'Connor will continue (Sessions, "Betty Hester" n. pag.).

Still another literary friendship of O'Connor's last year was with Robert Drake, at that time an aspiring young writer and teacher at the University of Texas. Drake, who spent most of his academic years at the University of Tennessee, has written several articles on O'Connor and her work and published four volumes of fiction himself. Though O'Connor wrote only a few letters to Drake (he says that he made no deliberate attempt to keep them), he did visit her at Andalusia in August 1963, almost a year to the day before she died. After that visit, Drake invited O'Connor to come to the University of Texas to talk or read; she agreed to the visit, but her surgery in February 1964 forced her to cancel the appearance. Drake recalls her letter to him: "The first we knew anything was wrong was when she wrote me and to the chairman of the lecture committee to cancel the engagement. She said, 'I've been ordered into the hospital for a totally unexpected operation and I won't be able to write you but you must continue to write me because I intend to survive this.' It sounded just like her, you know."[8]

Like nearly all of her other regular correspondents, Drake wrote to O'Connor after reading her fiction; he had just read the stories in *A Good Man Is Hard to Find*. From that first reading, Drake declares that he became an avid admirer of O'Connor's work, urging it on his friends and longing to visit her in Georgia. In 1960 he published a review of *The Violent Bear It Away* and sent a copy of it to O'Connor, who responded immediately; Drake describes her reaction to the review: "[She thought] it was about the best one she had gotten and I was a reviewer who seemed to share her prejudices. [. . .] And yes, she would be glad to see me when I was in the neighborhood" (Drake, "The Lady Frum Somewhere" 212).

Drake's recollections of the day he spent with O'Connor in August 1963 offer several new insights about O'Connor's interaction with the many admirers who came to Andalusia. Drake asserts that his reception by both O'Connor and her mother "couldn't have been nicer":

> Now, it took me a little while to learn that she didn't have any small talk. She looked you straight in the eye just like she wrote, and she said what she had to say; then she just quit. Most Southerners are scared of silence and then I realized [when she was quiet] that it was my time [to talk].
>
> We did not talk about the literary world, you see. We were talking most about the cultural world and what she and I both had in common as Southerners. [. . .] She wasn't much on literary gossip [though] she did tell me that Katherine Anne Porter always had to have a pink spotlight when she read. She didn't have anything to say about Faulkner; she didn't have anything to say about Eudora Welty. There was no particular literary cast to the conversation.

Drake and O'Connor lunched at the Sanford House in Milledgeville; he does not recall that anyone approached the table to speak to O'Connor, but, as a Southerner himself, reinforces the idea that in Milledgeville, O'Connor received little attention for her writing: he says neighbors "are not terribly impressed with people who do things like that; they're just homefolk."

Drake also retains a clear memory of his departure from Andalusia that afternoon: "When I left—this I will never forget—I parked in the big back yard and there's that portecochere where you went into the back door. She [O'Connor] stood there in the doorway and looked me in the eye, and she said, 'Well, now you know where we live. Come back.' And I thought, 'Now that was a genuine, from the heart invitation. She really means that.'"

After the one-day visit ended, a friendship developed between the two that resulted in O'Connor's reading some of his work and recommending it to her agent, Elizabeth McKee. The recommendation appears in a letter O'Connor wrote to McKee early in January 1964: "I suggested to a friend of mine, Robert Drake, that he send his stories to you. They've mostly been published in the *Christian Century* and I thought they might make a book that would have some kind of limited popular appeal" (*HB* 560). McKee did indeed become his agent "for a couple of years." Drake at least partly repaid O'Connor's generosity to him by writing the first monograph published on her work, a pamphlet in the series Contemporary Writers in Christian Perspective. His reading offers the theological interpretation of her works that O'Connor clearly intended.

The friendships, then, that O'Connor made with aspiring writers and intellectuals during the late 1950s and early 1960s enriched both her personal life and her writing. These friendships supplemented those she had made earlier during her five years away from Milledgeville and those she had formed soon after her return. People from the academic world helped her create characters like Sheppard in "The Lame Shall Enter First," but she also needed the emotional support her many correspondences supplied; Robert Drake recalls that Sally Fitzgerald once told him that O'Connor "lived for the mail." He correctly asserts, "She was a secluded person. It [the steady flow of letters] was communication."

CHAPTER ELEVEN

LECTURES AND TRAVEL
OUTSIDE MILLEDGEVILLE,
1955–1959

Above all else, Flannery O'Connor was a writer with a true sense of vocation; however, after illness forced her to return to Milledgeville, she formed, especially through correspondence, numerous friendships that helped broaden her emotional life; in addition, the readings and lectures she presented in the South, North Midwest, and Northwest added a wider dimension to her life. O'Connor's public lectures and readings were extensive: between 1954 and the end of 1963, she presented nearly sixty. To those with only limited knowledge of her later life, the extent of her travel may seem surprising, for it undercuts the traditional view that O'Connor languished in Milledgeville, the victim of chronic illness, able to write only a few hours a day under the protective eyes of her mother, Regina Cline O'Connor. Permanently trapped in Milledgeville, O'Connor was, this view expresses, an exile to illness, freed only by her creativity.

That O'Connor suffered from lupus, that she spent the last twelve years of her life in Milledgeville, that she lived with her mother at Andalusia, and that she wrote some of the best fiction of our time are indisputable facts; however, far from being physically trapped in Milledgeville, O'Connor left the town a number of times every year to speak both locally and nationally. Although many of her appearances *were* local—she often addressed the Macon Writers' Club and appeared fairly regularly at her alma mater, GSCW, and at Wesleyan College in Macon—O'Connor also traveled throughout the South and as far northwest as Minnesota. Even though she had to abandon plans for these trips, she also wanted to accept invitations from the universities of Missouri, Washington, Colorado, and Texas. In 1963, besides traveling to Northampton, Massachusetts, to accept an honorary Ph.D. from Smith College, O'Connor arranged a lecture tour that took her to Hollins College in Virginia, to Georgetown in Washington, D.C., and to Notre Dame of Maryland. At the end of 1963 and early into 1964, O'Connor was planning another trip: she expected to lecture at Boston College, Brown University, and the University of Texas, but she gave up the plans because "I have very shortly to go to the hospital and be cut upon by the doctors" (*HB* 566).

O'Connor's appearances as a reader and lecturer were an obvious outgrowth of her writing. She began to make public appearances locally in 1954 after the publication of *Wise Blood* but before she published *A Good Man Is Hard to Find*. She spoke at the January 1954 Convocation of GSCW and was a guest at a Penwomen's breakfast in Atlanta on 24 February 1955; she also made several presentations that year to the Macon Writers' Club. When Alta L. Haynes invited her to speak before the East Lansing, Michigan, branch of the American Association of University Women in the spring of 1956, O'Connor wrote in response: "I have made a good many talks in the past year but all in the South, which is like talking to a large gathering of your aunts and cousins" (*HB* 136). Gradually, however, she became more comfortable speaking to less parochial audiences, although the subjects of most of her lectures concerned, as she wrote to Granville Hicks, "regionalism and religion in fiction, or anyway my experience of it" (205–6).

Southern letters and the role of religion in fiction do predominate as the subjects of her lectures. O'Connor delivered her favorite talk, usually titled "The Catholic Novelist in the Protestant South," at least fifteen times. She did not, however, present this lecture or any other of her favorites without extensive revision before each presentation. Study of the manuscripts in the O'Connor Collection at Georgia College and State University reveals that O'Connor revised every specific lecture at least three times before she gave it; there are, for example, eight drafts of "Some Notes on the Combination: Novelist and Believer" that O'Connor presented at a symposium on Religion and Arts at Sweet Briar College in Virginia on 8 March 1963.

O'Connor had a genuine dread of sounding abstract and intellectual in public. Writing to Granville Hicks early in 1957, she asserted: "I'm not an intellectual and have a horror of making an idiot of myself with abstract statements and theories" (*HB* 202). In order to achieve both the clarity and concreteness that she demanded of herself, O'Connor labored over every lecture and, in the process of the writing, she formulated theories relative to the style and function of modern fiction. When illness forced her to cancel an appearance at the University of Missouri in May 1958, she wrote to Cecil Dawkins: "I haven't got over having to give up the Missouri business, particularly after I had spent a good five weeks writing myself a lecture for it" (284). After, however, O'Connor had produced the basic lectures in her repertoire—"The Fiction Writer in the South," "The Grotesque in Southern Literature," "The Catholic Novelist in the Protestant South"—she did make use of them a number of times, admitting before an appearance at Spring Hill College in April 1960, "I may reuse some of the coffee grounds" (363).

O'Connor actually preferred reading from her works to presenting formal lectures. In 1958 she admitted to Maryat Lee this preference for reading "mainly because the element of ham in me seeks release. I have a secret desire to rival Charles Dickens upon the stage" (*HB* 265). She read her preferred story for public presentation, "A Good Man Is Hard to Find," at least eight times. Before her trip to Hollins, Georgetown, and Notre Dame of Maryland in the fall of 1963, O'Connor wrote to Katherine Anne Porter that the story was the only one she could read "without laughing." Besides, she said, it was the right length.[1] To explain the story ahead of her reading, O'Connor wrote several versions of a rather elaborate preface that clarified her use of the grotesque in "A Good Man Is Hard to Find."[2] This introduction shows how, indeed, O'Connor reused "some of the coffee grounds" as she proceeded from lecture to lecture. Here she has incorporated many of the ideas, examples, even the actual words from her speech/essay on the grotesque to introduce a pivotal example of the genre.

O'Connor's enjoyment of reading her stories publicly offers a first major motive behind her willingness to become a lecturer. Though by nature she was reserved (both her appearance on Harvey Breit's television show *Galley-Proof* in 1955 and the tape recording of her panel appearance with Robert Penn Warren at Vanderbilt prove her reticence), she also possessed an innate desire to perform in public in order to achieve self-confidence and deserved recognition. She, in addition, wanted to help readers understand her works as she meant them to be understood. In her memorial comment on her friendship with O'Connor, Maryat Lee remembered O'Connor's enthusiasm for lecturing: "She complained about speaking engagements & writing speeches—complained acidly, saying it was the money. But she *loved* talking in front of people—she had a gift & [it was] most shocking to find it in her. Her passion was there & it warmed me deeply."[3] O'Connor, then, like most of us, occasionally enjoyed the spotlight, admitting to her friend, Roslyn Barnes, in 1960, "I am quite a ham" (*HB* 422).

Another incentive that convinced O'Connor to accept lecture engagements was money. When she applied for the grant-in-aid from the Ford Foundation in January 1959, she disclosed earnings of just over three thousand dollars in 1956 and a good deal less than that in 1957 and 1958. She explained her financial situation in a cover letter to W. McNeill Lowry: "I live on a farm with my mother where my living expenses are not great. I have managed to hold my own financially by selling a story about once a year, by royalties, and by accepting engagements to lecture. While a grant would not free me from any other job, it would free me from feeling that I have to accept every lecture engagement every time I am offered a fee. These things take time to prepare and are not what I feel I ought to be doing frequently."[4] O'Connor's words here make clear her need for money, and comments in other letters add more support. When she went to the University of Chicago in February 1959, she earned seven hundred dollars, later bragging to Cecil Dawkins, "I can live for a year on what they are paying me for a week" (*HB* 316). In 1962, again writing to Dawkins, O'Connor expressed a dislike for making appearances but gratitude for her earnings from them: "[A] little of this honored guest bidnis goes a long way, but it sure does help my finances" (472). In 1963, she wrote to John Hawkes that her trip North would allow her to by "another pair of swans" (548), and to Betty Hester that she would come home with enough money "to float me the next six or seven months" (543).

O'Connor, however, also asserted that "I get a lot out of it besides money. I see how the other half thinks and I come home raring to write" (*HB* 543). Her statement here contains one of the basic reasons for her many public appearances: she needed connection with the world outside Milledgeville to stimulate her artistic creativity. Although O'Connor wrote in 1962 that she preferred "to go to colleges rather than conferences [. . . because] [t]hat many writers gathered together can't be healthy" (493), her participation in conferences enabled her to meet other writers. In 1955 in Greensboro, she met Randall Jarrell and Peter Taylor. At Vanderbilt in 1959, Robert Penn Warren and Jesse Stuart also participated. After the Arts Festival at Wesleyan in Macon in 1958, she met Katherine Anne Porter and subsequently entertained her at Andalusia. At Converse College in April 1962, she appeared with Eudora Welty, whom she admired for her appealing lack of "presence." Meeting other writers integrated O'Connor into the community of her craft and helped her consolidate her identity as a serious writer.

In addition to establishing contact with other writers, O'Connor was also intellectually stimulated by the professors and students she met at the colleges and universities where she appeared. She joked about athletes being forced to attend her reading at Notre Dame in 1957: "I guess all the bumbling boys at Notre Dame will be forced in off the golf courses and football fields to squint at a live novelist" (*HB* 213); however, she also asserted that the students in her audience often "know more than I do" and allowed undergraduates from Wesleyan to visit her at Andalusia: "When they appear, they do all the talking and have fantastic but positive ideas about how everything is and ought to be; and they are mighty sophisticated on the outside. The visits leave me exhausted and yearning to go sit with the chickens" (249). Still, she enjoyed talking with students and even established correspondences with some of them. O'Connor also became friends with some of the professors she met at her appearances, among them Sister Bernetta Quinn from Minnesota, who became a correspondent and later a sympathetic critic of O'Connor's work.

One of the most significant reasons for O'Connor's lecturing evolves from her chief reason for writing: to guide the nonbelievers of her generation toward redemption through grace. Throughout her life, O'Connor was vitally concerned that her work be understood—that her fiction be read not as a study of grotesque monsters headed toward ruin but as the account of desperate seekers looking (sometimes without knowing it) to find God in a world where secularism has increasingly prevailed. O'Connor, then, obviously chose the public forum to further her work as "a Catholic novelist in the Protestant South." In a lecture presented at Sweet Briar College in 1963, O'Connor clearly stated her aim and the difficulties inherent in fulfilling it: "Today the central problem of the novelist who wishes to write about man's encounter with [. . .] God is how he shall make the experience intelligible to an audience in which religious feeling has become, if not atrophied, at least vague and soggy and sentimental, and for whom centuries of second-hand pulpit prose have made the language of religion somewhat comic when not simply meaningless" (Cash, "Flannery O'Connor as Lecturer" 5). O'Connor, by lecturing so widely, created her own pulpit, one from which she could and did use both clarity and humor to enlighten her listeners to the theological intention of her work.

In general, O'Connor richly benefited from lecturing and reading from her work. Appearing in public enabled her to develop a side of her talent and personality that would have lain dormant had she refused invitations to read and lecture. In conscientiously preparing the lectures, O'Connor also formulated concretely the ideas that under gird her fiction; in addition, presenting these ideas in public helped her advance the genuine focus of her work: like her letters for readers today, O'Connor's lectures helped her audience comprehend her works as she meant them to be understood.

Lecturing also gave O'Connor independence. She usually traveled alone, leaving behind the limited personal life she shared with her mother. She became Flannery O'Connor the writer, discarding her local identity as Regina Cline's invalid daughter. The money she earned from her readings and lectures also gave her financial independence. Though she was unable to hold a full-time job, the lectures (with a legacy from an aunt and the grants she received) allowed her to buy rental property in Milledgeville and to pursue her rather expensive avocation—the collection and nurturing of her exotic poultry.

Finally, and most significantly, traveling and lecturing gave Flannery O'Connor the opportunity to see, as she asserted, "how the other half thinks," and, though she expressed the desire, after interaction with this outside world, to get back to her writing, she needed to experience the world beyond Milledgeville in order to develop the full awareness that enabled her to create believable characters like Sheppard in "The Lame Shall Enter First," a man similar to the unbelieving "humanists" she met in the world of academia. Her interaction with other writers also built her self-confidence, helping her realize the validity of her own ideas and approaches to writing fiction. Meeting students gave her the opportunity to teach, to serve as a wise and knowing mentor to aspiring young thinkers and writers. Without this part of her life, O'Connor would have lived a far more limited existence, both as a writer and as a human being.

One of the first public appearances that O'Connor made was at her alma mater GSCW when she gave the convocation address "Some Aspects of Fiction" in January 1954.[5] In *The Habit of Being,* O'Connor first mentioned a future public appearance outside Milledgeville in a letter to Sally Fitzgerald the day after Christmas in 1954. She related that she had accepted an invitation to appear at the North Carolina Women's College in March 1955: "That is where Brother Randall Jarrell holds forth. I accepted but I am not looking forward to it. Can you fancy me hung in conversation with the likes of him?" (*HB* 74). Despite this initial reluctance, O'Connor participated in at least seven public meetings in 1955, beginning with her appearance at the Penwomen's breakfast in Atlanta on 4 February, where she was recognized for her story "The Life You Save May Be Your Own," which had been included in the O. Henry short-story collection in 1954. In a letter to her agent, Elizabeth McKee, in April 1955, she also related that at the meeting she had had to sit by her "old friend, Long John Selby" (77).

O'Connor traveled to Greensboro on 29 March 1955 to participate in the twelfth annual Festival of the Arts at North Carolina Women's College. Robert Frost had read at the festival ten days earlier. On the twenty-ninth, O'Connor, serving on a panel with Randall Jarrell, Robie Macauley, and Peter Taylor, read and critiqued student writing in the Festival of the Arts edition of *Corradi,* the college literary magazine. The next day she held individual conferences with the student writers whose work appeared in the journal. Jeanne R. Nostrandt, then an undergraduate at the college, remembers O'Connor's appearance on the twenty-ninth. She recalls O'Connor's short, bluntly cut dark hair, her demure style of dress, and her clear admiration for Randall Jarrell.[6] O'Connor, Nostrandt recalls, seemed pleased to be at the college, though a bit astonished at her own celebrity. O'Connor walked to the edge of the stage on her aluminum crutches and warmly recognized the students whose work appeared in *Corradi*. Nostrandt also remembers that O'Connor praised Jarrell and the college for giving its students the opportunity to participate in a forum devoted to the arts. O'Connor must have felt that participating in the arts festival was of positive value, for she soon wrote to the Fitzgeralds, "I said nothing intelligent the whole time, but enjoyed myself. Mr. Randall Jarrell, wife and stepdaughters I met and et dinner with. I must say I was shocked at what a very kind man he is—that is the last impression I expected to have of him. I also met Peter Taylor, who is more like folks" (*HB* 76). The New York public library holds a thank-you note from O'Connor to Jarrell dated 3 April 1955.[7]

O'Connor's other presentations that year were all in Georgia. Apparently her mother urged her to accept whatever invitations came. O'Connor showed her overall doubt about both her mother's attitude and the appearances themselves in a letter she wrote to Frances Cheney in May 1955: "My mother has a Chamber of Commerce approach to literature and she thinks that I must address all these DARs and Book Review Groups whenever called upon. [. . .] The last one I talked at was on April 23 and one of the ladies told me that it was a very important day—the birth of William Shakespeare, Harry Stilwell Edwards, and Shirley Temple" (*CC* 18).

O'Connor appeared before the Macon Writers' Club three times in the spring of 1955. Rosa Lee Walston described this organization "as a little group of those who want to write and who get a little article published here or a little story there, and they were just looking for someone who was embodying what they hoped for. I don't think Flannery ever thought much of them." Louise Gossett recalls having heard O'Connor read at the club: "She came and read "A Good Man Is Hard to Find" to this *very proper* club. It was a hat and gloves set. We sat in a very comfortable home. Flannery and I laughed [but] I think everybody else was a little bit taken-aback by the story." As a speaker, O'Connor was "delightful" and "likeable," Gossett recalls. "There was never any sense that she was working on the audience. She was just interested in what she was saying." After appearing before the Macon group at the end of April 1955, O'Connor wrote to Ben Griffith that "nobody [there] had ever heard of me, of course" (*HB* 79).

Late in 1955, she gave three presentations in Atlanta, one at the annual meeting on 1 December of the Georgia Writers' Association, where she presented "Some Problems of the Southern Writer." After meeting Lillian

Smith at this gathering, she wrote to the Cheneys: "I have now got to be famous enough to address this body. I set two down from Miss Lillian Smith who asked me to visit her on her mountain top. I allowed as how my infirmity prevented my going to the mountains right now" (*CC* 29). In a letter to Catherine Carver on 2 December 1955, O'Connor commented on the reaction of a member of the audience to her presentation: "After my talk, one lady shook my hand and said, 'That was such a nice dispensation you gave us, Honey.' Another said, 'What's wrong with your leg, sugar?' I'll be real glad when I get too old for them to *sugar* me" (*HB* 120). To Betty Hester, she also described another member of her audience: "There is one of them who attends all these things who reminds you of Stone Mountain on the move. She's a large grey mass, near-sighted, pious, and talks about 'messages' all the time. I haven't got her name yet but she is going to pursue me in dreams I feel" (125).

In 1956 O'Connor gave seven lectures or readings—all of them in Georgia except for her visit to Lansing, Michigan, in late April at the invitation of the Lansing–East Lansing American Association of University Women. Before she traveled to Michigan, however, O'Connor addressed the Georgia Council of Teachers of English in Atlanta on 16 March. Her topic was "The Georgia Writer and His Country." The trip to Michigan, though, took precedence in O'Connor's plans for 1956. As early as July 1995, Alta Haynes had invited O'Connor to come to Michigan as she (O'Connor) revealed in a letter to Catherine Carver: "I have been asked to talk on The Significance of the Short Story (UGH) at a wholesale gathering of the AAUW in Lansing, Michigan—next April. It will take me from now until next April to find out what the significance of the short story is" (*HB* 91). When she was making final arrangements for her visit to Michigan early in 1956, O'Connor, who had only recently been forced to use crutches, worried about the inconvenience they would cause her and her hostesses, but she agreed to travel to Michigan anyway and expressed her willingness to either talk or read from her works if she could find out what her audience was interested in. In an unpublished letter to Haynes, O'Connor also explained why she could not extend her visit through the weekend: she needed to get home so that her mother, who stayed at the Cline mansion in Milledgeville while her daughter was away, could return to Andalusia.[8] Just before leaving for Lansing, O'Connor wrote to Betty Hester giving details about her living arrangements in Lansing. She would be staying with the Hayneses, who were already unnecessarily solicitous about her being on crutches. She also ridiculed in advance Mrs. Haynes's desire to introduce her to other "young writers and intellectuals" in Lansing: "Anything I can't stand it's a young writer or intellectual" (53).

A detailed record of O'Connor's trip to Michigan exists: Alta Haynes compiled a scrapbook of O'Connor's visit, a sojourn that extended from 24 to 27 April. Mrs. Haynes described her reaction to O'Connor's arrival at her home at midnight on Monday, 23 April: "[I]t was for me a case of love at first sight. There she was, young and smiling, and fresh despite the late hour and the long trip. Her crutches, we'd all worried about them, seemed to enhance, to set off her attractiveness. And her deep Georgia drawl, in the middle of the chill Michigan night, was enormously appealing."[9] The next day O'Connor was guest of honor at a luncheon given by one of the AAUW members and a tea arranged by another; at 8:00 P.M., she presented her lecture, "Some Aspects of Contemporary Fiction," at Eastern High School in Lansing. The local newspaper included a brief article on the first day's activities, including a description of O'Connor's outfit for the luncheon: "For the party the petite writer of literary stature donned a soft, two-piece dressmaker suit of blue, grey and black plaided wool. Her small veiled hat was black and her pumps grey suede with Baby Louis heels. Her accessories included a pair of crutches which she hopes to shed within a year."[10] For the next two days, O'Connor continued to be wined and dined by the AAUW membership, culminating with parties Alta Haynes gave at her home on Thursday: "Rumsey [her husband] and I invited a number of literary folks to the house to meet her, some in the afternoon and others for dinner in the evening." The next morning, Haynes drove O'Connor to the airport: "It was this last morning that I had my best visit with her, perhaps the only one alone." While she was in Lansing, O'Connor also attended (probably on Wednesday), a "huge convention luncheon of the Nat. Asso. of Cat. Women," which she described in a letter to Betty Hester as "something suitable for the remission of temporal punishment due to sin": lasting three hours, it included speeches, endless introductions, and too many strangers (*HB* 155).

When O'Connor returned to Georgia, she wrote the obligatory thank-you note to Alta Haynes, asserting, "I enjoyed everything, but the best part of for me has been getting to know you and Rumsey and that is a pleasure that won't end with my visit to Lansing" (*HB* 154). In a letter to Betty Hester, written a few days later, O'Connor elaborated on her enthusiasm for Alta and Rumsey Haynes: "They were really very nice people and I enjoyed them. Rumsey collects postcards and gave me a bunch of them to send out. [. . .] You always like these people better than you had expected to and perhaps the dreary part is that you will never see them again" (155). Although O'Connor never saw the Hayneses again, she maintained a correspondence with Alta Haynes that Regina O'Connor continued even after her daughter's death. When the Flannery O'Connor Room opened at Georgia College in the early seventies, Haynes donated a peacock lamp from Poland that she had owned for many years.

On 22 May 1956 O'Connor gave "The Fiction Writer in the South" lecture to a meeting of the Friends of the Public Library in Savannah, a trip that allowed visits with her Savannah relatives, including Katie Semmes. After another appearance before the Macon Writers' Club, O'Connor addressed the Macon Parish Chapter of the National Council of Catholic Women on 27 September 1956. Her topic was "What Is a Wholesome Novel?" She reacted to that lecture in a letter to the Cheneys on 18 October, saying that she had told her audience "that the average Catholic reader was a Militant Moron. They sat there like a band of genteel desperados and never moved a face muscle. I might have been saying the rosary to them" (*CC* 45). On 2 November 1956, O'Connor received one of the Georgia Writers' Association's Literary Achievement Scrolls for 1955 "for her distinguished collection of short stories, *A Good Man Is Hard to Find.*" The comment that accompanied the award quite clearly shows how much other writers in her own state approved the texture of her work by late 1955, even if they didn't quite understand her vision:

> A sensitive and passionate observer, Miss O'Connor has trained her eyes to see what is significant among the details of our common environment, her ears to hear what is meaningful in the rhythms and trivia of our everyday speech, and her heart to feel that which causes each of us to know frustration and fulfillment, pride and humility, folly and wisdom, hate and love—especially love, which transcends the physical and temporal. And, most

important, she has trained her mind and her hand to set it all down with originality and wit and compassion. Hers is a great gift. Hers is a true art.[11]

In an unpublished letter to Denver Lindley, O'Connor ridiculed the occasion and the award. She was particularly amused that her name was misspelled twice on the scroll.[12] Her final appearance for the year was at Wesleyan, where she presented "The Fiction Writer in His Country" on 6 December. An article in the Wesleyan College newspaper on 13 December described the event: "Miss O'Connor explained the hardship a writer undergoes in that he has to make one's country do for all countries. He is limited and has to be universal at the same time. She told her audience that a writer's country is the country he is concerned with, his environmental country or region."[13]

Despite expressing some annoyance with the talks, O'Connor, in 1957, lectured or participated in workshops at Emory University, Agnes Scott College, GSCW (where she received the outstanding alumna award on 10 May 1957), and the University of Georgia. She also read "A Good Man Is Hard to Find" at the Macon Writers' Club on 5 February. She wrote to Maryat Lee in March that "all I seem to be doing these days is writing these stinking talks" (*HB* 209). Her most distant appearance that year was at Notre Dame University on 15 April 1957.

At Emory on 11 January 1957, O'Connor participated in an evening class in an adult education program titled "How the Writer Writes." The Emory University Community Education Service sponsored the program, which featured a different writer every week through the semester. Preparing for the lecture in late January, O'Connor wrote disparagingly to Maryat Lee that "adult education calls for the most elementary things you can think of in not more than two-syllable words"; she also said that she expected the "poor souls" to be more confused at the end of her lecture than at the beginning: "I am going to end my lecture on the note that it is as noble not to write as to" (*HB* 201).

She wrote to Roysce Smith that she planned to make the visit to Emory a one-day excursion because she could not tolerate spending the night in Atlanta during the winter.[14] "The Nature and Aim of Fiction," the composite essay compiled by the Fitzgeralds for *Mystery and Manners* certainly contains some of the material O'Connor presented at Emory, as she gives the title of the program in her first paragraph and makes some scathing comments about writing programs at the end. She also talked about symbolism in "Good Country People" as an identified manuscript at Georgia College and State University reveals. Celestine Sibley reviewed O'Connor's lecture in the *Atlanta Journal-Constitution* and, according to O'Connor in a letter to Betty Hester, "left the impression, which I did not intend to convey, that I had a great contempt for the audience." She also asserted that she felt uncomfortable at "the little dinner beforehand" attended by a "table full of College Liberals" with whom she was unable to converse. She sat there, she said, "expressionless as a clock" (*HB* 203).

In April, O'Connor gave her most stimulating presentation of the year at Notre Dame, where she presented "The Church and the Fiction Writer" and participated in a panel discussion. O'Connor first mentioned the planned trip to Notre Dame in a letter to Granville Hicks in early March 1957, when she told him that she had agreed to give the talk "against my better judgement" (*HB* 205). To the Cheneys she wrote, "I want to go look at all them Cathlick interleckchuls as you don't often see none around here" (*CC* 52). In a letter to Betty Hester, O'Connor showed more enthusiasm for the appearance; she liked the amount of money they were paying her and knew she would "get to see Robert [Fitzgerald] who will meet me in Chicago" (*HB* 207). To Maryat Lee, O'Connor confided her disgust with the travel necessary to reach Notre Dame: "I am the kind that would like to *be* somewhere but don't like to *get* there" (209). After her appearance at Notre Dame, O'Connor described her audience to Lee: "The audience of about 250 or 300 consisted of 25% Bumbling Boys, 25% skirted and beretta-ed simmernarians, 25% higher clergy, 25% faculty and wives, 25% graduate students, 25%. [. . .] I am over-extending the audience. Anyway the operation was successful and I have a hundred bucks to compensate for any damage that may have been done to my nervous system" (215). She elaborated even more in a letter to Betty Hester, describing the trip as "entirely successful" because she "escaped the snow by exactly one day and made all the necessary connections"; she also declared her audience interested: she was "a writer about 'Southern Degeneracy' and a Catholic at oncet and the same time." She reported that while she talked she "trained [her] gaze" on one of the young clerical students in her audience who "didn't believe a damm word of it" (216). She appreciated another non-Catholic member of the audience who approached her after the talk: "a girl came up to me and said, 'I'm not a Catholic, I'm a Lutheran but you've given me some hope for the first time that Catholic writers may do something.' I said, 'Well please pray that we will.' And she said, 'I will, I will in Christ.' And she meant it and she will and it is that kind of thing that makes these trips worth the effort" (216).

One of O'Connor's most personally gratifying appearances in 1957 in Georgia must have been the one at GSCW where she received one of two alumna awards for 1957. By the time the college chose to present O'Connor with this award, she had published *Wise Blood* (1951) and *A Good Man Is Hard to Find and Other Stories* (1955). Dr. Robert E. Lee, president of GSCW, presented the award to O'Connor at the annual Honor's Day ceremonies at the college on 15 May 1957. He remembers that she "had great rapport with the audience of students, [but it was] not her delivery; it was what she said [. . .] without adornment, without rhetoric, without any of the devices for holding an audience. [. . .] What you got was gold. Of course, people respond to this."[15] In her letters, O'Connor expressed both pleasure and skepticism at receiving the honor. On 17 April she wrote to Maryat Lee: "The next Occasion for me will be at the local college on something they call Honors Day and at which me and another worthy are to be "honored." I can do without all honors that do not carry stipends with them but if you convey the crude sentiment to your brother, I shall consider you a Skunk of the Third Water and will declare in public that you are a lier" (*HB* 215). O'Connor's brief acceptance speech demonstrates her facile humor, her actual delight in making public presentations, and the seriousness with which she formulated the theories behind the fiction.[16] O'Connor's remarks reflect both her own experience as a writer and, very briefly, her theories about writing. She had experienced by mid-1957 the insincere regard of celebrity seekers; for example, after *Time* magazine reviewed her collection of short stories in 1955, O'Connor had written to her friend Ben Griffith: "I have been getting some very funny fan mail—a lot of it from gentlemen who have got no further than the title—'Do you really think a good man is hard to find? I am 31 years old, single, work like a dog . . .' etc. etc. etc." (89). More seriously, O'Connor's comments in the speech are consistent with her assertion in "The Nature and Aim of Fiction" that the writer must be a person of absolute integrity whose greatest concern should be with the truth of his presentation. In miniature, O'Connor's acceptance speech at

GSCW reflects her concerns—both serious and comic—as a literary artist practicing her craft in 1957.

Her comment above about the writer's having her work "ceremoniously butchered on television" was also the result of personal experience. The Schlitz Playhouse, not the GE Theater as she at first thought, televised her short story "The Life You Save May Be Your Own" on 1 March 1957. In a letter to the Cheneys on 3 January 1957, O'Connor discussed what she considered to be the travesty of that production:

> If you all have the stomach for it, you can view "The Life You Save May Be Your Own," on the Schlitz Playhouse of Stars, Friday, February 1st [the actual showing was 1 March] at 9:30 P.M. New York time but something else your time. Starring Brother Gene Kelly. Who announces that there will be no singing and dancing in this but that he is going to ACT, a thing which he has had no opportunity to do in the movies. He also says, "[T]he story is a kind of hill billy thing in which I play a guy who *befriends* a deaf mute girl in the hills of Kentucky." Underlining mine. Another announcement described it as "Flannery O'Connor's backwoods love story." I don't know whether I should see the thing or not but my mother insists we are going to and she has notified all the kin and I know they are going to think that the TV version is better than the original. (*CC* 48)

Though during her lifetime none of her other stories was ever dramatized on television, she was not averse to the commercialization of her fiction as revealed in her years of encouragement to a young writer named Robert Jiras, who wanted desperately to film a version of "The River."

Between 28 July and 2 August 1957, O'Connor participated as a member of the Southern Writer's Workshop held by the Georgia Center for Continuing Education at the University of Georgia. She recorded her amusement with the workshop in a letter to Betty Hester on 9 August: "The jamboree was a real farce [. . .] There were forty or fifty [women] in the room and three men, the man who was running the thing [. . .] (he had to be there), a youth with the name of Mr. Phinizy Spalding, and an old man [. . .] who came from Louvail, Ga., sent I am sure by the Lord to be a plague on the penwomen. This was a poet and he had his poems in a paper bag from the ten-cent store;

he attended every session he could and tried wherever possible to get the floor away from the ladies" (*HB* 235). O'Connor also described her own talk and the insipid group response to the seven best stories presented at the workshop. The old man finally got the floor and told the women, metaphorically, that they were among the damned. O'Connor really enjoyed his performance: "The women were growling under their breaths for him to sit down, but he held on until the bell rang. He was worth my trip" (235).

O'Connor gave only one public lecture in 1958, this one at Birmingham Southern College on 25 November 1958, when she presented "The Freak in Modern Fiction" and held a creative writing workshop. She had planned to present the same lecture in May 1958 at the University of Missouri, but ill health—at least partly the result of her one trip abroad—prevented her making that appearance. That spring O'Connor also met Katherine Anne Porter when she (Porter) lectured at Wesleyan College on 28 March. O'Connor wrote to Cecil Dawkins that the Gossetts would bring Porter to Milledgeville for lunch, but that she could not attend the reading, even though she had been asked to introduce Porter.[17]

O'Connor's excursion to Europe came in April 1958 when she and her mother joined a seventeen-day pilgrimage (21 April to 8 May) to Ireland, Paris, Lourdes, Rome, and Lisbon organized by the archbishop of Savannah, Msgr. James T. McNamara. O'Connor's Savannah cousin—and patron—Katie Semmes paid for the trip on the condition that O'Connor bathe in the healing waters at Lourdes. As her many comments in letters reveal, O'Connor, from the beginning, had mixed feelings both about foreign travel and joining the pilgrims at Lourdes. Her first mention of the possibility of joining the tour occurred in a letter to Betty Hester early in November 1957. She wrote: "As this is about the only way either of us will ever get there, my mother is all for it. I am all for it too though I expect it to be a comic nightmare. It only lasts 17 days so I figure I should be able to stand it that long. What I see is a planeload of fortress-footed female Catholics pushed from shrine to shrine by the prelates McNamara and Bourke" (*HB* 250). One reason that O'Connor agreed to the trip to Europe in 1958 was that Sally and Robert Fitzgerald were then living in Levanto, Italy, and the pilgrimage would give her the opportunity to visit her longtime friends. As early as December 1957, O'Connor wrote to them, suggesting that they meet her at Lourdes. She vacillated, however, about actually bathing in the waters. In December 1957, she told Betty

Hester that she would "not be taking any bath. I am one of those people who could die for his religion easier than take a bath for it" (258). As the subsequent story of her visit to Lourdes reveals, O'Connor, despite these protests, did immerse herself in the holy waters.

Throughout the early months of 1958, her doctors debated about whether she was strong enough to make the trip at all. With the help of a Savannah travel agent and the Fitzgeralds, however, O'Connor and her mother made arrangements to join the pilgrimage on their own terms. Just before they left Savannah, O'Connor detailed these final arrangements to Ashley Brown, explaining that instead of traveling with the group of twelve pilgrims to Ireland and England, she and her mother would meet the Fitzgeralds in Milan and "spend four or five days with them in Levanto while the others disport themselves at Baloney Castle or whatever it is" (*HB* 277). The two would spend one night in London, where they would meet the group to visit Lourdes, Barcelona, Rome, and Lisbon.

From Rome, near the end of the trip, O'Connor wrote to Betty Hester, telling her that she had caught a head cold or sinus infection early in the trip, though she "had been taking the Msgr's aureomycin & so am enduring more or less." She also described the other members of the tour: "The fellow pilgrims consist in 4 old ladies who are always getting lost from the rest, 4 priests, 2 little boys 12 & 14, 2 secretaries, & me and ma. They are constantly buying junk of one kind or another for which they pay large sums. One of the old ladies has just lost her traveler's checks" (*HB* 280–81).

Sally Fitzgerald traveled with the O'Connors to Paris, Lourdes, and Rome, and it was she who insisted that O'Connor take the waters at Lourdes. From Rome, O'Connor wrote Hester that "Lourdes was not as bad as I expected" and that she had agreed to the bath "because it seemed at the time that it must be what was wanted of me" (*HB* 280). After her return to the United States, she told Hester that the only reason that she bathed in the waters was Sally Fitzgerald's insistence: "She has a hyperthyroid moral imagination. If I hadn't taken it she said it would have been a failure to cooperate with grace and me, seeing myself plagued in the future by a bad conscience, took it" (282). In a footnote to the above letter in *The Habit of Being*, Sally Fitzgerald admitted that she had made O'Connor enter the waters "but not because of an overheated moral imagination but because I was sure she would later feel she had disappointed her elderly cousin." She also remembered that O'Connor was a bit annoyed by her persistence, "but her irritation faded" (282).

In Rome, O'Connor also had a group audience with Pope Pius XII, Eugenio Pacelli, which she rated second only to her visit with the Fitzgeralds. She wrote to Betty Hester: "There is a wonderful radiance and liveliness about the old man. He fairly springs up and down the little steps to his chair. Whatever the special super-aliveness that holiness is, it is very apparent in him" (*HB* 280). Though O'Connor also spent a day or two in Paris, her cold kept her from viewing its attractions; however, French novelist Gabrielle Rolin visited her at the hotel; afterward, O'Connor facetiously wrote to Ashley Brown, "Instead of seeing Paris I saw her" (285). In her thank-you letter to the Fitzgeralds, she revealed how closely she observed the other pilgrims in a description of their behavior on the airplane as they traveled to Lisbon from Rome. She especially enjoyed the antics of the young boys who pretended to drop a coin into the gaping mouth of one of the sleeping pilgrims. She also wrote to Maryat Lee that she had not kept a travel journal of her European jaunt as Cousin Katie had directed but suggested that "[m]aybe some day I will write mine, when the reality has somewhat faded. Experience is the greatest deterrent to fiction" (284).

O'Connor may have planned to translate her experiences abroad into fiction, but, back in the United States, she returned with renewed enthusiasm to work on *The Violent Bear It Away*. In retrospect, she also gave credit to her immersion at Lourdes for what proved to be a temporary improvement in the density of her hip bones. In November 1958, she wrote to Caroline Gordon that her doctor had told her that her hip bone was "recalcifying." "Maybe," she said, "this is Lourdes" (*HB* 305). A week later she also reported to Betty Hester that Katie Semmes was dying but had felt relieved at knowing "that the trip to Lourdes has effected some improvement in my bones" (306). Overall, however, O'Connor was less than enthusiastic about her one trip to Europe; she wrote to Hester, "Now for the rest of my life I can forget about going to Europe, having went. Had I been ten years younger I might have enjoyed it" (282). The Lourdes experience, however, stayed with O'Connor; in February 1963, she wrote to a new friend, Janet McKane, both about having been there and the effect of "taking the waters" on her completion of *The Violent Bear It Away*: "I prayed there for the novel I was working on, not for my bones which I care about less, but I guess my prayers were answered about the novel, inasmuch as I finished it" (509).

Having returned from Europe and recovered both her health and equilibrium, O'Connor returned to lecturing and reading in 1959. O'Connor's two main appearances that year were at the University of Chicago in early February and at Vanderbilt University in April. As early as January 1959, she wrote to Cecil Dawkins of her scheduled appearance in Chicago. She was replacing Eudora Welty, she wrote, and would hold "two workshop classes" and present a "public reading" on in early February. I have to live in the dormitory and confer with the young ladies as to how to attain their ideals—this being a clause in some old lady's will who is providing $2/7$ of the money for this part of the engagement. Maybe you can get down" (*HB* 316).

In another letter—this one to the Cheneys—O'Connor told of the engagement, adding, "The fee persuadeth me" (*CC* 82). In an unpublished letter to Cecil Dawkins, O'Connor gave more details about her schedule in Chicago. She would arrive on Monday and leave the next Saturday at 12:15 from Midway Airport. She told Dawkins that she would be given a dinner before her presentation and suggested that she and Dawkins might have breakfast together on Saturday morning. She was to stay in a guest room at a women's residence hall on campus; she speculated about its convenience and quality. O'Connor also wrote to Betty Hester that she didn't plan to see any more of Chicago "than necessary," and that she was "going to read 'A Good Man Is Hard to Find,' deleting the paragraph about the little nigger who doesn't have any britches on. I can write with ease what I forbear to read" (*HB* 317). Just before she left, O'Connor asked Fr. James McCown to "pray for me that I will get to and from Chicago whole and be unscathed by the city interleckchuls. They are paying me well and unfortunately I have to earn me bread. I wish I didn't have to earn it this way in February" (318).

After the appearance on 22 February, O'Connor wrote to Cecil Dawkins about her pleasure in seeing her in Chicago and of the overall success of the air travel involved: "The plane not only went but went on time and arrived on time and some of my faith was restored" (*HB* 320). In still another letter—this one to Elizabeth Bishop—on 9 April, O'Connor gave more details about the dormitory part of her residency at Chicago and her reception at the reading:

The girls were mostly freshmen and sophomores and their questions gave out long before my patience. I had to sit with them drinking tea every afternoon while they tried to think of something to ask me. The low point was reached when—after a good ten-minute silence—one little girl said, "Miss O'Connor, what are the Christmas customs in Georgia?" I was mighty glad to leave after five days. They didn't have much in the way of writing students and at the public reading there was no public. And the weather was revolting. (*HB* 327)

O'Connor also mentioned in a letter to Cecil Dawkins that she had met Richard Stern at the university and liked him quite well. O'Connor and Stern subsequently established a correspondence that continued through the rest of her life. Stern recalled that the weather *was* indeed frightful when O'Connor came to Chicago:

> there was a blizzard and ice storm which forced her plane down in Louisville. She was put in a bus and spent nine hours riding to Chicago. I met her at two a.m. in the immense terminal building downtown. She was off the bus first, her aluminum crutches in complex negotiation with handrails, helping arms, steps. Tall, pale, spectacled, small-chinned, wearily piquant. I was to recognize her, she'd written, by the light of pure soul shining from her eyes. Fatigue, relief, wit-edged bile were more like it.
>
> The streets were studded with ice bits. The walking was worse than I'd ever seen it in Chicago. The difficulties drew bitter snorts from Flannery once she was safe in the car on our way to the dormitory. (Stern 6)

Stern, too, remembered O'Connor's difficulties with the young female students in the dorm where she stayed. Despite her problems, Stern also said that "she read her stories wonderfully," but seemed somewhat uncomfortable with the social features of her visit to Chicago. He reviewed their correspondence through the next five years and recalled that she sent him "peafowl feathers." A year after the visit, she recalled in a letter to Stern the "horrors" of her trip to Chicago; always in her correspondence with him, she seemed to facetiously play the Southern dolt to his Northern "academic"; for example, when he wrote to her during the last year of her life, she thanked him for "thinking of me. I think of you often in that cold place among them interleckchuls" (*HB* 574).

O'Connor first mentioned her planned trip to Vanderbilt in a letter to Betty Hester just before Christmas in 1958, asserting that she had to accept this invitation because of the $350 fee they offered her. Writing to Cecil Dawkins in February, O'Connor was considering reading "The Artificial Nigger" at Vanderbilt because there the story wouldn't hurt "anybody's feelings." She also asserted, "It is great to be at home in a region, even this one" (*HB* 321). The occasion at Vanderbilt was more than a reading: the English department was holding its annual Literary Symposium, with O'Connor, Robert Penn Warren, Jesse Stuart, and critic, Murray Kreiger from Illinois as its visiting writers. Warren and O'Connor stayed with the Cheneys at their home in Smyrna; O'Connor later wrote her positive impressions of Warren in an unpublished letter to Cecil Dawkins, describing him as ugly but likeable and nice. The literary symposium was held 21–24 April; O'Connor read "A Good Man Is Hard to Find" at the first session and later participated on a panel with the other writers.

Walter Sullivan, her former classmate at Iowa and by then a member of the English department at Vanderbilt, introduced O'Connor ahead of her afternoon reading. He mentioned the Ford Foundation grant that O'Connor had just received, asserting that "they couldn't have chosen a better recipient." He applauded her particular originality, asserting that he had followed O'Connor's fiction and career with

> a great deal of interest and a great deal of affection for a long time. My single claim to fame is that I was in school with her up at Iowa. She was awfully good then; she was a kind of legend, I think. She had published a story or two, began publishing while she was up there and those stories were awfully good and as her career progressed, within five years after that time, she was writing stories that a master could be proud of. But the thing that impresses me about Flannery O'Connor is that every story [. . .] shows an increasing excellence, a development in technique, a development in perception, and invention that certainly is rare in any case and certainly rare in one of Flannery O'Connor's tender literary years.[18]

O'Connor gave an introduction before reading "A Good Man Is Hard to Find" with obvious enthusiasm. The late David Hallman, a member of the audience for that reading, remembered O'Connor's crutches, the "scowl" on her face, and her lack of ease before the audience.[19] Her voice on the tape recording of the reading, however, sounds confident rather than diffident. Ted Spivey, who also attended the symposium, remembers that O'Connor seemed "sort of uptight" but "was very intense about reading that story. She was really caught up in it."

A recording of a panel session of the symposium, which included O'Connor, Warren, and Stuart, also exists; under the influence of Warren's extroverted personality and Stuart's egotism, O'Connor said very little. Walter Sullivan recalls how "out-of-place" Stuart seemed alongside the other two: "Jesse Stuart was a nice man [but] he wasn't up to snuff and he was here because Donald Davidson had insisted on it. That was an unlikely crowd to have him in. Mr. Davidson was very, very loyal to friends and he would bring in some unlikely people, just because he thought they ought to be brought in." Spivey remembers that Stuart "tended to dominate the whole thing. He was awful, just so egocentric. They had to play him up because he had been [a student] at Vanderbilt and was a popular writer. He had no ability compared with O'Connor and Warren." Immediately after returning from Vanderbilt, O'Connor herself wrote to Cecil Dawkins that Jesse Stuart was the polar opposite of the other participants. She also wrote to Ted Spivey that "Jesse Stuart's ego was like the light on the front of a train but as Warren remarked, we probably all have that much but just know how to keep it under cover better" (HB 331).

On the morning of 23 April 1959, O'Connor and Warren met with students and faculty members at Vanderbilt for a recorded interview. Through the course of the interview, as expected, Warren answered far more questions than O'Connor, but she did manage to make a number of significant comments about her methods of writing. When a student asked directly whether she began with a predetermined theme, O'Connor replied: "I think it's better to begin with the story, and then you know you've got something. Because the theme is more or less something that's in you, but if you intellectualize it too much you probably destroy your novel" (Con 20). She related the anecdote about how she found the title, "The Artificial Nigger," and told of John Crowe Ransom's objections to her use of the racial epithet. When one member of the group asked O'Connor whether she wrote from a theological point of view, she replied that a writer cannot "begin a story with a system. You can forget about a system. These are things you believe, they may affect your writing unconsciously. I don't think theology should be a scaffolding" (29).

Ted Spivey remembers that O'Connor seemed "very uncomfortable [throughout her visit to Nashville]. I talked to her some at Vanderbilt between meetings and during recesses. She seemed to be very much on her guard." Jane Sullivan (Walter Sullivan's wife) recalls O'Connor's behavior under serious questioning by the audience. She says, "They set out to give her a very difficult question deliberately," but O'Connor held up "quite confidently." Overall, despite seeming ill at ease to others, O'Connor enjoyed being at Vanderbilt. She wrote to Cecil Dawkins that she had had a pleasurable visit to Nashville and that her reading had been successful. She liked the large Southern audience and the atmosphere at Vanderbilt. To Maryat Lee, however, she wrote that she had had "enough writers for a while" and asserted that "[w]hoever invented the cocktail party should have been drawn and quartered. It was a good symposium for the most part but one a year is enuf for me" (*HB* 329).

On 8 May 1959 O'Connor made her last public appearance of the year when she read "A Good Man Is Hard to Find" at Wesleyan College. It was after this reading that she met with one of the literature classes to answer questions; in a letter to Ted Spivey, she described what happened: "There were a couple of young teachers there and one of them, an earnest type, started asking questions. "Miss O'Connor," he said, "why was the Misfit's hat *black*?" I said most countryman in Georgia wore black hats. He looked pretty disappointed. Then he said, "Miss O'Connor, the Misfit represents Christ, does he not?" "He does not," I said. He looked crushed. "Well, Miss O'Connor," he said, "what is the significance of the Misfit's hat?" I said it was to cover his head; and after that he left me alone" (*HB* 334).

As she moved into the 1960s, then, O'Connor had traveled fairly widely as a reader and lecturer and even visited Europe; she would enthusiastically continue to present lectures and readings in the next decade.

CHAPTER TWELVE

LECTURES, 1960~1963

Between 1960 and the end of 1963, O'Connor continued to lecture frequently and to read from her work at colleges and universities throughout the United States. Her fame had spread with the publication of *The Violent Bear It Away* in 1960 and the regular appearance of new short stories in journals and magazines. She became so comfortable appearing in public that she gave eleven readings or presentations in 1962. In 1960 between January and late October, O'Connor made eight public appearances, four of them in Georgia. On 7 January she was chapel speaker at GSCW, where she spoke on "Some Aspects of the Grotesque in Southern Fiction." In early April, her first trip out of the state was to Spring Hill College, a Jesuit institution in Mobile, Alabama, where she presented "The Catholic Novelist in the Protestant South" and visited at least one class the next day. It was for this appearance that O'Connor told Betty Hester that she might "reuse some of the coffee grounds" (*HB* 363). After her visit to Spring Hill, she wrote to Brainard Cheney: "I just got back from Mobile and the Jesuit College. You would like it. I enjoyed myself very much and had a good audience. They begin their classes with Our Father, close them with the Hail Mary, are integrated and lapped in azaleas" (*CC* 114). To Betty Hester, O'Connor wrote that "Spring Hill was peachy. I enjoy those things once I get there." With her usual broad humor on the subject, she also commented on the school's being integrated: "There were two grinning black faces in the class I talked to the day after my lecture" (*HB* 386).

On 20 March 1960 O'Connor addressed the Georgia Council of Teachers of English in Atlanta. In an unpublished letter to Paul Farmer, who invited her to the meeting, she wrote that she would be delighted to address the group and thanked him for putting her on the map of Georgia writers that he and the council had recently created.[1] Catharine Carver, who at that time was O'Connor's editor at Harcourt Brace, attended the meeting with O'Connor. In a thank-you note to Farmer, O'Connor wrote that she appreciated being allowed to bring Carver, who was in the South for the first time.[2] A few days later, O'Connor wrote to Farmer again, telling him how interested Carver was in the map of Georgia writers and in the luncheon menu that featured "Ransy Sniffle" potatoes.[3] Blanche Farley, who attended the meeting, recalls O'Connor's presentation: "She seemed in control, though rather timid and perhaps a little on the nervous side. After a pleasant remark or two—something to the effect that, but for the grace of God and the Ford Foundation, she too might have been an English teacher—she read us 'The Fiction Writer and His Country'" (Farley 83). A news story in the *Atlanta Journal-Constitution* about her presentation begins with a quotation from the speech: "The Georgia writer's true country is not Georgia but Georgia is an entrance to it for him." Later in the article the journalist uses still another now-famous statement from O'Connor's speech: "The region is something the writer has to use in order to suggest what transcends it. His gaze has to extend beyond the surface, beyond more problems, until it touches that realm of mystery which is the concern of prophets."[4] On 18 May O'Connor addressed the Atlanta area English Club on the topic "A Witness for the Map," probably a play on the fact that she had recently been included on the map of Georgia writers. That spring she also appeared again before the Macon Writers' Club, where she was now an honorary member.[5]

O'Connor's major trip in 1960 was her lecture and reading tour to Minnesota in mid-October. In July, she wrote of the projected trip to Brainard Cheney: "I've been asked to go to Minnesota in October for a week and talk at four or five Catholic colleges—the which I plan to do. The Sisters who have asked me have the idea that I'm quite decrepit and have asked if I would like to be lodged in their infirmary. I wants to mitigate this reputation, but not too much" (*CC* 118). O'Connor was in Minnesota from 17 October until noon on 21 October. For the first two days she was at St. Teresa's College in Winona, where she gave her talk, "Some Thoughts on the Catholic Novelist," on 18 October at the General Convocation of the College. On the seventeenth, she participated in a seminar for English majors titled "Distortion as a Technique of Fiction: The Short Stories of Flannery O'Connor," and visited a class, Seminar in Prose Fiction, directed by William Goodreau, a member of the English department. John J. Murphy, who describes himself then as a "green member" of the English faculty at the College of St. Teresa, recalls spending time with O'Connor:

> I had recently concluded my stint with the U.S. Army, most of it in Fort Benning, Georgia, and had begun my scholarly commitment to the fiction of Willa Cather and knew very little about Flannery O'Connor. In conversations with her at meals we discussed Georgia and avoided her fiction. She was easy to talk with, gracious and not a bit intimidating, and I was not inhibited by knowledge. Her wit, as I recall, was delicately perceptive, crisp but not harsh. She made her way on the aluminum crutches she christened her flying buttresses and had to be helped in and out of automobiles. (Murphy iv)

On Wednesday, 19 October, O'Connor arrived at St. Catherine's College in St. Paul Minnesota, where she gave, on the morning of the twentieth, the same convocation address that she had presented at St. Teresa's; in addition, she participated in an informal discussion with English majors. That evening, she also appeared at the University of Minnesota, where she presented "The Grotesque in Southern Literature." On Friday, 21 October, she left St. Catherine's for the airport to fly home, apparently none too soon. On returning to Milledgeville, she wrote to Brainard Cheney that the "sisters in Minnesota drained me of my anyway inconsiderable store of energy. [. . .] I am weary of riding upon airyplanes and being The Honored Guest. I think the reason I like chickens is that they don't go to college" (*CC* 122). To Cecil Dawkins, however, she wrote that she liked the two Catholic schools because the nuns there were quite different from the ones they had known as children in parochial schools.[6] She told Betty Hester that she was particularly impressed with Sr. Bernetta Quinn, her hostess at St. Theresa's (*HB* 414).

Almost as soon as she returned to Milledgeville, O'Connor went to Macon for her previously arranged appearance at the Southern arts festival with Caroline Gordon, Katherine Anne Porter, Madison Jones, and Louis Rubin. She told Cecil Dawkins that she hated such panels and planned to say very little. The festival was held between 27 and 28 October 1960. As O'Connor explained in a letter to John Hawkes, it was an annual affair subsidized by an "old lady [. . .] with a sizable fortune." The benefactor's only "stipulation [was] that the guests had to be Southerners and discuss Southern culture. [. . .] I think it's programs like this that are going to hasten the end of it" 412–13). At the festival, O'Connor appeared with the other participants and but also presented her lecture, "Some Thoughts on the Grotesque in Southern Fiction." The *Bulletin of Wesleyan College* published a transcript of the discussion among the panel in January 1961. As in every other such presentation —this one was ably guided by moderator Louis Rubin—O'Connor was the most reticent of the participants. Rubin began by asking the writers to describe their writing routines. O'Connor said, "I sit there before the typewriter for three hours every day and if anything comes I am there waiting to receive it."[7] She later said in a discussion of "place" in Southern literature that her own was "unadjustable. [. . .] I know if I tried to write stories about credible Japanese they would all sound like Herman Talmadge" (63). Later she said of her use of "community" in her work, "I don't feel that I am writing about the community at all. I feel that I am taking things in the community that I can show the whole western world, the whole edition of the present generation of people, of what I can use of the Southern situation" (70). She also made a particularly interesting comment about her use of symbolism: "I really didn't know what a symbol was until I started reading about them. It seemed I was going to have to know about them if I was going to be a respectable literary person. Now I have the notion that symbol is sort of like the engine in a story and I usually discover as I write something in the story that is taking on more and more meaning so that as I go along, before long, that something is turning or working the story" (73).

That weekend, after the festival had ended, O'Connor and her mother entertained the participants at a dinner party at Andalusia, for which, O'Connor wrote Betty Hester, they were "steeling" themselves. This was the occasion at which Katherine Anne Porter remembered chickens she had first met in 1958. In a letter to Roslyn Barnes shortly thereafter, O'Connor reacted more stringently to the gathering, declaring discussion rather superficial; she admitted, however, that she was well paid for her effort.[8]

O'Connor gave just three public presentations in 1961, probably partly because she was suffering from additional degeneration of her hip bones that spring; in addition, she was also busily arranging for the publication of *A Memoir of Mary Ann,* a book about a young girl who had died of cancer at Our Lady of Perpetual Help Home in Atlanta, a hospice operated by the Dominican nuns. In an unpublished paragraph in a letter to Cecil Dawkins in November 1960, O'Connor told how she became involved in the project, explaining that the nuns had first asked her to write the book about the child, who suffered from a huge, disfiguring cancer on one side of her face. O'Connor felt that she could not write the book but told the nuns that if they wrote it, she would edit their work and write an introduction for it. She did not expect them to produce the book, but they did and she subsequently wrote the introduction to help memorialize the brave little girl.

The introduction O'Connor wrote for the book is one of her most engaging essays: she describes how she became involved in the project and explains her inability to write a book about a dying child. She retells the story of how Nathaniel Hawthorne, by reputation a reserved, even cold man, was touched by the plight of a repulsive child in an orphanage he visited in Italy. Hawthorne's daughter, Rose Hawthorne Lathorp, O'Connor also reveals, founded the order of Dominican Nuns—the Servants of Relief for Incurable Cancer. Probably most significantly in the essay, O'Connor asserts that talking with the sisters about the project helped her to better understand one part of her own fictional technique:

> This [discussion] opened for me also a new perspective on the grotesque. Most of us have learned to be dispassionate about evil, to look it in the face and find, as often as not, our own grinning reflections with which we do not argue, but good is another matter. Few have stared at that long enough to accept the fact that its face too is grotesque, that in us the good is something under construction. The modes of evil usually receive worthy expression. The modes of good have to be satisfied with a cliché

or a smoothing down that will soften their real look. When we look into the face of good, we are liable to see a face like Mary Ann's, full of promise. (O'Connor, Introduction 17–18)

As O'Connor wrote in her letter to Dawkins, she did not believe the sisters would be able to write Mary Ann's story, but they surprised her. She submitted their manuscript to Farrar, Straus and Cudahy, who, to her amazement, accepted it for publication. In gratitude for her help, the Dominican sister gave O'Connor a television set, and O'Connor herself relished the considerable popular success of the book. In July she wrote to Dawkins, "The Sisters' book is going to be a runaway. *Good Housekeeping* is going to feature it in their Christmas issue. They paid $4,500. I get $1,125 of that" (*HB* 445).

After her work with this project, O'Connor, on 19 April, attended another fine arts festival, this one at Agnes Scott College in Decatur, Georgia. There she participated—with John Ciardi—in a panel discussion of the arts festival issue of *Aurora,* the college literary magazine. A brief article in *The Agnes Scott News,* published on 26 April 1961, reports O'Connor's reaction to the magazine: "Authoress Flannery O'Connor said that the short stories featured in the magazine were better than the usual 'college-girl story'" (Wurst n. pag.). Her criticism of the works was that the subject matter was "'slight.'" Betsy Fancher in the local newspaper *(The Decatur-DeKalb News)* the week of the arts festival, highlighted O'Connor as one of contemporary Georgia's four major women writers. She cites novelists Margaret Mitchell and Carson McCullers in addition to O'Connor and biographer Elizabeth Stevenson. When asked how she would account for this gender imbalance, O'Connor facetiously answered, "'Women just have more time'" (Fancher 5).

O'Connor participated in the Fifth Annual Southern Writers' Workshop at the University of Georgia between 6 and 9 August 1961. According to an article in the *Athens Banner-Herald* on 10 August O'Connor spoke to the workshop on 9 August. She apparently did not title her presentation but she spoke on the "mechanics of writing, the inherent difficulties of novels as opposed to short stories, and the need for Southern writers to be careful that they did not emulate too closely the work of Faulkner. She also said that the time to decide when to become a writer was after your first work had been published."[9]

Her last appearance in 1961 was at the Marillac College for nuns in Normandy, Missouri (near St. Louis), on 31 October. In 1961, Cecil Dawkins was teaching at Stephens College in Columbia, Missouri, and O'Connor thought her lecture at Marillac might give them the opportunity for a visit. She wrote to Sister Bertrande Meyers, D.C., then dean of Marillac, to ask whether Dawkins might attend the presentation, but Sister Bertrande's secretary replied that the college was definitely closed to those outside the order. Indicating both disappointment and reservations about the strictness of the order, O'Connor sent the note on to Dawkins.

O'Connor, appearing at Marillac as a speaker in their Lecture and Concert Series, presented "The Catholic Novelist in the Protestant South" under the general heading "Faith and Fiction." She apparently enjoyed being at Marillac, as she asserted in her "bread and butter letter" to Sister Bertrande. She told the nun how much she had enjoyed the liveliness of the students and asked Sister Bertrande to thank another sister who had apparently praised O'Connor in saintly terms after her presentation.[10] To Cecil Dawkins, whom she had planned to telephone from Marillac, O'Connor wrote on 4 November that the sisters had treated her as an invalid who needed to be put to bed after every event. She also related that the students there told her of their ability to empathize with Tarwater's experience. O'Connor also told Betty Hester how much she had enjoyed her visit to St. Louis, praising the sisters at Marillac for their clear understanding of *The Violent Bear It Away*. She also met their writing teacher, Sister Mariella Gable, who had earlier brought serious trouble onto herself for teaching *The Catcher in the Rye* in a Catholic high school.

O'Connor's busiest years as a reader and lecturer were 1962 and 1963, probably partly because, by this time, she and her work had achieved fame throughout the country. The widespread critical attention that *The Violent Bear It Away* received certainly stimulated the number of invitations she received during these years; in addition, by this time O'Connor had no doubt become more comfortable appearing in public. O'Connor's health had also stabilized during these years, so that she was physically able to travel widely; thus, between early April and 20 November 1962, O'Connor gave eleven readings or lectures, including her tour to Louisiana in November.

O'Connor's first two presentations in 1962 were in North and South Carolina in April; she followed them with visits to Rosary College in Chicago and to Notre Dame in May. In a letter to John Hawkes, O'Connor detailed her fairly hectic spring schedule; she listed her planned appearances at North

Carolina State, at the Southern Literary Festival in Spartanburg, at "a Catholic college in Chicago," and at Notre Dame. She said she would then head "home with my tongue hanging out and a firm resolve not to go anywhere else for as long as possible" (*HB* 471). She spoke on "The Grotesque in Southern Literature" at North Carolina State on 10 April, afterward calling the college "strictly a technical school [. . . but] the students are sharp" (472). She participated in the literary festival at Converse between 19 and 21 April, presenting "The Catholic Novelist in the Protestant South" on 20 April and writing her reaction to the festival in a letter to Cecil Dawkins on 25 April. She commented both on Welty's reading and the social obligations of being there: "She read a paper on "Place in Fiction." It was very beautifully written but a little hard to listen to as anything like that is written to be read. These affairs are powerful social. There was a coffee in the morning, a tea in the afternoon and a reception with a receiving line in the evening" (474).

In the same letter to Dawkins, O'Connor outlined the rest of her spring schedule, including the visits to Rosary College and Notre Dame and another appearance at Emory scheduled for late May. Her only recorded reaction to the visit to Rosary College was her discovery of the *English Journal* when the sisters there showed her a recent article in it on "The Artificial Nigger." She called the essay "about as dumb as you could get"; and, she liked knowing that "[t]he sisters thought it was dumb too" (*HB* 474). Apparently the best part of her visit to Notre Dame was meeting Thomas Stritch. She wrote to him that she had enjoyed being at Notre Dame, "particularly talking to you" (472). In early June, O'Connor traveled to Indiana again to be awarded an honorary doctorate by St. Mary's College at Notre Dame University. Just before receiving the award, she wrote to Fr. James McCown about both her birthday (she had just turned thirty-seven) and her "impressive" new degree. She also told Tom and Louise Gossett about the degree from St. Mary's, slyly wondering whether possessing it would admit her into the academic community.[11] After actually receiving the award, she wrote to Tom Stritch that her "degree hasn't done a thing for me so far"; she told him that "Regina wrapped the hood up in newspaper and put it away and unless I wear it Halloween, I guess it'll stay there" (483). Before her rather extended tour to Texas and Louisiana that fall, O'Connor made two appearances in Georgia; she lectured on "The South" at Emory on 20 May: it was after her talk here that O'Connor began her correspondence with Alfred Corn. On 26 October

1962 the Georgia Writers' Association in Atlanta awarded her a second Literary Achievement Scroll, about which she was again somewhat dubious; she wrote to Betty Hester that she had "declined in a polite way" to attend an awards dinner but agreed to accept the award at a box luncheon and to speak "some words of Thanksgiving": "I am telling them that awards are valuable in direct ratio to how near they come from. Don't give me no Nobel prize, give this here scroll, ahhh. What I really mean is, and what is true, is that the writer's check of himself is local where place still has meaning" (494–95).

O'Connor first mentioned her planned trip to Texas in a letter to Cecil Dawkins on 19 July when she said she would go because of the chance to visit a state she had never seen. On 27 October she told Maryat Lee, "I will be on the road, war permitting. I am going to East Texas College, University of Southwest La., Loyola at New Orleans, & Southeast LA. College, 4 talks in 6 days and too much too much. My bones are not up to it" (*HB* 496). On 9 November, in bed with a "common cold," O'Connor admitted to Lee, "I have bit off more than I can chew this time" (499).

Recovered, however, from both the cold and her doubts, O'Connor was in Texas by the middle of November; she delivered "Some Aspects of the Grotesque in Southern Literature" at East Texas University in Commerce on 16 November. By the next day, O'Connor was staying in the Town House Hotel in Lafayette, Louisiana, from which she wrote a long letter to Maryat Lee:

> My how you would love Texas. Just the place for you, cure your interesting disease. The gentleman who met me at Dallas is from Greenville, Texas, where there is a big sign at the city limits, "Greenville, Texas, Home of the Blackest Dirt and the Whitest People." This "white" means "fair & square," not Caucasian. In Greenville they say, "Our niggers are white too." I saw the home of General Walker in Dallas—a big two-story battleship grey clapboard house with a giant picture window in front in which there is a lamp with a ceramic Uncle Sam for a base. There was a U.S. & a Texas flag flying on the lawn. (*HB* 499)[12]

According to Sura Rath, O'Connor was met at the airport in Lafayette, Louisiana, by Fr. Edward J. Romagosa, a Jesuit priest with whom she had been corresponding since 1959. Rath writes: "Father Roma remembers several anecdotes from this time with Flannery. The rooms at her motel had doors, each a different color, and Flannery noticed the lavender on her door. During their drive through the town, Father Roma mentioned the name of Wellborn Jack in the course of conversation, and Flannery said the name would fit one of her characters" (Rath 4). O'Connor met with members of the Newman Club at the University of Southwestern Louisiana at a banquet on Saturday, 17 November. The next day, Father Romagosa introduced O'Connor at the forum lecture, which she gave at Jeanmard Hall on campus on Sunday evening, 18 November. According to Rath, the text of Romagosa's introduction was long: "five single-spaced, typed pages." In it, Father Romagosa emphasized the "'tardiness with which Catholic circles are catching up with the rest of the literary world in acknowledging Miss O'Connor's talents'" (9). Another excerpt shows how highly he, at least, valued her work: "What I find particularly Catholic about her work is its solidity. [. . .] By solidity I mean a certain tough-mindedness; an admission of man's actual condition, of his fall of his need for redemption; a truth-telling that refuses the escapes of facile optimism or facile pessimism" (9). According to Rath, a tape of O'Connor's presentation, "The Catholic Novelist in the Protestant South," shows that the audience greeted her lecture with "rousing applause" (8–9).

From Lafayette, O'Connor traveled to Loyola University in New Orleans, where she gave the same lecture to the Newman Forum on 19 November. To Father Romagosa on 26 November, she wrote that her audience there was "'very good and alert [. . . and] Walker Percy was there with his wife and daughter and I liked them very much'" (*HB* 5). Jay Tolson gives further details of the meeting between the two Catholic novelists who had long admired each other's work:

> Percy and Bunt [his wife] were invited to a reception that was to follow [O'Connor's lecture at Loyola]. By all rights, it should have been a lively encounter. Fellow Catholics, Fellow artists, Fellow graduates of the Caroline Gordon School of fiction, Percy and O'Connor had a great deal to talk about. In the annals of frustrating encounters, however, this one ranks regrettably

high. To begin with, Percy and O'Connor were both bad at the quick and public encounter. They were the kind of people who need a little time and privacy to get a conversation going, and the occasion denied the possibility of either.

Tolson also describes the second-floor setting of the reception and the necessity for two people to carry O'Connor up a flight of outside stairs; however, once O'Connor and Percy met,

> they hit it off immediately as Percy later related to his cousin Phinizy Spalding [whom O'Connor had met at the University of Georgia]. "Went a couple months ago to hear Flannery O'Connor. We had a drink after her lecture. When I said I had kinfolks in Atlanta, she said, do you mean Phin Spalding? She is great. But I was thrown at first by her deep Georgia accent."
>
> "I liked her a lot," Percy later recalled, "but it was as though we never had the chance to develop the friendship." [. . .] Percy's admiration for her grew with the passing of years. He thought of her as a model of personal courage and fierce faith, as well as an uncompromising artist. (Tolson 307–8)

In the recently published letters between Percy and Shelby Foote, Percy emerges as a strong defender of O'Connor's work against Foote, who declared O'Connor a "minor-minor writer" because she "died before her development had time to evolve" and before she had "time to turn her back on Christ, which is something every great Catholic writer (that I know of, I mean) has done" (Foote and Percy 136). In 1979 Percy sent Foote a copy of *The Habit of Being;* Foote claimed that he had read only *Wise Blood* and a "couple of short stories I read in magazines" (255). Percy included the following evaluation of the collection: "I attach great importance to it—a truly remarkable lady, laconic, funny, tough, smart, hard-headed, no-nonsense, the very best of US, South and Catholicism" (254).

O'Connor later wrote to Maryat Lee that she "had a great time in New Orleans," partly because she was reunited with her old friend, Richard Allen, as she related in a 24 November letter to John Hawkes:

> I have a friend in New Orleans (originally from Milledgeville) whose distinguished title is Curator of the Jazz Museum at

Tulane. He actually has a Ford grant to collect the stuff. In his charge I saw a lot of New Orleans that I wouldn't otherwise. We passed a Negro nightclub called "Baby Green's Evening in Paris," which I might some day like to investigate. If I had to live in a city I think I would prefer New Orleans to any other— both Southern and Catholic and with indications that the Devil's existence is freely recognized. (*HB* 500)

From New Orleans, O'Connor traveled to Hammond, Louisiana, where on 20 November she gave her fourth lecture in six days, again presenting "The Catholic Novelist in the Protestant South," this time to the Newman Club at the University of Southeastern Louisiana. She found her audience at Southeastern "rather grim," as she wrote in a letter to Father Romagosa: "Fr. Haddad [her host] was very nice but there were a lot of other priests there who I am sure had never lowered themselves to read a piece of fiction in their lives and were unprepared for what I had to say. That's a Dominican terri-tory and I gathered from the lady I spent the night with that they were all Boston Irish and a trial to the people. [. . .] They had their cocktail party, then the dinner, then after-dinner drinks, then me, and by the time they got to me, a great leaden calm had settled over them" (Rath 5). This hurried six-day trip must have exacted considerable physical stress on O'Connor, but on 28 November she wrote to Maryat Lee that she was still "ambulating," an indi-cation that the benefits of the excursion outweighed its liabilities.

In 1963 O'Connor continued the vigorous pace of reading and lecturing that she had maintained in 1962. Between March and October, she appeared on eight occasions, including her tour north to Hollins, Notre Dame of Mary-land, and Georgetown University in Washington, D.C., in October. On 13 January 1963 she wrote Cecil Dawkins about a planned trip to Sweet Briar in Virginia, to the University of Georgia, and a possible trip to Troy State in Alabama, about which she was yet uncertain because of a letter she had writ-ten to one of their students, who had solicited a cut-and-dried explanation of one of her stories. Considerably "exasperated" at receiving this letter, O'Connor advised the girl to read the story for enjoyment rather than as an algebra problem: "Presently I got a letter back from her full of profuse thanks; she had shown the letter to the head of her department and he is pro-foundly shocked. [. . .] So I figure they don't want me now" (*HB* 505).

O'Connor's first lecture in 1963 was at Sweet Briar College in Virginia, where she participated in a symposium on Religion and the Arts, lecturing on "Some Notes on the Combination: Novelist and Believer" on 8 March. Other participants in the symposium—including George Boaz, the dean of the Theological School at Drew, James Johnson Sweeney, and John Ciardi—were far more liberal than she: she described her revulsion with the proceedings in a letter to Fr. James McCown on 4 April. Hearing the liberal papers presented by the other participants troubled her greatly. Boaz talked about magic and art and John Ciardi offered a grandfatherly image of God. She told Father McCown that she had tried to counter their arguments with orthodoxy but felt that she was fighting a losing battle.[13] In a letter to the Fitzgeralds she declared, "The Devil had his day there" (*HB* 510), and, writing to Cecil Dawkins in early April, O'Connor repeated her comment about getting a stomachful of "liberal religion." She also wrote to Maryat Lee that she had met "about a million people [there] and earned my money the hard way" (516). Her friend Ted Spivey believes that her time at Sweet Briar was "her worst moment. [. . .] John Ciardi [and the others] really didn't like what she had to say. [. . .] Those people are all very nice on one level [. . . but] they just hate anything metaphysical."

Much more to O'Connor's liking was her reading of "A Good Man Is Hard to Find" at the University of Georgia on 27 March, where she "had a great time. My kind of folks" (*HB* 516). After being introduced by Marion Montgomery, later the author of *Why Flannery O'Connor Stayed Home,* she read both an introduction to the story and the story itself to a highly appreciative audience, as she wrote to Betty Hester on 30 March: "It was a perfect audience because they caught everything, it all being familiar to them. When I reached the point where Red Sammy Butts comes in, there was an appreciable titter of another order that rolled through the audience. (That case interested me greatly). Later somebody told me that the character of Red Sammy was not unlike the character of Wally [Butts, then football coach at Georgia]" (511).

She followed her reading at Georgia with the appearance at Troy State, which "happened" after all. She presented "The Grotesque in Southern Literature" on 24 April but reported to Cecil Dawkins that her appearance there was "pretty grim." Her next trip was to Smith College in Northampton, Massachusetts, where she received her second honorary doctorate on 2 June.

Her mother accompanied her to Boston, where they spent the weekend with O'Connor's aunts, cousins, and uncles, who attended the ceremonies at Smith. O'Connor told Robert Fitzgerald that her mother had said that these relatives "will go *anywhere*" (*HB* 519). She expressed her dubiousness about the award itself in a letter to Tom and Louise Gossett. She called the degree "stinking" and asserted that she would rather stay home and visit with them than to travel to the "fancy" college to receive the degree.[14] One positive benefit of the trip was that she was again able to see Robert Fitzgerald, who had returned briefly to the United States from Italy. In an unpublished letter to Maryat Lee, O'Connor elaborated on the occasion, asserting that other recipients belonged to the class of 1918 and that her sneezing brought on by allergy to New England pollen had interrupted the proceedings on thirty-two occasions.[15]

On 27 September O'Connor attended a luncheon for the Georgia governor at GSCW where she "got the official smile and the official handshake. My hand was being shaken while the last person got the smile and then I got the smile while somebody else's hand was shaken but this didn't worry me overly" (*HB* 541). Her main concern by September, however, was the rather extended tour she had organized for October. On 16 September she wrote to Cecil Dawkins that she was "refurbishing" the "same old talk" for appearances at Notre Dame of Maryland and Georgetown University; in addition she would spend three days as writer-in-residence at Hollins College, which was "filthy rich" and thus able to afford a different writer every month. She expected to give a "public reading" there and "I guess answer questions like *Why is the Misfit's hat black?*" (540).

Just before she left for this trip she wrote to Janet McKane, "I am off Monday for my rounds and will be mighty glad when it's over" (*HB* 542). Her first stop was at Hollins, near Roanoke, Virginia, where she read "A Good Man Is Hard to Find" on 15 October. By the next day, O'Connor had traveled to Baltimore, where she presented "The Catholic Novelist in the Protestant South" at Notre Dame College. Two days later she spoke at Georgetown as a part of Georgetown's 175th anniversary celebration. Presented on 18 October, her lecture "The Catholic Novelist in the Protestant South" was published in *Viewpoint,* the university's magazine in the spring of 1966. She also read "A Good Man Is Hard to Find" at Georgetown.

One particularly interesting episode, occurring during the Georgetown visit, was with Peter J. McCarthy, then a Ph.D. candidate in music at

Catholic University. A year earlier, McCarthy's former literature teacher at the State University College at Potsdam, New York, Grace Terry, had written to O'Connor in his behalf regarding the final episode between young Tarwater and the homosexual in *The Violent Bear It Away*. Terry wrote of how confused her young student was about this violent encounter; though she did not usually trouble writers with her questions, in this instance she wrote to O'Connor asking her to explain her purpose in including the episode.[16] O'Connor replied with an important letter not published in *The Habit of Being;* the letter contains her clearest explanation of her use of the homosexual rapist.[17]

When McCarthy approached O'Connor at Georgetown to remind him of the exchange of letters between Mrs. Terry and herself, she immediately recalled the entire episode. McCarthy also remembers that O'Connor sent him a copy of the *Sewanee Review* and an article about her work by a Jesuit priest. She probably sent him the summer 1963 issue that included her long story "The Lame Shall Enter First" and the two essays on her fiction by Robert Fitzgerald and John Hawkes. The article by the Jesuit was no doubt written by Fr. James McCown's brother, Robert M. McCown, S.J., who published "The Education of a Prophet: A Study of Flannery O'Connor's *The Violent Bear It Away*" in *Kansas Magazine* in 1962. O'Connor approved of this essay. McCarthy recalls that when he returned the articles to O'Connor, he also wrote her a long letter, to which she did not reply: "But I didn't expect it because she was not of this world."[18]

After returning from this jaunt, O'Connor wrote Janet McKane that she had "had a good trip, not a cloud in the sky all the way. The little plane landed on the sides of mountains all over West Virginia and I enjoyed it all no end. Good audiences, too, particularly at Georgetown" (*HB* 544). To Betty Hester she wrote that she appreciated the money she had earned, but that she had had a "stomach full of reporters," especially one in Roanoke who tried to imitate her accent and those in Washington who were avid to get her opinion on integration (543). In unpublished letters to Maryat Lee, her reaction to these reporters was even more frank.

Though at the time, O'Connor was clearly unaware of her future, final deadly bout with lupus, this tour north was to be her last. She had already planned another trip north to Brown University and Boston College for the spring of 1964; in fact, ironically, in an unpublished letter to Cecil Dawkins,

O'Connor had even said that she would travel to Boston in April 1964 if she was still alive. She was also talking with Robert Drake about a trip to Texas, and Rosa Lee Walston remembered that O'Connor was making plans for another appearance at GSCW: "She had said to me before Christmas that year that the college had been so good to her that she would like to do something for us." O'Connor and Walston subsequently planned to set up her appearance in a "very exclusive manner, to make people think it was hard to get in." They had the invitations printed before the holidays but when they returned, O'Connor had to cancel the appearance because of illness: "She said the medicine she took gave her the appearance of being inebriated and she didn't think that would be a very good example for the young ladies." The anemia from which she suffered led her doctors to diagnose an ovarian tumor. Surgery in February 1964 reactivated the lupus that ended all her plans.

CHAPTER THIRTEEN

Reviews, 1956~1964

In addition to her many public lectures and readings, one final intellectual pursuit stimulated O'Connor's life in Milledgeville between 1956 and 1964: the numerous reviews that she wrote for the diocesan publications *The Georgia Bulletin* and *The Southern Cross*. O'Connor began to review for *The Bulletin* early in 1956. On 11 February she wrote to Betty Hester that she had put aside her work on "Greenleaf" to prepare a talk for the Georgia Council of Teachers of English and to write a "book review for the *Bulletin*. This latter being my first emergence into the Catholic Press" (*HB* 137). A few days later, she wrote to John Lynch that she had just "had the doubtful honor of reviewing *All Manner of Men* for the diocesan paper, yclept the *Bulletin*. Of course, 'The Knife' [one of his stories] was one of the few good stories in it." She also gave Lynch her view of the official Catholic taste in fiction: "[T]he motto of the Catholic press should be: We guarantee to corrupt nothing but your taste" (138). In the review itself she wrote, "There are twenty-five stories in this collection all taken from the Catholic Press. Of this number, perhaps five are excellent. The rest are variously limited in range and depth and generally suggest that they were written in the Catholic college class room" (*PG* 13).

As Carter Martin writes in his introduction to O'Connor's collected book reviews, *The Bulletin* had a fairly long history in Georgia, having originated as a monthly publication in 1922, "when the state of Georgia was the Diocese of Savannah. In 1954 it began to appear every other week and continued to do so after the creation in 1956 of a separate Diocese of Atlanta. Beginning in 1963 O'Connor reviewed for both *The Georgia Bulletin* (now associated with the Diocese of Atlanta) and *The Southern Cross* (from the diocese of Savannah). Eileen Hall was the editor of the book page when O'Connor began her contributions" (*PG* 2). When Hall left *The Bulletin* to take a job in Florida in 1960, Leo J. Zuber, who had reviewed for the paper for some time, volunteered to replace her. At first, O'Connor, who had enjoyed a positive working relationship with Eileen Hall, was dubious about her replacement; however, as Martin writes, "In the following months and years she became quite pleased at just how wrong she had been [about Zuber]. Not only did the page continue, it flourished, and a strong personal friendship between her and Zuber quickly moved from her formal 'Mr. Zuber' letters to the familiar 'Leo' and visits to Andalusia farm by the entire Zuber family" (*PG* 2). Zuber, in fact, was organizing O'Connor's reviews for publication when he died suddenly in 1980; Martin finished his work.

Why did O'Connor, with her dedication to writing fiction, her extensive correspondence with numerous friends, and her desire to lecture as widely as she was able, take on the added responsibility of becoming a regular reviewer for *The Bulletin*? The answer to the question is not particularly complex but certainly true to O'Connor's overall outlook on the responsibilities of the Christian writer. At the personal level, writing regular reviews gave her the opportunity both to read and comment on books that she probably would have found and read anyway; however, writing about them helped her to focus her understanding of the ideas of the Catholic theologians whom she most admired, among them Romano Guardini, Baron Friedrich von Hügel, Karl Adam, Gustave Weigel, and Pierre Teilhard de Chardin. Reading and reviewing these works, in addition, added weight to her correspondence with various intellectual friends, among them Elizabeth Hester, Ted Spivey, and Williams Sessions.

Her reviews of novels by Catholic writers gave her the opportunity to set forth significant ideas about what she considered to the be mission of the Catholic novelist. She was equally averse to too much adherence to dogma and to too much sentimental sugarcoating. Soon after she began to review for *The Bulletin,* O'Connor asked Eileen Hall for permission to review Caroline Gordon's *The Malefactors.* On 10 March, she wrote Hall a letter that serves as an apologia for both her own writing and for her attitude as a reviewer. Apparently they had already discussed the kind of writing that many Catholic readers might have considered scandalous. She told Hall, "The fact is that in order not to be scandalized, one has to have a whole view of things, which not many of us have." In the same letter, O'Connor gave her views on bad taste:

> About bad taste, I don't know, because taste is a relative matter. There are some who will find almost everything in bad taste, from spitting in the street to Christ's association with Mary Magdalen. Fiction is supposed to represent life, and the fiction writer has to use as many aspects of life as are necessary to make his total picture convincing. The fiction writer doesn't state, he shows, renders. It's the nature of fiction and it can't be helped. If you're writing about the vulgar, you have to prove they're vulgar by showing them at it. The two worst sins of bad taste in fiction are pornography and sentimentality. One is too much sex and the other too much sentiment. You have to have enough of either to prove your point but no more.
>
> What offends my taste in fiction is when right is held up as wrong, or wrong as right. Fiction is the concrete expression of mystery—mystery that is lived. Catholics believe that all creation is good and that evil is the wrong use of good and that without Grace we use it wrong most of the time. It's almost impossible to write about supernatural Grace in fiction. We almost have to approach it negatively. As to natural Grace, we have to take that the way it comes—through nature. In any case, it operates surrounded by evil. (*HB* 143–44)

Hall allowed O'Connor to review Gordon's novel, and in the last paragraph of her comment on *The Malefactors,* her third review for *The Bulletin,* she set forth her basic conviction about Catholic fiction:

"The Malefactors" is profoundly Catholic in theme but it is doubtful it will receive the attention it deserves from the Catholic reader, who is liable to be shocked by the kind of life portrayed in it, or from the reader whose interests are purely secular, for he will regard its outcome as unsound and incredible and will look upon it merely as a *roman a clef*. The fact that the conversion is elaborately prepared for and underwritten by the force of Jungian psychology will be overlooked by those who are not willing to accept the reality of supernatural grace. Making grace believable to the contemporary reader is the almost insurmountable problem of the novelist who writes from the standpoint of Christian orthodoxy. "The Malefactors" is undoubtedly the most serious and successful fictional treatment of a conversion by an American writer to date. (*PG* 16)

Besides reading and commenting on her favorite Catholic theologians and setting standards for Catholic fiction, O'Connor stated her most important reason for becoming a reviewer in a letter to Betty Hester in April 1957: "Doing these things [writing reviews in the Catholic press] is doing the only corporal work of mercy open to me. My mother takes care of all the visiting the sick and burying the dead that goes on around here. I can't fast on acct. of what I've got. I can't even kneel down to say my prayers. Every opportunity for performing any kind of charity is something to be snatched at" (*HB* 214). O'Connor conceived of reviewing as legitimate exercise of charity, her unique means of assisting her fellow Catholics in understanding both the theology of their faith and in reading the kind of fiction necessary to their salvation.

From 1956 forward, then, O'Connor consistently wrote reviews for *The Bulletin;* Carter Martin tabulated that she wrote about twelve a year between 1956 and 1963; in 1964, the year of her failing health, she wrote only two reviews. Martin has counted and categorized her reviews: "She chose a broad range of works, reviewing 143 titles in 120 separate reviews between 1956 and 1964. The works were distributed as follows: 50 religious and homiletic, 21 biographies and saints' lives, 19 sermons and theology, 17 fiction, 8 literary criticism, 6 psychology, 6 philosophy and science, 4 history, 4 letters, 4 periodicals, 3 intellectual history and criticism, 1 art criticism" (*PG* 3).

Given that *The Bulletin* was a Catholic organ, that she herself was a highly spiritual person, that she read theology with great enthusiasm, it is not surprising that much of her comment in her terse reviews concerns religion.

A look at some of her reviews, chosen for the overall interest that she had in the writers and their ideas, shows how her general outlook on life, religion, and writing permeates even these brief commentaries, all of which are under three hundred words. Between 1956 and October 1960, O'Connor reviewed sixteen works of Catholic fiction; in her last three years as a reviewer, she commented on only one novel, J. F. Powers's *Morte d' Urban* in November 1963. The novels or works of short fiction that she reviewed were—almost by necessity since she was writing for two Catholic papers—written by Catholic writers. Overall, in the reviews she used her own situation as a successful Catholic novelist to define what Catholic fiction should be and what Roman Catholic readers should demand of that fiction.

Her three earliest reviews in *The Bulletin* were of fiction. In discussing *All Manner of Men,* the collection of twenty-five stories previously printed in Catholic journals, she considered only five to possess literary merit: "In most of the stories, the meaning is not well carried by the characterization; a good deal of piety is portrayed but not always at a depth that would make it acceptable; sin is conspicuous by its absence" (*PG* 13). At the end of the review, O'Connor called for the Catholic press to demand a "high quality of writing" and to allow its contributors "to make the effects of the Redemption believable in fiction" by writing about "a wide range of experiences [. . .] at a depth which will often seem dangerous to the peace of popular taste" (14).

O'Connor certainly chose to review *The Malefactors* both because Caroline Gordon was its author and because it was receiving unfavorable reviews in the secular press. When O'Connor asked Eileen Hall for permission to review the novel, she told her: "Don't feel you have to review the Gordon book if you think it would cause the *Bulletin* embarrassment or trouble. I will certainly understand. Most of your readers wouldn't like *The Malefactors* if it were favorably reviewed by Pius XII" (*HB* 144). Hall, however, commissioned O'Connor to write the review and, even though O'Connor herself had some reservations about Gordon's novel, her comments in the review show that she felt the work was a superb example of what Catholic fiction should be.

O'Connor also reviewed two works of fiction by her early teacher at Iowa, Paul Horgan. In June 1956, she reviewed *Humble Powers,* a collection of three novelettes, declaring that Horgan's stories possess a "calm classical quality" because "he seems able to assume an audience which has not lost its belief in Christian doctrine. The rest may be laid to the fact that he is by nature an artist" (*PG* 19). In October 1957, she reviewed his novel *Give Me Possession* in a joint review with Evelyn Waugh's *The Ordeal of Gilbert Pinfold.* She wrote that the Waugh novel "is worked out with the usual finesse that one might expect from a writer of his quality and it is always good to see even a slight book as this done with style and a certain flourish" (43). O'Connor asserted that the "theme [of Horgan's novel] becomes fairly obtrusive in the last part of the book, where the bones of symbol and allegory begin to stick out alarmingly" (43).

O'Connor's interest in the Roman Catholic writer J. F. Powers and his fiction began long before she reviewed his works. When she published *Wise Blood* in 1952, she wrote to the Fitzgeralds that she approved their asking Powers to review her novel. She asked them to send a copy of his review when it appeared in the *Hudson Review* because "it wouldn't be possible to get a copy around here as nobody ever heard of it" (*HB* 42). A year later, she read and liked one of his stories, "The Devil Was a Joker," in *The New Yorker,* which the Fitzgeralds had also sent to her. In December 1955, she wrote to Betty Hester that she believed Powers ranked with Peter Taylor and Eudora Welty as the best contemporary short-story writers; in the same letter she told Hester that both Truman Capote and Tennessee Williams "make me plumb sick" (121).

O'Connor reviewed Powers's collection of short stories, *The Presence of Grace,* in *The Bulletin* on 31 March 1956. Although she criticized his use of a cat "for the Central Intelligence" in two of the stories, she praised him for having "an inner eye which can discern the good as well as the evil which may lurk behind the surface." She also asserted that Powers "knows how to write and that writing is his vocation" (*PG* 14–15). She sent a copy of her review to Powers with a brief note: "This is a review from the backwoods and it is very backwoodsy of me to send it to you but I would like you to know that I admire your stories better than any others I know of even in spite of the cat who, if my prayers have been attended to, has already been run down" (*HB* 151). Her sending the review started a correspondence between them; he apparently approved of the review, for O'Connor reported to the Lowells that "he wasn't going to use that cat anymore so I could quit praying for it to be dispatched" (252). In late 1956, when she sent him a copy of "Greenleaf," he must have expressed reservations about O'Connor's ending the story with Mrs. May's death, for she wrote to Betty Hester: "I ought to defend Powers. I don't take him as meaning it was a mistake to kill Mrs. May for a short story, but only that I should have left her alive so that I could write a novel about her. Powers' instincts are too good on what to do with short stories for him to mean anything else" (190).

O'Connor's interest in Powers increased when she learned that both of them had published their first stories in *Accent,* and in the fall of 1958 O'Connor wrote to Cecil Dawkins that the journal, *Critique,* would devote its fall issue to her work and that of Powers; she also offered her critical opinion of his stories: "Powers' stories can be divided into two kinds—those that deal with the Catholic clergy and those that don't. Those that deal with the clergy are as good as any stories written by anybody; those that don't are not so good" (*HB* 287). Though Powers was a member of the English department at the University of Minnesota when O'Connor read there in 1960, they did not meet because Powers, as he told Sally Fitzgerald, was "in the black books of the department" at that time and was not invited to the reception given for O'Connor at the university (291).

O'Connor wrote a review of Powers's novel *Morte d'Urban* in 1963, after the book page of *The Bulletin* had been discontinued. She wrote to Betty Hester that she "had not expected to like the Powers book" because she had read chapters ("they all sounded pretty much alike") that he had published separately in the *New Yorker* and *Esquire;* she had turned down the chance to review the novel for *Commonweal,* but had changed her mind about its quality when she read the completed novel: "As it turned out, I liked it very much. The whole adds up to a great deal more than the parts would suggest. [. . .] it has many quiet virtues that should not be disdained. I think Powers precisely is a novelist" (*HB* 496). While the review she wrote was still in limbo, she wrote to Powers that she could not send it to him because "I can't even find a copy of it. But it was so favorable someone might have thought I was in your employ. I chiefly said that it was a novel and all the people who said otherwise were nuts. I thought it really hung together as a whole piece and that it was worth holding on to for ten years or however long you held on to it" (505). When *Morte d'Urban* won the National Book Award in the spring of 1963, O'Connor wrote to the Fitzgeralds that she "was much cheered at that." Ultimately, her laudatory, even defensive, review of the novel appeared in *The Southern Cross* on 27 November 1963. In the last paragraph she wrote: "In some circles this novel will be read as if it were an essay entitled 'The Priest in America.' Some reviewers will point out that Father Urban is not typical of the American priest; some will imply that he is. This reviewer would like to point out that Mr. Powers is a novelist; moreover a comic novelist, moreover the best one we have, and that Father Urban represents Father Urban. If you must look for anyone in him, Reader, look for yourself" (*PG* 167–68).

Besides reviewing fiction by fairly well-known Catholic novelists (one interesting omission is Graham Greene), O'Connor also reviewed works by inferior writers who carried the approval of the Catholic establishment. O'Connor courageously stated her skepticism, even disgust with, these inferior works. Of Franc Smith's *Harry Vernon at Prep,* she wrote, "The heel hero is also basically innocent and with a heart of gold and though he is not a Catholic, he feels a strong attraction to good Catholic living. All this makes a painful book more painful" (*PG* 70). Of Charles B. Flood's *Tell Me, Stranger* (1959), she asserted that "[i]n fiction there is nothing worse than the combination of slickness and Catholicism"; she also criticized Flood for failing to make his main character "come alive as a person. He is depthless and the author doesn't seem to be aware of it. The result, fictionalized apologetics, introduces a depressing new category: light Catholic summer reading" (*PG* 73). She liked Charles Koch's *Light in Silence* better, but wrote that the "book is about a hundred pages too long" (73). Overall, O'Connor believed that Catholic writers had to be good on the artistic and universal levels before they could have force in the Catholic community.

Though she began with reviews of fiction, O'Connor, as time passed, turned more and more to reviews of works by her favorite Roman Catholic theologians, among them the German thinker Friedrich von Hügel (1852–1925), whose *Letters from Baron Friedrich von Hügel to a Niece* she reviewed for the 13 June 1956 issue of *The Bulletin.* On 31 August 1957 she also reviewed his *Essays and Addresses on the Philosophy of Religion.* According to William Kirkland, O'Connor then owned a "well used copy" of this book and declared, "I think he's wonderful!" (Kirkland, "Baron von Hügel" 328). As her letters in *The Habit of Being* reveal, O'Connor apparently discovered von Hügel when she read a book by Evelyn Underhill (1850–1941), a theologian and mystic whose work *Mysticism* she read early in 1955. O'Connor soon recommended it to Betty Hester and asked her to try to find Baron von Hügel's *The Mystical Elements in Religion* in the Atlanta Public Library. Hester was unable to find the book (it was out of print) but offered O'Connor biographies of Baron von Hügel, which O'Connor said she would "pass up"; she had, however, ordered a copy of his *Letters to a Niece,* which she soon reviewed for *The Bulletin*. O'Connor recommended the book to Hester with the comment, "according to me [in the review] it is absolutely finer than anything I've seen in a long long time. You can read one letter a night without straining yourself much" (*HB* 156).

By July 1956 Hester had found O'Connor a copy of von Hügel's essays and addresses as well as Michael De La Bedoyere's biography of the theologian. In a letter that month to Hester, O'Connor expressed both her thanks to her friend and her enormous appreciation for the writer: "The old man I think is the most congenial spirit I have found in English Catholic letters, with more to say, to me anyway, than Newman" (165). In his essay on the connections between the two Catholics, William Kirkland reviews the humanistic liberalism of von Hügel and suggests that readers of both von Hügel and O'Connor might wonder at the vast difference between them. Von Hügel was a member of the Modernist movement in Roman Catholicism, which developed just after 1900 and focused on making the Church less dogmatic and more open to individual practice.

Kirkland suggests that O'Connor may not have agreed with this part of von Hügel's outlook but did identify with him in two other areas—his belief in the interconnectedness of religion and science and his understanding— like that of O'Connor herself—that suffering is an essential component of spiritual belief. Of their shared interest in religion and science, Kirkland writes: "Like von Hügel, O'Connor believed that the supernatural is known in and through the natural: the God of Grace is also the God of Nature. This concept was crucial for her as a believer and as writer of a unique kind of fiction; burning bushes, close at hand, were where she looked and listened for the muse and for the presence of God" (Kirkland, "Baron von Hügel" 29).

In her review of von Hügel's *Letters from Baron Friedrich von Hügel to a Niece,* O'Connor emphasized the basic purpose behind the letters: to help direct the young woman's reading as she moved from Anglicanism toward Catholicism. O'Connor approved of von Hügel's warning his niece "against the mentality that reads only religious literature, however good, and allows the fascinations of Grace to deaden the expressions of nature and thereby 'lose the material for Grace to work on.'" According to O'Connor, von Hügel also advised his niece against being "churchy" and directed her to avoid "'opening a Church paper or magazine'" (*PG* 21). O'Connor felt relief at his "subversive" stance. In her later (31 August 1957) review of von Hügel's *Essays and Addresses on the Philosophy of Religion,* O'Connor again applauded the theologian, primarily because his "always measured and intellectually just tone [. . .] would serve as an antidote to the frequently superficial methods by which many popular American Catholic writers approach and sidestep the problems of faith or meet them with the Instant Answer." She admitted that von Hügel's "style is often cumbersome," but his essays are certainly worth reading (42).

Between 1956 and 1961, O'Connor also reviewed five works by Romano Guardini, who during this period was professor of philosophy at the University of Munich; he had been named house chaplain to the pope in 1952. She articulated her strong support of Guardini's work in the last of his works she reviewed, *Freedom Grace and Destiny* (1961): "In all his work Msgr. Guardini's directive is this attempt to view the pattern of Christian existence as a whole, as it was viewed in early and medieval Christian thought before philosophy became separate from theology, empirical science from philosophy, and practical instruction from knowledge of reality" (*PG* 123). She approved of Guardini's theological directness, his ability to write in a straightforward style that could be comprehended by most Catholic readers, and his ability to hold onto traditional Catholic beliefs in the confusion of the modern world. In her April 1956 review of his *The Rosary of Our Lady* (1955), she wrote, "The first most noticeable characteristic of Monsignor Guardini's writing is the total absence of pious cliché. When he considers the doctrine or liturgy or practice of the Church, he rethinks these in the light of modern difficulties and preoccupations" (16–17). After reading his *Meditations Before Mass* (1955), O'Connor, in her November 1956 review, applauded Guardini's ability to restore the Mass "to its proper perspective for the individual and the congregation and the Church making its way in history" (28). Reviewing his *Prayer in Practice* (1957) in February 1958, O'Connor wrote, "His concerns are very much for the problems of modern man, in whom faith is often no more than a possibility" (53).

A third Roman Catholic theologian—Pierre Teilhard de Chardin—fascinated O'Connor from the spring of 1959 until her death; she reviewed three of his works, *The Phenomenon of Man* and *The Divine Milieu* in *The Bulletin,* and *Letters from a Traveler* in *Southern Cross.* Teilhard, a French Jesuit thinker who lived between 1881 and 1955, combined the studies of paleontology and theology. He was a part of a group of paleontologists who discovered the Peking man in the early 1930s; at the same time, however, he retained his original faith in Catholicism and made a serious attempt to accommodate the two areas of his interest. In an article in *Intellect* in April 1978, Kay Kinsella Rout summarized Teilhard's basic ideas:

> [He . . .] combined his knowledge of evolutionary data and his theological training to arrive at a theory about God's plan for the universe. He believed that, at the end of time, all creation will have returned to is creator through Christ, the Omega point. It would not be merely the spirits of men that would blend with God's as with an Oversoul, but all the created world would somehow move, with a united human race, forward and upward to the divine. (421)

O'Connor used one of Teilhard's most significant phrases, "everything that rises must converge," as the title of both a pivotal story in her last collection and of the collection itself. John J. Burke, S.J., asserts that the stories in *Everything That Rises Must Converge* "point [. . .] to God's grace working in [the lives of their characters]; each story reveals a spiritually converging world where the universal domination of Christ, as an intrinsic energy, has acquired an urgency and intensity" (Burke 46).

O'Connor first mentioned Teilhard in a letter to Ted Spivey in May 1959; she had not yet read *The Phenomenon of Man* but was interested in his iconoclastic approach to Jesuit theology. In counseling Cecil Dawkins about her waning devotion to Catholicism in late 1959, O'Connor pointed out the breadth of Catholic diversity when she reminded Dawkins that about the same time that an "old priest" was calling her (Dawkins) a "heretic" for "inquiring about evolution," Teilhard de Chardin was "in China discovering Peking man" (*HB* 366).

By January 1960, she had read *The Phenomenon of Man* and found it "stimulating to the imagination." She urged Betty Hester to read it before the Church placed it on the index. In March, she was carrying on a dialogue about the book with Ted Spivey, who apparently was unable to see strong similarities between Teilhard and Jung. On 16 March O'Connor wrote to him: "There are parallels between Jung and Teilhard that are striking. They have both the evolutionary view except that Teilhard believes the Church fulfills a continuing evolutionary purpose that will be completed at the end of time in Christ" (*HB* 383). In an April 1960 letter to Spivey, O'Connor asserted that Teilhard's direction was to guide the scientific age toward Christ, a mission that she herself assumed as a writer of fiction.

O'Connor reviewed *The Phenomenon of Man,* along with a commentary on the work by Claude Tresmontant, in *The Bulletin* on 20 February 1960. Commenting on the meager reputation of Teilhard's work in the United States, she also revealed that, although he had written the book as early as 1938, his Jesuit superiors had not allowed its publication until after Teilhard's death. The book was published in 1959. She wrote, "Only a man of profound Catholic piety could have sustained his love for the Church and his order under these circumstances, but Teilhard was a great Christian; his vision of Christ was as real as his love for science; his mind dealt in immensities" (*PG* 86). At the end of the review, O'Connor made statements that showed the real sources of her interest in Teilhard and his work: "Because Teilhard is both a man of science and a believer, the scientist and theologian will perhaps require a long time to sift his thought and accept it, but the poet, whose sight is essentially prophetic, will at once recognize in this immense vision his own. Teilhard believed that what the world needs now is a new way to sanctity" (87–88).

A year later (1961), O'Connor, after describing Teilhard to Betty Hester as a "great mystic," reviewed *The Divine Milieu* in *The Bulletin* on 4 February 1961. Surveying Teilhard's career as a scientist and Jesuit, she recommended that *The Phenomenon of Man* and *The Divine Milieu* be read together, for "[i]t is doubtful if any Christian of this century can be fully aware of his religion until he has reseen it in the cosmic light which Teilhard has cast upon it"

(108). By the fall of 1961, O'Connor had chosen "everything that rises must converge" as the title for her story and collection. In 1962, when she was counseling Alfred Corn, she recommended that he read *The Phenomenon of Man* as a means of stretching his spiritual imagination.

O'Connor also mentioned Teilhard several times in letters in 1963 to Janet McKane. In a February 1963 letter, she defined his concept of "passive diminishments" as "those afflictions that you can't get rid of and have to bear" (*HB* 509). This concept, particularly, must have had special appeal to O'Connor during her last year of suffering. O'Connor's final private word on Teilhard in her letters was to Fr. James McCown when she named the Jesuit paleontologist as "the most important [Catholic] non-fiction writer" of the twentieth century.

Reviewing books like those of Teilhard and the others for the Catholic press certainly allowed O'Connor to further her knowledge of Catholic writing—both good and bad—and offered her the opportunity to comment on it, to increase her own knowledge, and to continue to follow the mission of leading the nonbelievers of her generation nearer to Christ. Combined with her public lectures, this area of her work enabled her to promote both her reputation as a writer of fiction and as an advocate of her faith, one willing to help others accept Catholicism intellectually as well as emotionally.

CHAPTER FOURTEEN

ILLNESS, DEATH, AND LEGACY

Although she never overemphasized her suffering, Flannery O'Connor clearly had to accommodate to the illness that dramatically changed her life after 1951. When she returned to Milledgeville, O'Connor had to accept chronic illness as an indisputable fact of her existence, particularly after she realized that lupus erythematosus was the disease from which she was suffering. When she first became so desperately ill, she did not know, as is clear from her correspondence, that she had developed the disease. In a letter to Betty Boyd written shortly before Christmas 1950, O'Connor, in fact, identified her illness as arthritis: "I am languishing on my bed of semi-affliction, this time with AWTHRITUS of, to give it all it has, the acute rheumatoid arthritis, what leaves you always willing to sit down, lie down, lie flatter, etc. But I am taking cortisone so I will have to get up again. [. . .] I will be in Milledgeville Ga. a birdsanctuary for a few months, waiting to see how much of an invalid I am going to be" (*HB* 22). In *The Habit of Being,* Sally Fitzgerald wrote that O'Connor did not learn the "true nature of her illness" until the summer of 1952 (37).

Even when she learned that the disease was lupus and that it and its treatment were painful, debilitating, and ever present, O'Connor did not become a psychological martyr to suffering. When Margaret Turner, in a 1960 interview, asked her about how her illness affected her work, she tersely replied, "[T]he disease is of no consequence in my Writing, since for that I use my head and not my feet" (Turner 43). When she revealed the nature of her illness to friends, she was usually humorous and self-deprecating about its severity. Telling Robert Lowell and Elizabeth Hardwick of her illness in March 1953, she described its chronic nature but expressed relief that ACTH could control it. She told them, "I have enough energy to write with and as that is all I have any business doing anyhow, I can with one eye squinted take it all as a blessing. What you have to measure out, you come to observe closer, or so I tell myself" (*HB* 57). The calm and rational attitude that O'Connor took toward her illness is no better expressed than in her letter of application to W. McNeil Lowry at the Ford Foundation in 1959. She identified her disease as lupus erythematosus and told him that she was well enough to write several hours a day. She admitted that the crutches she had to use sapped her energy, but also described the cortisone treatments that controlled the disease. She said her doctors had predicted that she could expect to have a normal life span.[1]

Although O'Connor refused to be conquered by lupus after its onset, she struggled valiantly to control the disease so that she could continue to write and to lead a fairly active life. Even though none of her friends recall her complaining about her bad health, the illness adversely influenced her daily life. Her main concerns, however, remained her writing, her practice of Roman Catholicism, her literary friendships, and her lectures and reviews. O'Connor's most poignant and revealing comment on the personal importance of her illness occurred in a letter to Betty Hester in June 1956: "I have never been anywhere but sick. In a sense sickness is a place more instructive than a long trip to Europe, and it's always a place where there's no company, where nobody can follow. Sickness before death is a very appropriate thing and I think those who don't have it miss one of God's mercies" (*HB* 163). This comment shows the positive attitude that O'Connor consistently took toward her illness: it became central to her existence and contributed to her feeling of isolation, but it *still* operated as an "appropriate thing" that allowed her to understand "God's mercies" more fully. In this deeply moving statement, O'Connor revealed her ability to endure the illness with admirable courage based on acceptance and faith.

Apparently, after her first recovery by 1952, O'Connor was able to take a fairly sanguine attitude toward her condition: she prepared the final manuscript of *Wise Blood,* saw it through publication, and even enjoyed the book signing party at GSCW. Only after the disease and the drugs she was ingesting to treat it started to destroy her joints did she begin to mention the disease to her friends. O'Connor first wrote of its crippling effects in a letter to Elizabeth Fenwick early in 1954 when she described having developed "a decided limp," which she still believed was the result of rheumatism. She wrote, "I am not able enough to walk straight but am not crippled enough to walk with a cane so that I give the appearance of being a little drunk all the time" (*HB* 67). By December 1954, she told Sally Fitzgerald that she was using a cane, and by September 1955, she was "learning to walk on crutches and I feel like a large stiff anthropoid ape [. . . ;] my crutches are my complete obsession right now" (104–5). She also told Betty Hester that using crutches "is not as great an inconvenience for me as it would be for somebody else, as I am not the sporty type. I don't run around or play games. My greatest exertion and pleasure these last years has been throwing the garbage to the chickens and I can still do this, though I am in danger of going with it" (107).

Traveling to Michigan early in 1956 for her first literary appearances outside Georgia, O'Connor wrote to her hostess Alta Haynes that she felt it "an imposition" to ask to be met in Detroit, but "[c]rutches have changed the tempo of my existence and I can no longer get anywhere without inconveniencing someone else" (*HB* 136). By April 1956, O'Connor knew that the crutches would become a permanent part of her life: "So, so much for that," she wrote to Hester. "I will henceforth be a structure with flying buttresses" (151). O'Connor did remain on the crutches for the rest of her life, a reality that she deplored but dealt with stoically. After her visit to Lourdes in 1958, O'Connor believed for a few months that her bones were regaining density. She wrote to Caroline Gordon that her doctor was allowing her to "walk around the room and for short spaces without the crutches. If it continues to improve, I may be off them in a year or so. Maybe this is Lourdes. Anyway, it's something to be thankful to the same Source for" (305).

This hope for improvement, however, was short-lived. By December 1960, O'Connor knew that the continued deterioration was the result of the steroids she had so long taken to control the lupus; in addition to her hip joints, the drugs were affecting her jawbones. On 24 December 1960 she wrote to Betty Hester that her doctors were going to "withdraw the steroids and see if I can get along without them. If I can't, as Dr. Merrill says, it is better to be alive with joint trouble than dead without it. Amen" (*HB* 423).

Besides references to the chronic hip problems, in her correspondence with close friends, O'Connor often spoke of the various medications she took to control the disease. She commented most dramatically on her reaction to early cortisone treatments in two letters to Betty Hester in the mid-1950s. She recalled the frightening side effects of the large doses of the steroid: It "prevents your sleeping. I was starving to sleep. Since then I have come to think of sleep as metaphorically connected with the mother of God" (*HB* 112). In a slightly later letter, she elaborated even more dramatically: "cortisone makes you think night and day until I suppose the mind dies of exhaustion if you are not rescued. I was, but during this time I was more or less living my life and H. Motes's too and as my disease affected the joints, I conceived the notion that I would eventually become paralyzed and was going blind and that in the book I had spelled out my own course, or that in the illness I had spelled out the book" (117–18). In December 1957, O'Connor wrote to Caroline Gordon that she was "staggering around home" because she had been overdosed by a new medication. She elaborated, "Every time something new is invented I get in on the ground floor with it. There have been five improvements in the medicine in the 7 years I've had the lupus, and they are all great improvements" (257). Because of the chronic nature of her illness and her natural intelligence and curiosity, O'Connor became fascinated with medicine and shared that interest with Maryat Lee, whose own serious hypochondria drove her to great lengths in conducting medical research for herself and others.

Encouraged particularly by Lee in the early 1960s, O'Connor considered the possibility of hip replacement surgery, then still in its experimental stages and obviously risky because of the lupus. She was suffering a great deal of hip pain, and injections of cortisone and Novocain gave only temporary relief. On 31 May 1961 he wrote to Lee that she was "meditating those steel hips daily" (*HB* 441). When she broached the idea to Dr. Merrill, however, he objected so strongly that she gave it up. Still, in January 1962, O'Connor wrote to Lee: "I am on the trail of a new operation. This one they take a piece of bone out of your leg (bone with blood vessels in it) and graft it into your hip bone & that furnishes a blood supply to that hip. This is only performed by one man & he is at the University Hospital at Iowa City. They probably won't let me have this one either but I am looking into it" (462). This operation was never performed, probably again because of the danger of surgery. It is therefore sadly ironic that mandatory surgery for another condition—a large ovarian tumor—did indeed reactivate the lupus that killed O'Connor. Dr. Merrill earlier had made judicious decisions in prohibiting life-threatening, elective surgery.

During the last year of her life, in letters to friends, O'Connor traced the onset and negative progress of her final illness. She first described her problems with the ovarian tumor and later the return of lupus. In November 1963, after her most active year as a lecturer, she wrote to Betty Hester that she was almost too sick to write; by Christmas, she had suffered a fit of fainting that "gave my pore mother a turn." She also described her anemia in a letter to Maryat Lee written 18 January 1964: "I been sick. Fainted a few days before Christmas and was in bed about 10 days and not up to much thereafter. Blood count had gone down to 8 & you can't operate on that" (*HB* 562). By 18 February 1964 she knew that her anemia was the result of an ovarian tumor and that her only alternative was surgery; she wrote to Louise Abbot, "I have a large tumor and if they don't make haste and get rid of it, they will have to remove me and leave it. So this operation is going to take place this Tuesday (the 25th)" (567).

Although O'Connor described the surgery itself as "a howling success," it "awakened" the lupus that soon attacked her kidneys. She described her treatment for the kidney infection in a letter to Janet McKane; the antibiotics she was taking hadn't "done anything to the infection though they have done several things to me—torn up my stomach and swollen shut my eyes. Then the cortisone comes along and undoes the swollen eyes but gives you a moon-like face" (*HB* 572).

Despite her struggle with the illness, O'Connor did receive one final honor in the spring of 1964. Louis Dollarhide, later a longtime professor in the Department of English at the University of Mississippi, was chair of the Division of Humanities at Mississippi College in Clinton, Mississippi. He was also a member of the Board of the Henry H. Bellamann Foundation of Jackson, Mississippi. Katherine Bellamann, author of *Parris Mitchell of King's Row,* a sequel to her husband's popular novel *King's Row,* had established the foundation in honor of her husband.

The foundation awarded prizes to American writers who had made significant contributions to United States literature. Louis Dollarhide, a fan of O'Connor's work since the 1950s, had written a particularly cogent review of *The Violent Bear It Away* in 1960; O'Connor appreciated his reading, and Dollarhide continued to promote her work, nominating her for the $500 Bellamann prize in 1964. In a letter to Dollarhide on 6 April 1964, O'Connor gave her reaction both to the nomination and to receiving the award. She appreciated his nominating her and particularly thanked him for having it brought to her in Milledgeville. She also told him that she was happy with his news that Eudora Welty was about to publish another book; she said she herself had planned to publish a collection of stories in the fall of 1964 but her operation had intervened.[2]

By May of 1964 O'Connor was aware that she was again suffering from active lupus; she received blood transfusions that gave her temporary relief. She wrote to Maryat Lee that "[t]his time is not as bad as the last—because I know what's wrong with me"; even though she "was hearing the celestial chorus—'Clementine'[. . .] [o]ver & over. . . .[,] [t]he transfusion cut that out. Must come from not enough blood getting to the head" (*HB* 578). Back in the hospital by the end of May, she wrote to Louise Abbot that she expected to be there at least ten days. On 8 June she told Maryat Lee of more blood transfusions and of her uncertainty about her condition: "I don't get any information out of them that I particularly understand but then I'd have to study medicine if I wanted to keep up with myself with this stuff. I don't know if I'm making progress or if there's any to be made" (583). In her next letter to Lee on 1 July, she facetiously asserted, "As far as I can see the medicine and the disease run neck & neck to kill you" (590). By 8 July, when she wrote to Janet McKane, she realized how serious her condition had become: "Yesterday the priest brought me Communion as it looks like a long time before I'm afoot. I also had him give me the now-called Sacrament of the Sick. Once known as Extreme Unction" (591). About the same time she also told Sr. Mariella Gable, "I'll count on your prayers" (591). A few weeks later, on 3 August 1964, at 12:40 A.M. in the Baldwin County Hospital, O'Connor died of kidney failure brought on by the lupus; her mother found her last note (dated 28 July 1964)—this one to Maryat Lee—on her bedside table:

Dear Raybat,

Cowards can be just as vicious as those who declare themselves—more so. Don't take any romantic attitude toward the
call. Be properly scared and go on doing what you have to do, but
take the necessary precautions. And call the police. That might
be a lead for them.

Dont know when I'll send those stories. I've felt too bad to
type them.

Cheers,
Tarfunk (*HB* 596)

It seems typical that, even as O'Connor was dying, she was more concerned
about the welfare of her New York friend, who had just received an obscene
telephone call, than about her own impending death. This heroic lack of
self-concern suggests how well she had managed to adapt to the disease that
finally killed her.

O'Connor's funeral services were held at 11:00 A.M. on Tuesday, 4 August, at the Sacred Heart Catholic Church in Milledgeville. Louise Abbot,
whom Regina O'Connor invited to attend the funeral, recalls that the church
was full but not crowded. She also remembers the serenity of the occasion.
Msgr. Joseph Cassidy officiated at the funeral, after which O'Connor's body
was buried beside that of her father in Memory Hill Cemetery.[3] Notices of
O'Connor's death appeared in local newspapers and in the Atlanta papers—
with a number of tributes, including the following from the *Atlanta Journal-
Constitution:* "It is likely that critics and readers in Europe had more
appreciation for her as an artist than did her own people, so quietly did she
live among us."[4] In its account of her death of 4 August, the *New York Times*
called her "one of the nation's most promising writers."[5] Writing to Alta
Haynes, about five weeks after her daughter's death, Regina Cline O'Connor
gave her personal reaction. She said that she did not blame God for her
daughter's early death, partly because Flannery had lived many years longer
than she (Regina) had expected. Mrs. O'Connor expressed her gratitude for
having had each day of these final years with her daughter.[6]

Had Flannery O'Connor lived beyond 1964, what directions—both in life
and in her literary career—might she have taken? Certainly, she would have

continued to write fiction; when she died, she left multiple drafts of sections of a new novel, "Why Do the Heathen Rage?" some of which were published posthumously. Because literary and personal friendships had become so important in her life, it is also certain that she would have maintained these relationships and added even more as time passed. Although occasionally she complained about the lectures and readings that consumed so much of her writing time, she had made plans for lecture trips to Texas and Boston in 1964. The enthusiasm that Maryat Lee noted in O'Connor when she performed in public would certainly have motivated her to continue to promote her work in the public forum. She also would have continued to read and review books for *Southern Cross,* the diocesan paper, and probably would have written more essays for other journals and magazines. As Ted Spivey believes, it seems likely that, had she lived, O'Connor would have become a full-fledged woman of letters who would have gone on to produce significant works of nonfiction.

Louise Westling has suggested that O'Connor's work in fiction might also have taken a more feminist direction: "If Flannery O'Connor had lived long enough for the feminist movement to arouse her awareness of society's injustices to women and of her own repressed rage, surely she would have confronted these problems consciously in her stories" ("Flannery O'Connor's Mothers and Daughters" 522). Had she lived to the end of the twentieth century, O'Connor would have continued to exercise her genius in her unique and straightforward fiction and nonfiction, surpassed in its originality by that of few of her contemporaries. She would also have been surprised and wryly amused with the success and recognition that her work has achieved in the thirty-eight years since her death.

As long as they lived, Robert and Sally Fitzgerald contributed significantly to the expansion of O'Connor's literary reputation after 1964.[7] Robert Fitzgerald, named O'Connor's literary executor, arranged for the posthumous publication of *Everything That Rises Must Converge* in 1965. His introduction gave readers the first significant biographical information about O'Connor. Together he and Sally arranged for the publication of *Mystery and Manners* in 1969 and, with Robert Giroux, O'Connor's *Complete Stories* in 1971. The Fitzgerald family was also responsible for the film version of *Wise Blood,* made in 1979 and directed by John Huston. The Fitzgeralds' son Michael produced the film, another son, Benedict, wrote the script, and Sally herself designed the sets and costumes. Sally's collecting and editing of the letters in *The Habit of Being* in 1979 piqued many readers' interest in the woman behind the stories; that O'Connor's *Collected Works* became a volume in the Library of America Series is surely the result of the Fitzgeralds' collective efforts.

Academic and popular interest in O'Connor and her work have exploded during the past thirty-eight years. In 1972, Rosa Lee Walston and Mary Barbara Tate founded *The Flannery O'Connor Bulletin,* which Sarah Gordon continues to edit, under its new name, *The Flannery O'Connor Review.* It has operated as the chief outlet for articles by scholars of O'Connor's life and work. In 1992 Sura Rath established The Flannery O'Connor Society, which publishes a newsletter, *Cheers!* edited by Virginia Wray; the society offers panels yearly at the American Literature Association conference and other conferences. Between 1965 and 2001, scholars and other readers have produced hundreds of interpretative articles about O'Connor and her work. The MLA bibliography cataloged 403 entries between 1963 and 1980 and 1,030 entries from 1981 to January 2001. Among them were more than seventy-five doctoral dissertations and at least fifteen full-length studies of her work, including those by Frederick Asals, Robert Brinkmeyer, Robert Coles, John Desmond, Marshall Bruce Gentry, Richard Giannone, Sarah Gordon, Carter Martin, Marion Montgomery, Suzanne Paulson, Louise Westling, and Ralph Wood.

Academic conferences throughout the United States feature panels related to O'Connor and her work every year. In 1994 the Habit of Art Conference held at Georgia College and State University in 1994 drew more than five hundred participants who read or heard papers from a wide variety of scholars, writers influenced by O'Connor, and even some of her friends, such as Cecil Dawkins. In 1996, Brigham Young University held another nationwide Flannery O'Connor conference. One result of this conference was the 1997 collection of essays published by *Literature and Belief* under the title *Flannery O'Connor and the Christian Mystery.* O'Connor's fiction in translation, like that of Faulkner, has become popular throughout the world. Japanese scholar Hagime Noguichi, for example, has written at least four critical studies of her work. Noted French scholar André Bleikasten has published many essays on O'Connor's fiction, and the French journal *Delta* devoted a full issue to her work in March 1976. It included an interview with O'Connor's French translator, Maurice Coindreau, and a selection of letters she wrote to him in the late 1950s and early 1960s around the time he visited her at Andalusia in June 1960.

Because she herself was fascinated by the absurdities of popular culture, she would no doubt have been amused to learn that she has become something of an icon to pop musicians and movie stars. Jimmy Buffett, U2, and Billy Bob Thornton have all claimed an early interest in her work. Most recently, a folk-rock musician from Georgia named Robert Burke Warren has recorded a CD with songs titled "Milledgeville," "Falling into Grace," "Radio Church," and "I Want Her Faith." Both actor Tommy Lee Jones and late-night talk-show host Conan O'Brien wrote senior honors' theses at Harvard on her fiction. Younger writers, including Lee Smith, Sue Miller, Louise Erdrich, Larry Brown, A. Manette Aansay, Reginald McKnight, and Valerie Sayers have acknowledged their debt to O'Connor. Her work has also provided subject matter for a number of visual artists. Some of the most fascinating of these are by Martha Dillard of Blacksburg, Virginia, who in the early 1990s produced a series of semi-representational paintings illustrating eleven of O'Connor's short stories; among them, "Good Country People," "Everything That Rises Must Converge," and "A Good Man Is Hard to Find." The painting illustrating "Everything That Rises Must Converge" today hangs in O'Connor's childhood home in Savannah. Chris Daunt's haunting engravings also evolved from his appreciation of O'Connor's work. Particularly striking are his illustrations of "The Artificial Nigger," "The Life You Save May Be Your Own," and "Everything That Rises Must Converge," which contains a portrait of O'Connor herself imbedded between the angry black woman and Julian's mother. Douglas Powers's "Flannery O'Connor's Treelines" is a series of twenty prints illustrating her work. If alive in 2000, O'Connor would have enjoyed this popular attention to her work. But she would also have been disturbed by its mostly secular basis, the result of the continuing movement away from spirituality in the postmodern world, a direction that she had so clearly predicted.

Notes

Abbreviations

Published Primary Works

CC	*Correspondence of Flannery O'Connor and the Brainard Cheneys.* Ed. C. Ralph Stephens. Jackson and London: UP Mississippi, 1986.
Con	*Conversations.* Ed. Rosemary Magee. Jackson and London: UP Mississippi, 1986.
CW	*Collected Works.* Ed. Sally Fitzgerald. New York: Lib. of America, 1988.
HB	*The Habit of Being.* Ed. Sally Fitzgerald. New York: Farrar, Straus & Giroux, 1979.
MM	*Mystery and Manners.* Ed. Sally and Robert Fitzgerald. New York: Farrar, Straus & Giroux, 1969.
PG	*The Presence of Grace and Other Book Reviews.* Comp. Leo J. Zuber. Ed. Carter W. Martin. Athens: U Georgia P, 1983.

Collections

ChC, V	Frances and Brainard Cheney Collection. The Jean and Alexander Heard Lib., Vanderbilt U, Nashville.
	MC Papers Malcolm Cowley Papers. Newberry Lib., Chicago.
O'CC, GCSU	Flannery O'Connor Collection. Ina Dillard Russell Lib., Georgia College and State University, Milledgeville.
O'CC, Duke	Flannery O'Connor Collection. William E. Perkins Lib., Duke U, Durham, NC.
O'CC, Emory	Flannery O'Connor Collection. Robert W. Woodruff Lib., Emory U, Atlanta.
O'CC, Tulsa	Flannery O'Connor-Cecil Dawkins Correspondence. McFarlin Lib, U of Tulsa.
PE Papers	Paul Engle Papers, Flannery O'Connor File, Stephen Wilbur File, and Jean Wylder File. U of Iowa Lib., Iowa City.
TLG Papers	Thomas and Louise Gossett Papers. William E. Perkins Lib., Duke U, Durham, NC.

Introduction

1. Unpublished letter to Olive Bell Davis, 21 Aug. 1958, Olive Davis Bell Papers, Atlanta History Center, Atlanta.
2. Autobiographical sketch written at Iowa, O'Connor Collection, Ina Dillard Russell Lib., Georgia College and State University, Milledgeville.

Chapter 1. Savannah, 1925~1938

1. Patricia Persse, Winifred Persse, and Margaret P. Trexler, personal interview, 6 Aug. 1990; subsequent references to this interview included without citation.
2. Elizabeth Maguire Johnson, personal interview by mail, Sept. 1990; subsequent references to this interview included without citation.
3. Dan O'Leary, interview with Hugh R. Brown, 10 Feb. 1990.
4. Sister Consolata, personal interview, 8 Aug. 1990; subsequent references to this interview included in text without citation.
5. Loretta Feuger Hoynes, telephone interview, 6 Aug. 1990; subsequent references to this interview included without citation.
6. Sally Fitzgerald, "Root and Branch: O'Connor of Georgia," *Georgia Historical Quarterly* 44.4 (Winter 1980): 377. All data about the O'Connor-Cline family history, except as otherwise cited, comes from this essay; no further citation included.
7. Unpublished letters from Edward O'Connor to Erwin Sibley, O'CC, GCSU.
8. Katherine Doyle Groves, interview with Hugh R. Brown, 4 Feb. 1990.
9. Katherine Doyle Groves, telephone interview, 6 Aug. 1990; subsequent references to this interview included without citation.
10. Newell Turner Parr, interview with Hugh R. Brown, 10 Feb. 1990.
11. Tony Harty, interview with Hugh R. Brown, 4 Feb. 1990.
12. Tony Harty, personal interview, Savannah, 8 Aug. 1990; subsequent references to this interview included without citation.
13. After O'Connor's death, Regina sold the house on Charlton Street. It remained in private hands until July 1990, when a campaign launched by Hugh R. Brown, then professor of English at Armstrong State College in Savannah, raised $47,000-enough money for a down payment on the house. Today the home is owned by the O'Connor Home Foundation and, as a Savannah landmark, is open to the public. Just after the foundation bought the house, Brown contacted a number of O'Connor's cousins and other acquaintances who still live in Savannah; he subsequently recorded a series of interviews with them that he generously made available to me. Although Professor Brown died in 1994, the work of the foundation continues. For more details, see Brown's article, "Savannah Landmark: Flannery O'Connor's Childhood Home, *Flannery O'Connor Bulletin* 18 (1989): 43-45.
14. Lillian Dowling Odom, telephone interview, 5 Aug. 1990; subsequent references to this interview included without citation.
15. Regina Sullivan and Gerry Sullivan Horne, interview with Hugh R. Brown, 10 Feb. 1990.
16. Loretta Feuger Hoynes, interview with Hugh R. Brown, 11 Feb. 1990.
17. Sr. M. Jude Walsh, interview with Hugh R. Brown, 11 Feb. 1990.
18. Hugh R. Brown, personal interview, 5 Aug. 1990.
19. Autobiographical account written at Iowa, O'CC, GCSU.

20. Unpublished letter to "Helen"; no date but clearly written during the summer of 1937, Flannery O'Connor Collection, Robert W. Woodruff Lib., Emory U, Atlanta.
21. Flannery O'Connor-Maryat Lee Correspondence, O'CC, GCSU.
22. The booklet is today in O'CC, GCSU.
23. Vertical File, O'CC, GCSU.
24. Unpublished letter to "Helen," Summer 1937, O'Connor Collection, Emory.

Chapter 2. Milledgeville, 1938~1942

1. Regina O'Connor-Betty Boyd Love Correspondence, O'CC, GCSU.
2. Personal interview, 5 Oct. 1992; subsequent references to this interview included in text without citation.
3. Personal interview, 7 Oct. 1992; subsequent references to this interview included in text without citation.
4. Personal interview, 8 Oct. 1992; subsequent references to this interview included in text without citation.
5. Personal interview, 8 Oct. 1992; subsequent references to this interview included in text without citation.
6. Manuscript in O'CC, GCSU.
7. Flannery O'Connor-Maryat Lee Correspondence, O'CC, GCSU.
8. Interview, 5 Oct. 1992; subsequent references to the interview included in text without citation.
9. Telephone interview, 28 Feb. 1992; subsequent references to this interview included in text without citation.
10. Peabody High School no longer exists, having been replaced in 1956 by the Baldwin County High School, which also included Midway High School, formerly considered the county's vocational school.
11. Interview, 6 Oct. 1992. This interviewee preferred to remain anonymous, and in subsequent references I have not included citations. I have identified her as a Milledgeville classmate or acquaintance.
12. Autobiographical manuscript in O'CC, GCSU.
13. Telephone interview, 17 July 1989; subsequent references to this interview included in text without citation.
14. "Peabodite Reveals Strange Hobby," *Peabody Palladium* 16 Dec. 1941, n. pag. Rpt. in *Flannery O'Connor Bulletin* 19 (1990): 54.
15. Manuscripts of both stories and the poem are in O'CC, GCSU.
16. Letters from Flannery O'Connor to Mary Virginia Harrison are in O'CC, GCSU.
17. Interview by mail, Nov. 1992.

Chapter 3. Milledgeville, 1942~1945

1. In the summer of 1990, I sent questionnaires to every surviving member of the class of 1945 at the Georgia State College for women; I received numerous responses, and in this chapter I quote from many of them, including those from Mary Louise Bobo Haley, Elsie Parker Danielly, Grace Womble, Sarah Rudolph Miller, Fran Richardson, Lena Jo Tabb Chambers, Nora Moorhead Baker, Hazel Smith Ogletree, Mildred Sauls Bradley, Betty Boyd Gallop, Marian Nelson Poats, Bess Saye McFarland, Hilda Gray Mayo, Carmen Singletary Schatz, Kathryn

Donan Kuck, and two anonymous respondents. I therefore include no specific citations within the text.

2. Edna S. Weiss, letter, *New York Times* 4 Feb. 1979: 28.
3. The O'Connor Collection at the Ina Dillard Russell Lib. at Georgia College and State University holds a complete set of the major campus publications during the years O'Connor was at GSCW: *Colonnade* (school newspapers); *Corinthian* (literary magazine); and *Spectrum* (yearbook). All descriptions, specific and general, are based on material in these files.
4. Margaret Uhler, interview by mail, 26 Oct. 1992.
5. Unpublished letter to Katherine Scott, General Correspondence, O'CC, GCSU.
6. Interview by mail, 2 Aug. 1989.
7. Vertical File, O'CC, GCSU.
8. *Nashville Tennessean* 31 July 1956: 4E.

Chapter 4. Iowa, 1945–1948

1. Undated interview with Stephen Wilbers, Wilbers File, U of Iowa Libraries, Iowa City.
2. "University Hopes That Iowa Will Lead Nation in Creative Writing," *Des Moines Sunday Register* 21 Dec. 1947: n. pag., and "How Creative Writing Is Taught at the University of Iowa Workshop," 28 Dec. 1947: n. pag. Engle file, PE Papers.
3. Interview with Walter and Jane Sullivan, 8 Aug. 1992; subsequent references to this interview included in text without citation.
4. Interview by mail, 4 Dec. 1992; subsequent references to this interview included in text without citation.
5. "The Geranium: A Collection of Short Stories," MFA thesis, U of Iowa, 1947. A copy of the thesis is in O'CC, GCSU.
6. Unpublished postcard to Paul Engle, Aug. 1948, Engle Correspondence, PE Papers.
7. Unpublished letter to Jean Williams Wylder, Summer 1949; today in the possession of Wylder's son, Bill Wylder, of Coralville, IA.
8. Unpublished letter to Paul Engle, 9 May 1949, Engle Correspondence, PE Papers.
9. Telephone interview, Iowa City, 19 June 1993.
10. Interview by mail, 2 Aug. 1993.
11. Personal interview, Monteagle, TN, 26 July 1993; subsequent references to this interview included in text without citation.
12. Interview by mail, 8 Oct. 1993; subsequent references to this interview included in text without citation.
13. Interview by mail, 16 Sept. 1993; subsequent references to this interview included in text without citation.
14. Unpublished letter to Stephen Wilbers, 26 Mar. 1976, Wilbers file, PE Papers.
15. Anonymous interview by mail, 29 June 1993; interviewee referred to in a second reference as a workshop participant.
16. Unpublished letter to Earl J. McGrath, 9 Aug. 1947, Introductory Engle file, PE Papers.
17. Unpublished letter to Stephen Wilbers, 26 Mar. 1976, Wilbers file, PE Papers.
18. Unpublished letter to Paul Engle, 22 Feb. 1948, Engle Correspondence, PE Papers.
19. Unpublished letter to Thomas H. Carter, undated, Thomas H. Carter Papers, Univ. Lib., Washington and Lee U, Lexington, VA.

20. Unpublished letter to Thomas H. Carter, 24 June 1952, Thomas Carter Papers, University Lib., Washington and Lee U, Lexington, VA.
21. "Flannery O'Connor Wins Rinehart-Iowa Award for Novel," *Daily Iowan* 29 May 1947: n. pag.
22. Unpublished letter to Jean Wylder, 26 Dec. 1972, Wylder file, PE Papers.
23. Unpublished letter to Paul Engle, 24 Apr. 1948, Engle Correspondence, PE Papers.
24. All information about O'Connor's years at the Currier House comes from an interview by mail with Mrs. Sprieser, 30 Nov. 1992; subsequent references to this interview included in text without citation.
25. Unpublished letter to Martha Bell Sprieser, 25 Apr. 1952; in the possession of its recipient.
26. Unpublished letter to Jean Wylder, 28 Dec. 1952; in possession of Bill Wylder, Coralville, IA.
27. "Honoring talent for glowing praise," *Des Moines Sunday Register* 28 Sept. 1986: n. pag. O'Connor file, PE Papers.
28. Unpublished letter to Jean Wylder, 5 Mar. 1962; in possession of Bill Wylder, Coralville, IA.
29. Unpublished letter to Paul Engle, 16 Feb. 1948, Engle Correspondence, PE Papers.
30. Engle file, PE Papers.
31. Unpublished letter to Stephen Wilbers, 21 July 1976, Wilbers file, PE Papers.
32. Unpublished letter to Stephen Wilbers, 16 Apr. 1976, Wilbers file, PE Papers.
33. Thomas Kennedy, "A Last Interview with Robie Macauley," *AGNI*, Web Issue 4 (Summer 1993). Available: webdelsol.com/AGNI/
34. Flannery O'Connor Correspondence with Cecil Dawkins, McFarlin Lib., U of Tulsa.
35. Unpublished Allen Maxwell Letters, General Correspondence, O'CC, GCSU.
36. Introduction to O'Connor's reading at Vanderbilt U, 21 Apr. 1959; transcribed from a tape of her reading.
37. "Former SUI Student Has Book Published," *Daily Iowan* 28 Mar. 1952: n. pag.
38. "Ex-SUI Student Gets O. Henry Award," *Daily Iowan* 10 Jan. 1957: n. pag.
39. "Honoring Talent for Glowing Praise," n. pag.

CHAPTER 5. YADDO, NEW YORK CITY, AND CONNECTICUT, 1948~1950

1. Unpublished letter from Elizabeth McKee to Flannery O'Connor, 23 June 1948, O'CC, Duke.
2. Unpublished letter to Elizabeth McKee, 21 Sept. 1948, O'CC, Duke.
3. Telephone interview, 27 July 1994; subsequent references to this interview included in text without citation.
4. "Yaddo," promotional brochure, Saratoga Springs, N.Y., privately printed by the Yaddo Corporation, 1998.
5. Robert Fitzgerald, "Open Letter" to T. S. Eliot, Allen Tate, John Crowe Ransom, Robert Penn Warren, W. C. Williams, J. F. Powers, Randall Jarrell, Peter Taylor, Katherine Anne Porter, Louise Bogan, Leonie Adams, Elizabeth Bishop, Marianne Moore, John Berryman, Richard Blackmur, and George Santayana; Katherine Anne Porter Papers, McKeldin Lib., U of Maryland, College Park.
6. St. Thérèse of Lisieux (1873-1897) was a fourteen-year-old French girl when she experienced a conversion on Christmas Eve through the intervention of the Baby

Jesus. She joined the Carmelite order of the Catholic Church at the age of fifteen. Noted for her intense piety, she soon began to sign her letters "Thérèse of the Child Jesus." Already suffering from tuberculosis, she took her final vows at the age of seventeen. When she was twenty-two, she began to write her ultimately influential memoir, the *History of a Soul*. She died on September 30, 1897, after stating on her deathbed that she was no longer suffering: "all suffering is sweet to me." The publication of *History of a Soul* in 1898 helped created a cult following for her within the Church, which canonized her in 1925. From *Lives of the Saints*. Available at www.ewtn.com/therese/therese3.htm.

7. Letter to author, 2 July 1994.
8. Minutes of a special meeting of the directors of the Corporation of Yaddo, held at the office of the corporation, in the garage at Yaddo, Saratoga Springs, NY, on 26 Feb. 1949, Malcolm Cowley Papers, Newberry Lib., Chicago. Subsequent references to the history of the Yaddo episode are from these minutes.
9. Petition signed by forty-four supporters of Elizabeth Ames, 21 Mar. 1949, MC Papers.
10. Minutes of the Meeting of the Yaddo Board, 26 Mar. 1949, MC Papers.
11. Unpublished letter to Betty Boyd Love, 6 Mar. 1974, Regina O'Connor-Betty Boyd Love Correspondence, O'CC, GCSU.
12. Unpublished Flannery O'Connor-Betty Boyd Love Correspondence, O'CC, GCSU; subsequent references to these letters in this chapter included without citation.
13. Unpublished letter to McKee, 19 Apr. 1956, O'CC, Duke.
14. Unpublished letter to Malcolm Cowley, 16 Apr. 1949, MC Papers.
15. Interview by mail, June 1992; subsequent references to this interview included in text without citation.
16. Unpublished letter, 3 Apr. 1959, O'CC, Duke.
17. Notice of dues paid through October 1953, Vertical File, O'CC, GCSU.
18. Unpublished letter to Jean Wylder, [Mar. 1949], in possession of Bill Wylder, Coralville, IA.
19. Unpublished interview with Virginia Wray, 1999; subsequent references to this interview included in the text without citation.
20. Unpublished letter to O'Connor, 16 Feb. 1949, in O'CC, Duke.
21. Unpublished letter to O'Connor, 16 May 1949, in O'CC, Duke.
22. Unpublished letter to Paul Engle, 9 May 1949, O'CC, Duke.
23. Unpublished letter to Elizabeth McKee, 30 Dec. 1949, O'CC, Duke.
24. Mark Horowitz and Marietta Abrams Brill, *Living with Lupus: A Comprehensive Guide to Understanding and Controlling Lupus While Getting on with Your Life* (New York: Penguin, 1994), 15.
25. "White Cells Control Incurable Disease," *Science News Letter* 21 July 1956: 40.
26. "New Steroid Helps Treat Rare, Fatal Disease, *Science News Letter* 20 Sept. 1958: 185.

CHAPTER 6. RETURN TO MILLEDGEVILLE AND A PIVOTAL DECISION

1. An earlier version of this material appears in my article "Flannery O'Connor: "'art demand[s] celibacy.'" *Postscript* 15 (1998): 67-76.
2. Haynes Scrapbook, O'CC, GCSU; subsequent references to material in this scrapbook included without citation.
3. Personal interview, 6 Oct. 1992.

4. The unedited version of this letter is the Flannery O'Connor-Betty Boyd Correspondence, O'CC, GCSU.
5. Unpublished letter from O'Connor to Betty Boyd, 17 Oct. 1949, O'CC, GCSU; subsequent references to unpublished letters from this collection included in this chapter without citation.
6. Personal interview, 28 Aug. 1990.
7. Maryat's brother, Robert E. Lee, objects strongly to my interpretation of her lesbian interest in O'Connor; he says, "When Maryat professes her love for Flannery in several letters, it should be made clear that this is *familia* love, or *agape* love rather than the more common *eros* or physical love."
8. Journal, 28 Dec. 1956. Subsequent references to Lee's journal included without citation. Journals in the West Virginia and Regional Collection, West Virginia University Libraries, Morgantown.
9. Unpublished letter from Lee to O'Connor, 31 May 1957, Flannery O'Connor-Maryat Lee Correspondence, O'CC, GCSU; subsequent references to Lee's letters to O'Connor included without citation in text.

Chapter 7. Regina and Flannery

1. Unpublished letter to Maryat Lee, Flannery O'Connor-Maryat Lee Correspondence, O'CC, GCSU; subsequent reference to letters from this collection included without citation.
2. Unedited version of this letter to Lee, OCC, GCSU.
3. In 1953 O'Connor wrote a poem called "The Peacock Roosts," today in the O'Connor Collection at Georgia College and State University; also published in *The Habit of Being* (56):

The Peacock Roosts

The clown-faced peacock
Dragging sixty suns
Barely looks west where
The single one
Goes down in fire.

Bluer than moon-side sky
The trigger head
Circles and backs.
The folded forest squats and flies.
The ancient design is raised.

Gripped oak cannot be moved.
The bird looks down
And settles, ready.
Now the leaves can start the wind
That combs these suns

Hung all night in the gold-green wood
Or blown straight back until
The single one
Mounting the grey light
Will see the flying forest
Leave the tree and run.

4. Christmas card to Alta Haynes, Flannery O'Connor/Regina O'Connor-Alta L. Haynes Correspondence, OCC, GCSU.
5. Personal interview, 27 Oct. 1989; subsequent references to the interview included in text without citation.
6. Unpublished letter to Tom Gossett, 23 Feb. 1973, Gossett Papers, William E. Perkins Lib., Duke U, Durham, NC.
7. Interview by mail, July 1992.

CHAPTER 8. MILLEDGEVILLE~EARLY FRIENDSHIPS

1. Unpublished letter to Betty Ferguson and the library staff at GSCW. General Correspondence, O'CC, GCSU.
2. "Introduction of Flannery O'Connor at G.S.C.W. Chapel on January 7, 1960," Vertical File, O'CC, GCSU; the text of the introduction follows:

> When our lecture committee decided to bring to our campus a writer, they sent out to find the most stimulating person possible. Accordingly they wrote to a number of colleges and universities to find out who had been most effective with their students. They wrote to the University of Chicago and to Vanderbilt. They wrote to Notre Dame and Agnes Scott and Wesleyan and Birmingham-Southern. From each came the answer, "Get Flannery O'Connor." . . .
>
> When Thomas Wolfe wrote *You Can't Go Home Again,* most people pondered his title and mused, "How true." But it's as if Miss O'Connor said, "Wait a minute. I'm not so sure. I'd say rather, "'You can never leave home after all.'" And her stories are directed toward revealing to us insights about home that we might have missed without her penetrating analysis. By this I do not mean that she is writing about Georgians. She is writing about people who happen to be in Georgia in a way that shows the traits which they share with men the world over. There is of course a difference when these characters are seen through the artist's eye. Presenting things in a different light is the artist's function.
>
> Perhaps the best way to explain this is to quote from Wallace Stevens' poem.
>
> > They said, "You have a blue guitar
> > You do not play things as they are."
> > The man replied, "Things as they are
> > > Are changed upon the blue guitar."
>
> In this change lies the artist's subtle alchemy.
> > This morning it is my great privilege to present to you "Jessies" the most famous "Jessie," Flannery O'Connor, "Lady with the blue guitar."

3. Unpublished letters to Father McGown, TLG Papers. Specific comments occur in a number of letters O'Connor wrote to McGown.
4. Unedited letter to Father McGown, 15 Nov. 1958, TLG Papers.
5. Letter to Father McGown, 23 June 1961, TLG Papers.
6. Unpublished letter to Father McGown, 20 Sept. 1959, TLG Papers.
7. Interview with Tom and Louise Gossett, 2 May 1991; subsequent references to this interview included in text without citation.

8. Unpublished letter to Father McGown, 3 Mar. 1958, TLG Papers.
9. Interview by mail, July 1992; subsequent references included in text without citation.
10. Her description follows:

> In the fall of 1959 the O'Connors were adding on to the house, a "back parlor," Flannery called it, and a bedroom and bath. [. . .] Flannery chose the colors and furnishings for the parlor, a delightful room hung with her own Rouault-like paintings, full of light, full of books, dominated in fact by a massive bookcase with glass doors, a gift from her Cousin Katie. [. . .] A comfortable sofa, slip-covered in grey, was placed under two large windows at the end of the room with a low, glass-topped table in front of it. The bookcase was flanked by two more large windows. [. . .] Another chair, covered in wine material and supported by carved wooden legs, became my regular "pew." I sat in that chair; she sat at the corner of the sofa between the side and front windows. [. . .]
>
> Her bedroom [. . .] was an interesting, comfortable room, too. Books not only lined the walls, but a bookcase also divided the room so that her single bed, next to the door to the front hall, and her writing table were closed off in one area. On the other side of this bookcase were a comfortable chair with a reading lamp, a stool to prop her feet on, and a record player. One of the paintings in the room was a large portrait of the housekeeper Louise, done by a visitor from Florida. Along the mantel were various small objects which Flannery as a child might have collected. [. . .] By her bed, on the wall next to the hall door was a simple crucifix.

11. Interview, 12 July 1989; subsequent references included in text without citation.
12. Unpublished letter to Elizabeth Ferguson, 8 Jan. 1953, General Correspondence, O'CC, GCSU.

Chapter 9. Later Friendships

1. Unpublished letter to Brainard Cheney, 30 Dec. 1951, Cheney Papers, Jean and Alexander Heard Lib., Vanderbilt U, Nashville.
2. Personal interview, Nashville, 8 Aug. 1992; subsequent references included without citation.
3. In a letter to the author, 18 June 1985, Andrew Lytle expressed reservations about referring to Gordon as O'Connor's mentor: "I feel that mentor is a strong word for the occasion. I had the feeling that Caroline in a way was too much for Flannery."
4. Letter to Alta Haynes, 19 May 1956, O'Connor-Haynes Correspondence, OCC, GCSU.
5. Unpublished letter to Thomas Stritch, 1 Oct. 1952, ChC, V.
6. Unpublished letter to Brainard Cheney, 4 Feb. 1953, ChC, V.
7. Unpublished letter to Robert Penn Warren, 28 June 1953, ChC, V.
8. Unpublished letter to Robert Fitzgerald, 14 Aug. 1953, ChC, V.
9. Unpublished letter to Frances Cheney, 3 Dec. 1956, ChC, V.
10. Personal interview, 23 Sept. 1992; subsequent references to the interview included in text without citation.
11. Letter to C. Ralph Stephens, 28 Dec. 1984; qtd. in Stephens 84.
12. "Obscure Flannery O'Connor Penpal Dies at Age 75," *Macon Telegraph Online* 30 Jan. 1999.

13. Dawkins Letters, O'CC, Tulsa; subsequent references to unedited, unpublished letters included without citation in this chapter.
14. Elizabeth Hester named Williams Sessions her literary executor; he will thus control permission to look at this material when it becomes available 12 May 2007.
15. Unpublished Lee letters, OCC, GCSU; subsequent references to O'Connor's unpublished or unedited letters to Maryat Lee and Lee's letters to O'Connor included in this chapter without citation.

Chapter 10. Last Friendships

1. O'Connor letters to Cecil Dawkins, O'CC, Tulsa; subsequent references to these unedited or unpublished letters included in text without citation.
2. Kay Bonetti, "Interview with Cecil Dawkins" (Columbia, MO: American Audio Prose Lib., 1983). Subsequent references to this interview included in text with "B" in parentheses.
3. W. Tazewell, ed., *Hawkes Scrapbook: A New Taste in Literature,* 6. Online, 12 Aug. 1998, www.geocities.com/Athens/Parthenon/7993/hks-sb.html#photo.
4. Ibid.
5. "An Encounter with O'Connor and 'Parker's Back,'" *Flannery O'Connor Bulletin* 24 (1995-96): 106; subsequent references to this article included in text without citation.
6. Spivey published the poem in his *A City Observed, Poems of the New Age* (Atlanta: Oconee Press, 1988), 67.
7. Interview, 9 Oct. 1992; subsequent references to the interview included in text without citation.
8. Telephone interview, 1 June 1992; other references to the interview including in text without citation.

Chapter 11. Lectures and Travel Outside Milledgeville, 1955~1959

1. Unpublished letter to Katherine Anne Porter, 17 Aug. 1963, Katherine Anne Porter Collection, McKeldin Lib., U of Maryland, College Park.
2. An unpublished introduction to her reading of "A Good Man Is Hard to Find," Vanderbilt, 22 Apr. 1959, exists on a tape recording made and owned by Walter Sullivan.
3. Lee journal.
4. Letter to W. McNeil Lowry, 11 Jan. 1959, Archives, Ford Foundation, New York; qtd. in my article "Flannery O'Connor as Lecturer: 'a secret desire to rival Charles Dickens,'" *Flannery O'Connor Bulletin* 16 (1987): 3.
5. "Communication through Writing," *Alumnae Journal: The Georgia State College for Women"* 19.3 (Spring 1954).
6. Personal interview, Fall 1998.
7. Unpublished note to Randall Jarrell, 3 Apr. 1995, Berg Collection of English and American Literature, New York Public Lib.
8. Unpublished letter to Alta R. Haynes, 21 Mar. 1956, O'Connor-Haynes Correspondence, O'CC, GCSU.

9. Haynes scrapbook, O'CC, GCSU; subsequent references to material from Haynes's scrapbook included in text without citation.

10. "Mary Flannery O'Connor Local Guest," *Lansing Michigan State Journal* 25 Apr. 1956: n. pag.

11. Flannery O'Connor Papers, John M. Olin Lib., Washington U, St. Louis.

12. Unpublished letter to Denver Lindley, 17 Dec. 1956, General Correspondence, O'CC, GCSU.

13. "O'Connor Speaks on Writers," *Town and Country* 13 Dec. 1956: 1.

14. Unpublished letter to Roysce Smith, 20 Jan. 1957, Flannery O'Connor Correspondence, John M. Olin Lib., Washington U, St. Louis.

15. Interview, 28 Aug. 1990; subsequent references to the interview included without citation.

16. O'CC, GCSU; also included in my article "O'Connor as Distinguished Alumna: Wit and Wisdom," *English Language Notes* 29.1 (Sept. 1991): 67-70. The complete text of her remarks follows:

> Dr. Lee, it's very pleasant to accept this alumnae award this afternoon, not because it has been given to me personally, but because it has been given to someone whose occupation is writing stories, and I have found that these are times when the story writer is considered a mighty trifling member of society.
>
> It's not that we get no attention paid us. I've found that when it's learned that you've written anything, everyone shakes your hand but no one has read your book.
>
> The story teller has managed to maintain a status as a kind of third-rate celebrity, where he ranks somewhat below Miss Watermelon of 1950 and a little above the Lone Ranger's horse, but he attains this distinction as an oddity, and not as an artist. He's apt to receive the heartfelt approval of the public only after something of his has been made into a movie, or has been ceremonially butchered on television.
>
> This afternoon, however, the emphasis on these awards would seem to be on the arts, and so I presume that you are doing the story teller the honor of looking upon him as an artist, and I am very grateful.
>
> The artist in his essential capacity is something very simple. He is simply a maker, dedicated to the good of the thing he makes, to its order, proportion and clarity. This is a very humble but a very exact demand. It leaves no room for pretensions on the part of the artist or for sentimental requirements on the part of the public.
>
> St. Thomas Aquinas, in the 13th century, taught that art was a virtue of the practical intellect and that the work of art was a good in itself. It was good because in its perfection of form, it reflected the creator. And I can only hope that this kind of attention this afternoon to a story writer, is a tribute to that definition of art.

17. Unpublished letter to Cecil Dawkins, 15 Mar. 1958, O'CC, Tulsa; subsequent references to these unpublished letters included without citation.

18. Unpublished introduction to O'Connor's reading at Vanderbilt, 22 Apr. 1959; transcribed from Sullivan's tape and quoted with his permission.

19. Personal interview, Fall 1988.

CHAPTER 12. LECTURES, 1960~1963

1. Unpublished letter, 23 Nov. 1959, O'CC, Emory.
2. Unpublished letter, 21 Mar. 1960, O'CC, Emory.
3. Unpublished letter, 31 Mar. 1960, O'CC, Emory.
4. "Writer O'Connor Cites Georgia Topics," *Atlanta Constitution* 19 Mar. 1960: n. pag.
5. "Writers Club to Ask Guests to Hear Author," *Macon Telegraph and News* 3 Feb. 1957: n. pag.
6. Unpublished letter to Cecil Dawkins, O'CC, Tulsa; subsequent references to these letters included without citation.
7. "Recent Southern Fiction: A Panel Discussion," *Conversations* 62.
8. Unpublished letter to Roslyn Barnes, 14 Nov. 1960, TLG Papers.
9. Gilbert Head to author, 6 Jan. 1987.
10. Unpublished letter to Sr. Bertrande Meyers, D.C., 4 Nov. 1961, Archives, Marillac Provincial House, St. Louis.
11. Unpublished letter to Tom and Louise Gossett, 16 May 1962, TLG Papers.
12. The unedited version of the letter, in the O'Connor-Lee Correspondence, O'CC, GCSU, contains a rather unsavory joke about African American influence in the Kennedy White House. O'Connor repeated the offensive joke in an unpublished letter to Cecil Dawkins on November 24.
13. Unpublished letter, 11 Apr. 1963, TLG Papers.
14. Unpublished letter to Tom and Louise Gossett, 4 Apr. 1963, TLG Papers.
15. Unedited letter to Maryat Lee, O'Connor-Lee Correspondence, OCC, GCSU.
16. Grace Terry to author, 26 July 1985.
17. Letter to Grace Terry, 27 Aug. 1962, General Correspondence File, O'CC, GCSU; published in my article "O'Connor on *The Violent Bear It Away:* An Unpublished Letter," *English Language Notes* 26.4 (June 1989): 67-71. The complete text of the letter follows:

> Thank you for your letter. I sympathize with your friend's feeling of repulsion at the episode of Tarwater and the man in the lavender and cream-colored car. It was a very necessary action to the meaning of the book, however, and one which I would not have used if I hadn't been obliged to. I think the reason he doesn't understand it is because he doesn't really understand the ending, doesn't understand that Tarwater's call is real, that his true vocation is to answer it. Tarwater is not sick or crazy but really called to be a prophet-a vocation which I take seriously, though the modern reader is not liable to. Only the strong are called in this way and only the strong can answer. It can only be understood in religious terms. The man who gives him the lift is the personification of the voice, the stranger who has been counseling him all along; in other words, he is the devil, and it takes this action of the devil's to make Tarwater see for the first time what evil is. He accepts the devil's liquor and he reaps what the devil has to give. Without this experience of evil, his acceptance of his vocation in the end would be morally a dishonest manipulation by me. Those who see and feel what the devil is turn to God. Tarwater learned the hard way but he has a hard head.

18. Letter to the author, 28 Feb. 1988.

CHAPTER 14. ILLNESS, DEATH, AND LEGACY

1. Jan. 1959, Ford Foundation Archives.
2. Unpublished letter to Louis Dollarhide, 6 Apr. 1964, the Louis Dollarhide Papers, John E. Williams Lib., U of Mississippi, Oxford. The reference to a new Welty publication is interesting, for she published no book in 1964.
3. "Death Takes Novelist Flannery O'Connor, Funeral Rites Slated for This Morning," *Baldwin News* (Milledgeville) 4 Aug. 1964: 1.
4. "Flannery O'Connor Leaves Inspiration," *Atlanta Constitution* 4 Aug. 1964: 4.
5. "Flannery O'Connor Dead at 39; Novelist and Short-Story Writer," *New York Times* 4 Aug. 1964: n. pag.
6. Unpublished letter to Alta Haynes, 12 Sept. 1964, Haynes Scrapbook, O'CC, GCSU.
7. Robert Fitzgerald died in January 1985 and Sally Fitzgerald in June 2000.

SOURCES CITED

Abbot, Louise H. Personal interview by mail. July 1992.

———. "Remembering Flannery." *The Southern Literary Journal* 2.2. (Spring 1970): 3-25. Revision rpt. in *The Flannery O'Connor Bulletin* 23 (1994-95): 61-82.

Alexander, Alice. "The Memory of Milledgeville's Flannery O'Connor Is Still Green. *Atlanta Journal-Constitution* 28 Mar. 1979: 1B, 3B.

Allen, Reynolds. Telephone interview. 17 July 1989.

Anonymous. Personal interview (Milledgeville). 6 Oct. 1992.

———. Personal interviews by mail (GSCW Class of 1945). Summer 1990.

———. Personal interview by mail (Iowa). 29 June 1993.

Armour, Yvonne Giles. Personal interview. 5 Oct. 1992.

"Autograph Party." *Alumnae Journal: The Georgia State College for Women* 17.4 (Summer 1952): 7.

Baker, Nora Moorhead. Personal interview by mail. Summer 1990.

Bassett, Beth Dawkins. "Converging Lives." *Emory Magazine* 58.4 (Apr. 1982): 17-23.

Beiswanger, George R. Personal interview by mail. 2 Aug. 1989.

Bishop, Elizabeth. *One Art, Letters.* Ed. Robert Giroux. New York: Farrar, Straus & Giroux, 1994.

Blau, Sheldon Paul, and Dodi Schultz. *Living with Lupus: All the Knowledge You Need to Help Yourself.* Boston: Addison-Wesley, 1993.

Blitch, Lila. Telephone interview. 28 Feb. 1992.

Bongartz, Roy. "Yaddo at 60." *Publishers Weekly,* 24 June 1986, 33.

Bonner, James C. *Milledgeville: Georgia's Antebellum Capital.* Macon: Mercer UP, 1985.

Bradley, Mildred Sauls. Personal interview by mail. Summer 1990.

Breit, Harvey. "*Galley Proof:* A Good Man Is Hard to Find." In *Conversations with Flannery O'Connor.* Ed. Rosemary M. Magee. Jackson and London: UP of Mississippi, 1987. 5-10.

———. "In and Out of Books: Visitor." Magee 11-13.

Brooks, Cleanth. "Flannery O'Connor-A Tribute." *Esprit* 8.1 (Winter 1964): 17.

Brown, Ashley. Personal interview. 23 Sept. 1992.

Brown, Hugh R. "Flannery O'Connor: The Savannah Years." NEMLA Convention, Buffalo, NY, Spring 1992.

——. Personal interview. 5 Aug. 1990.

——. "Savannah Landmark: Flannery O'Connor's Childhood Home." *Flannery O'Connor Bulletin* 18 (1989): 43-45.

Brzenk, Gene. Unpublished letter to Jean Wylder. 26 Dec. 1972. Wylder File, U of Iowa Lib., Iowa City.

Burford, Kay. Telephone interview. 19 June 1993.

Burke, John J., Jr., S.J. "Convergence of Flannery O'Connor and Chardin." *Renascence* 19 (1966): 41-47, 52.

Cash, Jean W. "Flannery O'Connor: 'art demand[s] celibacy.'" *Postscript* 15 (1998): 67-76.

——. "The Flannery O'Connor-Andrew Lytle Connection." *Flannery O'Connor Bulletin* 25 (1996-97): 183-92.

——. "Flannery O'Connor as Lecturer: 'a secret desire to rival Charles Dickens.'" *Flannery O'Connor Bulletin* 16 (1987): 1-15.

——. "Maryat and 'Flanneryat': An Antithetical Friendship." *Flannery O'Connor Bulletin* 19 (1990): 56-72.

——. "Milledgeville, 1957-1960: O'Connor's 'pseudo-literary and theological gatherings.'" *Flannery O'Connor Bulletin* 18 (1989): 13-27.

——. "O'Connor as Distinguished Alumna: Wit and Wisdom." *English Language Notes* 29.1 (Sept. 1991): 67-70.

——. O'Connor in the Iowa Writers' Workshop." *Flannery O'Connor Bulletin* 24 (1995–96): 67-75.

——. "O'Connor on *The Violent Bear It Away*: An Unpublished Letter." *English Language Notes* 26.4 (June 1989): 67-71.

Chambers, Lena Jo Tabb. Personal interview by mail. Summer 1990.

Cheney, Brainard. Unpublished letter to Frances Cheney. 3 Dec. 1956. Brainard and Frances Cheney Collection, Jean and Alexander Heard Lib., Vanderbilt U, Nashville.

——. Unpublished letter to Robert Fitzgerald. 14 Aug. 1953. Cheney Collection, Jean and Alexander Heard Lib., Vanderbilt U, Nashville.

——. Unpublished letter to Thomas Stritch. 1 Oct. 1952. Cheney Collection, Jean and Alexander Heard Lib., Vanderbilt U, Nashville.

——. Unpublished letter to Robert Penn Warren. 28 June 1953. Cheney Collection, Jean and Alexander Heard Lib., Vanderbilt U, Nashville.

Cheney, Frances. Personal interview. 8 Aug. 1992.

Claffey, Charles E. "She returned to Milledgeville, and then she began her Work." *Boston Globe* 7 July 1981, n. pag.

"Communication through Writing." *Alumnae Journal: The Georgia State College for Women* 19.3 (Spring 1954): 1-2.

Corn, Alfred. "An Encounter with O'Connor and 'Parker's Back.'" *Flannery O'Connor Bulletin* 24 (1995-96): 104-18.

Corse, Lucia Bonn. Personal interview by mail. Nov. 1992.

Cowley, Malcolm. Unpublished letter to C. Everett Bacon. 16 Mar. 1949. Malcolm Cowley Papers, Newberry Lib., Chicago.

———. Unpublished letter to Granville Hicks. 1 Mar. 1949. Cowley Papers, Newberry Lib., Chicago.

Danielly, Elsie Parker. Personal interview by mail. Summer 1990.

Dawkins, Cecil. Letter to the author. 2 July 1994.

———. Interview with Kay Bonetti. American Audio Prose Lib., Columbia, MO, 1984.

———. "Introduction to Reading." "The Habit of Art: An Interdisciplinary Celebration of the Legacy of Flannery O'Connor." Milledgeville, 16 Apr. 1994.

Day, Jeffrey. "Symposium Remembers Flannery O'Connor." *Union-Recorder* 17 Apr. 1984, sec. 1.

"Death Takes Novelist Flannery O'Connor, Funeral Rites Slated for This Morning." *Baldwin News* [Milledgeville] 4 Aug. 1964: 1.

Dinger, Ed., ed. *Seems Like Old Times.* Iowa City: U of Illinois P, 1986.

Drake, Robert. *Flannery O'Connor, A Critical Essay.* Grand Rapids, MI: William B. Eerdmans, 1966.

———. "The Lady Frum Somewhere: Flannery O'Connor Then and Now." *Modern Age* (Summer 1985): 212-23.

———. Telephone interview. 1 June 1992.

Eichelbaum, Melanie C. "Systemic Lupus Erythematosus." English 398, James Madison U. 4 Dec. 1994: 1-17.

Engle, Paul. "University Hopes That Iowa Will Lead Nation in Creative Writing." *Des Moines Sunday Register* 21 Dec. 1947: n. pag.

———. "How Creative Writing Is Taught at the University of Iowa Workshop." *Des Moines Sunday Register* 28 Dec. 1947: n. pag.

———. Unpublished letter to Flannery O'Connor. 16 May 1949. O'Connor Collection. William E. Perkins Lib., Duke U, Durham, N.C.

"Ex-SIU Student Gets O. Henry Award." *Daily Iowan* 10 Jan. 1957: n. pag.

Fancher, Betsy. "Authoress Flannery O'Connor Is Evidence of Georgia's Bent to the Female Writer." *Decatur-DeKalb News* 13 Apr. 1961: 5.

Farley, Blanche. Review of *Conversations with Flannery O'Connor.* Ed. Rosemary Magee. *Flannery O'Connor Bulletin* 16 (1987): 82-85.

Fitzgerald, Robert. "Introduction." *Everything That Rises Must Converge.* By Flannery O'Connor. New York: Farrar, Straus, & Giroux, 1965.

———. Notes. *The Complete Stories.* By Flannery O'Connor. New York: Farrar, Straus & Giroux, 1971.

———. "Open Letter." Mar. 1949. To T. S. Eliot, Allen Tate, John Crowe Ransom, Robert Penn Warren, W. C. Williams, J. F. Powers, Randall Jarrell, Peter Taylor, Katherine Anne Porter, Louise Bogan, Leonie Adams, Elizabeth Bishop, Marianne Moore, John Berryman, Richard Blackmur, and George Santayana. Katherine Anne Porter papers. McKeldin Lib., U of Maryland, College Park.

Fitzgerald, Sally. "Chronology." *Collected Works.* By Flannery O'Connor. New York: Lib. of America, 1988.

——. "The Invisible Father." *Christianity and Literature* 47.1 (Autumn 1997): 5-18.

——. "Flannery O'Connor: Patterns of Friendship, Patterns of Love." *Georgia Review* 52 (Fall 1998): 407-25.

——. Letter to C. Ralph Stephens. 28 Dec. 1984. Stephens 84.

——. "A Master Class: From the Correspondence of Caroline Gordon and Flannery O'Connor." *Georgia Review* 33 (Winter 1979): 827-46.

——. "Root and Branch: O'Connor of Georgia." *Georgia Historical Quarterly* 44.4 (Winter 1980): 377-87.

"Flannery O'Connor Dead at 39; Novelist and Short-Story Writer." *New York Times* 4 Aug. 1964: n. pag.

"Flannery O'Connor Leaves Inspiration." *Atlanta Constitution* 4 Aug. 1964: 4.

"Flannery O'Connor Wins Rinehart-Iowa Award for Novel." *Daily Iowan* 29 May 1947: n. pag.

Foote, Shelby, and Walker Percy. *The Correspondence of Shelby Foote and Walker Percy.* Ed. Jay Tolson. New York: Norton, 1997.

"Former SUI Student Has Book Published." *Daily Iowan* 28 Mar. 1952: n. pag.

Freedman, James O. "Honoring Talent for Glowing Praise." *Des Moines Sunday Register* 28 Sept. 1986: n. pag.

Fugin, Katherine, Faye Rivard, and Margaret Sieh. "An Interview with Flannery O'Connor." Magee 58-60.

Fulton, Lyman A., M.D. Interview with Virginia Wray. Summer 1999.

Furman, Laura. "The Benign Ghosts of Yaddo." *House and Garden* 6 June 1986: 75.

Gallop, Mary Boyd. Personal interview by mail. Summer 1990.

Georgia Journal 10 May 1815. n. pag.

Georgia Writers' Association. Citation accompanying the Literary Achievement Scroll for 1955 awarded to Flannery O'Connor. O'Connor Papers. John M. Olin Lib., Washington U, St. Louis.

Gilman, Richard. "She Writes Powerful Fiction." Magee 37-40.

Giroux, Robert. Introduction. *The Complete Stories.* By Flannery O'Connor. New York: Farrar, Straus & Giroux, 1971. vii-xvii.

Godwin, Gail. "House Parties and Box Lunches: One Writer's Summer at Yaddo." *New York Times Book Review* 10 Aug. 1986: 3.

Gordon, Caroline. "An American Girl." In *The Added Dimension, The Art and Mind of Flannery O'Connor.* Ed. Melvin J. Friedman and Lewis A. Lawson. New York: Fordham UP, 1966. 123-37.

——. "Heresy in Dixie." *Sewanee Review* 76 (1968): 263-97.

——. "Rebels and Revolutionaries: The New American Scene." *Flannery O'Connor Bulletin* 3 (1974): 40-56.

——. "Flannery O'Connor-A Tribute." *Esprit* 8.1 (Winter 1964): 28.

——. Unpublished letters to Brainard Cheney. 30 Dec. 1951 and 4 Feb. 1953. Cheney Collection. Jean and Alexander Heard Lib., Vanderbilt U, Nashville.

Gossett, Tom, and Louise Gossett. Personal interview. 2 May 1991.

——. Thomas and Louise Young Gossett Collection. William E. Perkins Lib., Duke U, Durham, N.C.

Greene, Dr. Helen I. Personal interview. 8 Oct. 1992.

——. "Mary Flannery O'Connor: One Teacher's Happy Memory." *Flannery O'Connor Bulletin* 19 (1990): 44-48.

Griffith, Benjamin. "After the Canonization, Flannery O'Connor Revisited." *Sewanee Review* 97 (1989): 575-80.

——. "Ten Years of Letters and Visits Showed a Witty, Friendly, Sincere Woman." *Atlanta Journal-Constitution* 10 Apr. 1994: M4.

Griffith, Paul. Unpublished letter to Paul Engle. 16 Feb. 1948. Paul Engle Correspondence. U of Iowa Lib., Iowa City.

Groves, Katherine Doyle. Interview with Hugh R. Brown. 4 Feb. 1990.

——. Telephone interview. 6 Aug. 1990.

Haley, Mary Louise Bobo. Personal interview by mail. Summer 1990.

Hall, James B. Personal interview by mail. 8 Oct. 1993.

Hallman, David A. Personal interview. Fall 1988.

Hamilton, Ian. *Robert Lowell: A Biography.* New York: Random House, 1982.

Hardwick, Elizabeth. Personal interview by mail. June 1992.

Harty, Tony. Interview with Hugh R. Brown. 4 Feb. 1990.

——. Personal interview. 8 Aug. 1990.

Hawkes, John. "Flannery O'Connor's Devil." *Sewanee Review* 70.7 (Summer 1962): 395-407.

——. "An Interview." *Wisconsin Studies Is Contemporary Literature* 6 (Summer 1965): 141-55.

Hawkins, Peter S. "Faith and Doubt First Class: The Letters of Flannery O'Connor." *Southern Humanities Review* 26 (Spring 1982): 91-103.

Haynes, Alta L. Unpublished correspondence with Flannery and Regina Cline O'Connor. O'Connor Collection, Ina Dillard Russell Lib., Georgia College and State University, Milledgeville.

——. Unpublished scrapbook. O'Connor Collection. Ina Dillard Russell Lib., Georgia College and State University, Milledgeville.

Head, Gilbert. Letter to the author. 6 Jan. 1987.

Hicks, Granville. "Literary Horizons." *Saturday Review* 10 May 1969: 30.

Hill, Mary Anne. Letter to the author. 8 Jan. 1987.

Hines, Nelle Womack. "Mary O'Connor Shows Talent as Cartoonist." *Macon Telegraph and News* 13 June 1943: n. pag.

Horne, Elizabeth. Personal interview. 5 Oct. 1992.

Horowitz, Mark, and Marietta Abrams Brill, *Living with Lupus: A Comprehensive Guide to Understanding and Controlling Lupus While Getting on with Your Life.* New York: Penguin, 1994.

Hoynes, Loretta Feuger. Interview with Hugh R. Brown. 11 Feb. 1990.

——. Telephone interview. 6 Aug. 1990.

Johnson, Elizabeth Maguire. Interview with Hugh R. Brown. 11 Feb. 1990.

——. Personal interview by mail. Sept. 1990.

Kazin, Alfred. *Bright Book of Life.* Boston: Little, Brown, 1973.

——. *New York Jew.* New York: Knopf, 1978.

——. Telephone interview. 27 July 1994.

Kellam, Kitty Smith. Personal interview. 7 Oct. 1992.

Kennedy, Thomas. "A Last Interview with Robie Macauley." *AGNI* 4 (Summer 1993): n. pag. Available: webdelsol.com/AGNI/

Kirk, Russell. "Memoir by Humpty Dumpty." *Flannery O'Connor Bulletin* 8 (1979): 14-17.

Kirkland, William M. "Baron von Hügel and Flannery O'Connor." *Flannery O'Connor Bulletin* 18 (1989): 28-42.

——. "Flannery O'Connor: The Person and the Writer." *East-West Review* 3 (1967): 159-63.

——. Personal interview. 12 July 1989.

Kuck, Kathryn Donan. Personal interview by mail. Summer 1990.

Lee, Maryat. "Flannery, 1957." *Flannery O'Connor Bulletin* 5 (1976): 39-60.

——. Letter to the author. 20 Aug. 1989.

——. Unpublished journals, 1956-1965. The West Virginia and Regional Collection, West Virginia Universities, Morgantown.

——. Unpublished letters. Flannery O'Connor-Maryat Lee Correspondence. Flannery O'Connor Collection. Ina Dillard Russell Lib., Georgia College and State University, Milledgeville.

Lee, Robert E. Personal interview. 28 Aug. 1990.

——. Letter to the author. 11 Oct. 2000.

Lewis, Jay. Personal interview. 8 Oct. 1992.

Lochridge, Betsy. "An Afternoon with Flannery O'Connor." Magee 37-40.

Love, Betty Boyd. "Recollections of Flannery O'Connor." *Flannery O'Connor Bulletin* 14 (1985): 64-71.

——. Manuscript version of "Recollections of Flannery O'Connor." With penciled comments by Margaret Meader. O'Connor Collection, Ina Dillard Russell Lib., Georgia College and State University, Milledgeville.

Lytle, Andrew. Personal interview. 26 July 1993.

——. Letter to the author. 18 June 1985.

——. Unpublished Letters to Thomas Carter. Undated and 24 June 1952. Thomas H. Carter Papers, University Lib., Washington and Lee U, Lexington, VA.

——. Unpublished Letter to Paul Engle. Aug. 1947. Engle Correspondence. U of Iowa Lib., Iowa City.

——. "Flannery O'Connor-A Tribute." *Esprit* 8.1 (Winter 1964): 33-34.

Macauley, Robie. Unpublished Letter to Stephen Wilbers. 16 Apr. 1976. Wilbers File. U of Iowa Lib., Iowa City.

——. "Flannery O'Connor-A Tribute." *Esprit* 8.1 (Winter 1964): 34.

——. Personal interview by mail. 4 Dec. 1992.

Magee, Rosemary M., ed. *Conversations with Flannery O'Connor.* Jackson & London: UP of Mississippi, 1987.

Martin, Carter. Introduction. *The Presence of Grace and Other Books Reviews.* By Flannery O'Connor. Athens: U Georgia P, 1983. 1-8.

Martin, Hansford. Unpublished letters to Paul Engle. 22 Feb. 1948 and 24 Apr. 1948. Engle Correspondence. U of Iowa Lib., Iowa City.

"Mary Flannery O'Connor Local Guest." *Lansing Michigan State Journal* 25 Apr. 1956: n. pag.

Maxwell, Allen. Unpublished letters to Flannery O'Connor. General Correspondence. Flannery O'Connor Collection. Ina Dillard Russell Lib., Georgia College and State University, Milledgeville.

McCarthy, Colman. Reprint of "The Servant of Literature in the Heart of Iowa." *Washington Post* 27 Mar. 1983.

McCarthy, Peter. Letter to the author. 28 Feb. 1988.

McCown, James H. "Flannery O'Connor." Lecture presented at the U of Alabama, Mobile. 26 Apr. 1985. 1-19.

——. Unpublished Letters. Gossett Papers. William E. Perkins Lib., Duke U, Durham, N.C.

——. "Remembering Flannery O'Connor." *America* 8 Sept. 1979: 86-88.

McFarland, Bess Saye. Personal interview by mail. Summer 1990.

McKee, Elizabeth. Unpublished letter to Flannery O'Connor. 23 June 1948. Flannery O'Connor Collection. William E. Perkins Lib., Duke U, Durham, N.C.

Meaders, Margaret. "Flannery O'Connor: 'Literary Witch.'" *Colorado Quarterly* 10.4 (Spring 1962): 377-78.

Messick, Hank. Unpublished letters to Stephen Wilbers. 26 Mar. 1976 and 21 July 1976. Wilbers File. U of Iowa Lib., Iowa City.

Miller, Sarah Rudolph. Personal interview by mail. Summer 1990.

Miller, Warren. Unpublished letter to Paul Engle. 29 Feb. 1948. Engle Correspondence. U of Iowa Lib., Iowa City.

Minutes. Special Meeting of the Board of Directors of the Corporation of Yaddo. Held at the office of the Corporation in the Garage at Yaddo, Saratoga Springs, NY. 26 Feb. 1949. Cowley Papers, Newberry Lib., Chicago.

Minutes. Special Meeting of the Board of Directors of the Corporation of Yaddo. Held at Spencer Trask and Co., New York City. 26 Mar. 1949. Cowley Papers, Newberry Lib., Chicago.

Mullins, C. Ross, Jr. "Flannery O'Connor: An Interview." Magee 103-7.

Murphy, John J. "Another Way of Seeing, Editor's Foreword." *Flannery O'Connor and the Christian Mystery, Literature and Belief* 17 (1997): iv-viii.

"New Steroid Helps Treat Rare, Fatal Disease." *Science News Letter* 20 Sept 1958: 185.

Nichols, Acosta. Letter to Malcolm Cowley. 16 Apr. 1949. Cowley Papers, Newberry Lib., Chicago.

Nichols, Loxley F. "Flannery O'Connor's 'Intellectual Vaudeville': Masks of Mother and Daughter." *Studies in the Literary Imagination* 20.2 (Fall 1987): 15-29.

Nipson, Herbert. Personal interview by mail. 16 Sept. 1993.

Noguchi, Hajime. *Criticism of Flannery O'Connor.* Tokyo: Bunkashobouhakubunsha, 1985.

Nostrandt, Jeanne R. Personal interview. Fall 1998.

"Obscure Flannery O'Connor Penpal Dies at Age 75." *Macon Telegraph Online.* 30 Jan. 1999.

O'Connor, Edward. Unpublished letter to Erwin Sibley. O'Connor Collection. Ina Dillard Russell Lib., Georgia College and State University, Milledgeville.

O'Connor, Flannery. *Collected Works.* New York: Lib. of America, 1988.

——. *Conversations with Flannery O'Connor.* Ed. Rosemary Magee. Jackson: UP Mississippi, 1987.

——. "The Fiction Writer and His Country. In *Mystery and Manners.* Ed. Sally and Robert Fitzgerald. New York: Farrar, Straus & Giroux, 1969.

——. "The Geranium: A Collection of Short Stories." Thesis. U of Iowa, 1947.

——. *The Habit of Being.* Ed. Sally Fitzgerald. New York: Farrar, Straus & Giroux, 1979.

——. Introduction. *A Memoir of Mary Ann.* By the Dominican Nuns Who Took Care of Her. New York: Farrar, Straus & Giroux, 1961. 3-21.

——. "The King of the Birds." *Mystery and Manners* 3-21.

——. *The Presence of Grace and Other Book Reviews by Flannery O'Connor.* Comp. Leo J. Zuber. Ed. Carter W. Martin. Athens: U Georgia P, 1983.

——. Letter to Grace Terry. 27 Aug. 1962. General Correspondence. O'Connor Collection. Ina Dillard Russell Lib., Georgia College and State University, Milledgeville.

——. Unpublished introduction to "A Good Man Is Hard to Find." Tape recording in possession of Walter Sullivan, Nashville.

——. Unpublished letter to Roslyn Barnes. 14 Nov. 1960. O'Connor Collection. William E. Perkins Lib., Duke U, Durham, N.C.

——. Unpublished letter to Olive Bell Davis. 21 Aug. 1958. Olive Bell Davis Papers. Atlanta History Center, Atlanta.

——. Unpublished correspondence with Cecil Dawkins. Cecil Dawkins File. McFarlin Lib., U of Tulsa.

——. Unpublished letters to Louis Dollarhide. Dollarhide Collection. John E. Williams Lib., U of Mississippi, Oxford.

——. Unpublished letters to Paul Engle. Aug. 1948 and 9 May 1949. O'Connor Collection. William E. Perkins Lib., Duke U, Durham, N.C.

——. Unpublished letters to Paul Farmer. 23 Nov. 1959, 21 Mar. 1960, and 31 Mar. 1960. Robert W. Woodruff Lib., Emory U, Atlanta.

——. Unpublished letters to Tom Gossett and Louise Gossett. Gossett Collection, William E. Perkins Lib., Duke U, Durham, N.C.

——. Unpublished letter to Alta Haynes. 19 May 1956. O'Connor-Haynes Correspondence. O'Connor Collection. Ina Dillard Russell Lib., Georgia College and State University, Milledgeville.

——. Unpublished letters to Maryat Lee. Flannery O'Connor-Maryat Lee Correspondence. O'Connor Collection. Ina Dillard Russell Lib., Georgia College and State University, Milledgeville.

——. Unpublished letter to Denver Lindley. 17 Dec. 1956. General Correspondence. O'Connor Collection. Ina Dillard Russell Lib., Georgia College and State University, Milledgeville.

——. Unedited letters to Betty Boyd Love. Flannery O'Connor-Betty Boyd Love Correspondence. O'Connor Collection. Ina Dillard Russell Lib., Georgia College and State University, Milledgeville.

——. Letter to W. McNeil Lowry. 11 Jan. 1959. Archives. Ford Foundation, New York.

——. Unpublished letters to Fr. James McCown. 3 Mar. 1958, 3 Apr. 1959, 20 Sept. 1959, 23 June 1961, and 11 Apr. 1963. O'Connor Collection. William E. Perkins Lib., Duke U, Durham, N.C.

——. Unpublished letters to Elizabeth McKee. 21 Sept. 1948, 30 Dec. 1949, and 19 Apr. 1956. O'Connor Collection. William E. Perkins Lib., Duke U, Durham, N.C.

——. Unpublished letter to Sr. Bertrande Meyers, D.C. 4 Nov. 1961. Archives. Marillac Provincial House, St. Louis.

——. Unpublished letter to Katherine Anne Porter. 17 Aug. 1963. Porter Collection. McKeldin Lib., U of Maryland, College Park.

——. Unpublished letter to Roysce Smith. 20 Jan. 1957. Smith Papers. John M. Olin Lib., Washington U, St. Louis.

——. Unpublished letter to Martha Bell Sprieser. 25 Apr. 1952. In the possession of its recipient.

——. Unpublished letters to Jean Williams Wylder. Undated 1948, undated letter 1949, 28 Dec. 1952, 27 Dec. 1961, and 5 Mar. 1962. In the possession of Bill Wylder of Coralville, IA.

——. Unpublished note to "Helen" [unidentified relative]. Summer 1937. O'Connor Collection. Robert W. Woodruff Lib., Emory U, Atlanta.

——. Unpublished note to Randall Jarrell. 3 Apr. 1955. Berg Collection of English and American Literature. New York Public Lib.

——. "The Writer and the Graduate School." *Alumnae Journal: The Georgia State College for Women* 13.4 (June 1948): 4.

O'Connor, Regina Cline. Unpublished notes to Alta Haynes, 12 Sept. 1964 and Christmas 1966. Haynes Scrapbook. O'Connor Collection, Ina Dillard Russell Lib., Georgia College and State University, Milledgeville.

——. Unpublished letters to Betty Boyd Love, undated. Regina Cline O'Connor-Betty Boyd Love Correspondence. O'Connor Collection, Ina Dillard Russell Lib., Georgia College and State University, Milledgeville.

——. Unpublished letter to "Helen" [unidentified relative]. Summer 1937. O'Connor Collection. Robert W. Woodruff Lib., Emory U, Atlanta.

"O'Connor Speaks on Writers." *Town and Country* [Wesleyan College, Georgia, newspaper] 13 Dec. 1956: 1.

Odom, Lillian Dowling. Interview with Hugh R. Brown. 11 Feb. 1990.

——. Telephone interview. 5 Aug. 1990.

Ogletree, Hazel Smith. Personal interview by mail. Summer 1990.

O'Leary, Dan. Interview with Hugh R. Brown. 10 Feb. 1990.

Parr, Newell Turner. Interview with Hugh R. Brown. 10 Feb. 1990.

Persse, Patricia. Interview with Hugh R. Brown. 2 Feb. 1990.

___. Winifred Persse, and Margaret P. Trexler. Personal interview. 6 Aug. 1990.

Poats, Marian Nelson. Personal interview by mail. Summer 1990.

Porter, Katherine Anne. "Gracious Greatness." *Esprit* 8.1 (Winter 1964): 50-58.

Rath, Sura. "An Evolving Friendship: Flannery's O'Connor's Correspondence with Edward J. Romagosa, S. J." *Flannery O'Connor Bulletin* 17 (1988): 1-10.

"Recent Southern Fiction: A Panel Discussion." Magee 61-78.

Reuman, Ann E. "Revolting Fictions: Flannery O'Connor's Letter to Her Mother."
    Papers on Literature and Language 29.2 (Spring 1993): 197-214.
"Reynolds Allen Wins Four-Year College/Scholarship with Essay on Congressman
    Vinson." *Milledgeville Union-Recorder* 14 May 1942: n. pag.
Richardson, Fran. Personal interview by mail. Summer 1990.
Rout, Kay Kinsalla. "Flannery O'Connor and the Role of the Intellectual." *Intellect*
    Apr. 1978: 421-22.
Ryan, Elizabeth Shreve. "I Remember Mary Flannery." *Flannery O'Connor Bulletin* 19
    (1990): 49-52.
Schatz, Carmen Singletary. Personal interview by mail. Summer 1990.
Schemmel, Bill. "Southern Comfort." *Travel-Holiday* June 1988: 72.
Selby, John. Unpublished Letter to Flannery O'Connor. 16 Feb. 1949. O'Connor
    Collection. William E. Perkins Lib., Duke U, Durham, N.C.
Sessions, William. "Betty Hester: 'A Noble Soul.'" *Cheers! The Flannery O'Connor
    Newsletter* 6.2 (Fall/Winter 1998-99): n. pag.
———. "Flannery O'Connor: A Memoir." *National Catholic Reporter* 23 Oct. 1964: 9.
Shannon, Margaret. "The World of Flannery O'Connor." *Atlanta Journal-Constitution
    Magazine* 20 Feb. 1972: 8-9, 37-39.
Sherry, Gerard E. "An Interview with Flannery O'Connor." Magee 97-102.
Sister Consolata. Personal interview. 8 Aug. 1990.
Snodgrass, W. D. "A Liberal Education: Mentors, Fomenters and Tormenters."
    Southern Review 28.2 (July 1992): 445-68.
Spivey, Ted R. *A City Observed, Poems of the New Age.* Atlanta: Oconee Press, 1988.
———. "The Complex Gifts of Flannery O'Connor." *Essays in Arts and Sciences*
    14 (May 1985): 49-58.
———. *Flannery O'Connor: The Woman, the Thinker, the Visionary,* Macon, GA: Mercer
    UP, 1995.
———. Personal interview. 9 Oct. 1992.
Sprieser, Martha Bell. Personal interview by mail. 30 Nov. 1992.
Stephens, C. Ralph, ed. *The Correspondence of Flannery O'Connor and the Brainard
    Cheneys.* Jackson and London: UP of Mississippi, 1986.
Stern, Richard. "Flannery O'Connor: A Remembrance and Some Letters." *Shenandoah*
    16.2 (Winter 1965): 5-10.
Stritch, Thomas. *My Notre Dame.* Notre Dame, IN: Notre Dame P, 1992.
Sullivan, Regina, and Gerry Sullivan Horne. Interview with Hugh R. Brown.
    10 Feb. 1990.
Sullivan, Walter. Undated interview by mail with Stephen Wilbers. Wilbers File.
    U of Iowa Lib., Iowa City.
———. Unpublished introduction. O'Connor's reading at Vanderbilt U, 21 Apr. 1959.
    In writer's possession, Nashville.
———, and Jane Sullivan. Personal interview. 8 Aug. 1992.
Tate, Allen. "Flannery O'Connor-A Tribute." *Esprit* 8.1 (Winter 1964): 48-49.
Tate, James. "An O'Connor Remembrance." *Flannery O'Connor Bulletin* 17 (1988): 65-68.
Tate, J. O. "On Flannery O'Connor: Citizen of the South and Citizen of the World."
    Flannery O'Connor Bulletin 13 (1984): 26-43.
———. "An Introduction to 'An O'Connor Remembrance.'" *Flannery O'Connor Bulletin*
    17 (1988): 62-64.
Tate, Mary Barbara. "Mary Flannery O'Connor at Home in Milledgeville." *Studies in
    the Literary Imagination* 20.2 (Fall 1987): 31-35.

——. Personal interviews. 20 July 1989 and 7 Oct. 1992.

Tazewell, C. W., ed. *Hawkes Scrapbook, A New Taste in Literature:* 6. Online, 12 Aug. 1998. www.geocities.com/Athens/Parthenon/7993/hks-sb.html#photo.

Terry, Grace. Letter to the author. 26 July 1986.

Tolson, Jay. *Pilgrim in the Ruins: A Life of Walker Percy.* New York: Simon & Schuster, 1992.

Turner, Margaret. "Visit to Flannery O'Connor Proves a Novel Experience." Magee 41-43.

Uhler, Margaret. Personal interview by mail. 26 Oct. 1992. *Nashville Tennessean* 31 July 1956: 4E.

Waite, Maria Peabody. *Yaddo, Yesterday and Today.* Albany, NY: Argus Press, 1933.

Walsh, Sr. M. Jude. Interview with Hugh R. Brown. 11 Feb. 1990.

Walston, Rosa Lee. "An Affectionate Recollection." *Flannery O'Connor Bulletin* 1 (1972): 43-47.

——. "Flannery O'Connor as Seen by a Friend." *Carrell* 14.1-2 (June and Dec. 1973): 16-24.

——. Personal interview. 27 Oct. 1989.

——. "Introduction of Flannery O'Connor at G.S.C.W. Chapel on January 7, 1960." Vertical File. O'Connor Collection. Ina Dillard Russell Lib., Georgia State College and State University, Milledgeville.

Weiss, Edna S. "Letters: Memories of Milledgeville, Ga." *New York Times* 4 Feb. 1979: 28.

Westling, Louise. "Flannery O'Connor's Revelations to 'A.'" *Southern Humanities Review* 20.1 (Winter 1986): 15-22.

——. "Flannery O'Connor's Mothers and Daughters." *Twentieth Century Literature* 24.4 (Winter 1978): 510-22.

"White Cells Control Incurable Disease." *Science News Letter* 21 July 1956: 40.

Wiatt, Mary Mudge. Personal interviews by mail. 7 July 1993 and 2 Aug. 1993.

Wilbers, Stephen. *The Iowa Writers' Workshop.* Iowa City: U of Iowa P, 1980.

Womble, Grace. Personal interview by mail. Summer 1990.

Wood, Ralph. "Where Is the Voice Coming From? Flannery O'Connor on Race." *Flannery O'Connor Bulletin* 22 (1993-94): 90-118.

"Writer O'Connor Cites Georgia Topics." *Atlanta Constitution* 13 Mar. 1960: n. pag.

"Writers Club to Ask Guests to Hear Author." *Macon Telegraph and News* 3 Feb. 1957: n. pag.

Wurst, Marianne. "O'Connor Calls Stories 'Slight,' Ciardi Analyzes Student Poetry." *Agnes Scott News* 26 Apr. 1961: n. pag.

Wylder, Jean. "Flannery O'Connor: A Reminiscence and Some Letters." *North American Review* 225.1 (Spring 1970): 58-65.

"Yaddo." Promotional brochure. Saratoga Springs, N.Y.: privately printed by the Yaddo Corporation, 1998.

INDEX

Flannery O'Connor was designed and typeset on a Macintosh computer system using QuarkXPress software. The text is set in Granjon and the chapter openings are set in UpperWestSide. This book was designed by Cheryl Carrington, typeset by Kimberly Scarbrough, and manufactured by Thomson-Shore, Inc. The paper used in this book is designed for an effective life of at least three hundred years.

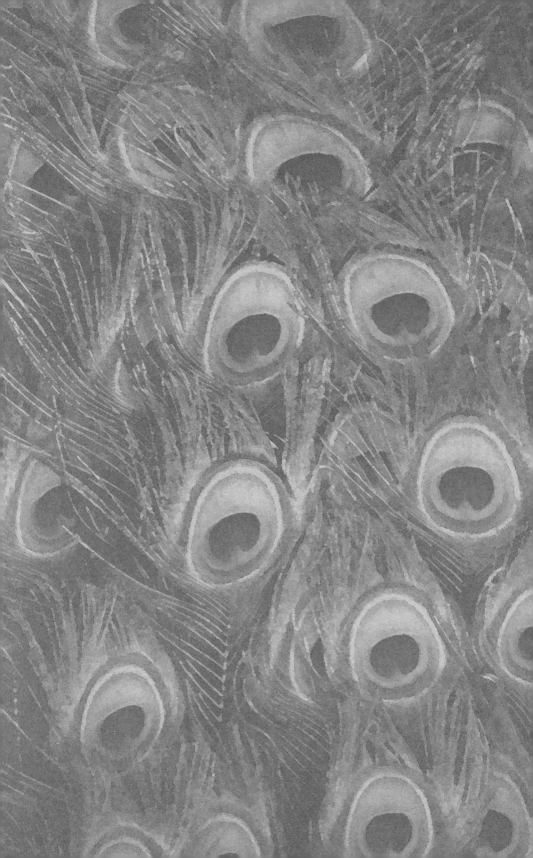